AF512390

JNU STORIES

JNU STORIES

THE FIRST 50 YEARS

Edited by

Neeladri Bhattacharya
Kunal Chakrabarti
S. Gunasekaran
Janaki Nair
Joy L. K. Pachuau

ALEPH

ALEPH

ALEPH BOOK COMPANY
An independent publishing firm
promoted by ***Rupa Publications India***

First published in India in 2020 by
Aleph Book Company
7/16 Ansari Road, Daryaganj
New Delhi 110002

Introduction Copyright © Neeladri Bhattacharya and Janaki Nair
This edition copyright © Aleph Book Company 2020

Copyright for individual essays vests with respective authors
Credits for section openers: pp. 1, 31, 57, 123, 175, 217, 323, 365, 385, and 409 (courtesy Samim Asgor Ali);
p. 281 (courtesy *Deccan Herald*, 25 November 2019, and *edexlive*, 25 November 2019); and p. 301 (courtesy Café Dissensus, 11 April 2016, and Samim Asgor Ali).
All rights reserved.

The views and opinions expressed in this book are those of the authors and the facts are as reported by them, which have been verified to the extent possible, and the publisher is not in any way liable for the same.

The publisher has used its best endeavours to ensure that URLs for external websites referred to in this book are correct and active at the time of going to press. However, the publisher has no responsibility for the websites and can make no guarantee that a site will remain live or that the content is or will remain appropriate.

No part of this publication may be reproduced, transmitted, or stored in a retrieval system, in any form or by any means, without permission in writing from Aleph Book Company.

ISBN: 978-81-948741-9-5

3 5 7 9 10 8 6 4 2

Printed at Parksons Graphics Pvt. Ltd, Mumbai

This book is sold subject to the condition that it shall not, by way of trade or otherwise, be lent, resold, hired out, or otherwise circulated without the publisher's prior consent in any form of binding or cover other than that in which it is published.

CONTENTS

IX: THE WAY THINGS WERE

X: PROMISES TO FULFIL

XI: MEMORIES FROM AFAR

INTRODUCTION

A RED-BRICK UNIVERSITY WITH A DIFFERENCE

NEELADRI BHATTACHARYA AND JANAKI NAIR

It is only rarely that an Indian public institution makes a commitment to the preservation of institutional memory. JNU—surprisingly given its reputation—appears to have been no exception. To look back, therefore, on fifty years of an institution's existence minus the vital prop of an official archive calls for a different kind of reconstructive effort, especially when the structures and processes that have been carefully nurtured and built up through a process of debate and discussion, trial and revision, are severely strained today. Yet, now more than ever, when even the past is no longer safe from the determined effort to refashion memory—thereby threatening institutions themselves—such reconstruction is not an option but an imperative, an archival effort in itself, a debt owed to all those whose lives were touched and transformed by the life of this institution. More importantly, the way institutions like JNU think and function is crucial to the history of higher education in India and the sociology of knowledge more generally. A crisis can thus be turned into an opportunity and this book is a small step towards creating that opportunity.

Institutions develop within and against moulds. The biography of such an institution cannot afford to be a mere laundry list of achievements; rather, it must equally record and confront the failures, the struggles, sometimes unsuccessful, in breaking out of preconceived moulds as well as in creating alternatives. What are the 'thought worlds'[1]—here not to be confused with 'schools of thought'—that have been enabled in a space like JNU? Did it live up to the dreams and aspirations of those responsible for its early existence? What was the distinctive culture of teaching and learning built up at JNU and to what pressures, changes, and developments did this

[1]Mary Douglas, *How Institutions Think*, Syracuse: Syracuse University Press, 1986, p. 16.

culture respond and adapt? Were there also unanticipated consequences of this culture of learning and teaching? Most important, to what extent can the more positive of these be replicated in other locations?

The Idea of a New University

Jawaharlal Nehru University has had a complicated history as an idea. By the late 1950s, Delhi University was facing a crisis: there had been an exponential increase in student population, colleges were mushrooming, finances were inadequate, the infrastructure was under pressure, and administration from the university office in North Delhi was stretched to a breaking point. C. D. Deshmukh and others in the University Grants Commission felt that a second campus in South Delhi would resolve the immediate problem, relieving pressure on the North Campus and dividing administrative responsibilities.[2] When persuaded to join as the Vice Chancellor of Delhi University, Deshmukh participated in concretizing the project. The idea was to split the university of Delhi into two, somewhere close to Ajmeri Gate, but for historical reasons, retaining Delhi College within the jurisdiction of the North Campus.

The UGC discussed the scheme and sent a plan to the Education Ministry; in 1963 an Expert Committee was set up by the Ministry to work out the broad proposal, and M. C. Chagla, the Education Minister, talked to Nehru about the idea. In his memoir, Chagla recounts the conversation:

> I had once told Nehru that if I had his approval, I would establish another university in Delhi. I explained that Delhi was growing and one university was not adequate for its student population. Nehru agreed. I then mentioned with some hesitation a more delicate point. I said: 'Panditji, I would like to name this university after you. You have been the Prime Minister of this country since its independence, and you have ruled over our destinies from this city.' Nehru flared up: 'You know my views about raising memorials to living persons. It is entirely wrong. No statues should be raised to living persons

[2]C. D. Deshmukh, *The Course of My Life*, Hyderabad: Orient Longman, 1974, p. 254. Deshmukh was appointed the first UGC Chairman in 1956 and remained in office until 1961. He would subsequently go on to be the Vice Chancellor of Delhi University in 1962.

> and no institutions should be named after them.' I persisted that the only appropriate name for the university was Nehru University. He refused to give way, and reminded me that there were several names to choose from. Delhi had been called differently at different times in its history, and I could select one of these names. He suggested 'Raisina' as a possibility; it is a very fine sounding name.[3]

When Nehru died on 27 May 1964, a committee was already working out the details of this new university, imagined as the South Campus of Delhi University.[4] The name Raisina had appealed to those involved in the discussion, and Deshmukh liked it too. However, after Nehru's death, there was a rush to memorialize him. Chagla persuaded others that the university should be now named after Nehru. When the bill for the establishment of Jawaharlal Nehru University was tabled on the Rajya Sabha floor on 24 December 1964, the proposed Raisina University was reanointed as Jawaharlal Nehru University.

For a while, nothing changed much, except the name. How was the old idea to be reworked? No one was very clear. Chagla and many others were caught in a dilemma, pulled in seemingly contrary directions. From 1960 when the idea was first mooted to May 1964, the moment of Nehru's death, the proposal for the new university was intimately connected to the history of Delhi University and its problems. Was it possible to be wedded to that conception and yet imagine something radically new? Would not the burden of the past weigh upon the present, constraining the possibility of innovation and experimentation? Caught in a bind, Chagla pleaded for time. When the bill was introduced in the Rajya Sabha on 24 December 1964, there was no discussion.

◆

In the meantime, the idea of an institution in Nehru's memory was discussed at a different level outside the Parliament. Two common ideas appeared in most of the proposals. First, Nehru's name should not be associated with a pre-existing institution: it was necessary to plan for a new

---

[3]M. C. Chagla, *Roses in December: An Autobiography*, Bombay: Bharatiya Vidya Bhavan, 1975, p. 372.

[4]See *Rajya Sabha Debates*, 24 December 1964; *Lok Sabha Debates*, 20 September 1965, pp. 6,508ff.

kind of institution. And, second, this should be a special institution—in a sense, elite and exclusive. The Jawaharlal Nehru Memorial Fund (JNMF) was set up on 17 August 1964. Soon after, a panel of experts was formed to advise on the possible establishment of the Nehru Memorial Institute of Advanced Studies and the Committee was to finalize its report within three months. The Convener of the panel was Romesh Thapar, one of the founding editors of the journal *Seminar*, and the other five members were: J. K. Chowdhury, R. N. Dogra, B. N. Ganguly, P. N. Kirpal, and K. G. Saiyidain.

The industrialist, J. R. D. Tata, one of the Trustees of the JNMF, had strong views on how institutions of higher learning ought to be developed in India. Somewhat suspicious of the left-leaning Thapar, he persuaded the JNMF to set up another working group to prepare a concrete project report for 'a high-level educational institution as a memorial to Jawaharlal Nehru'.[5] It was another high-powered committee consisting of Professor Jean Capelle, formerly Rector of several universities in France and Director-General, Ministry of Education, Paris, Dr S. Dhawan, Director, Indian Institute of Science, Bangalore, Dr A. G. Evstafiev, Chief of the UNESCO Mission in India, Dr Malcolm M. Willey, formerly Vice President for Academic Affairs at the University of Minnesota, and Professor R. Choksi, Managing Trustee, Sir Dorab Tata Trust, Bombay. Instead of a regular university, they recommended the setting up of a Nehru Academy—an institution of excellence, distinctive and exclusive. It was visualized as a high-level post graduate institute providing special education to 'exceptional men and women'. There was to be only one course of study, integrating natural sciences, social sciences and humanistic studies, that would produce men and women of action with wide ranging knowledge and deep moral values. No more than a hundred students were to be admitted to this institute.

Tata himself was committed to this idea of excellence and exclusivity. In his own note to the Nehru Memorial Fund, which summarized a lecture he had given at the Indian Institute of Science in Bangalore, he advocated the creation of an institute on the lines of the French 'Grandes Écoles', as an

[5]'Project Report on Educational Institution in the Name of Jawaharlal Nehru', Douglas Ensminger Papers, Box 3, Folder 106, call number: MS 1315 Series, Yale University Library.

alternative to the usual university.[6] In France, since the days of Napoleon, the state had taken the initiative to train an elite for public service, quite apart from the work of universities. This was done through these Grandes Écoles to which only the 'most gifted' could ever hope to enter. While agreeing that the state should spread education as widely as possible, Tata underlined a compelling need 'to train to the highest level a select few'.[7] The progress of the country, he believed, would depend greatly on the 'creative and constructive abilities of an elite of brilliant administrators, managers, scientists and innovators whose example and leadership will inspire others'.[8] Instead of being complacent with the ordinary, Indians had to aspire for the finest: 'It is essential that amid the arid stretches of mediocrity there be here and there an oasis of excellence.'[9] From such focal points of distinction, Tata felt, influence would radiate outwards.

◆

Dr Douglas Ensminger of Ford Foundation (FF), a good friend of J. R. D. Tata, was also asked to submit a note to the JNMF outlining his proposal for the Institute of Advanced Studies to be established in memory of Jawaharlal Nehru.[10] This eight-page note was entitled 'A Prospectus of a New National Institution of Higher Learning in India'.[11]

Having come to India in 1952, Ensminger had become a powerful figure in Indian political circles.[12] He had won the confidence of Indian

---

[6]Note of J. R. D. Tata, Bombay, Dr K. G. Saiyidain Papers.

[7]Ibid.

[8]Ibid.

[9]Ibid.

[10]Dismayed with the public university system and keen on an alternative, Ensminger had tried to persuade Tata, much before Nehru's death, to start a private university in the name of Nehru. The plan never took off. See Douglas Ensminger, 'Oral History Transcript', 23 August 1972, Rockefeller Archive Centre, New York, Collection Ford Foundation, FA 744, Series B, Box 2, Folder B23, pp. 63–64.

[11]'Prospectus for a New National Institution of Higher Learning in India', forwarded by M. V. Rajan, to all members of the Panel of Experts to set up the Institute of Advanced Studies, to be established in memory of Jawaharlal Nehru, 19 September 1964. Dr K. G. Saiyidain Papers.

[12]Nicole Sackley, 'Foundation in the Field: The Ford Foundation New Delhi Office and the Construction of Development Knowledge, 1951-1970', *American Foundations and the Coproduction of World Order in the Twentieth Century*, edited by Ulrich Herbert and Jörn Leonhard, Göttingen: Vandenhoeck & Ruprecht, 2012, pp. 232–60.

politicians by resisting politically sensitive projects emanating from the US head office, shielding the Indian FF from the direct interference of the US government, and actively participating in the rural reconstruction projects of the time.[13] He hated the existing educational system in India and wanted it to be radically overhauled.[14] Everything, he felt, was wrong with the system. It was driven by examinations, and sustained by memorization. Its object was to produce degree holders and clerks, not an enlightened citizenry. It held out the promise of government jobs, not new realms of knowledge. He was convinced that education could not be radically transformed unless the British system was thoroughly rejected.[15] What a great difference it would have made, he said, if the Indian political leaders had been 'as strongly motivated to throwing out the British pattern of education as they were in throwing out English as a language along with the British'.[16] But Indians, he felt, did not want to do that. They respected the British and embraced the system the British masters instituted.

Ensminger knew the pressure for mass education in India. Everyone, he felt, wanted to enroll in some college and get a degree—the imagined but illusory passport to a secure job. But he had no sympathy for this hankering for degrees. The quality of education is what mattered. He was cynical about the idea of mass access to higher education, and was convinced that such access only creates a sick system, a rut, that drags quality down. As an official of the FF, support had to be extended only to institutions of higher learning that promised excellence, and to select departments in existing universities that demonstrated their potential for brilliance.

So when Ensminger penned his 'Prospectus', he too was thinking of an elite institution—exclusive, somewhat secluded, protected from the 'undesirable effects' of metropolitan life—that would break away from the existing mould of Indian universities. It ought to be 'free to experiment

---

[13]Ibid.

[14]See Douglas Ensminger's Oral History transcript, 23 August 1972, Rockefeller Archive Centre, New York, Collection Ford Foundation FA 744, Series B, Box 2, Folder B23, pp. 2–6.

[15]Ibid., p. 4.

[16]Ensminger said 'If the nation's institutions of higher learning turn out educated clerks, the nation will develop a clerk mentality. India is in danger of having a clerk mentality'; Ibid.

with and develop new practices and procedures that would be difficult or impossible for the existing universities to undertake'. The faculty should be well paid and chosen with the greatest care, for only 'superior faculty' attract good students. Students too should be wisely chosen, through innovative tests. 'Performance on traditional type examinations,' Ensminger emphasized, 'must not be the criteria for admission.' As was the case in the US, pay and promotion ought to be based on merit, not seniority. In lieu of the traditional structure of faculties and departments, the Academy should have institutes involved in academic work that was of use to India's developing needs. Senior faculty members should not be 'burdened with unnecessary administrative tasks or any other kind of routine work'.[17] The carefully drafted note that Ensminger submitted envisioned an Academy where merit counted above everything else—it was to determine admission, appointment, pay—and the academy would be a space where scholars would pursue high level research without disturbance. The name did not really matter—it could be Nehru National Academy or Institute—as long as it was radically different from Indian universities shaped by British minds.[18]

◆

The Romesh Thapar committee had three meetings between September–October 1964, discussed all the notes and memoranda that it had received, and finalized its report within a month.[19] It proposed the establishment of a Nehru Academy in Sohna, within 33 miles of Delhi, that would coexist with other institutes within the jurisdiction of the Nehru Memorial Fund. The Academy would be a graduate and postgraduate institute, exploring the frontiers of different disciplines and engaged in interdisciplinary

---

[17]Ibid.

[18]Ensminger was critical of the Education Ministry backing off from the commitment made to Deshmukh about creating a second campus for Delhi University. Ibid., pp. 72–73. He does not discuss the Jawaharlal Nehru University in his long 100-page oral testimony on 'Ford Foundation Interest and Involvement in Indian Education', dated 23 August 1972. Ibid, while talking a lot about FF involvement in developing the language departments, the Centre for Chinese Studies, and the Library in DU. Our reading of the significance of Ensminger's note 'Prospectus for a New National Institution of Higher Learning in India' is different from Gyan Prakash. See below.

[19]'Report of the Committee of Experts on the Establishment of the Nehru Memorial Institute of Advanced Studies', Dr K. G. Saiyidain Papers.

research. Though an autonomous academy, it would be under the control of the Nehru Memorial Trust. The number of students was not to exceed 1,000, since the pressure of numbers could 'dilute the quality of work'. The model upheld was that of advanced research centres such as those at Princeton, Stanford, and Hawaii. Once again, we see in the proposal a fear of numbers, and the fantasy of an exclusivist research centre, far removed from the university that was to come into being later.

◆

Over the subsequent months the discussion took many different turns. More committees were set up, memos circulated, representations were made, and the tenor of the discussion kept changing. Yet, the vision of the new university could not emancipate itself easily from the idea of being the south campus of Delhi University. In his short speech on the bill on the floor of the Rajya Sabha eight months later, on 31 August 1965, Chagla emphasized once again the problem of booming numbers and the unbearable pressures on Delhi University. The population of Delhi, he said, had grown exponentially since Independence, the number of colleges had increased from 7 in 1947–48 to 35 in 1964–65, and the enrolment of students had shot up from 4,583 to 30,640 in the same period.[20] This university, however, was not to be 'a mere duplication of the old'. It had to be imagined, Chagla emphasized, by drawing on the experiential insights of the finest educational institutions of the world. In what way it was to be different was not yet adequately clear.

This lack of clarity was systematically unpacked by several members of the House even before the bill was sent to the Joint Committee. Perhaps the clearest statement came from G. Ramachandran, a Gandhian educationist who was a nominated member of the Rajya Sabha. He urged Chagla to show some originality, move away from the trodden path, think of something new, rather than a repetition of the old. The name of Nehru, he pleaded, ought not to be affixed to a university cut from the old cloth, and had been planned to solve an administrative problem, not to create something new. The claims being made were big, but the ideas were unclear, amorphous, and traditional. If 14 colleges with 14,000 students

[20]The same argument was put forward when the bill was presented in the Lok Sabha on 20 September 1965. See Jawaharlal Nehru University Bill, 20 September 1965, *Lok Sabha Debates*, pp. 6,508–70.

were being affiliated to the new university, how was it possible to innovate? The university would be tied to the existing structure of Delhi University, to its curriculum and syllabus as well as the terrible old examination system. The claim that the university would 'embody a unique synthesis of the humanities, the sciences and technology worthy of the great son of India and so on' was no more than empty rhetoric.

> This kind of thing has been said every time a new university has been started. I remember the starting of the Kerala University long ago. I knew very clearly what was happening when the Annamalai University was being started. Great claims were made. I remember, on the floor of the Kerala Legislature, it was said that what was going to be started would kindle the lamp of Kerala culture and that the light of that lamp will shine across the world. When the Annamalai University was started, it was said that the genius of the Tamil language and culture will be brought out by this University and that it will be presented as a great offering to the rest of the world and so on.... All those dreams are gone.[21]

Warning against the implementation of a project without a substantive vision, Ramachandran insisted that some time be spent in thinking of the way the new university could embody the principles and ideals Nehru stood for.

After introduction, the bill was referred to a joint committee of the two houses. In the meetings that followed many eminent academics were called to offer their opinion. Almost unanimously they argued against existing colleges being affiliated to the new university. To innovate without constraints, it had to start with a clean slate, unfettered by existing structures. To be worthy of the name it was supposed to bear, the new institution had to represent the principles that infused Nehru's life—secularism and cosmopolitanism, social justice and scientific temper, as well as his interest in international affairs and his commitment to world peace. It had to be a university of an 'entirely new type'.

[21] *Rajya Sabha Debates*, 1 September 1965, p. 2,293.

The Pillars of an Edifice

In the stimulating discussion that followed on the floor of the house on 1 and 6 December 1965, each of these ideas was debated at length, the meaning of each term was interrogated, and the ideals that Jawaharlal Nehru University was to represent were thought through. In what way was it to be a university of an 'entirely new type'? What was to be unique about the university? What elements were to define its identity?

First: criticality. Many in the house were opposed to the naming of a university after an individual. To do so, they felt, was to perpetuate a cult, propagate the ideas of an individual, instead of creating a space for debate and dialogue. Allaying such fears, Chagla argued passionately that he was aware of the danger of canonizing individuals, and creating prophets. Prophets' words are glorified, quoted, and misquoted. They congeal and harden into ideas that become sterile and barren. 'Nehru believed in dynamism,' said Chagla, 'and it is not the intention of this University that we should study these principles (the general principles encoded in the First Schedule) as Nehru believed in them. It would be open to the students to criticise these principles, to push them forward, to give them a dynamic edge.'[22] The general ideals of secularism and social justice, he urged, were not the ideals of one individual alone, 'those are the principles to which the whole nation subscribes'.[23] But even a 'national legacy' could not be ossified. It was important for students and teachers to probe these ideas, discuss and critique them, even as they are committed to them. Dialogue and debate, thus, were to be integral to the culture of the university

Second: secularism. The First Schedule of the JNU Bill declared that the university would be committed to secularism. How was this secularism to be defined? What was this ideal that was to express the very essence of the new university? This is how Chagla elaborated the idea:

> Now, what is secularism in our country? I agree that the Constitution does not use the word. But secularism, as we understand it, means equality before the law, fundamental rights guaranteed to all our citizens, no discrimination between one citizen and another on the

[22]*Rajya Sabha Debates*, 6 December 1965, p. 3,797.
[23]Ibid.

> grounds of race, caste, community or religion.... And finally—most important—no officially established Church in this country. The distinction is between the secular society in India and the theocratic society in Pakistan.[24]

As the debate on secularism unfolded on the floor of the house, Chagla was pushed from opposite sides. Maridas Ruthnaswamy, the most eloquent Rajya Sabha member of the Swatantra Party, feared the use of the term, for secularism to him was 'anti-religion', hostile to all religion.[25] Such a notion could not be celebrated in a country like India with its many religions. On the other hand, Professor M. B. Lal, a socialist, argued passionately that secularism alone could hold the country together. For Lal, secularism was not mere tolerance: it was an ethical doctrine advocating a moral code independent of all religious considerations or practices; and in a multireligious country like India, secularism alone could be the basis of democracy. [26]

In concluding the discussion on the issue, Chagla underlined the intimate constitutive link between secularism and all the other ideals the nation valued. Only secularism could ensure equality, justice, and democracy. If India aspired to be a democracy it had to be secular. To depart from the ideals of secularism was to destroy democracy. If the state was partisan, favouring one religion against another, the ideals of justice and equity would be thrown overboard, and the multicultural, multireligious fabric of Indian democracy would be torn apart.

Third: inclusivity. This institution of 'an entirely new type' was not to be an exclusive academy of higher research. Pedagogic practices had to be integrated from the finest universities of the world, and innovative courses introduced, but the university had to open up to diverse social groups. Imagined as a national university, not a provincial one, it had to embody the nation. And it could be truly Indian only by incorporating the diversity that was India. So, the First Schedule of the bill stated that the university had to 'take special measures to facilitate students and teachers from all over India to join the University and participate in its

[24]Ibid., p. 3,800.

[25]Ibid., pp. 3,800 and 3,810.

[26]Ibid., p. 3,820ff.

academic programmes'.[27] Meeting fellow students from different parts of India would itself be a learning experience, an encounter that would help students understand the meaning of cultural diversity and create the basis of a truly composite culture.

The university, moreover, could not become the preserve of the rich. While aspiring for excellence it had to be committed to social justice. Chagla was assertive: '[H]igher education is not the monopoly or the privilege of a few. In our country we want to give higher education to as many people as possible.'[28] Everyone agreed that those who could not afford education had to be offered scholarships, some in fact argued with passion that no one should be charged for education.

Fourth: interdisciplinarity. The existing courses of studies in Indian universities were seen as too specialized, creating hard boundaries between disciplines. Students lived in segregated worlds, unaware of the advances of other disciplines. Chagla was keen that the students study a common course—somewhat like the PPE at Oxford—that combined natural sciences, social sciences, and the humanistic disciplines; others felt the common course should include philosophy and mathematics too.[29] After a prolonged discussion, the Select Committee decided that academic activity should be organized within overarching Schools with a set of Centres. The School would create a space for interaction between disciplines, and the Centres would offer different sets of specialization.

Fifth: autonomy. The ideal of institutional autonomy was part of the discourse of the time. The Radhakrishnan Committee had emphasized:

> Higher education is, undoubtedly, an obligation of the State but State aid is not to be confused with State control over academic policies and practices. Intellectual progress demands the maintenance of the spirit of free inquiry. The pursuit and practice of truth regardless of consequences has been the ambition of universities.[30]

The principle of autonomy, the Radhakrishnan Committee had argued, was intimately connected to the idea of liberty and freedom. Liberty

---

[27]*Rajya Sabha Debates*, 1 December 1965.

[28]Ibid., 6 December 1965, pp. 3,801–2.

[29]PPE is the Oxford undergraduate programme on Philosophy, Politics, Economics.

[30]*The Report of the University Education Commission*, December 1948–August 1949, Vol. 1, Government of India Press, 1949, p. 48.

cannot be fully exercised without autonomy from control, and exercise of government control would suffocate democracy:

> Exclusive control of education by the State has been an important factor facilitating the maintenance of totalitarian tyrannies.... We must resist, in the case of our own democracy, the trend towards the Governmental domination of the educational process.[31]

This ideal was distinct from its neoliberal version that is gaining currency today, one that would argue for a radical distance between the state and education, freeing the government of all social responsibility, transferring education to the realm of individual initiative, private capital. What was emphasized in the Radhakrishnan Report, and later in the Kothari Report, was the state's obligation to fund education, but not to interfere with its day-to-day functioning.[32] That would be a violation of autonomy, freedom, and liberty enjoined by the Constitution. Only under totalitarianism was this seen as acceptable, natural, and normal, not within the working of democracies. The Parliament could provide a broad frame, create enabling conditions, but the Vice Chancellor and the faculty were to develop the academic programme and work out the institutional structures of administrative functioning. They were to devise new programmes of study, new courses, new modes of examination.

Finally: love and trust. To build a new institution of an entirely new type, students and teachers had to be empowered and trusted, given the space to innovate. This was asserted by many of those who spoke on the JNU Bill on the floor of the house. Irritated with the talk of regular Visitorial review and assessment, Tara Chand declared that no great institution could be built unless the teachers and administrators were trusted and respected. It was essential, urged Tara Chand, to trust the teachers and students, listen to their voice, and integrate them within representative structures of the university.[33] Only such trust could generate

[31]Ibid., p. 48.

[32]*Report of the Educational Commission, 1964-66*, Chaired by D. S. Kothari, Ministry of Education, New Delhi: Government of India, 1966.

[33]*Rajya Sabha Debates*, 6 December 1965, p. 3,484ff. Tara Chand said: 'The functioning of the University depends upon the trust that you place in the teaching staff of the University, they depend upon the arrangements that you make for dealing with the students of the University. Some friend over there made this point that greater trust

the energy that could fashion a great institution.[34] Ramachandran's vision was even more radical. Not just the teachers, the students had to be trusted, he said.

> I would like this University more to be a students' university than a professors' university or lecturers' university. The students must be allowed a full hand in the shaping of the curricula, of the syllabi and the entire work and life inside the University so that ultimately in the name of Pandit Nehru we establish a unique institution, in the name of a unique person functioning in a unique way and particularly as a Students' Republic.[35]

These were elements of a frame—enunciation of ideals, the outlining of a vision. What would happen to the frame was for history to tell. Not everyone agreed fully with Ramachandran, but JNU as it evolved was undoubtedly fashioned through the active participation of teachers and students.

Red-Brick Buildings on a Rocky Terrain

While the first Vice Chancellor, G. Parthasarathi was entrusted with the task of developing the academic and administrative structure of the university, the government went around looking for a suitable space where this new university could come up. Near Munirka village, it had identified 300 acres for the South Campus of Delhi University. This was too small for such an ambitious project of institution-building. After frantic efforts, over a thousand acres were acquired by mid-1965.[36]

This area was a bare and rocky plateau—part of the Mewat branch of the Aravallis that extends into Delhi from its southern end and stretches in a thin strip northeast up to Wazirabad. After 1860, the central and

should be put in the students. I entirely approve of that sentiment. The students that are coming to the University are not children; they are grown-up people...why not develop in the University such bodies and institutions as will give a chance to these young men and young women to have their say on matters which will, after all, affect them most intimately?' p. 3,485.

[34] *Rajya Sabha Debates*, 2 December 1965, pp. 3,583ff.

[35] Ibid., 1 September 1965, p. 2,298.

[36] Ibid., 19 March 1965; Ibid., 12 September 1966, pp. 5,237–38.

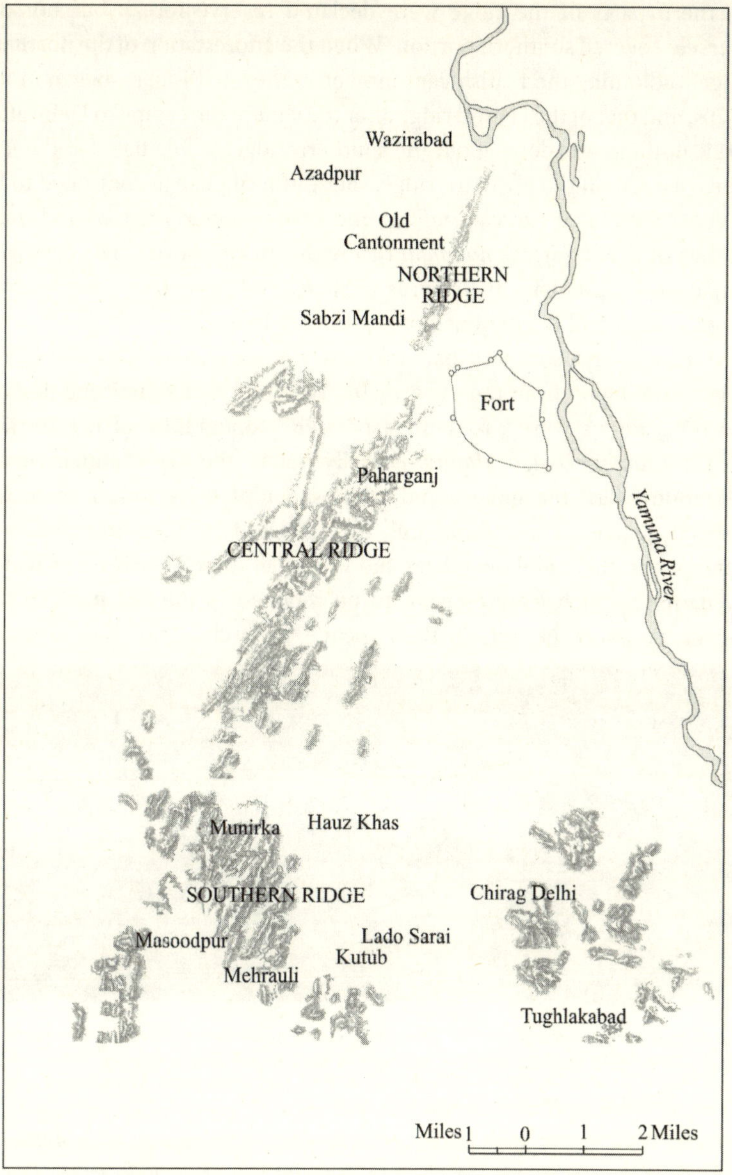

Map of the Delhi ridge, 1870s.
This map has been drawn on the basis of a revenue map produced in the 1870s by W. H. Wilkins. Place names are spelt the way they were in the 1960s. JNU campus is to the south of Munirka.

northern parts of the ridge were declared reserve forest, but not the sparsely covered southern portion. When the afforestation of the northern ridge—adjoining the British cantonment in the Civil Lines—began in the 1870s, and that of the central ridge after the shift of the capital to Delhi after 1911, nothing was done about the southern ridge. While babul and neem were planted on the northern ridge, the southern plateau continued to be covered with kikar (*acacia arabica*) and karil (*campari aphylla*) and small bushes of beri (*zizyphis nummularia*) with prickly thorn.[37] For centuries Gujar pastoralists with their herds of sheep and goats had traversed this ridge, their small habitations dotting the landscape.

On this arid southern part of the Delhi ridge, red-brick structures began coming up from the early 1970s. The architects submitting designs for the campus were asked to respect the topography of the terrain. As the *Campus Design Manual* lyrically put it 'the dry channels of the monsoon nalas, the gulleys and ravines, sculpted by soil erosion, the disused quarries, the residual hill, the scattered boulders over gulleyed pene plains, the undulating dales and vales—all these have been provided by nature'.[38] Such features were to be retained as integral parts of the university landscape. Yet, Sir Basil Spence, the architect of the University

The JNU campus in the early 1970s. This image of the rocky terrain on which the architects were to plan the university complex was part of the campus design manual.

Source: A Study in Campus Designs

[37]Oswald Wood and R. Machonachie, *Final Report on the Settlement of Land Revenue in the Delhi District*, Lahore, 1882, p. 3ff. Kalpavriksha, *The Delhi Ridge Forest: Decline and Conservation*, 1991.

[38]*A Study in Campus Designs: National Competition for the Master Plan of Jawaharlal Nehru University Campus*, Department of Advertising and Visual Publicity, Delhi: Ministry of Information and Broadcasting, 1974, p. 6.

of Sussex which JNU hoped to emulate in some respects, had this to say about the initial campus design:

> In the programme approved by the UGC, there is no place for what is called 'waste space'—the colonnade or cluster where friends can walk and talk, discussing the latest seminar or the last piece of research, or the distinguished lecture. Yet the addition of spaces like these lifts a mere group of buildings to the level of a place of higher learning.[39]

Fifty years later, we could agree that Basil Spence's idea has been more than amply met in the design of a campus that enhances rather than engulfs or flattens the natural features. 'Waste spaces'—or 'open spaces'—have become the defining features of the JNU landscape. We could even say that the open spaces continue to dominate the 1,000-acre campus (today, due to a process of institutional proliferation on its edges, reduced only to 600 acres). The built space combines with open space for exactly the kinds of discussions and debates that have made it a place of higher learning. Well into the 1980s however, JNU retained its aridity almost as a badge of honour, as if the very challenge of this topography was in the sheer efflorescence of ideas and in the flourishing of diversity—of languages and lifestyles from across India. The rocks around the library complex, or around Ganga Dhaba, have been turned into dialogic spaces and debating arenas—places of intellectual ferment, away from the far shoddier built spaces of classrooms and seminar halls, whose poor maintenance and upkeep have dealt them a far greater blow than weathering has the rocks.

Still, how far we have travelled from that barren image of the Aravallis to the green campus of today, evident not only in the cascading bougainvillea of the summer months, but the plentiful jamun, red-silk cotton trees, clumps of bamboo and bottlebrush that have thickly taken root in the campus, before natural modes of propagation took over. Many features of the C. P. Kukreja Plan (the architect chosen from sixty-eight applicants for the design of the campus) and the imagined university never came into being: the three seasonal waterbodies that were to be turned into lakes; the bold rose garden in memory of Jawaharlal Nehru; or even the provisions for stables and horse-riding. Folklore has it that Kukreja planned the stepped storeys of both the hostels and the Academic Complex

[39]Ibid., p. 6.

as pyramids and inverted pyramids respectively but at least the design submitted for the competition betrayed no desire beyond the ecological.

To trace the path of a snake that might have just crossed before you, to catch the glimpse of the golden jackal cubs, or the groups of shy nilgai—the campus offers diverse pleasures to those who wish to explore this wealth. It is the open spaces of JNU that have nourished incomparably diverse forms of plant, animal, bird, and insect life, despite the fact that the planned museum/archive/gallery/deer park/butterfly garden which would have formally showcased such diversity have not come into existence. It is still to these open spaces that many from the surrounding areas return each morning, to provide water and simple sustenance to forms of life from which they have today been completely estranged. The exponential growth of buildings, including multi-storeyed apartments which are segregated from the rest of the campus, was inevitable given the rise in the student and faculty populations (more than 8,000 and 600 respectively). In some cases, as in the proposed motorable road through Parthasarathi Rocks, the habitat has been saved from 'improvement'. But it is the relentless idiom of 'improvement' in the form of well-laid, brightly lit pavements—signs of the recent desire for a stultifying institutional homogeneity—that have seriously disturbed the wildlife of the night.

Fifty years later: JNU campus in 2019. The forest cover has now transformed the landscape of the university, with the buildings partly hidden between the dense growth of trees. Whether all the trees planted are ideal for this terrain is a different issue that needs to be addressed.

Photo courtesy: Samim Asgor Ali

Between Autonomy and Accountability

The building of an institution which had neither campus nor teachers was a challenge that was taken up by the first Vice Chancellor, G. Parthasarathi—a highly respected diplomat and administrator.[40] He was given enormous powers to make the initial appointments and build a team that would work out a concrete vision plan. Inviting several teachers from outside the country—at least fifteen of them—and from other institutions within the country, he gave his first recruits six months in which to brainstorm and produce a syllabus.[41] He urged them to be part of an intellectual adventure and visualize an academic programme that would be exciting and unique. Numerous accounts in this volume speak of the freedom and autonomy he gave to the faculty to innovate and experiment.

It is a thin line indeed between the freedom and autonomy given to institution builders such as GP (or P. C. Mahalanobis, Homi Bhabha, or V. K. R. V. Rao) and their practices which will certainly be seen as arbitrary today. But those were early days. Rulebooks were yet to be created to regulate the activities of the institution. What institutional architecture was put in place to ensure that exceptional power was not consolidated? What norms were to be devised and rules codified? GP expressed his optimism that the 'new and innovative' approach would bring about excellence. 'We are also keen to adopt,' he said, 'in our academic organization, the democratic instead of the hierarchical pattern, and to establish traditions of intimate and close cooperation between the teachers and students who will be selected on a nationwide basis, with adequate provision for fellowships and scholarships. I am sure that these objectives and programme would attract brilliant young Indian scholars, here and abroad to the University.'[42] JNU lived up to the promise in both senses, fostering a democratic spirit in its functioning from the start, with the involvement of students and teachers, and also in establishing programmes and disciplines—environmental sciences for instance—which were truly visionary for their times.

The red-brick university with a difference was brought into being

---

[40]Ashok Parthasarthi, *GP: 1912-1995*, New Delhi: Academic Foundation, 2018, esp. pp. 135–83.

[41]Ibid., p.141.

[42]Ibid.

through a deliberative process, assuring applicants and prospective students a degree of fairness and transparency that is relatively rare in our university ecosystem. To look back on a founding moment when liberties were taken with the process of appointment, thus, is neither to applaud nor to condemn but to historicize, to place the pioneers in their context, and to acknowledge the structures of privilege which may have been effaced in the name of merit, a category which has since not only been questioned but critically reviewed within JNU itself.

◆

Yet what is autonomy which does not also imply accountability? In its early years, JNU, like most other institutions in the country, developed its own norms of accountability, without which the question of autonomy could become meaningless. Rather than the growing millennial obsession with an audit culture and with international rankings, to which we are witness today, JNU sought its own way of being accountable to the tax-payer: through the development of a pluralistic, secular, and democratic process of institution-building, and by mentoring many who were the first generation to enter higher education. JNU strove to be accountable to students through modes of democratic self-governance (such as regular faculty meetings, as well as the meetings of the Student Faculty Committee [SFC], Centre for Advanced Scientific Research, Boards of Studies, and of course vigorous and active participation in the Academic Council and Executive Council) which were built into both the norms and statutes of the university. A reasonably efficient administrative structure thus came into place, in which faculty themselves played a critical role, often participating in time-consuming consensus-building processes. Rather than an infantilizing system of recording 'attendance' for its own sake, which goes against best practices of academic institutions worldwide, most teachers were participants in regular weekly seminars, within and beyond the department, student presentations, conferences organized at JNU, etc.[43]

---

[43]Following the arbitrary imposition of compulsory attendance for teachers in 2018, which has currently been stayed by the High Court, JNUTA sought responses from a wide range of universities worldwide to the idea of compulsory attendance; responses overwhelmingly confirmed (in a survey of seventy-five universities in twenty-one countries) that compulsory attendance impeded cultures of research and teaching

The opportunities that JNU provided to its faculty resulted in a large and very respectable body of scholarship in every recognized and newly pioneered field. Its status as India's premier research and teaching institution (JNU enjoys a NAAC rating of 3.77 (A++) on a four-point scale for the five-year period ending 2018) has partly arisen from this dedication to research and writing. Well over 600 PhDs and approximately 900 MPhils are produced each year. It has been also widely acknowledged that JNU contributes a disproportionately large number of research articles and books in the social sciences compared with most Indian research institutions and universities put together.[44] Whether there have been methodological and conceptual innovations in different fields of research—and if so how influential they have been—perhaps should be assessed more in terms of path-breaking programmes established at JNU and their trajectories.[45]

JNU teachers' engagement with the popularization of research, or its thought worlds, to which we give the name of public intellection more generally, has been equally impressive, with a large number of teachers contributing to newspapers, and now social media platforms, on a regular basis. True, much of that writing occurs in English, which immediately confines the reach of such writing in a country such as India, (we return to the growing predicaments and limits of the language of higher education below) but there have been few important policy and administrative measures, relating to both domestic and international affairs, in which scholars from JNU have not only participated but also shaped public opinion. On another register is the contribution of JNU teachers to efforts such as the writing of textbooks, particularly for high schools and undergraduate teaching. For instance, both the single author

---

that were creative and consistent (with the notable exception of the University of Malaya, Kuala Lumpur) *JNUTA Report: Global Practices of Attendance for Academic Accountability*, January 2019.

[44]Partha Chatterjee, citing the 2001 SSRC sponsored study of social science research in India, shows that JNU accounted for between 9.92 and 14 per cent of articles in specific fields, alongside Delhi University and Nehru Memorial Museum and Library. 'Institutional Context of Social Science Research in India,' *Economic and Political Weekly,* 31 August 2002, pp. 3,604–12.

[45]For instance, a 2011 DFID (South Asia Research Hub, September 2011) report *Social Science Research in India: A Mapping Report*, lists JNU among a handful of institutions producing—both in quantity and quality—high quality social science research.

NCERT books in history which were in circulation from 1976–2002, which continue to be profitably consulted by millions across the country, and the multi-authored and thematically arranged textbooks in history since 2006 have had significant contributions from JNU scholars. Faculty members from the Centre for the Study of Social Systems, Centre for Political Studies, and Centre for the Study of Regional Development also participated actively in the production of these textbooks.

Innovations

The significance of interdisciplinary studies was strongly emphasized when JNU was established. In the subsequent decades, this ideal was to unfold in three ways. First: each Centre was to be an interdisciplinary space, operate with an interdisciplinary vision. Courses were expected to be formulated in ways that broke down the old disciplinary boundaries, incorporating insights of other disciplines, and encouraging students to read beyond narrowly defined confines of a subject. Second: the Schools were to be interdisciplinary spaces beyond the Centre, encouraging faculty members and students to interact across Centres and across disciplinary boundaries. Information, ideas, and knowledge were supposed to flow between Centres. Third: this idea of interdisciplinarity was to shape the relationship between Schools. Intellectual interaction between Schools was to be encouraged, with students from one School crediting or auditing courses in other Schools, and faculty members of different Schools coming together to participate in collective intellectual projects. Subsequently a number of smaller interdisciplinary centres and programmes that were set up: Centre for the Study of Law and Governance, Centre for Women's Studies, Centre for North East Studies, School of Arts and Aesthetics, have pioneered the way forward in drawing on the strengths of several disciplines.

As a university, JNU proved equal to the task of responding to important national developments and critical events: following the dramatic changes ushered in by the Mandal Commission Report, there was intense debate and discussion on the need for a centre exclusively focused on a unique Indian problem. Questions of caste had been debated and discussed across several centres at the university, and, in its first incarnation, the formula for deciding deprivation points took into account caste identities.[46] The setting up of the Centre for the Study of Discrimination and Exclusion, therefore, was not only a timely and creative innovation in response to India's most unique and persistent forms of hierarchy, it also served as a model for other such centres that were opened across the country by the UGC thereafter.[47] Similarly, the Centre for the Study of Law and Governance and the Centre for Women's Studies broke new ground in their methods and courses, and provided models in form and substance in several universities thereafter. In other words, research at JNU particularly in the social sciences, has remained interdisciplinary and context-sensitive in the richest sense of the term. While it is true that interdisciplinarity has become part of an accepted ideal at JNU, much more can be, and ought to be, done to develop this ideal.[48]

Other innovations of the teaching and learning culture of JNU included the semester system (a first in the public university system), a tutorial system and a robust system of internal assessment. (Teachers' rooms were in fact designed as tutorial cum teacher rooms.) Followed in the breach rather than in practice in some other parts of the country, this form of intensive discussion, based on the student's own writing and evaluated by the individual teacher, was at first an attempt to recall the finest mentoring traditions of the Oxbridge model. But the tutorial system very often reaffirms the power of privilege: the assertive voice of certainty often dominates, silencing those who are hesitant and uncertain, quiet and introverted. JNU sought to build a culture where the tutorial and discussion system derived from the elite institutions of the west were refigured. Tutorials were not only to be spaces where the meritorious were trained to excel, they were to be spaces where a culture of dialogue and debate could be nurtured, enabling students with diverse competencies to converse. Tutorials allowed effort and thinking capacity to be assessed,

---

[46]On deprivation points see pp. xxxix, 243–44 below.

[47]Begun in 2005 as a Programme for Studies in Discrimination and Exclusion, with special reference to Scheduled Castes, Scheduled Tribes, and Minorities. (Item No 6. /AC(A)/31.3. 2005.), it was renamed as the Centre for Social Exclusion and Inclusive Policy in 2012. See Sukhadeo Thorat, 'An Unique Experiment', in this volume; see also <https://www.jnu. ac.in/sss/csde>.

[48]In the vision committee report of 2014, a set of suggestions were made to further strengthen the ideal of interdisciplinarity. See *JNU Vision 2020 and Beyond: The Recommendations of the Group*, 2014.

and not just the merit of the essay written.

In its early decades, the tutorial system flourished, reliant as it was on low student teacher ratios, but the system was bound to be challenged not only by the ever-growing numbers but also by the emerging inability or unwillingness to use English as the language of higher education. The tutorial discussions today, maintained with difficulty in some departments, such as CHS, strain to achieve the quality that was initially intended and may even be unsustainable over the long term. A comparable system of teaching-learning appropriate to our changing student body and its capabilities and interests is yet to be imagined.

There has been an unprecedented enhancement of student diversity: their varied linguistic backgrounds posing fresh challenges to practices of teaching and learning that had long gone uncontested. In part, the mandated inclusion of larger sections of Indian society has been a true achievement of the Indian public university system of which JNU has once more been among the pioneers. There have been not only persistent calls to build a more inclusive academic culture but also to consciously go beyond the narrow social bases from which Indian higher education drew its beneficiaries in the early decades: this was no mean achievement of the Indian public university. In places like JNU, caste, and other forms of discrimination, rather than being seen as an intellectual drag or as a challenge to the functioning of democracy, were revisualized as enabling democratic functioning. The ideal of inclusiveness expressed in the founding debates could remain empty rhetoric. The vigorous and energetic students' movement of JNU ensured that these ideals were concretized, given robust form. As JNU's first students' union president put it: 'Perhaps, it is for the first time in the history of Indian universities that a Students' Union fought for giving specific weightages to socio-economic backwardness during admissions and got these implemented to some degree.'[49] In its early incarnation, JNU's famously fashioned 'deprivation points' included, by 1974, a policy of weightages for regional, class, and caste deprivations, to create a level playing field,

[49]V. C. Koshy, 'Jawaharlal Nehru University: A Model University?: Perspective and Ideal', *Social Scientist*, Vol. 2, No. 2, September, 1973, pp. 46–51 and p. 49. See also Prakash Karat, 'Student Movement at Jawaharlal Nehru University', *Social Scientist*, Vol. 3, No. 10, May 1975, p. 48. From 1994, five deprivation points were also awarded to women applicants.

where the socially and economically deprived could hope to compete with the privileged. Although removed in 1984 following an unusually disastrous period of student–teacher antagonism, it was restored only after sustained and momentous struggles by the student body in 1994.[50] Today it stands threatened once again.

Among the other achievements of the student movement were unusual forms of protection against possible victimization under the system of internal assessment: the right to appeal a grade was a hard-won right of the union.[51] It is a sign of how resilient these structures of assessment and protection against their possible misuse were that fifty years have passed without any major challenge, a significant achievement in the Indian setting. The bedrock of these decisions was that not only were students entitled to re-evaluation as a right, their presence in most decision-making bodies ensured that no decisions that concerned them were made without their participation or understanding.

Relearning at JNU

A university is not just its academic programme: innovative syllabi, experimental courses, thoughtful ways of evaluation. It is much more. It is the culture of intellection, the forms of sociality, the spirit and energy, the excitement and passion that permeates the institution. All this cannot be simply planned by bureaucrats and politicians; they have to be fashioned by students, teachers, karamcharis, and enlightened administrators, along with the many small figures—invisible to the outside world but intimately connected to the everyday life of the campus. There is a reason why so many stories in this volume are saturated with nostalgia—celebrating a seemingly idyllic time of the past—of excitement and creativity, fun and joy. But nostalgia is equally about loss: what flourished in the past, is under severe strain now.

From its inception, JNU has been a residential university with a difference. Partly since its students and teachers have enjoyed a larger

[50]See 'Administrative Change over the years (Committee Paper)', Kanjiv Lochan (ed.), *JNU—The Years: An Anthology by the Silver Memoir Committee*, Bombay: Popular Prakashan, 1996, pp. 24–30.

[51]Karat, 'Student Movement at Jawaharlal Nehru University', *Social Scientist*, Vol. 3, No. 10, May 1975, p. 49.

than usual role in determining institutional life, a genuine alternative to some aspects of life outside the university was imagined and has been sustained over the last half century. There are several significant pointers to the truly alternative values the institution has managed to fashion and protect over the decades. In the first place, from very beginning, there has been an attempt at JNU to break the traditional hierarchy and distance between teachers and students, allow a greater space for discussion, critique and debate. Questioning the teacher's argument was not seen as a sign of indiscipline, insolence and disrespect. Knowledge had to develop through dialogue and critique; the authority of the pedagogue was to be earned, not pre-given; constituted through intellectual capital, not punitive discipline. It is true not everyone has believed in the ideal, nor has everyone practised it; and it is equally true that the rhetoric of collective interaction and dialogue cannot elide the structures of power that mediate all relationship between teachers and students. Yet there is no doubt that the culture of intellectual sociality at JNU has been more democratic than anything seen in higher educational institutions generally.

Second, the resetting of gender hierarchies, rare and even unimaginable in a society that has been deeply scarred by misogyny, violence against women, and harassment of women in daily and academic life. The JNU campus has enabled female students and teachers to feel relatively freer in their daily lives and academic transactions, within and beyond the classroom, in hostels and in public spaces. So many of the stories in the volume talk of what Ganga Dhaba or Parthasarathi Rocks have meant as spaces where students have engaged in passionate discussions till late night, opening up minds, forging friendships, sharing intimacies. Caste/class/religious/regional and ethnic differences are dissolved, as women enjoy forms of respect that are rarely accorded to them outside. The torment that female students feel in other parts of Delhi (leading to the spectacular rise of the Pinjra Tod movement) and the country is generally absent at JNU: a good sign of this sense of well-being and safety is the harassment-free celebration of Holi year after year on the JNU campus, enjoyed by residents and visitors alike. This too is likely to change, as growing resentment about the perceived 'permissiveness' of the campus has periodically called for the re-imposition of more familiar gender hierarchies and segregation. Still, for now, JNU exists as a small haven relatively free of the sexism of the city.

Third: JNU has also led the way in pioneering institutional mechanisms to redress student grievances, not just against fellow students but teachers as well. The establishment of GSCASH (in 1997) has been hailed by both national and international agencies as among the most well-designed procedures for combating sexual harassment on campuses, protecting female students (and some male students) from assaults on their sense of self and personhood that might impair their functioning and careers as academics. As the Justice Verma Committee Report of 2013 said: 'We are also aware that in compliance with the judgment in *Vishaka vs State of Rajasthan 1997*, universities such as the Jawaharlal Nehru University and the University of Delhi have formulated policies and constituted mechanisms to prevent and redress complaints of sexual harssment. We have taken note of the suggestion that those universities whose anti-sexual harassment policy rules and committee mechanism meet the standards of Vishaka are proposed to be exempted from the purview of the Sexual Harassment Bill, 2012, *as these committees are more democratic and are better related to ensure prevention and prohibition of sexual harassment in educational institutions*.' (emphasis added).[52] Much more needs to be done to nurture gender sensitivity, and deepen our understanding—whether as students or as teachers—of the subtle and almost invisible ways in which gender discrimination works in the everyday life of the campus. Unfortunately, administrative action of the last few years threatens to dismantle all that has been achieved.

Finally: all these achievements have been sustained by the unusually high level of participation of the student body in the conduct of student elections through a widely acclaimed constitutional process which has kept JNU free, until date at least, of the kinds of violent, money-driven, election processes that have become the norm in most universities in Delhi, as well as the country. This relatively dispute-free election process, in addition to being inexpensive and ecologically sustainable, and run by an Election Commission composed of students

[52]It is a matter of serious concern that the well-tested and acclaimed mechanism, which represented all sections of the JNU community, was abruptly dismantled in 2017, in favour of a nominated (rather than elected) Internal Complaints Committee, ostensibly to comply with the new norms laid out in Sexual Harassments of Women at the Workplace Act, 2013. For a view of the work of GSCASH, see <https://www.jnu-gscash-archive.org/blog/date/2017-10>.

themselves, consciously gives every political formation—from extreme Right to every shade of Left—a chance to contest and deliberate during the elections. If JNU is relatively free of forms of deference that are only too well known elsewhere, a rare degree of democratic civility marks student life on the campus, where discussion and debate, even if it is sometimes tediously long, rather than violence in word or deed, govern student interactions. This exceptional student-body behaviour was warmly appreciated even by the Lyngdoh Commission though such a model was considered suitable only for smaller universities: 'The JNU/ University of Hyderabad mode of elections, where direct elections are held in a peaceful manner and are conducted entirely by the students, where election-related expenditure is kept to a relative minimum due to strict norms on the use of posters and election propaganda, has a major drawback inasmuch as this form of election is suitable only for small universities of the single campus type.'[53] However, the Committee accepted this as one possible model:

> 6.2.1 A system of direct election of the office bearers of the student body whereby all students of all constituent colleges, as well as all students of the university departments vote directly for the office bearers. This model may be followed in smaller universities with well-defined single campuses (for e.g. JNU/University of Hyderabad), and with a relatively smaller student population.

◆

The platitudinous statement bears repetition: how long it takes to build institutions, and how little time to destroy them. Over the last fifty years, enlightened administrators trusted students and teachers, listened to their voices, opened the doors of dialogue. It is through collective discussions that rules and norms were devised, institutional structures built, democratic functioning ensured. Now, in the last few years, these spaces of dialogue are shrinking rapidly, institutional structures are being

[53]Report of the Committee Constituted by Ministry of Human Resource Development, Government of India as per the Direction of the Hon'ble Supreme Court of India to frame Guidelines on Students' Union Elections in Colleges/Universities, New Delhi: MHRD, GOI, 23 May 2006, pp. 42 and 43. On p. 43 the report said: 'The general consensus was that the model to be followed was the JNU model which, however, in the Committee's opinion is not suitable for very large universities.'

subverted, established norms violated, seniority rules dishonored, expert committees arbitrarily formed, norms of selection overturned. What were seen as normal and natural at JNU—the right to debate and discuss, the right to inclusive and affordable education, the right to intellectual adventure, the right to dream of justice and equity—are no longer so. If JNU has to hold out hope for the future, its spirit has to be saved, the constitutive elements that defined its uniqueness have to be protected. At this moment, as we celebrate the fiftieth anniversary of JNU, students and teachers of the institution are involved in a desperate effort to protect its democratic and intellectual traditions—the spirit of JNU.[54]

On 5 January 2020, a series of extraordinary events took place on the JNU campus that shook the very foundations of the institution. A mob of 60–100, armed with lathis, stones, and bottles, unleashed a reign of terror on students and teachers in hostels such as Periyar and Sabarmati, New Transit House, and in public spaces such as Sabarmati T-point and Godavari Dhaba. The attack came following a long and sustained struggle of more than seventy days by the students of JNU resisting a proposed fee hike, which would have made education at JNU unaffordable to at least 40 per cent of the existing student population. On 5 January, the JNUTA had called for a public meeting at 4 p.m. to be followed by a peace march to quell student restlessness about unresolved and festering issues, growing anxieties and fears regarding the registration process, (which was largely being boycotted by students) and the increasingly tense atmosphere on the campus. The ease with which several armed outsiders were able to enter the campus, launch their targeted attack on teachers and students, leaving a trail of damaged cars, hostel buildings and public spaces, while seriously wounding several teachers and students, raised justifiable speculations about the complicity of the administration and police in this premeditated event.

Meanwhile, each and every aspect of JNU's carefully built heritage, as a space that allowed free discussion and debate, but not violence; as a

[54]A concerted intellectual, political and administrative assault on JNU began in February 2016. Among the many forms of resistance put up by the students and teachers was the 'teach-in' on nationalism and on the idea of freedom—Azaadi. For a brief introduction to the events leading to the teach in, and the lectures themselves, see Rohit Azad, et al, *What the Nation Really Needs to Know: JNU Nationalism Lectures,* New Delhi: HarperCollins, 2017.

space that was safe for women; as a space in which students and teachers were respected by the administration in the running of the university—all this and more has been severely damaged in ways that will now take a long time to rebuild. The physical attacks have been only the latest in a series of academic, political, and psychological assaults on the institution. Such a quick descent into chaos was not envisaged at the time of planning this book.

In documenting some aspects of what has been called a part of India's cultural heritage,[55] we hope to preserve memories that may be of use to all those who will, we hope, salvage and rebuild the institution, reinventing it to meet fresh challenges in the decades to come.

[55]Romila Thapar, *Indian Cultures As Heritage: Contemporary Pasts*, New Delhi: Aleph Book Company, 2018.

I

SPACES AND PLACES

1

LANDSCAPE STORIES: THE ARCHAEOLOGICAL PASTS AND PRESENTS OF THE JNU CAMPUS

MUDIT TRIVEDI

The Delhi ridge, amidst which the JNU campus is located, has long been described as 'lean but wiry fingers', as ancient rocks sinking into the geologically younger alluviums of the Yamuna River. This romantic juxtaposition of the old and the new—an allegory for the nation and its capital—does little justice to the archaeological landscape of the campus. The JNU campus is a perfect microcosm, containing within its approximately 400 hectares much of the archaeological pasts of the Delhi region, ranging from the prehistoric to the recent. The fact that the large area enclosed within its walls remains relatively untouched by the infrastructural and construction processes that have transformed all else around—allows one to think not of archaeological sites, but rather of landscapes.

On this landscape, the distinctive grey rock of the JNU hills is a quartzite with a specific history of its own. Its origin from deeply weathered parent sandstones means that it is at once a typical metamorphic product of the Delhi Aravalli group of rocks, but also distinctively marked by a pyrite (FeS_2) impurity. Over geological time, rainwater and the iron within interact to create a series of distinctive forms—most commonly, a series of rinds that accrue around the grey rock as layers of increasingly red and friable, sandlike weathering products. Fresh breaks on the rocks, as seen along the campus roads, redirect these processes and lead to a dirty, ferrous-red bleeding trail. In other places, the iron impurity has leached out and precipitated as thin black 'crusts'. Excavation to bedrock on campus usually ends in metre-thick layers of decomposing quartzite in the form of red, sandy regolith. Most memorably for lives on campus, these processes lead to large rounded 'tor' formations, or the boulders that cap the ridges, best seen at 'PSR' or Parthasarathi Rocks. In addition, the JNU hills are marked by the intrusive veins of a milky transparent and white quartz as well as a micaceous pegmatite.

Anyone who has ridden into campus on the 615 DTC bus has found their eyes drawn to some or all of these features. Diagonally opposite the Kendriya Vidyalaya on campus, the rock as cut back for the road towards the Administration Block shows almost all of these features together. Further on, past the Academic Complex, the rise before the valley to Poorvanchal yields one of the best vistas of the open lands to the south. In the 1990s, a scholar at the School of Environmental Sciences noted that the campus hills were marked by thin sediment deposits that appeared like grassy vegetation mats, and decided to take a closer look at their origin. Using facilities and labs at the school, J. K. Tripathi (now faculty at SES) established that these sediments were neither the weathering products of the local hill quartzites nor were they related to the Yamuna alluviums. Instead, he explained, the campus was mantled, almost blanketed by airborne sediment from the Thar Desert. This had also occurred previously when the desert was larger and its processes of entrainment and redeposition of sand were far more intense than today.

The JNU campus and its long-term geomorphology are significant as the interplay of weathering, erosional, and regional aeolian processes has meant that between its ranges, the broad valleys are marked by distinctive rolling stepped landscapes. Crossing from the western hostels to the academic block, entering into the valley, one traverses recently gullied, reworked Thar-derived sediments and crosses one of the streams that drain the hills. On either side of the valley floor, paths climb onto hillsides where very old rock surfaces wear thin patinas of long duree weathering processes where they remain unburied by fine sands and the grass they support. After every rain the grey rock, the red detritus, and the yellow sands commingle, and walking the JNU landscape means encountering an interweaved set of traces of different epochs all at once and subtly modified by each other.

For instance, to level the area for the statue of Jawaharlal Nehru at the Administration Block, a number of tors were cleared mechanically, one of which was covered with a range of old cupules. Sets of such features, usually found as dual rows of small holes pecked into the eroding rinds of the quartzite preserve one of the most widespread kinds of archaeological traces on campus. Some sets of these dots are more complex, occasionally intersecting with sets of two or four rows and are usually on large flat rocks. While such finds of petroglyphs have attracted symbolic interpretation elsewhere, on campus they helpfully occur alongside a range of other motifs: graffiti in Nagari (names), animals, stars, and a range of other expediently and informally chiselled-in forms. Before its acquisition by the government as institutional land, the campus was a part of the pastoral landscapes of Munirka and other villages and, thus, these cupules and art forms are the game boards and material ruminations of those who watched over their ruminants. Occasional footing courses of walls survive and suggest ridge-top casual structures and cattle pens. Close to these, on flat boulders, often are the cupule game boards—usually variations of pacchisi (ludo). Together, these traces suggest ways in which within the usually solitary exercise of grazing goats or cattle, a game and a meeting point were devised.

Ceramics are the most common archaeological finds and yet on the JNU campus they are almost entirely absent. What the archaeological survey did find was that when they are found, and when they can be identified, they are usually distinct kinds of medieval and early medieval lamp forms. It is tempting to think of these as related to the closest site of Lalkot, its walls barely a kilometre to the east of campus. While no distinct paths or routes survive archaeologically, to walk from Lalkot towards the Tughlaq-era madrasa, tombs and gardens at Muradabad Pahari or to head towards Munirka and further north-west, travellers would likely have passed through the campus area. One can almost envision these hills sitting quietly on the fringes of the city in its medieval past. At the very southern end of the campus, within the yawning, deep valley, there exist remains of what appears to be a small medieval quarry, exploiting the natural propensity of the exposed outcrop to foliate into rock sizes useful for medieval masonry. Elsewhere on campus we find the tell-tale wedge-and-split marks of similar medieval efforts to quarry and split boulders. Beyond this, while the Delhi region is dense in diverse evidence and sites for the early medieval, early historic and prehistoric/ Iron Age, and even Late Harappan periods—no such evidence is found within the walls.

What the campus does yield, however, are rich and complex finds that relate to the deeper pasts of the Delhi region. Several of the ridges on

I.1. Distinctive weathering visible on freshly broken rocks
Photo courtesy: Mudit Trivedi

I.2. Characteristic view of the stepped rolling tor-strewn hillslopes that distinguish the JNU Campus area from other parts of the Delhi ridge
Photo courtesy: Mudit Trivedi

I.3. Cupule game-board and Nagari graffiti alongside tool-sharpening grooves on a large, flat boulder
Photo courtesy: Mudit Trivedi

I.4. Typical wedge and split marks of medieval attempts to quarry boulders
Photo courtesy: Mudit Trivedi

campus were found to bear the traces of microlith stone tool production. Microlith scatters, or remains of the waste stone left in reducing a nodule to a final tool, are distributed widely across the campus. They represent a time when people who knew the hills and its rocks very well ranged across it widely. These tools are fashioned on the distinctive quartz sourced from the rare but regular veins in the hills. They also used an exotic, tuffaceous sandstone, which is not known geologically on campus, but is well known, in the Delhi region. Together, the microlith scatters appear to tell an ill-understood story that is one of repeated expedient tool production by communities who knew the landscape and its lithic resources well. Their residues are found across every ridge, at both locations that afford commanding views over the landscape and are a sign of how they lived and used the land. Their largest footprint on campus is at a location outside of Paschimabad where the stream exits the hillside and fans out in the valley. While we do not know exactly when these persons lived, we do know that they created the kinds of tools (scrapers and backed blades) that are usually involved in the processing of a range of materials like plants, hides, etc. Based on the present evidence, the microlith scatters suggest the picture of a community that knew its landscape well and likely ranged far and traded with other communities in the Delhi region.

Older still are arresting and exceptionally regular finds of much older tools, part of a tradition of stone tools that are amongst the oldest hominin occupations in South Asia. These date prior to at least 100,000 years ago, and are very likely two to three times that age. A diverse range of acheulian tools, hand-axes, cleavers, side-scrapers, end-scrapers, cores, and considerable numbers of what appear to be waste reduction flakes (byproducts of the process of making these tools), have been found. Notably, the JNU landscape comprises a range of sediments and rocks of different ages that persist on the surface, sometimes buried and re-exposed, in other cases never fully buried even over such timescales. This has meant that such old traces of the pre-modern human past also are regularly stumbled upon.

As a result, over the past years, some faculty members, guests and even students running across the valley to class have stopped in their tracks to observe the artifact in front of them. A detailed archaeological survey of a sample of the campus recorded the precise locations of these finds and their relative states of erosion. On this basis, it was able to establish that each tool, depending on where it was found, bore traces of not only the range of depositional, erosional, and weathering processes within which it was found but also of the ancient hominin landscapes of use and discard. When the major phase of campus infrastructure expansion took place, the excavation of each new building afforded a new window into these pasts. The present School of Physical Sciences sits upon one of the many 'sites' from the Palaeolithic age on the campus, and its foundation excavations yielded a buried acheulian floor, where half-finished tools, waste flakes, and large cores were recovered.

The evidence on campus for both the microlithic and Palaeolithic deposits speak to the evidence from the larger Delhi region. At both scales, campus and regional, we do not have exact dates of the older occupations and the campus itself remains a palimpsest of varied and challenging archaeological pasts awaiting further research and investigation. While India does not have any national policy of archaeological clearance before excavation, the campus provides an ideal space within which to test such ideas and to recover information prior to and alongside the destruction that accompanies new constructions vital to institutional growth. More than any singular 'site', the JNU campus provides, in the midst of the rapidly unrecognizable landscapes of Delhi, an area within which the varied accumulations of the past are available, allowing insight, opportunity as well as challenges.

As the campus grows and the present-day 'JNU culture' occupies a larger footprint, it too has distinctive accumulations. In 2016, many decided that this was a discursive site to make evaluations of what transpired at JNU and the modern nation. Gyandev Ahuja of the BJP infamously claimed to have first-hand knowledge of the material detritus of the distinctive and, to him, scandalizing freedoms that campus life affords. That episode alone alerts one to the unique materiality of campus life, set against the city outside and poses further questions. To consider these is to ask questions of the rhythms of material life across the campus and its own distinctive accumulations and erosions. One such opening is provided by attention to how state infrastructural projects have their own rhythms of supply and discard. For years the central courtyard in the iconic JNU library stood closed, as a site where generations of old furniture accrued, waiting for bureaucratic sanction to be disposed. In the contest over public spaces and order, concrete paths direct desired academic subjects in certain ways, but also directed the feet of many

I.5. Selection of distinctive microliths
Photo courtesy: Mudit Trivedi

I.6. View of the major stream that drains the western part of campus looking towards the Paschimabad Dam.
Photo courtesy: Mudit Trivedi

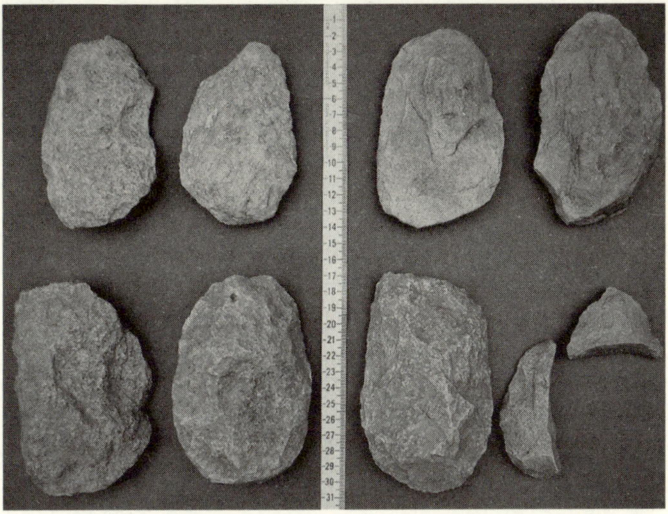

I.7. Selection of the Palaeolithic Acheulian Bifaces: The top row displays the kind of patination that results from long exposure to surface processes and contact with the Thar-derived sediments. The lower row is stained red by being buried in contact with the decomposing and weathering quartzite at the site below the present SPS building.
Photo courtesy: Mudit Trivedi

I.8. View of the trench excavated for the construction of the SPS building. Significant evidence for the Delhi Palaeolithic was recovered from this trench.
Photo courtesy: Mudit Trivedi

off these on to paths beaten underfoot. Ceremonial entrances to power structures have been recast as freedom squares. Just as no one 'site', nor one architectonic plan of campus could communicate *the* JNU story, the material landscapes, past and present of the campus reveal object lessons to us. They exhort us to consider at once the inseparable spatial, material, geological, geomorphological, and cultural landscapes underfoot.

2

THE ARCHITECTURAL IMAGINATION OF A NEW UNIVERSITY

VIPUL JHINGTA

Competition Requirements

The Campus Committee of Jawaharlal Nehru University laid out the terms and conditions for a nationwide competition to design a unique campus on the suggestions of Chancellor Indira Gandhi.[1] The University was to house 10,000 students and 1,250 faculty members finally, but would begin with 3,200 students and 400 faculty, doubling numbers only in the second stage.[2] There were to be seven multidisciplinary Schools of Studies, each one envisaged as a community of scholars from disciplines that were linked to each other in a single organic complex; the Centres and Departments in turn made up the Schools, as communities of scholars. The architect had to formulate designs keeping these nuances in mind.[3]

Both national and global perspectives were to be fostered in the community life of residents. In the seven Schools that were envisaged, there were to be fifty centres and about thirty departments, all of them

---

[1] S. G. Puthli, Chief Project Engineer, Jawaharlal Nehru University 'Introduction', *A Study in Campus Designs: National Competition for the Master Plan of Jawaharlal Nehru University Campus,* New Delhi: Ministry of Information & Broadcasting, Government of India, 1974, hereafter *Campus Design Book.* The Committee included: Chairman, G. Parthasarathi (Vice Chancellor), Members: Padmaja Naidu, Mohan Sinha Mehta, R. N. Dogra, L. G. Selvam, S. G. Bose Mullick, G. D. Bahri, R. K. Chhabra, J. B. Mathur, J. M. Benjamin, Veera Raghavan, and M. L. Sobti.

[2] 'Stages of Development', *Jawaharlal Nehru University: National Competition for the Design of the Master Plan of the University Campus,* New Delhi: Directorate of Advertising & Visual Publicity, 1974, p. 18. (Hereafter *Competition Manual*); *Campus Design Book,* p. 10.

[3] 'Preamble', *Campus Design Book,* p. 3.

situated in an Academic Complex, which was to be preferably located on the main plateau. The buildings had to be in close proximity to each other, and linked so that they would form a single nucleus, breaking disciplinary boundaries. The Library-Computer Centre would be the 'cynosure' of the campus, knitting the entire Academic Complex together.[4]

On the other hand, the residential complex was supposed to reflect the diversity of the country, with democracy and social justice as ideals, dispersed throughout the campus in nucleated sectors, connected with each other through formal and informal paths. The sixteen residential sectors would house students and teachers from all regions of India.[5] The sensitivity of the architect was also drawn to the larger topographical setting of the campus, including the Qutab/Palam Mosque, the Hauz-i-Khas, and other medieval structures.

A radical suggestion made by the Committee was that student and faculty residences, canteens, and informal spaces should be in close proximity, to foster friendlier relations between these two parts, though there was also a hint of a 'disciplining' aspect to this arrangement, in which students were seen as potential 'delinquents'.[6] The Administrative Block, the auditorium, and an open-air theatre were to be placed around the Academic Complex in an equilateral triangle schema, with the road leading directly to the Academic Complex, with the Qutab Minar as the backdrop to the library building.

Sir Basil Spence, the architect of the University of Sussex, also saw the undulating terrain and scattered rocks as having the potential to make this space conducive to higher learning. The natural features of the site were to be kept intact as far as possible; maintenance of the buildings was to be low and the materials used were to be inexpensive.[7] Landscaping became critical to such a project because the seemingly unfriendly terrain and minimal vegetation would otherwise subdue the designed buildings. A 75-acre (approximately) green belt was intended to cover the eastern

---

[4]'Some suggestions to the Architect', *Campus Design Book,* pp. 5–9.

[5]Ibid.

[6]Ibid. Since JNU was envisaged as a residential university, perhaps there were anxieties about disciplining the female students. The word *delinquent* used by the Committee need not have referred only to the potentially rebellious young man.

[7]'Design Requirements,' *Campus Design Book*, p. 14.

side of the campus.[8]

The budget for such a large-scale, prestigious project was low, and Parthasarathi had stated this handicap:[9] air conditioning, for instance, was planned for only a few buildings, complemented by the landscaping of the site.[10]

The national competition for the design of the Master Plan of Jawaharlal Nehru University Campus in 1970 was won by a young architect, C. P. Kukreja, of C. P. Kukreja Associates,[11] who saw the three water bodies as complementing the academic and residential complexes. Kukreja's design maximized the site space, with proper thought for the planting of trees along the roads, which was a great step towards landscaping. Since the university was to come up in three phases, with significant time gaps, Kukreja must have been concerned about achieving a sense of completeness in Phase I itself.

The Academic Complex was to be visible on entering from the east gate; two lakes situated at different heights would present themselves alongside the road. The major landmark in the Academic Complex would be the library building, referred to as 'Library Block' by Kukreja. The School buildings in the Academic Complex were to be placed in close proximity to each other. The buildings would be square-shaped, in a single line looking towards the southeastern direction, and facing the Qutab Minar and the two lakes. Each School building in the next phase were to follow a similar pattern, and would be constructed towards the southwest of its respective school, the square shape of the buildings connected to each other by their corners.

The library and computer centre would be built on the western side of the Academic Complex, towards the northwest of the School buildings, both in a single building. The original site for the library was where the School of Computer and Systems Sciences currently is, and would thus be visible from the Administrative Block. The Administrative Block would come up towards the north of the School buildings, and three structures meant to serve as lecture halls would come up to the east of

---

[8]'Description of the Site', *Campus Design Book*, pp. 10–13.

[9]'Foreword', *Campus Design Book*.

[10]*Competition Manual*, p. 14.

[11]This was to be Kukreja's first project, and was followed by a long list of achievements. He passed away in August 2018 at the age of seventy-nine.

I.9. Photograph of the model designed by C. P. Kukreja
Source: Campus Design Book, p. 23.

the Administrative Block.

Kukreja seemed to have been unable to fit the Administrative Block, the auditorium, and an open-air theatre in an equilateral triangle schema, and hence the auditorium and open-air theatre sprang up outside the Ring Road, towards the area which became known as Parthasarathi Rocks (PSR). The Ring Road surrounding the Academic Complex would be served by the main approach road from the east gate, and five other roads from various directions. There were sixteen residential sectors, containing three hostel blocks, each hostel with a capacity of 200 residents, further divided into four parts of fifty residents forming a single hostel, with a common dining facility. Other facilities for debating, games, and meeting places were also provided. Also, twenty-four staff residences were grouped around each hostel block.

A Nehru Memorial Court was to be budded near the Administrative Block, with several varieties of roses, where a museum was proposed for the future. For the green belt, a proposal was made to extend it towards the southern edge. The area to the south of the lake near the Academic Complex was to be developed into a natural garden, for conversion into a bird and deer sanctuary with planted trees and shrubs, the lakeside to be developed for sitting in the sun during winters. Kukreja in his book *Tropical Architecture* mentions the need to minimize surface area for walkways so as to reduce the heating effect of the sun.[12]

[12]C. P. Kukreja, *Tropical Architecture*, New Delhi: McGraw-Hill, 1978.

The Buildings and Landscape

It seems as if Kukreja went off course on only a few things—the equilateral triangle schema of Administrative Block, the open-air theatre, and the auditorium—though he tried his best to incorporate even these elements as close as possible to the desired location. But did Kukreja commit a blunder in arranging the School buildings of the Academic Complex?

The design had only a minimal, linear interconnection between Schools, since the proximity of Schools was not utilized. Kukreja's design could not nurture the interdisciplinary ethos of JNU, although one of the sketches shows an outdoor bridge connecting two buildings in the academic block.

The earliest of the Schools to be constructed was the School of Life Sciences—a magnificent example of the architectural technique of achieving maximum efficiency ratio of the useful area to the plinth area, with a torch-like design extending towards heaven, as if hanging in the air without support. It was attempted to be linked with School of Social Sciences-1 (SSS-I) via a bridge; this distasteful addition to these marvellous structures was perhaps a late realization by Kukreja on the need for organic linkages between schools. The attempt was so unaesthetic no such linkage was tried between the SSS-I and SSS-II, and other schools beyond. Also, as the buildings came up, some design features seen in the earliest of buildings were either reduced or diluted: for example, the overhanging-slanting brick-wall exterior in SLS and

I.10. The proposed Academic Complex in the plan.
Source: Campus Design Book, p. 44.

SSS-I, transforms into a step-wise slanting brickwork when it reaches SSS-II and School of Environmental Sciences (SES). Later, in both School of International Studies (SIS) and School of Language, Literature and Culture Studies (SLL&CS), it does not remain as impressive.

Another important building is the School of Computer and Systems Sciences both because it is the oldest building on the campus, and because it purportedly won a prize for its design.[13] The unusual-looking structure with a pointed concrete half-roof like design has giant protruding red-brick window-like formations over the actual windows which lie hidden beneath them. This was to protect the building from solar heating, and the resultant insulation effect was phenomenal. However this building is the most isolated School inside the Academic Complex, even today.

The designs of the residential complex reflect an intent towards community living and diversity. Kukreja's image of hostel blocks is sketched with sensitivity to the undulating terrain of the site, the sectional view of the rooms with various residents going about their ways, and the court where male and female students are seen interacting, with some vegetation and trees. This was a powerful statement reflecting the proposed life of a world-class university, coming up in India in the 1970s.

The first hostels to come up were Kaveri, Periyar, and Godavari, as per Kukreja's design in 1972,[14] although with many changes. The terrain was left as it is and no levelling effort was made, so that the western wing of both Periyar and Godavari hostels lie on a slope, with their ground floor almost invisible from the ground floor of the eastern wings. The two wings of the hostels have been connected through a bridge which goes over the common mess. Interestingly, most of the designs show hostels having a slanting structure, with rooms becoming smaller as one goes upwards. If there was an obtuse-angled brickwork in the Academic Complex buildings, there was an acute-angled brickwork in the early hostel buildings, which runs as an extension to the room walls, serving as a partition in the

---

[13]It was the first building in the academic block to be completed, followed by School of Life Sciences. 'Foreword', *Campus Design Book*. The prize was mentioned by Mr Gopal Dutt, JNU draftsperson, and his associates to me in a personal exchange. Unfortunately the name and agency of the prize could not be ascertained by them, but they are certain that Kukreja was given a prize for that particular building.

[14]Rakesh Batabyal, *JNU: The Making of a University*, Noida: HarperCollins, 2014, p. 187.

I.11. Envisaged inter-school linkages in the plan
Source: 'The Odd Goings on at Nehru University', *Design Journal,* Vol. 20, No. 11, November 1976.

balconies. Kaveri and Periyar hostels have a stepwise red-brick slant, but Godavari hostel and others that came later have that stepwise red-brick slant converted into a continuous red-brick slant, arranged with careful lining of the bricks to produce an uninterrupted line of brickwork.

The earliest three hostels were served by a common recreational complex, known as Nilgiri. Later on, three hostel blocks came up to the north of these hostels: Ganga, Sutlej, and Jhelum; but the 'dilution of one or the other elements' principle worked here too, as in the case of other buildings in the Academic Complex. The staff residences came up simultaneously around the first hostels, in Dakshinapuram.

The landscape effort was probably the hardest thing to do while building the whole campus and the officials of the engineering department vouch for the dedication and hard work of CPWD authorities who were assigned this task. Labourers travelled great distances to fetch water for the saplings.[15]

Not everything in the Master Plan materialized, and after the first Vice Chancellor Parthasarathi, there was a sharp deterioration in the relations between the University and Kukreja. The trouble began after

[15]I wish to thank the JNU draftsperson Gopal Dutt and his associates for providing me with this information and their thoughts on the effort by Kukreja.

the second Vice Chancellor, B. D. Nag Choudhuri, unimpressed by the six designs produced by Kukreja over two years, wanted to enforce his own sensibilities on the design of the upcoming library building. To prevent Nag Choudhuri's design from materializing, Kukreja approached the Delhi Urban Arts Commission which took his side, and over a series of sessions, agreed upon a new concept of the library building. The new design, consisting of a tower block on a podium, had a mature and complete look when compared to the eye-sore attributed to Nag Choudhuri's imagination.[16]

Although Kukreja's design ultimately prevailed, the University barred him from designing any more buildings on the campus and created bureaucratic hurdles for him thereafter. He was to work in conjunction with newly appointed architects, even though Kukreja was solely responsible for the Master Plan according to the National Competition Clause 18.[17]

The dissonance between the various architectural imaginations, old and the new, was minimized and the campus is aesthetically pleasing despite all its flaws and lack of adherence to the Master Plan—due to the landscaping! The Master Plan was developed for a semi-arid landscape consisting of scanty vegetation, where the vision was unhindered in all directions, but the later designs of the buildings had to take the trees and greenery into account.[18] The University is a rare case of positive environmental impact with the trees and vegetation adding charm to the spaces. A hostel building such as Godavari, with its rocks and boulders and red-brick architecture would greet someone going along the road from the North Gate in the early years. Later, it would lie mysteriously hidden behind trees and shrubs with its barren rocks completely taken over by the vegetation. The roads studded with bougainvillea and cassia fistula with their short bloom cycles on both sides create a sensory pleasure which one associates with brightness and enthusiasm. Due to the landscaping, all that was planned and unplanned

---

[16]'Architecture as a Victim of Irrational Attitudes', *Design Journal*, June 1976, Vol 19, No. 10, pp. 29–31.

[17]'The Odd Goings on at Nehru University', *Design Journal*, November 1976, Vol. 20, No. 11, pp. 21–22.

[18]To give a perspective to the reader, one could easily view the Qutab Minar from the ground level without requiring any advantage of height! Photographs of the site in the *Competition Manual* attest to this fact. *Competition Manual*, p. 21.

I.12. Sectional view of the residential court as envisaged in the plan. Notice the way different levels are designed with an eye to the undulating terrain.
Source: 'The Odd Goings on at Nehru University', *Design Journal,* Vol. 20, No. 11, November 1976, p. 31.

merge into one, creating a new aesthetic expression for future architectural imaginations.

3

LIVING WITH NATURE

SURYA PRAKASH

It is indeed a privilege to have experienced the beauty of thirty-five springs in Jawaharlal Nehru University, a green lung in the crowded capital city of India. I have been lucky enough to know JNU from its adolescent years and have seen it transform into the beautiful lush green natural landscape that it is now.

Historical Background

On page xxvi is a photograph of the JNU terrain in the early 1970s. It was printed as part of a note (published in *A Study in Campus Designs*) that sought to give architects an idea of the site on which they were expected to create the campus, which we see today. While extremely barren, it was a site that had seen human habitation for more than a millennium. From the JNU campus, the Archaeological Survey of India (ASI) has obtained late Stone Age tools and microliths used in making sickles for cutting grass.[1] The campus has also revealed rock engravings and if ASI is to be believed, a few of them date back to the fifth century CE. Such evidence, including pictures engraved on rocks, suggest that the barrenness depicted in the photos was neither natural nor eternal.[2] A fact we must not ignore is that due to natural weathering and anthropogenic stress over many years, a substantial amount of evidence has been lost; a lot of rocks have also been converted into gravel for construction purposes. The Government of India had allotted 13.8 square kilometres for the University campus, which has eventually been transformed, with the conscious efforts of

[1] See Chapter 1 above, pp. 1–12.

[2] Neha Lalchandani and Richi Verma, 'Rock carvings unearthed at JNU, but ASI prefers to bury history', *Times of India,* 16 July 2011.

earlier visionaries, into the verdant JNU campus that we see today. It was categorically mentioned in the minutes of the first Campus Development Committee that the natural water bodies and other natural ecosystems should be left undisturbed or only minimally disturbed. The biodiversity of the campus is improving with each passing year due to the collective efforts of the entire JNU community.

Biodiversity

Broadly speaking, the Delhi-NCR had two major ecosystems that sustained its thriving floral and faunal diversity. However, they have lost their pristine glory and are not able to provide their ecological services to Delhi NCR any longer. The need of the hour is to rejuvenate both. The first of these is the Aravalli range, which is older than the Himalaya, on which our campus is located, and are the last stretch of the hills as they merge into the north Indian plains. The second are the river Yamuna and its floodplains.

With constant community conservation efforts and sustainable development, JNU has managed to enhance the ridge ecosystem within the heart of the city. I remember the first time I stepped into JNU some three-and-a-half decades ago. It was barren, dry, and desolate. Over the years, however, JNU campus has evolved into a lush green lung over the rocky plateau.

The master plan of JNU had suggested: 'A portion of the campus site which is too rugged for building purposes may be developed as a bird sanctuary and a deer park where students and faculty members may profitably spend their leisure time in the natural surroundings.'[3] Today that dream has come true as I have documented more than 200 species of birds. There were 172 at the time I published my book that documented the birds of the university, *Feathered Friends of JNU,* in 2011. The number is still rising.

The university also took advantage of the vast system of natural drains and dry wells which used to remain dry for most of the year due to their inability to retain water as the catchment areas were located on steep gradients. The campus design document had proposed: 'There is a scope for converting a part of the drainage system into an artificial lake or pool

[3]*A Study in Campus Design*, 1974, p. 17.

of water by providing an escape weir at an appropriate place.'[4] As a result, today, the campus has a couple of natural water bodies and three check dams attracting many migratory and resident water birds. This is due to the north-south flow of river Yamuna which is on the major Central Asian Flyway (CAF) of migratory birds who annually fly from Central Asia and Europe to India, especially in winter when they arrive in Delhi NCR.

Efforts were also made to plant native Aravalli species of trees within JNU apart from naturally growing vegetation. That is the reason today one can see and enjoy many fruit-bearing trees and plants that are useful to all of us apart from providing shelter and food to wildlife. To date, I have documented the presence of over a dozen large and small mammals and lizards, a little over twenty species of snakes and around ninety species of butterflies, including seven new species for Delhi and this work has been recognized by WWF-INDIA.

Here I must recount my own experience of engendering the natural habitat of JNU. My wife and I decided that charity begins at home, and hence took the initiative to provide water, food, and shelter to birds that frequent the campus. And our work was rewarded. Bulbuls, babblers, mynas, barbets, treepies, flameback, doves, white-eyes, sunbirds, parakeets, and many other birds, difficult to sight in the city, have become regular visitors to our balcony. Encouraged by the balcony birding, we thought we would step out into the backyard and try our luck there as well. It took us nearly three months to get the garden in shape since it had previously been used as a dump yard by us and the nearby residents. We planted many trees like orange, lemon, guava, papaya, pomegranate, drumsticks, caster, kalanchoe, ashoka, curry leaf, wild plants, including lantana and milk weed, that have been felled indiscriminately everywhere because they were perceived to be common weeds, but are actually favourites of butterflies and many other insects. We didn't remove any dead trees, but, in fact, placed a dead branch horizontally for birds to perch upon. This was stage-III of Mission Backyard Wildlife that proved to be a real success. Butterflies like lime butterfly, common mormon, common jay, plain tiger, common castor, red pierrots, etc., whose larval host plants we had planted, started visiting and laying eggs. Many terrestrial and shy birds like peacocks, grey francolins, Asian koels, the elusive golden orioles,

[4]Ibid., p. 7.

I.13. Check Dam at Paschimabad
Photo courtesy: Surya Prakash

the boisterous Indian plaintive cuckoo, prinias, Indian scops owls, spotted owlet, jungle crows, house crows, parakeets, white-breasted waterhen, pied crested cuckoo, white-throated kingfisher and green bee-eater were just some of the birds that started dropping in regularly for water and food during summer.

Soon, black-shouldered kites, oriental honey-buzzards, black kites, shikras, accompanied by mongooses, cats, monitor lizards, rat snakes, and wolf snakes flocked to the area for not just water, but also to optimally utilize the opportunity to show their hunting skills. The water we kept out also attracted jackals, nilgais, and Indian crested porcupines, these too could not resist grabbing a bite or two from our garden plants, especially from the papaya tree. From a barren piece of land littered with rubbish, my backyard had turned into a mini universe. One only needed a little time and patience to witness nature at its best; a squirrel feeding its two babies on a branch, a purple sunbird building a nest in the hanging chimes, bulbul chicks calling out to their parents every few minutes. Parakeets, after having raised four chicks on a nearby neem tree, brought them to our balcony before their first flight, presumably to say goodbye to us.

To spread awareness about the biodiversity within JNU, the administration has also been a wonderful support over the years. It has published annual calendars of birds, butterflies, trees, greeting cards, and bookmarks of JNU on a regular basis, which reflects the biodiversity of our campus. Many schools of JNU have produced souvenirs and cover photographs of wildlife of JNU on the front and back covers of various conference folders. In the recent past, some of the former Vice Chancellors of JNU proposed the creation of a butterfly park and also launched a bimonthly magazine in Hindi entitled *Patrika*, *JNU-Parisar.* The front colour pages of each issue contains an article on the wildlife and biodiversity of the campus for those who cannot read English. These conservation efforts by JNU authorities and the community are very encouraging. JNU has led the way in inspiring such awareness programmes among Indian universities. Efforts are also being made to make JNU a zero polybag zone. The introduction of battery rickshaws and bicycle rides and implementation of biodegradable earthen pots for tea-coffee by the canteen owners of the campus are positive steps to improve the environment of JNU. The 'Big Bird Day,' an annual event organized in Delhi-NCR, has also received the support of the JNU administration.

I.14. Nilgais roam the residential quarters, not just the forests around.
Photo courtesy: Samim Asgor Ali

I.15. Black Kite
Photo courtesy: Surya Prakash

I.16. Long-legged Buzzard
Photo courtesy: Surya Prakash

I.17. Oriental Magpie Robin
Photo courtesy: Surya Prakash

I.18. Yellow Wattled Lapwing
Photo courtesy: Surya Prakash

I.19. Sirkeer Malkoha
Photo courtesy: Surya Prakash

I.20. Black-rumped Flameback
Photo courtesy: Surya Prakash

However, the University also faces challenges similar to those faced by Delhi's citizens—rising traffic density, both on the surface and in the air, is a serious concern. A lot of wildlife is killed as a result of road accidents, while noise pollution is adversely affecting the auditory system of humans. Another issue that needs immediate attention is the proliferation of the feral dog population on campus that has killed a significant proportion of wildlife, apart from biting and attacking humans, especially affecting differently abled people and children. Also, technology and development are inevitable but, at the same time, they often have a negative impact—the erection of mobile towers at many places that generate high frequency electromagnetic fields around them has had an adverse effect on bird life.

I request the entire JNU community to support the conservation projects not only of JNU campus but also those of the nation.

Jai Hind.

II

IMAGINING THE UNIVERSITY

4

A UNIVERSITY IS SET UP*

RAKESH BATABYAL

Right from the introduction of the JNU Bill in the Rajya Sabha in 1964, the intention of making the institution unique was the overwhelming sentiment, and discussion revolved around the theme of uniqueness rather than on other details. The Joint Committee enthusiastically responded to this sentiment.

The first person who gave evidence in the Joint Committee was V. K. R. V. Rao. G. S. Pathak set the tenor of the committee's proceedings when he posed his first question to Rao: What in Rao's opinion was going to be the 'uniqueness of the proposed university'? Rao, speaking from his rich experience, explained that 'uniqueness' had a twofold meaning here. First, it should be different from all other universities in this country[1].... Second, as a university bearing Jawaharlal Nehru's name, it should embody three basic principles: national integration, establishment of a decent society, and a universalistic philosophy....

One of the instruments to foster national integration Rao proposed was to have a department of Indian languages and a truly national student body. In his opinion, the 'national representation' in Delhi University consisted of Bengalis and the south Indians of Delhi, which gave the university a superficial semblance of a national university although it was not.[2] He suggested there be a quota system allocated to students from each state.[3]

When JNU's uniqueness was being discussed, Rao emphatically

*Excerpted from Rakesh Batabyal, *JNU: The Making of a University*, New Delhi: HarperCollins, 2014. This excerpt has been edited for this volume.

[1]V. K. R. V. Rao in the 'Verbatim Report of Evidence given before the Joint Committee on the Jawaharlal Nehru University Bill, 1964' (Hereafter *Report of Evidence*), p. 2.

[2]Ibid.

[3]Ibid.

recommended a *federating* and *postgraduate university* rather than a new university serving merely as an extension to the old Delhi University colleges; according to him, most of these lacked standards and would merely be deadweight on the new institution....

Rao was aware that it was advanced studies and research—not undergraduate studies—which gave a degree of consequence to a university and he wanted this to be the 'hallmark of this university'.[4] However, he acknowledged that a university also needed life and laughter as opposed to the scholarly sobriety of a purely postgraduate university and he wanted a small part, *only a small part,* of the university to be dedicated to undergraduate studies, just so the university would have versatility and vitality.[5]

According to the original idea, as the education minister, M. C. Chagla, indicated, the new university would be the first of its kind to include advanced levels of research and tie in with existing institutions like the All India Institute of Medical Sciences (AIIMS), Indian Agricultural Research Institute (IARI), and the Indian Institute of Technology (IIT). This idea was wholeheartedly supported by J. S. Jha, D. S. Kothari, and V. K. R. V. Rao. However, the bill did not include any specific proviso as to when and how these technical institutions would become part of the new university. Rao and Kothari, who were very knowledgeable about academic administration, asserted that these institutions needed to be brought into the ambit of the bill before actually passing the Act.[6] But according to Chagla, the autonomy of these institutes was just as important as the new JNU....

Kothari and Rao's determination to bring the institutions engaged in high technology within the ambit of the JNU Act so that the new university could commence as a postgraduate institution inspired the members of the committee. Jayaben Shah, a member of the Joint Committee, endorsed their opinion and assured them the government ministries could convincingly negotiate with the institutes and bring them under the confederation of JNU. Although Chagla continued to be ambivalent, another member of the Joint Committee, Amarnath Vidyalankar, was convinced that the government could achieve anything it set its mind to

[4]Ibid., p. 8.
[5]Ibid., p. 9.
[6]Ibid., p. 15.

do; therefore amending the bill to include the affiliation of the science and technology institutions to JNU would not be impossible. Kothari felt this would be the right way to do things, because Chagla's plan of action to pass the bill without further ado would be tantamount to putting the cart before the horse, and the new university would not have the benefit of affiliations to the high-technology institutions....[7]

Chagla was unwilling to be high-handed with the institutes and dictate terms to them, hence his equivocation. Kothari suggested he be guided by expert academicians who could look at the situation objectively....[8] He reiterated that it was a pointless exercise to waste time deliberating on how to set up an exemplar university and then wait decades for it to actually materialize....[9]

The report of the Joint Committee had clarified some important features of the new university: it would not include the Delhi University colleges and it would in all likelihood be a postgraduate university....

It was a first for India to conceive an institution with such a comprehensive national character. It was meant to provide unlimited access for people from all the regions and states of the country....

The plan was for JNU to chart a new course for national integration. V. S. Jha and Triguna Sen felt that a good faculty with prominent and eminent professors would attract good students from all over the country. Kothari maintained that the focus should be on countrywide accessibility to a new postgraduate university....

Rao felt that the core value of the new university was going to be national, therefore the principles and sentiments of national solidarity and national integration should be inculcated.[10] Kothari saw it differently and wanted the national character of the university to be facilitated by keeping a 'much greater proportion of postgraduate students than is the case of other universities'.[11]

The Joint Committee returned the bill after amending several clauses in light of the evidence given by the educationists. The bill was then moved to the Rajya Sabha on 1 December 1965. The minister acknowledged the

---

[7]Ibid.

[8]Ibid.

[9]Ibid.

[10]Submission by V. K. R. V. Rao, ibid., p. 25.

[11]D. S. Kothari, p. 4.

II.1. M. C. Chagla, the Education Minister who piloted the Jawaharlal Nehru University Bill through the Parliament between 1964–65

revisions and changes, the foremost being the decision not to affiliate the existing seventeen to eighteen colleges of the Delhi University and start a university de novo.[12]

Although three-and-a-half hours were allotted to the discussion of the bill, it took three whole days to discuss it, and as many as 174 amendments were suggested, many of which were accepted, including the amendment of some extremely important clauses and the first schedule itself. Professor Mukut Bihari Lal, a member of the Joint Committee, was the most impassioned critic of the bill. He was against naming the university after Jawaharlal Nehru as he was opposed to fostering personality cults. The socialist had also taken a stand against using Nehru's name for the university and the substance of the first schedule....

Chagla was adamant in his insistence on using Jawaharlal Nehru's name for the new university even while agreeing that it may not be proper to name universities after individuals. But he urged that an

[12] *Rajya Sabha Debates,* 1 December 1965, c. 3,406.

exception be made to this principle when men of outstanding stature were involved.[13]

The schedule was now amended as below:

> The university shall endeavour to promote the study of the principles for which Jawaharlal Nehru worked during his lifetime, namely, national integration, social justice, secularism, democratic way of life, international understanding and scientific approach to the problems of society.[14]

Chagla agreed with the amendment and concurred that a university exists to study and not to propagate. JNU would prove its worth by its own merit and be worthy of the great leader's name....

The debates on the bill in the Lok Sabha and the Rajya Sabha were focused on the name of the university and its possible national and international ethos. The emphasis shifted to the composition of the university faculty when the Joint Committee invited the evidence of the eight leading educationists. This panel made it clear that it was vital that the new university had brilliant teachers at the heart of this enterprise.

V. S. Jha and Triguna Sen had disagreed with V. K. R. V. Rao who wanted a state-wise quota system to bring students to JNU. Jha and Sen were of the opinion that a faculty consisting of eminent professors would invite good students from across the country. Jha, with his background in academic administration, had intervened to say that unless the proposed university had worthy teachers, it had no great future....

Most obvious, throughout this debate, was the underlying urge to create a completely autonomous institution, and this could be done by making the teachers the custodians of the university.

---

[13]M. C. Chagla., *Rajya Sabha Debates,* 1 December 1965, Vol. 54, No. 20, c. 3,401.

[14]*Rajya Sabha Debates,* 6 December 1965, Vol. 54, No. 23, c. 3,898.

5

A PROSPECTUS FOR A NEW UNIVERSITY*

GYAN PRAKASH

Why did JNU attract the punitive eye of the state? For one thing, it was—and still is—unique and enjoyed the prestige of being named after Indira's father and India's first prime minister, Jawaharlal Nehru. Although M. C. Chagla, a jurist and the education minister, introduced the JNU Bill in the Parliament at the end of 1964, the discussions on the university's establishment began soon after Nehru's death on 27 May. In August 1964, the Jawaharlal Nehru Memorial Fund formed a committee of experts to discuss the establishment of an institution of higher learning named after Nehru that would be different from existing universities.[1] The committee solicited opinions from noted individuals, including the nuclear scientist Homi J. Bhabha and the industrialist J. R. D. Tata, who suggested something modeled on the French Grandes Écoles.[2]

The most detailed advice came from Dr Douglas Ensminger of the Ford Foundation in Delhi. His nine-page note titled 'Prospectus for a New National Institution of Higher Learning in India', proposed a small residential institution named Nehru Academy, or the Nehru National Institute for Higher or Advanced Studies, or the Nehru National University. It advised the passage of special legislation to create the institution

---

*Excerpted from Gyan Prakash, *Emergency Chronicles*, Gurgaon: Penguin Random House India, 2018, pp. 22–27.

[1]This information is from the papers of Dr K. G. Saiyidain (1904–71), a noted educationist who was a member of a panel of experts formed to consider proposals for establishing an educational institution named after Nehru. His papers are not yet in the public domain. Neeti Nair generously shared her digital copies with me. Rakesh Batabyal, *JNU: The Making of a University*, New Delhi: HarperCollins India, 2014 seems unaware of the activities of the Jawaharlal Nehru Fund and attributes the university's formation solely to M. C. Chagla.

[2]Notes from Homi J. Bhabha and J. R. D. Tata, as well as from Romesh Thapar, K. T. Chandy, and B. F. H. B. Tyabji, K. G. Saiyidain Papers, Delhi.

to ensure that it would be independent and free from government interference. The note also contained specific suggestions on the structure of the institution, a nontraditional and interdisciplinary curriculum, and the recruitment of talented faculty and students housed in a residential campus. It recommended that the campus be located near an urban and industrial centre, not in Delhi but possibly Bangalore, Nasik, Hyderabad or Trivandrum.[3]

The expert committee headed by Romesh Thapar, a left-wing journalist and the founding editor of the noted public affairs journal *Seminar*, developed Ensminger's proposal into the final plan.[4] Proposing Nehru Academy or the Nehru Institute of Advanced Studies as possible names, the Thapar committee envisioned the establishment of a small, research-oriented institution of a different kind. It was to advance Nehru's ideas on national integration and his global outlook. In keeping with Nehru's broad-minded scientific perspective, the new institution would stress interdisciplinary study and research and abandon the annual examination system of Indian universities. It would recruit top Indian faculty from within the country and abroad and teach a select body of students. Disagreeing with Ensminger's view, the committee strongly recommended it be located near Delhi, both because that would be more convenient for international exchanges and because Nehru's reign as prime minister was in the city.

The left-wing student body of JNU in the 1970s would have been inflamed if they had known of the role played by Ensminger in the foundation of the university. Not only were the student activists stridently anti-American, India's image under Nehru and Indira was also pro-Soviet Union. But Nehru, in spite of his socialist leanings, was not averse to American assistance. While securing Soviet help in establishing highly visible steel plants and heavy engineering projects in the public sector, he was receptive to expertise and assistance for modernization from everyone, including the Ford Foundation. The Foundation recruited Ensminger, a rural sociologist who had earned his doctorate from Cornell University and had previously worked in the Department of Agriculture in the United States, to establish and lead its field office in India to promote

[3]Dr Douglas Ensminger, 'Prospects for a New National Institution of Higher Learning in India,' 29 August 1965, K. G. Saiyidain Papers.

[4]'Report of the Committee of Experts on the Establishment of Nehru Memorial Institute of Advanced Studies,' 20 November 1964, K. G. Saiyidain Papers.

its agenda of 'human welfare'. He proved to be an excellent choice, for Ensminger recognized that the Foundation's success as a philanthropic organization depended on keeping its distance from the US government. Recognizing Indian political sensitivities, he positioned the Foundation in India as a purely technocratic body of development and social engineering. He defended India's goal of achieving a 'socialist pattern of society', fought Ford's New York headquarters to secure local veto power over projects, and made sure that they were partnered with Indian scientists.[5] During the nineteen years of his tenure in New Delhi, Ensminger succeeded in inserting the foundation in shaping key areas of development initiatives. In addition to spearheading programmes such as family planning and rural community development, the Ford Foundation helped establish several important institutions like the Indian Institute of Public Administration, the National Institute of Design, and the Indian Institutes of Management in Ahmedabad and Calcutta.

The key to Ensminger's success was the rapport he established with Nehru. Upon arriving in New Delhi in 1951, he concluded, 'Nehru was India'. Not only was he the prime minister, the external affairs minister, and the head of the Planning Commission, he 'told the people of India what was expected of them, and the people looked to Nehru to tell them what he wanted them to do'.[6] Accordingly, Ensminger quietly forged a productive working relationship with Nehru, regularly informing him of and discussing with him all of the Foundation's activities, which he presented as technical advice and financial assistance on priorities determined by the Indian government. At no time did he have to wait longer than three days to meet with Nehru, and they frequently exchanged messages on ongoing projects. Over time, Ensminger thought that they had developed a relationship 'truly Indian in character'. Evidently, his ready access to Nehru made him appear such an influential figure that the American architect Albert Mayer, who headed the formulation of

---

[5] For a full treatment of Ensminger and the Ford Foundation in India, see Nicole Sackley, 'Foundations in the Field: The Ford Foundation New Delhi Office and the Construction of Development Knowledge, 1951–1970,' Ulrich Herbert and Jörn Leonhard (eds.), *American Foundations and the Corporation of World Order in the Twentieth Century*, Göttingen: Vandenhoek and Ruprecht, 2012, pp. 232–60.

[6] 'Douglas Ensminger Oral History; Relationships with Nehru,' FA 744, Box 1, Folder A8, Ford Foundation Records, Rockefeller Archive Center (RAC).

the Delhi Master Plan, remarked in 1959 that Ensminger was 'the second most powerful man in India'.[7]

Nehru's death in 1964 profoundly saddened Ensminger, but his productive relationship with the Indian government continued. It is no surprise therefore that he was asked for advice on setting up a university that was to be named after a leader he so admired and with whom he had worked so consequentially during independent India's formative years.

Ensminger's proposal was revised and redrafted into a plan for JNU. As the Ford Foundation chief had suggested, special legislation was introduced in the Parliament, which passed the Jawaharlal Nehru University Act in 1966.[8] The university formally started functioning in 1969 under the newly appointed vice chancellor, Gopalaswami Parthasarathi, or GP, as he was popularly known. It was housed temporarily in the unoccupied buildings originally constructed for the National Academy of Administration on the southern outskirts of the city while construction for a permanent campus began on the adjacent rocky outcrops of the Aravalli mountain range. The government held a design competition for a master plan of the new JNU campus, which attracted sixty-eight proposals. It invited the competing architects to design a campus that reflected Nehru's educational philosophy of unity of knowledge and reflected the 'unity in diversity of India' and embodied 'the spirit of democracy and social justice'. The injunction that the plan should incorporate the states and cultures of India did not mean an institution 'where Kerala students live in Kerala House' and 'Bihar students live in Bihar house'. The ideal was that the students and teachers from all of India would live together in the spirit of unity in diversity. Just as Nehru was 'thoroughly modern and still rooted in and took sustenance from the past—not its fossils', so should be the university named after him.[9] JNU was to literally embody the ideal of a pedagogic state, teaching its citizens to be Indian in the fashion that Nehru envisaged. The irony was that this was being built precisely when the ideal itself was coming apart on the streets.

---

[7]Cited in Sackley, 'Foundation in the Field,' p. 251.

[8]For JNU's history since the introduction of the JNU Bill by Chagla, see Batabyal, *JNU: The Making of a University*.

[9]Jawaharlal Nehru University, A Study in Campus Designs: National Competition for the Master Plan of Jawaharlal Nehru University Campus, New Delhi: Directorate of Advertising & Visual Publicity, Ministry of I & B, GOI, 1974, pp. 4–5.

II.2. G. Parthasarathi, the first Vice Chancellor of JNU
Photo courtesy: The Hindu Photo Archive

The architectural competition, however, went ahead. The winning entry was by C. P. Kukreja Associates. It planned for a campus built of red bricks set amid rocks and shrubs, designed to reflect the terrain. The student dormitories were named after India's rivers as a nod to national integration. By 1973, the New Campus was ready to house students while teaching and administration remained on the Old Campus. The university itself had become fully operational a year earlier. Vice Chancellor Parthasarathi, an Oxford graduate, a former barrister, and a diplomat, recruited top faculty from across India and abroad. Initially, many of the admitted students were from privileged and anglicized families and were graduates from elite institutions. To diversify the student body, the system of admission introduced in 1974 was designed to give preference to applicants from economically deprived families and to those belonging to the officially classified backward regions of the country.

Both Parthasarathi and his subordinate N. V. K. Murthy, the Registrar, were suave cosmopolitan individuals, cut from the Nehruvian liberal cloth.

They were open to diverse views and opinions, tolerated dissent, espoused a plural view of India, held progressive social and political values, and exuded an international outlook. They fostered JNU as a place of academic excellence and free exchanges of ideas between the administration and faculty and students. Radicalism thrived in this milieu. Many of the leading historians and social scientists recruited to the faculty also belonged to the Left. Graduate students formed the overwhelming majority of the student body, while the undergraduates were confined to the School of Languages, where the prime minister's younger daughter-in-law, Maneka Gandhi, the wife of Sanjay Gandhi, was a student of German. The university was small—under 800 students and 200 faculty until 1975.[10] This fostered an atmosphere of a close-knit community woven together with informal face-to-face relationships and exchanges. The residential campus and the close proximity of the dormitories of men and women also produced a liberal atmosphere of conversations and friendships across genders, which was unusual for India.

[10]Kanjiv Lochan (cd.), *JNU: The Years*, Bombay: Popular Prakashan, 1996.

6

HEADY, INFORMAL, INCLUSIVE: THE EARLY YEARS

ATIYA HABEEB KIDWAI

JNU is an educational institution considered by many as enigmatic in its conception and unacceptable in its form. Paradoxically, it has been able to produce some of the best minds in the country. The people and events I will discuss created that paradox in the 1970s.

Here, I share some memories of the first cohort of JNU teachers and students, and recall how the university broke traditional moulds of education in India; how norms were reworked when things needed to be done; how young minds were respected and nurtured; what freedom and tolerance meant in a university, and, how a centre of study became the laboratory for testing new ideas. I write, in particular, about the vision and the efforts of two men who knitted students, teachers, and karamcharis into a modern liberated gurukul.

On 21 June 1971, I joined the university in the Annexe of Vigyan Bhavan where it was located. I was in my early twenties, non-metropolitan, and naive in many ways. I had been, perhaps, identified as a 'potential' candidate after a chance meeting I had with our first Vice Chancellor, G. Parthasarathi (GP) for a post subsequently advertised by the Centre for the Study of Regional Development (CSRD). At the time, I was happily employed as an Assistant Professor at IIT Kharagpur where I had studied professional regional and urban planning and had been selected to go to Poland for a year to associate with a leading theoretician in socialistic spatial planning. Excited about my first trip abroad, I forgot about JNU the moment I left Delhi. However, I was captivated by GP's charisma. But I wondered why he was trying to start a new university when there were already too many, and that too in the Annexe of Vigyan Bhavan. I was sure he was made for bigger things.

Within a couple of months I was contacted by Professor Moonis Raza, a professor of geography, an officer on special duty at JNU and GP's aide-de-camp and think tank. He knew me through his brother, my teacher at Aligarh Muslim University. The CSRD posts had been advertised and I was asked to apply. Professor Pathak, my teacher and my colleague at Kharagpur, was also keen on one of the senior posts and suggested we give JNU a try. The play of subsequent events landed me and Dr Pathak at JNU. Poland had to be shelved on GP's behest and I took a big leap into uncertainty.

My first home in Delhi was a guest room at Sapru House, now the Gomti Guest House. This building accommodated the hostel of the School of International Studies, which was then the only functioning School of JNU at Ferozeshah Road, where ICHR is now located. Professor Bimal Prasad, Bimal Babu as he was fondly called, was our warden and lived with us. Bengali Market and Triveni were close by, and the students of the National School of Drama (NSD) were an almost permanent fixture at the Sapru House Canteen. For the first time, I was exposed to a metropolis and to a hub of radical culture around Mandi House.

In Vigyan Bhavan, the JNU faculty was growing in number. Coming from the backwaters of Kharagpur, I did not know the who's who of social sciences. I saw a very impressive and attractive woman, perhaps in her mid-thirties, always with a smile and twinkling, penetrating eyes. I tried to find out about her. 'She is the brilliant Romila Thapar', I was told. The most suave among the men was S. Gopal, the son of President Radhakrishan. We also had Imtiaz Ahmad, a Lucknawi, Rashiduddin Khan, and the Registrar, N. V. K. Murthy, both Hyderabadis with their characteristic style and sense of humour. Very distinctive, but desi like us, was the firebrand Bipan Chandra, and then there was the serene Yogendra Singh, the erudite T. K. Oommen, the boisterous Javed Ashraf, and the affable C. P. Bhambhri, whose laughter reverberated joy in all the rooms of the Vigyan Bhavan Annexe. All had been handpicked by GP.

And, of course, there was Moonis Raza. Module by module, GP and he had conceptualized the idea of a university for a country like India—unified yet diverse, inclusive, egalitarian, and academically innovative. Many questions had to be addressed. But there was one that was critical in defining the character of JNU: how to reach out to students from the remote backwaters of the country, to the most deprived strata of our society, and to women. This was done through a unique admission policy

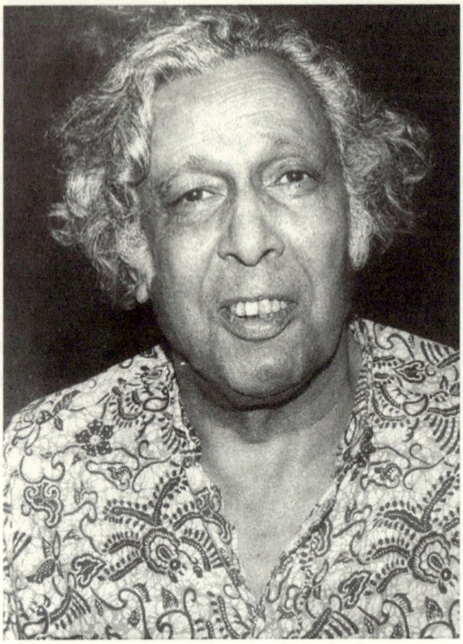

II.3. Moonis Raza, the first Rector of JNU
Photo courtesy: Gul Mooni

they evolved wherein, along with the traditional written test and interview, students were given deprivation points to overcome the systemic disadvantages they had faced in life earlier. The academic programme too was unique. Instead of compartmentalized departments we had 'Centres of Studies' within different Schools where allied disciplines converged and interacted.

Where else was this idea to be tested in full earnestness but in the Centre for the Study of Regional Development (CSRD), Moonis Raza's own centre. When we interviewed the first batch of MPhil students in Vigyan Bhavan, the panel comprised: Biplab Dasgupta, Boudhayan Chattopadhyay, Amitabh Kundu, S. K. Rao (economists), C. R. Pathak, R. S. Sharma, K. P. Dhrandher (geographers), Sanjay Chandra, V. K. Asthana (geologists) Ashok Rao (engineer), and me, an urban and regional planner.

Moonis Raza led the flock. His master's degree labelled him as a geographer but he was part philosopher, part poet, part serious, part fun—an intellectual 'bindaas'. He was an ardent student of philosophy as enshrined in books and taught by his life's struggles—a life which had been about fighting injustices of all kinds. Part of this struggle had been incognito and politically underground, during the national movement, when he lost one of his lungs to tuberculosis.

When I look back I am amazed at what CSRD enabled the first batch of MPhil and MA students to achieve later in life. Ashok Lata Jain, Suneet Chopra, Harjit Singh, Keya Deb, Shakti Kak, Sohail Hashmi, Kamala Menon, Poonam Natarajan, Mujeeb Kidwai, Ashok Malick, Ruma Chandra, Mala Banerjee, to name a few. I distinctly remember the admission interview of Ashok Lata, a petite and charming young girl from the small town of Bijnor, Uttar Pradesh. She broke down when the first question was put to her in English. Even our persistent assurance that she would lose no marks if she replied in Hindi could not stop her tears and I had to take her out of the room to console her. Within a span of four years, the same Ashok Lata became the chairperson of the JNUSU Council, organized the Janwadi Mahila Samiti and addressed huge rallies on the lawns of India Gate. Death snatched her from us very early but she left behind a rich legacy of social activism. CSRD is proud of her. Another student activist who made us all proud was Baburam Bhattarai of Nepal who led a revolution, freed his country and became the prime minister.

Following the admissions, in early September 1971, we shifted from Vigyan Bhavan to the building complex on New Mehrauli Road, originally built for new Civil Service entrants. Later, it came to be called the Old Campus. Interestingly, the Old Campus now houses the police academy. Its four blocks, each five-storeyed, were originally built to house the civil service academy which was to shift here from Dehradun. These four blocks consisted of 14×16 feet single rooms, with attached bathrooms. The faculty residences, offices, classrooms, and students—all had to be accommodated in them. Ingeniously, the administration converted these rows of rooms for multiple uses. The faculty occupied the first four storeys in Block 2. The fifth storey was turned into the girls' hostel. The Professors were given four rooms, Associate Professors three rooms and Assistant Professors two rooms. The so-called 'flats' were separated by sheets of plyboard and made an interesting jigsaw puzzle. The fact that your kitchen was a converted bathroom and its counter sat on a commode was not a matter oft-discussed.

Water from the new pipes was chalky or loaded with cement. For about two weeks, until the water pipes cleared, the finicky amongst us would walk to IIT Delhi hostels to get our daily supply of drinking water.

Flats were allotted to the faculty by a lottery system. Elevators had not been installed yet. Despite his one lung, Moonis sahib voluntarily took a flat on the fourth floor. While climbing the stairs when he wanted to sit down and rest his one lung, he would knock on the door of any of the flats along the flight of stairs. A halt could extend to an hour or more if the conversation got going or if he was in the mood to recite Faiz and Majaz.

Life in this small campus was intimate, cosy, and eventful. Cultural events were organized on a small scale and not advertised. To meet friends and encourage the experiment that was JNU, came Faiz Ahmad Faiz, M. S. Sathyu, Shyam Benegal, Tariq Ali, and many more. Habib Tanvir lived across the road in Ber Sarai with his troupe, and the first show of most of his plays was invariably staged on the campus. Not many people know that we also had a music club in the Old Campus. I happily took charge of it. The teacher invited to train students was none other than Anil Biswas, playback singer and music director, who brought orchestral music into Indian cinema. He was a close friend of Faiz Ahmad Faiz and composed the musical rendering of his poems. Faiz had sent his famous poem 'Hum ke Thahre Ajnabi Itni Mulaqaton ke Baad', written after the creation of Bangladesh in 1971, to Anil da to set to music. Sometimes he would stay after the class to try out different versions of this poem and many others with just me as audience.

The close proximity of workplace and residence in the Old Campus had a flip side. The working day had little meaning. CSRD functioned almost 24x7, as the cartographic lab and documentation unit, managed by students, were open late into the night throughout the year. For Moonis Raza, 'vacations' were merely notional. We were made to believe that you could be working and still 'feel' like you were on a vacation if you enjoyed your work. This work ethos, however, was not coercive.

The New Campus came to life when we shifted there in February 1974, two months after I got married. It had been taking shape, brick by brick, since 1970. We had picnicked amidst its rocks and bushes, gone there for long walks, explored its Neolithic sites as identified by Javed Ashraf, eaten the small ber from the bushes native to the ridge, and collected shining souvenirs of mica from its mines. In those days, the New Campus consisted of Dakshinapuram and Uttarakhand faculty residences and the Ganga, Kaveri and, Godavari hostel complexes. There were no School buildings. I was made one of the four wardens of the Godavari Hostel for girls. There was as yet no separate approach to my flat, since the hostel happened to be the last building on the South Delhi periphery. There was no construction after Godavari and no Vasant Kunj at the time. My husband had to come to our house through the hostel wing. I was later told that he was held in awe by the girls, perhaps because we had shifted to the hostel in winter, and they first encountered him in his rather worn-out three-button Dunn's Harris Tweed coat with leather elbows, looking very scholarly.

Protests and rebelliousness were a part of the JNU culture. Their resolution was fast and friendly. Let me refer to two instances that took place in chronological order. Imagine the CSRD classroom with Sohail Hashmi, a student of MA first semester, a compulsive smoker. In Moonis Raza's first lecture to the class, Sohail feels the urge to smoke, and decides his strategy. To overcome your opponent, make the first move. He takes out a cigarette pack from his pocket and puts it determinedly on his desk. Then comes out the matchbox and is placed next to the pack, all the while eyeing the professor and the professor eyeing him. Then in a brave attempt a cigarette is taken out and lit. The professor quietly asks, 'akele akele?' (smoking alone?) A second cigarette is then lit, handed over to the professor to be accepted cheerfully by him. The class laughs and is won over.

On another occasion, the JNUSU President, D. P. Tripathi, leads a protest march one evening to the house of the Dean of Students, who again happened to be Moonis Raza. Hearing the slogans he comes out and tells the students that however legitimate be the cause of their protest, the timing was inappropriate. Evenings were meant for other things. They were welcome to come inside his house, share food with him. They could come to his office the next morning and call him 'Bourgeois, Bourgeois'.

JNU was sensitive to students' freedom to choose their own paths in life. Professor Sopory recently told me that when he was a warden he had asked Moonis, then Rector, to make pucca footpaths connecting hostels and Schools as the rugged ground was inconvenient and dangerous to walk on. Moonis Raza had told him, 'Not now. Students will not walk on the footpaths you make. In our informal layout plan the students will discover their own convenient paths. Time will tell us which paths they prefer. Let them choose. We will then pave them.'

Hark this message. Students will not walk on the paths you make. They discover their own paths. Let them choose.

II.4. Paths ordained and paths followed (towards the academic block from the western hostels and valley)
Photo courtesy: Mudit Trivedi

7

A UNIQUE EXPERIMENT

SUKHADEO THORAT

Not many realize that the emergence of Jawaharlal Nehru University in Delhi in the 1970s, as a centre of excellence in teaching and research, was a unique development in the history of university education in India. As the chairman of University Grants Commission (UGC), I had an opportunity to closely watch the university system in the country, and as the chairman of the National Assessment and Accreditation Council (under UGC), was also witness to the assessment of the quality of research and teaching in the universities. But I am yet to see a public university in India which has acquired the top position in the country in such a short time, besting older, established universities. Some of the centres in other universities (like Bombay, Calcutta, Madras, Banaras, Aligarh) acquired excellence in some subjects, but as an integrated system of teaching and learning at the postgraduate and PhD level, JNU remains unparalleled. The JNU experiment began in 1970, and by the early 1980s people began to compare it with Oxford and Cambridge in the West. It is therefore useful to understand the basis of this success, preserve the best features of the university, and learn from it.

What accounts for the success of the JNU experiment? Reflecting on my forty years at JNU (1975–2014), I would like to list some of the features that, in my opinion, have helped convert JNU into an outstanding centre of teaching and research. At the cost of some simplification, I would include the following in this list: the inclusive admission policy, the unique selection procedure for admission of the students, the decentralized, inclusive, and democratic process of governance, the unique academic programme with a semester system, the freedom given to the faculty to devise courses and academic programmes, the excellence of the teaching faculty, the accessible residential system for the teachers and students and, above all, an unprecedented level of autonomy to the faculty. Much of the credit for devising the overall framework goes to the first Vice Chancellor G. Parthasarathi, the Rector cum Planning Officer Professor Moonis Raza, and the faculty members that joined the university in the early 1970s.

Even before the statutory reservation policy came into effect, JNU had introduced deprivation as a factor to be considered in admission, granting points for regional and economic backwardness. This was an admirable effort to provide space to those who were deprived and lacked access to quality education. While merit had its space, some weightage was given to those who were first-generation learners, those coming from backward districts, those with relatively low income, as well as to women. This provided opportunities to those who lag behind in higher education. This system brought in students who valued the opportunity and worked hard to excel. JNU was quick to accept the policy relating to reservation as soon as it became a statutory ruling. The early acceptance of the policy of reservation for Dalits, Adivasis, and later OBC students, consolidated the space for marginalized groups within the university.

There is one more important aspect of the admission policy, namely the method of assessment for admission. In the early years, JNU had both written examination and interviews for selecting the students for undergraduate, masters and MPhil/PhD programmes. The decision of interviewing thousands of students for selection was a bold step as it extended the process of admission by weeks. But it provided the faculty an opportunity to meet the candidates face to face, and evaluate their academic competence, social and economic background, and general interests. It was a laborious process and yet very useful: it helped in choosing the finest candidates, keeping in mind their merit, social location, and experience of deprivation. The admission policy also sought to admit students from all parts of the country. After 1984, this was facilitated by the decision to conduct the entrance examination at various centres in the country, including many remote places. All-India representation with social diversity is the hallmark of JNU. Having visited many central universities as the chairman of UGC, I've seen how central universities tend to be regional universities, serving primarily the students of their states. We are yet to see an admission system comparable to that at JNU, one which combines so well inclusiveness and diversity, while maintaining quality and excellence.

JNU also set up an Equal Opportunity Office. Initially this was to help the students in improving their competence in the English language, but later, remedial assistance was extended to the core subjects. This capability enhancement programme is a hallmark of JNU, and was later adopted by UGC for the entire university system in the country.

The second element that accounts for JNU's excellence, in my view, is the structure of the academic programme: the semester system, the system of course work and assignments, and the method of assessment. It needs to be recognized that while many universities in India have adopted the semester system now, JNU did this from the very beginning. So it did not have to face the problem of converting from a yearly to a six-monthly system. The assessment system too was unique from the start: we had reviews of literature, analytical exercises, and presentations of assignments, tutorials, and seminars. This continuous process of writing, presentations, and assessments, drew out the best from the students and allowed them to develop their research capabilities. The end-of-term written examinations, in fact, constitute a small component of marks within the overall assessment. Equally important is the freedom given to the faculty to develop courses. As against the uniform structure of courses in most Indian universities, JNU allowed variations across the centres/departments. The number of courses varies from centre to centre, which is not the case in other universities, where uniformity is the rule. While some centres had three-credit courses, others had four-credit courses. This freedom and flexibility provided the opportunity to develop a system that promoted excellence.

JNU also tried to ensure, at least until recently, that the faculty had enough freedom and opportunity for their academic development. The university introduced a liberal leave policy: this included sabbatical leave of six months once in three years, or for one year once after six years, in addition to study leave and extraordinary leave. All these provided a milieu and incentive for research for the faculty.

The reservation policy helped individuals from scheduled castes and tribes to join the faculty at JNU, from its early days in the late 1970s. It also reformed the reservation policy by introducing the roster system at the university level, rather than at the centre level. During my tenure as the UGC chairman, this reform was adopted by UGC for all central universities in India.

The third factor is the decentralized mode of governance, where the administration, the faculty and the students are all, in some ways involved. JNU is possibly exceptional in having students as members of the Academic Council. The decentralization meant a bottom-up governance system: from the centres to the schools, from the Committee of Advanced Studies and the Board of Studies in each School, to the Academic Council and then the Executive Council. In this sense, all decisions in some ways reflect the views and opinions of the larger academic community, arrived at through an inclusive process.

Thus the inclusive admission policy, the unique academic programme, the bottom-up structure of governance, and the decentralized decision-making process, among other attributes, have made JNU a high-ranking centre of teaching and research. I also want to emphasize that the written framework of rules and regulations—the ordinances—are very important, but at the same time the ethos and the practices developed over years are also invaluable. It is this ethos and these practices that have helped JNU implement rules sensitively. In my view, the freedom granted to teachers and students and the respect for democratic practices have enabled JNU to sail through many troubled times. An administrative system can become democratic in its functioning, provided the stakeholders also develop a supportive moral ethos and social practices. I will give one example as evidence of the importance of this democratic ethos. I remember an incident when the JNU Students' Union had gone on a hunger strike for some demands, which the administration and many within the faculty thought unreasonable. The hunger strike went on for over a week, disturbing the academic session. One choice for the Vice Chancellor was to call the police and forcefully end the hunger strike. But Professor Y. K. Alagh, the then Vice Chancellor, who came from Gujarat, was desperate to find a different solution. In the end, he fell back on Gandhiji's method of hunger strike. He erected a tent in front of the protesting students, and went on a counter-hunger strike against their unreasonable demand. This peaceful method had an immediate and profound impact. The students withdrew the hunger strike and entered into negotiation, ending the deadlock. This is a rare and exceptional example of a democratic way to resolve issues through discussion and reason. But this requires commitment to high values, a faith in democratic ways, and the courage to use them.

The emergence of JNU as a premier university, also attracted the attention of policy-making bodies like the Ministry of Education/ Ministry of Human Resources, and the UGC. During my tenure as the UGC Chairman, the insights that I developed on the success of JNU helped me devise policies for other educational institutions. A few schemes were adopted straight from JNU. The Equal Opportunity Office set up at JNU to address the specificities of SC/ST/OBC/Physically Handicapped as well as women was introduced as a scheme for all universities and colleges at the national level. JNU had set up a Centre for the Study of Discrimination and Exclusion (CSDE) to undertake studies on the problems experienced by the socially marginalized groups. The UGC adopted the scheme, and set up thirty-two Centres of Social Exclusion and Inclusive Policies in different universities. The reform in the PhD admission procedure that the UGC introduced was also drawn from the JNU experience. It reduced the biases in PhD admission in universities where the admission method for PhD was ad hoc and non-transparent.

Those from JNU who joined various positions of authority in the country carried with them their JNU experience, especially, the importance of being sensitive to the legitimate demands of people. During 2006–11, the Rajiv Gandhi fellowships for the SC/ST students were introduced to enable them to undertake research. I was approached by students from minority groups of JNU for similar fellowships. I persuaded the minority minister at the time, A. R. Antulay, to introduce the fellowship, which he did. The general students from JNU approached me with a complaint that nothing was being done for those who do not get NET fellowship. So I pursued the matter with the officials in the ministry, who finally agreed to the proposal after six months. A new scheme was introduced that entitled all non-NET students to Rs 3,000 per month during their MPhil, and Rs 5,000 per month during their PhD. The logic was that PhD students in central universities like JNU entered the system through a rigorous admission test. They became a human resource for the country, and it would be unfair to expect them to self-finance their studies for four years.

Similarly, the salaries of teachers in universities were increased, making them almost on par with that of the Indian Administrative Services. The accountability system through APP and other academic reforms were inspired by JNU, where the faculty did have the same salaries as other central universities, but they also received funds from research projects and other academic engagements which facilitated their academic work.

The JNU experiment is unique. We should not allow anyone to undermine this experience which the academicians at JNU have evolved with great effort, step by step. If the institution is damaged, which seems to be happening now, it will be not just an enormous loss for the higher education system in the country: it will be a national calamity and a profound tragedy.

III

OF SCHOOLS AND CENTRES

8

THE CENTRE FOR RUSSIAN STUDIES*

RITOO M. JERATH

History

It is a wonderful day in the history of any institution to celebrate fifty years of its existence. It is also a time to assess its achievements, its shortcomings, and to chart out the possibilities of its growth directions over the next fifty years.

The Centre for Russian Studies was founded in 1965. The aim and objective of its foundation was to promote special learning and scientific research work in the field of Russian language and literature and for the systematic study of the life and culture of the USSR. The decision to establish such a Centre of Learning was arrived at during the discussions between the Education Ministers of the two countries, Shri M. C. Chagla and Professor V. P. Yelutin. This was first discussed in February 1965 and then in July 1965, and formalized through an agreement signed on 27 October 1965.

The Centre of Learning was inaugurated as an autonomous body on 14 November 1965, the birthday of Jawaharlal Nehru, and was called the Institute of Russian Studies. Initially the institute was housed on the IIT campus in a building that was located near the IIT gate leading to Essex Farms. According to one of the students of the first batch, when Jawaharlal Nehru died in 1964, the government wanted to set up a university in his memory, and so this institute was established with the tacit understanding that it would eventually become a part of the university.

---

*Excerpted from Ritoo M. Jerath, *CRS through the Decades*, (1965-2015), Centre for Russian Studies, School of Language, Literature and Culture Studies, Jawaharlal Nehru University, New Delhi, pp. 1-3. The text has been edited for this volume.

In the meantime, the Institute of Russian Studies was set up very fast. Its first director, Professor C. N. Chakravarty, was teaching Russian in Delhi University and heading the Department of Modern European Languages at the time. The IRS soon got its own building, hostels, library, and the best Soviet specialists to come and teach. The students who came to study completed a one-year intensive foundation course and then a three-year BA degree after which they were sent to Moscow for further qualifications. The very first batches were sent to Moscow after less than one year. Interestingly, some of the students in the first batch already knew some Russian. The batch included the daughter of the then Indian Ambassador to the Soviet Union. It also included some army and air force officers.

In 1969, when JNU was established, IRS became a part of the School of Foreign Languages and its graduates got their degrees from JNU before going to Moscow. They received their degrees from Indira Gandhi at a convocation ceremony. This was probably the first and last time JNU had a convocation and Indira Gandhi was allowed on our campus. My memory of one of JNU's non-convocations is that of Mrs Gandhi not being allowed on campus by the JNUSU.

So, IRS became CRS and, from a four-year course, it became a five-year MA integrated course. The batch during the transition studied six years of Russian to get their MA degrees and then those who were interested in higher studies went to Moscow. While IRS was basically dominated by Soviet teachers, when IRS became CRS, the number of Russian teachers teaching in the centre was cut down to five. By this time many from the first batch of IRS had returned from Moscow and had been appointed Assistant Professors in CRS. Among them were Professor R. Kumar, Professor Varyam Singh, and Professor R. N. Menon.

The mid-seventies and the beginning of the eighties was a very radical period in the history of JNU and that radicalism entered CRS. Physically, CRS was isolated from the rest of the university, located in its own building away from the main centre of activity. The Soviets continued to send their five specialists to our Centre and we received books, newspapers, and journals from the Soviet Union. It would not be fair to say that the syllabus was controlled by the Soviets but there was a very (perhaps naturally) heavy Soviet influence in terms of the authors we studied and the point of view from which we got our education. But as students in the mid-seventies and early eighties, we could not help being influenced by the 'down' campus. Simultaneously, scholarships for higher studies were getting more difficult to come by. Although we had a very strong MA programme with a choice of specialization in either language and literature or translation and interpretation, CRS did not have a very well worked-out PhD programme. By this time some of us felt the need to do a PhD in our own Centre. We also chose to be somewhat radical in our choice of subjects for research. Our topics were not necessarily Soviet friendly. The PhD programme developed and grew with us. There was Rashmi Doraiswamy who chose to work on Bakhtin, there was Ranjana Saxena who wanted to research the women's question and I initially wanted to work on Mayakovsky's suicide. A small example of how these topics were not Soviet friendly was the fact that when we did go to Moscow for material collection in 1985, Ranjana came across an article in the archives that said there was no longer a women's question because the women's question had been solved with the invention of the potato peeler!

In CRS we did not study Bulgakov, Pasternak, Solzhenitsyn, the formalists, the émigré writers etc., until the mid-eighties when Mikhail

III.1. Centre for Russian Studies moved into this building in 1990, from its earlier isolated location near the Old Campus.
Photo courtesy: Samim Asgor Ali

Gorbachev announced his policies of glasnost and perestroika. It was around this time that we changed our syllabus to a common MA with very minor specialization. Our new syllabus came into effect with the batch that joined in 1988 and they studied some of the previously forbidden writers and the earlier sanctioned writers such as Ostrovsky, Fadeyev, and Sholokhov were removed. Soviet specialists also were not sent that easily. Books, journals, and newspaper supplies became erratic.

In 1990, we moved to the new building. From being housed in one building and all of us living next to each other five days a week from 9 to 1, our Centre was split over four floors of the new building. We were also left with only one Soviet specialist. In 1991, the Soviet Union collapsed and, just like the Russians who had to search for a new identity, our Centre also had to search for a new identity. It has taken a while but we are now in the process of restructuring our syllabus, and we are also in the process of finding and strengthening our research areas. It has been a long and interesting journey over the last fifty years. Despite some of the hurdles that have come our way, from the very material and physical problems of resources, scholarships and research opportunities, our Centre still remains one of the best centres for learning Russian and for Russian studies.

9

CHS THAT WAS

NEELADRI BHATTACHARYA

I often wonder why I felt so happy joining JNU as an MA student back in 1973. I had completed my BA in a college that was generally considered prestigious. I had some wonderful friends and some great teachers. Dwivedi Saheb always had an interesting take on themes in Ancient Indian History; Dr Baker introduced us to some of the finest writing on British History; Amin Saheb made history fun; and Robi Chatterjee was brilliant and inspiring. Yet there was something I missed during my undergraduate days. In a college packed with students from 'Ivy League' schools, as someone from an 'ordinary' school, I was made to feel I did not really belong. Performing well academically did produce grudging recognition. But I remained somewhat of an outsider. Above all, the entire system of the end-of-the-year exams in Delhi University was torturous, as I could never finish writing five essay-type answers in three hours. It seemed to me as much a test of fast writing as of rote memory. It devalued reading, thinking, and reflection. So when I heard of JNU, a new university that had a semester system, and where students had to write essays which were then collectively discussed in regular tutorial meetings before being graded, where the system did not hinge on a year-end exam, I made up my mind to try getting in. From the moment I joined the university I knew I belonged.

In the first semester itself, we were taught by a galaxy of great teachers: Professors S. Gopal, Romila Thapar, Bipan Chandra, Sabyasachi Bhattacharya or Bappa as he was called. Each had a distinct pedagogic style. Gopal, supremely regal and grand, looked at us with a mischievous twinkle in his eyes, lectured with nonchalance, and impressed us with his natural lucidity and familiarity with a vast range of readings from across the world. Romila with her gravitas and attractive presence taught us a wonderful course on Ancient Society, moving with a grand sweep from

Rome and Greece to India, her lectures carefully structured and her points flowing seamlessly from one to the next. Bipan was passionate about his ideas and impassioned in his lectures. He wanted to persuade, make you see the world through his eyes, be convinced of his truth. Bappa was not a believer who wanted you to think his thoughts. He celebrated scepticism as a mode of being, as a style of intellectual thinking. Between these four, in my very first semester, I felt a whole world of history and ways of thinking open up. And there was an excitement in this discovery.

The course structure at CHS was a contrast to what I was used to in my undergraduate days. In those days the BA courses in Delhi University were all encompassing. The course on Ancient India spanned the entire period temporally categorized as ancient, with all that was considered important packed into the course. So were the courses on Medieval and Modern Indian History, or on British, European, and Chinese History. The object of each course was to cover the entire period and all the themes and events that were seen as important. In JNU, the logic of the course structure was radically different. In Modern India, we were introduced to four courses in the first semester. One was the compulsory-for-all, overarching foundational course on Ancient Society, and the other three were Colonial Economy, British Policies, and National Movement, with each course focusing only on the period between 1857 and 1947. We did little of the earlier century (1757–1857), generally seen as part of any course on Modern India, and within each course the focus was more on themes rather than the chronological flow of events. In the subsequent semesters the courses panned out, focusing once again on intensive studies of specific themes: intellectual history, peasant movements, the history of Indian capitalism. As Bipan told us time and again, the idea was to make us think, familiarize us with different historiographies, demonstrate the linkages between economic history, intellectual history, British politics and nationalism. Once we understood these linkages, studying one period in some depth, and became sensitive to different ways of understanding history, we could easily study other periods on our own. Doing a general survey course did not allow the possibility of engaging intensively and critically with any theme, mull over ideas, or reflect on the meaning of specific paragraphs of a text. Students then had to skim over the course, sliding rapidly from one topic to the next, hurrying to cover as much as possible and prepare for the exam. True, even in our undergraduate days we did read many of the 'topics' intensively, referring to multiple books, reflecting on historiography. But the system did not encourage this and one had to struggle against the constraints.

What was unique to CHS was the practice of weekly tutorial discussions. Even in our undergraduate days we had had tutorials but it had no relationship with the system of grading. Those who scored high in the exams often borrowed others' tutorials, never wrote one of their own. Here at CHS, the entire structure of teaching was grounded on the effectivity of discussions. These discussions were energizing and fun. You came to know your fellow classmates, engage with them, question their ideas, and be questioned by them. You also came to know your teachers more intimately: their capacities to listen, their openness to differences of opinions, their ability to empathize with a student's problems, their ways of conducting the discussion.

I remember my first tutorial with Bipan. I had worked hard on my essay on early nationalist thought and had taken pains to think through my ideas. As I presented, Bipan first looked at me with penetrating eyes, then closed his eyes gently, concentrating, but kept shaking his head vigorously—left, right, left. I hesitated, wondering what I had said that he so vehemently disagreed with. Uncertain whether to continue with my presentation, I stopped. Bipan opened his eyes. Realizing his head movement had disturbed me, he explained with a smile that he nodded when he disagreed and shook his head sideways when he approved of an argument.

In subsequent discussions, I realized that Bipan's nod was a prelude to an intense and spirited discussion. When he disagreed, Bipan would relentlessly question your ideas, emphatically affirm his argument, and passionately spell out his logic. But when you stood your ground, argued back, persisted in elaborating your own idea, you earned his respect. It was an honour earned through an intellectual battle. Dialogue here was an encounter. A rite of initiation into intellectual adulthood.

Bappa was radically different. Most often when I presented an argument with passion and enthusiasm, excited about my own formulation, Bappa reacted with stoic silence—he was sceptical of the logic, and unmoved by the evidence. He offered a defence of the argument I set out to critique, and questioned my logic. This was both frustrating and empowering. As a student I wanted affirmation and encouragement. I wanted him to tell me the argument was important and original and, if possible, to declare that no one had made such an argument before. But Bappa would do no such thing. During early days as a student, I was often left disappointed. But then I realized that the art of being contrary, staging disagreement, was part of his pedagogic style, and his innate scepticism. He wanted me to push the logic of my argument, see my ideas through the eyes of a critic. In returning to my argument with a critical eye, and reworking some of the formulations, I inevitably strengthened the argument itself.

What made me most comfortable at JNU is the fact that it was not a club, whether of smart public-school boys, or some other closed group. Its social body was immensely diverse. The innovative admission policy with its 'deprivation points', and the commitment of the faculty to look not just for merit but potential, ensured that students came from different social, economic, regional, and linguistic backgrounds. JNU was a polyglot, multicultural, and socially diverse space. Living within such a space was itself a learning experience. In interacting with each other we learned about cultural and social diversity, and about the meaning of deprivation. Even students who came with a sense of self-conceit and arrogance mellowed rapidly, learning to listen to each other, respect each other, and befriend each other.

Within a year of finishing my MA, I started teaching at CHS. Teaching those who were just two years younger than me, many of them my friends, was a bit forbidding, but I enjoyed the challenge. There were, however, other more difficult challenges in teaching at JNU. First: I had to learn quickly that it was not enough to be eloquent and knowledgeable—it was important to get across to all the very diverse students we had there. When students come armed with vastly different levels of knowledge, and with linguistic and analytic competencies that differ widely, the critical challenge is to try reaching them all—neither making some feel you are talking above them, nor allowing the attention of others to flag. Over the years I felt it necessary to articulate ideas in different ways, at varying levels of simplicity and complexity, building arguments in a form where even complex ideas could become comprehensible to all: so that what is difficult does not appear to be so. It was necessary to try and make sure every student understood what I was saying. But intention does not always translate into effect. I have always wondered whether as teachers we are really able to communicate to all those who sit in the class with

III.2. Centre for Historical Studies and Centre for the Study of Regional Development shifted to this building (SSS-I) in 1979. It was one of the first few buildings of the Academic Complex in the new campus.
Photo courtesy: Samim Asgor Ali

such rapt attention, their eyes sparkling with curiosity. Are we able to empathize adequately with their problems relating to the course, and the ideas being discussed in the class?

Second: Teaching in a place where you have studied can be reassuring but also intellectually incestuous. There is always a danger of being sucked into the dominant frame of the centre's or institution's discourse, work within that frame, nuancing it, elaborating it, but remaining within it. While becoming socially diverse, the institution could turn out to be intellectually homogenous. How was it possible to belong without dissolving your identity, retain your personal voice, and develop ideas that may connect with others without merging with them?

In the early years of CHS, it came to stand for a Left nationalist history. Many among the faculty were part of the wider movement in India to develop a secular vision of history, critiquing colonial and communal frameworks, elaborating an understanding of colonialism and nationalism. This vision of the secular national—naturalized and taken for granted—shaped the syllabus and course structures in CHS, and provided an energy that animated the Centre. From the late 1980s, however, the frame was under strain, as different forms of critical thought swept through Indian academia. Some historians within CHS, as elsewhere, began to explore what the nationalist frame excluded and erased, and unpacked its homogenizing frame, its universalizing discourse. They asked the questions that were being asked within the new intellectual conjuncture of the time. How could one respect the voices of the subalterns even as they refused to fuse with that of the nation; or explore the region without marginalizing it, without searching within it the story of the nation? How could we move from the history of the homogenous national to that of the heterogeneous social? When a frame comes to be taken for granted, questioning and criticism are not always enthusiastically welcomed, and are often misunderstood. Breaking out of a frame that is naturalized is never easy. But as long as there is a vibrant space for dialogue—such as JNU offered—differences can be openly debated. From the nineties, with many new faces in the faculty, several new courses were offered, some focusing on caste and region (themes nationalist historiography had been uncomfortable with); others on discourses and cultural practices (a focus that Marxists are often suspicious of); yet others on gender and family (issues that male-centric frames had comfortably ignored). Each course was exhaustively discussed before it was passed, and the engaged discussions allowed us all to reflect on the new visions opened up by the courses.

One of the most stimulating discussions I have ever participated in was on the refashioning of the historical methods course. From 1973, when CHS started its MA and MPhil/PhD programme, there was a compulsory course on Historical Methods. In the late 1980s there was a move to abolish the course, since it was seen as somewhat amorphous, run by the entire faculty, and not tied together with a strong thread. Some said historical method was embedded in the practice of history, revealed in the way history is written: it could not be taught. Others, including me, disagreed strongly. True, the framing ideas historians operated with were not spelt out explicitly, but they were embedded in the texts they produced. These ideas had a lineage that needed to be understood; they were mediated by powerful trends of conflicting thought that students should be familiar with. Only then could students unpack the texts, critically engage with the hegemonic frames, and develop their own distinct arguments. Over two semesters we discussed the structure of the course. The were numerous notes, intense discussions, engaged and lively arguments with the entire faculty participating. Teaching the course as it finally emerged has been an energizing experience for me.

The structure of the curriculum also changed over time. Within the academic programme of the CHS as it was formulated in the early 1970s, students had to choose a stream—Ancient, Medieval, or Modern. Committed to the idea of interdisciplinarity, there was always space for students from other disciplines, but this space was limited. By the 1990s there was a powerful pressure for change. The argument was: if indeed we are serious about interdisciplinarity, should we not allow more easy movements between the disciplines—with history students taking more optionals from economics, sociology or philosophy—and make the borders between Ancient, Medieval and Modern more permeable? Should there be these strong specializations? Once again, through long and animated discussions over the years, we changed the structure of the curriculum, and began a process of opening up. The process, however, has been slow. While the boundaries were made more malleable, they were difficult to tear down.

These debates were not limited to academic issues alone. CHS has always been concerned with the public life of history. Keen on building a wider network of historians across the country, many faculty members have been active in the organization of the Indian History Congress. When the Ram Janmabhoomi movement gathered momentum in the late 1980s, several faculty members came together to write a much-debated pamphlet, 'The Political Abuse of History', and subsequently produced a book, *Anatomy of a Confrontation*, reflecting on the politics of the movement. Almost two decades later, in 2010, when the Allahabad judgment on the Ayodhya issue was announced, a day-long workshop was organized to engage with the text of the judgments and the issues they raised. Aware of the importance of history-teaching in schools, many CHS faculty members, in the past and the present, took the initiative to write the NCERT history textbooks.

CHS has been a vibrant and exciting place, a space where productive and energizing discussions—on both academic and public issues were always possible. I can only hope that this tradition does not disappear.

10

JNU IN THE FIRST DECADE: A PLACE OF INTELLECTUAL DISCOVERY

JAYATI GHOSH

It is hard to convey the sheer intellectual excitement and the exhilaration of academic discovery that marked JNU when I was a student there in the 1970s.

It was a new and small university, with all the teaching still based in the Old Campus, and most students knew each other by face, as well as the faculty in other centres. It made for a more exploratory approach to pedagogy: curricula and syllabi had only recently been introduced and were still being developed; readings were not presented only at the start of the semester in the standard list but could be tossed off during a lecture as the instructor suddenly thought of an appropriate reference, or even a less appropriate but still interesting item; a course itself could change and shift as the teacher and students' interests dictated.

The lectures were mostly engaging and often enthralling, delivered by a dominantly young faculty still caught in its own process of working things out and seeking answers to theoretical and empirical concerns. Because of this, there was also a remarkable democracy in the pedagogical process, a sense of probing questions and discovering the answers (or even more questions) together, rather than a top-down process of instruction. The faculty in my Centre (Centre for Economic Studies and Planning, or CESP) even attended one another's lectures on occasion, to grapple with particular ideas and approaches together—thereby displaying both supreme confidence and a lack of self-consciousness that was infectious.

I remember one particular occasion quite early in my MA programme, when I had gone to meet S. K. Rao, who taught us a course on sectoral problems in the Indian economy, to ask him about a point he had made in class on investment and inflation that I had not fully understood. He happened to be in his room chatting with Prabhat Patnaik and Amal Sanyal (chatting in super relaxed fashion, true adda style—I seem to remember one of them had his feet on the desk) but they insisted I should come in anyway and ask my question. S. K.'s response sparked off an animated discussion between them, as his answer to me was interrogated by the others, who came up with their own interpretations, and a lively debate ensued that lasted for at least an hour. I remember sitting there enthralled, not fully understanding everything that was said, but fascinated and feeling privileged to be witness to this lively interaction of minds.

Much of this pedagogic generosity also resulted from the fact that the vision of the founding faculty of the CESP was to provide access to different approaches to economic analysis: neoclassical, Marxian, Ricardian, Keynesian; and allowing students to decide for themselves after a thorough exposure to each. This could have been confusing, but surprisingly, it was not—possibly because those who taught each subject were so deeply committed and convinced of it themselves, and typically clear in their expression. It was also exciting, because the students also got drawn into debates over different approaches and perspectives, and developed strong opinions which we were then forced to justify with arguments.

The faculty were also heavily involved in analytical and policy discussions about the Indian economy—something that has happily continued to this day. This meant that each issue of the *Economic and Political Weekly* was eagerly awaited and then devoured, most often because there would be some article or note that would either be authored by one of our teachers, or be in response to one of them, or relate directly to a discussion that was occurring in the classes. There was a sense of being (even indirectly) in the midst of the important economic policy discussions that could affect millions of people—but always informed by strong theoretical perspectives.

Of course, there were the stars among the faculty, professors whom everyone talked about, whose lectures students flocked to even when they were not necessarily doing that course. It was a prestige issue for those of us studying economics that CESP had so many of the stars, but then we also grew to be comfortable with them in a way that others less fortunate (such as our fellow students in the Delhi School of Economics) could not even begin to imagine. Krishna Bharadwaj would not just take you wandering down the fascinating alleyways of the evolution of economic thought; she would share her personal books and materials (including carefully preserved photocopies of original books that were unavailable or unaffordable) and offer beguiling reminiscences of her interactions with some of the people whose books we were reading, like Sraffa and Dobb.

Prabhat Patnaik was of course a dominant influence because of the sheer force of his intellect and the intensity and precision of his lectures, but he was also someone who encouraged us to ask questions and got us into all sorts of other reading. And this extended well beyond his particular passions of Lenin and Rosa Luxemburg. Because Utsa Patnaik was on maternity leave in the semester when she would have taught us a course on the evolution of the Indian economy, the course was taught by Prabhat—and even if he could not always provide a comprehensive list of historical writing on a particular subject, he opened up the world of relevant literature. For example, I was first introduced to the writings of Dinabandhu Mitra through Prabhat's reference to *Neel Darpan*, the historical play that captured the exploitative practices of indigo farming introduced by the colonial rulers of Bengal.

But much of the learning also came from other students. Reading widely and well beyond disciplinary boundaries was taken for granted; social status was conferred by greater erudition; daytime debates on the

III.3. SSS-II. Centre for Economic Studies and Planning shifted from the Old Campus to this building in 1986.
Photo courtesy: Samim Asgor Ali

library steps and late-night discussions on the New Campus rocks (long before the Ganga Dhaba became a thing) were heavily intellectual in content even when they turned emotional. The need to win a particular argument forced us to go into deeper and wider reading to justify our case; often unwittingly, the addas then became springboards for further intellectual exploration.

Of course, this did not mean we were all eggheads or nerds. But certainly, eggheadery was indulged and celebrated even in social interactions and extracurricular cultural activities. I still maintain that much of my youth was destroyed by the large number of very heavy films (representatives of 'alternative cinema') presented by the JNU film club, followed by endless (and pointless?) discussions on them over tea or rum in smoke-filled rooms.

A lot has been written about the strongly political atmosphere on campus. This was certainly true, and had multiple impacts on world views and subsequent life choices of many of the students. Since my MA programme coincided with the Emergency, active engagement with politics was obviously inescapable. But perhaps not enough is said about how this occurred within a very strongly intellectual and rational framework, when arguments could not be based only on sentiment but had to be reasoned and held up against counter positions.

So JNU in the 1970s was an extraordinary place for a student, not just socially and politically, but most of all intellectually. It proved to be a defining experience of my life, and remains for me a standard of what a university can and should be.

11

NEW LIFE AT JNU: ISIS TO SIS

PUSHPESH PANT

I joined JNU as an Assistant Professor in the Diplomatic Studies division in the 'reborn' School of International Studies (SIS) in September 1971 soon after the first batch of students was admitted to the newly established university. By that time I had finished my PhD from the Indian School of International Studies (ISIS), a deemed university, functioning from Sapru House on Barakhamba Road and taught for two years at a college in Delhi University.

There were two jokes frequently cracked about the ISIS. That 'it was a great lawn with a good library and a reasonable canteen attached to it' and that 'the place needed renaming as the South Indian School of International Studies'. Founded by the legendary H. N. Kunzru and Tej Bahadur Sapru, the first Director of ISIS was A. Appadorai. He had retired by the time I joined in 1965, and was succeeded by M. S. Rajan, who made all of us who did not hail from the region beyond the Vindhyas feel that we were children of lesser gods. But I digress.

When it was proposed that the ISIS be integrated to JNU, Dr Rajan, the then Director, resisted it for as long as he could. He certainly did not like the idea of losing his unchallenged authority as the Director and accept a much less prestigious position as a Dean—that too for a period of two years. The school was starving for funds, most of the faculty members were stagnating, and the atmosphere was stifling. Hierarchical order was rigid and the 'best and the brightest'—Sinologist V. P. Dutt, and the rising star in South Asian Studies, K. P. Karunakaran—had already moved to Delhi University and elsewhere. Those who lingered were perpetually weighed down with the burden of their own sterile 'scholarship'.

What rejuvenated the SIS was the infectious enthusiasm of young students and faculty in other newly established schools like the School of Social Sciences. The Centre for Historical Studies and the Centre for the Study of Social Systems boasted of faculty that enjoyed international reputations and were accessible to their students. Dissent and debate were encouraged in the classroom. The exchange of ideas continued at the Kashiram ka Dhaba into the wee hours of the morning. Members of the stuffed shirt older generation at the SIS were scandalized but their school could not remain untouched by winds of change.

As the school expanded, students of the MA programme soon outnumbered those doing research. Newly appointed Professors like Sishir Gupta and Bhawani Sengupta (heading Diplomatic and Disarmament divisions respectively) effortlessly outshone their pompous seniors. Others like Professor M. L. Sondhi and Professor R. P. Anand came into their own—no longer stymied by those at the helm envious of their originality and brilliance. The area studies programmes that had dominated theoretically oriented departments were now reduced to irrelevance. The newer centres like the one I joined brought together International Law, International Economics and Diplomatic Studies. The Centre for International Politics, Organization and Disarmament (CIPOD) was another centre within SIS that made the dinosaurs like Commonwealth Studies uncomfortable.

The SIS was transformed almost overnight by the arrival of students from other schools who opted for courses there. I recall vividly how refreshing it was to have youngsters (then!) in my class like Kamal Mitra Chenoy, Niraja Gopal, and Gurpreet Mahajan. Soon all of them became colleagues and some remain valued friends. The list is long: S. Jaishankar and D. P. Tripathi from the Centre for Political Studies, Chitra Harshvardhan from the School of Languages. Those admitted to the MA programme in SIS were no less stimulating. Curious and irreverent, they kept me constantly on my toes. Harshvardan Raju, Anuradha Duda, R. Venu, Rahul Kulshreshtha, Sunil Lal, Amitabh Mattoo, Varun Sahni, Shama Jain, Amrita Narlikar, Medha Bisht, to name just a few. They made SIS so different from the ISIS at Sapru House! As years passed, some gravitated towards civil services or journalism, and even electoral politics. It was as if the merger with JNU had exorcized ghosts of Sapru House.

Some of the 'veterans' continued to complain that the younger schools were treated better and that none of the renowned historians, economists, and sociologists treated the 'area studies experts' as peers, and suspected that their research lacked academic rigour. They rarely

III.4. SIS-I: School of International Studies now has an additional new building (SIS-II) to accommodate its rapid expansion.
Photo courtesy: Samim Asgor Ali

found a sympathetic audience.

In the newly established JNU, the trinity of G. Parthasarathi, the Vice Chancellor, Moonis Raza, the Rector, and N. V. K. Murthy, the Registrar, had put in place innovative structures for democratic governance not weighed down by hierarchies or seniorities. The interdisciplinary approach, the semester system, the equal opportunity to interact with visiting faculty, seminars open to all, broke old fetters that had crippled Sapru House inmates, releasing them from bondage to tyrannical supervisors and sycophantic senior fellow scholars.

It was more than a whiff of fresh air that revived us. Being a part of JNU in that blissful dawn was electrifying. Suddenly, everything seemed possible. As an exciting future beckoned, we at the SIS no longer remained prisoners of our (mostly imaginary) 'glorious' past. Indian School of International Studies was obsessed with its self-assumed role as adviser to the Ministry of External Affairs. It basked in the reflected glory of the work done by its parent institution—the Indian Council of World Affairs.

The change involved much more than availability of resources or a change of scene from the heart of urban New Delhi to the wilderness beyond the city, on a spur of the Aravalli. Age or rank did not mean much at JNU. Everyone shared the same dreams of equity and excellence. Most students and faculty members in the SIS began to proudly identify with JNU. There was a new sense of belonging to a family where striving matters more than reputation. The days of promising protégés dependent on powerful patrons for protection and promotion were over. It was impossible for SIS to continue living in a world of make believe, in splendid isolation.

When the school celebrated the golden jubilee of its foundation in 2005, there were few who recalled the Sapru House days. The Founder-Director, a benign old man and a dedicated scholar of the old school, and his successor had faded like old soldiers. In a little over a quarter-century after the merger, more than a dozen Deans had played musical chairs but none could claim the SIS to be their fiefdom. A School at JNU was judged on merit, by the brilliance of its faculty and students.

The vision of JNU was to provide the experience of education as an adventure of ideas. This shock treatment is what gave a new life to the SIS.

Much has changed at JNU and the SIS in the last five years, not necessarily for better. But that is another story.

12

SCIENCE LABORATORY TO ADMINISTRATIVE BUILDING

SUDHIR K. SOPORY

It is a matter of pride for the nation that JNU has completed fifty years of glorious existence. During this amazing journey of experimentation, JNU has contributed immensely towards knowledge creation in various domains, towards achieving academic excellence, contributing to national development through its alumni and research, and etching its presence in the national and international community. The university has competed very well with older and established universities like Delhi University, Calcutta University, Madras University, and many others. Within a short time span, it has become one of the top-ranked universities of India, as accredited by NAAC, NIRF, and other agencies, and has received the university-of-excellence status twice. Needless to mention, all these achievements have been the result of joint efforts of all the earlier VCs, dedicated teachers, committed students, and staff members.

The Early Years: At the Old Campus

I joined JNU in 1973 as an Assistant Professor in the School of Life Sciences (SLS) and became a Professor in 1985. In 1996, I left JNU but returned in 2011 as the Vice Chancellor, continuing until January 2016. Thus, I have been at JNU for almost twenty-eight years and since I left in between, I had an opportunity to view this institution from within—as a teacher and an administrator—and as an outsider.

During the early 1970s, the university was located at the Old Campus. The first batch of MPhil/PhD students at SLS joined in 1972 and six of us who constituted the faculty, had to take regular classes and supervise their research. For me it was an exciting experience. In the first class I taught, I was surprised to find M. C. Sharma as one of the students taking my course. Mr Sharma was an Assistant Professor at the University of Jammu and Kashmir, Srinagar, where I had done my masters, and he was one of our favourite teachers. He comforted me, which allowed me to carry on with my teaching and evaluation of that course.

The student-faculty relationship was very cordial and informal, which made teaching and learning very joyful. All of us were committed to give our best to the subject and to the university, as well as learn from each other. There was a dynamic interaction between teachers and students, sometimes in the form of after-dinner seminars. At the time, the establishment of a School of Life Sciences was a novel experiment in Indian universities. It not only dissolved the boundaries between various biological fields but also integrated chemistry, physics, and mathematics with biology. Students from all these backgrounds could join the programme. Unfortunately, this concept has only been successfully implemented at JNU. In other universities that followed our model, the overarching interdisciplinary category slowly separated into distinct subdisciplines—plant sciences, animal sciences, biochemistry etc. (as in Hyderabad University). Developing interdisciplinary studies has remained a core idea of all the schools of studies at JNU. During my tenure as VC, I got to know that the faculty members with early educational background, for example, in physics, were teaching economics or were associated with education studies. This was unique in the Indian university system. Today, however, UGC rules and regulations prohibit bright minds from voyaging into different areas in search of new ideas.

In the New Campus: Many Spaces, Many Roles

In 1974, I shifted to the New Campus as one of the first wardens of Kaveri Hostel at Dakshinapuram. The first VC of JNU, G. Parthasarathi, chose me for this role. My qualification for this role: not being married (at that time). Life in the New Campus was initially difficult: transport facilities were inadequate, building constructions were in full swing, the rocky terrain was still devoid of greenery. New trees were being planted along with new construction. The shopping complex was just coming up, with a medical shop, a barber shop, and a vegetable shop. Even after many years of staying outside, when I came back to JNU as VC, I enjoyed going to

III.5. The School of Life Sciences building, located next to SSS-I, was one of the first to come up in the new campus, in 1979.
Photo courtesy: Antony Thomas

the same shops. My most frequent visits were to the chemist to buy my medicines and to the barber shop for haircuts.

During the next twenty years that I stayed on campus, I took on other responsibilities besides my academic work at SLS. I was chosen as the provost of Uttarakhand, and elected the Vice President of JNUTA. I was even involved with the JNU community in the construction of the flats in the JNU group housing society at Pitampura, and served first as its secretary and later as president. Further, I was appointed as the chair of the committee to develop the internet facility on the New Campus during Professor Y. K. Alagh's tenure. I lived in Dakshinapuram, Poorvanchal, and Uttarakhand and am thus acquainted with almost all the living spaces at JNU as well as its community life. I got married after joining JNU and my children grew up on the campus. Once, my son got lost when he was around four years old. All the faculty members and students were worried. Finally, after a hunt of about seven to eight hours, the JNU security personnel found him in the nearby RK Puram area. I was conferred a new identity that day, the 'father of the lost son'! The wonderful time of my association with the JNU faculty, students, staff, and, in fact, the entire campus environment itself, is forever engraved in my mind.

Let me relate an interesting incident that took place in 1975 when I was the warden of Kaveri Hostel. The hostel president along with a few students approached me saying the Dean of Students, Professor K. J. Mahale (he was from Centre of French Studies), wanted to meet all the wardens to discuss something serious. When we reached Professor Mahale's house, he asked what he could do for us. It took us a while to figure out that the students were playing a prank on us: it was, after all, 1 April. The students, in fact, had met Mahale and told him that the wardens wanted to discuss some serious issues. We laughed and, thereafter, had tea and chats with the students.

Another time, the Dean of Students' Welfare called the president of the students' union and a few student representatives to hear their demands. The president stated, 'Sir, the students at present do not have a table tennis room and we find that the drawing room of Dr Sopory is not being used.' Later, Professors Mahale and Raza called me and advised me to put up at least curtains in my drawing room, which had glass walls, so that the house would appear occupied. Paying heed to their advice, I

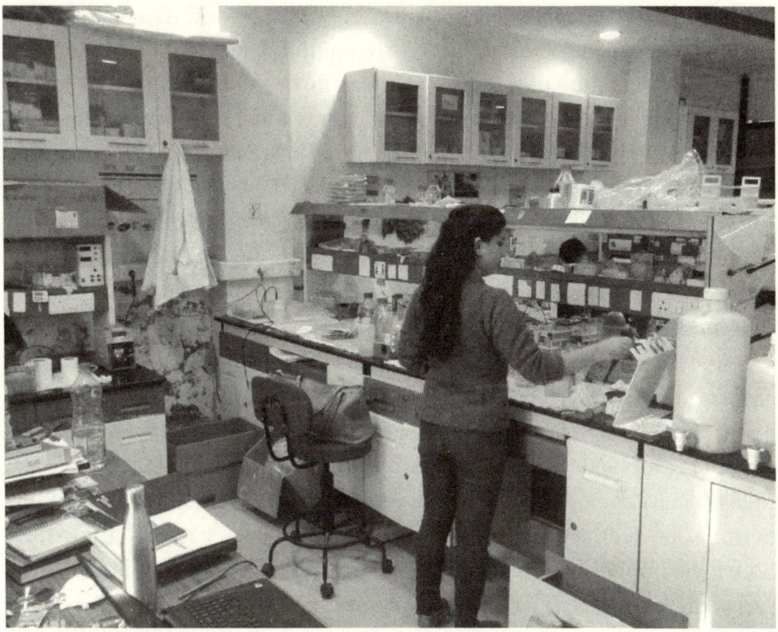

III.6. Inside the laboratory of the Special Centre for Molecular Medicine (SCMM). *Photo courtesy: Pangertoshi Walling*

borrowed some money and bought curtains. When I asked the students' union president why he had made such an unusual demand, he replied, 'it is just to put pressure on you to furnish your rooms, get married, and settle down.' This was the kind of bond we had with the students.

At the School of Life Sciences

Working in the laboratories was equally exciting. In the Old Campus, as it was called, initially, we did not have adequate equipment and facilities in the laboratories. One day the students started a demonstration in front of the Academic Council meeting. Despite being a member of the council, I supported their demands. Reacting to this, the VC joked that I should be outside with the students in that case. Nevertheless, he accepted our need for equipment and immediately constituted a committee. Since it was not possible to import equipment from abroad due to lack of foreign exchange, our initial consignment of equipment came from East Germany. As we moved to the New Campus and each one of us started getting project grants, we were able to equip our laboratories. As a cooperative gesture, we decided that all the costly equipment would be kept at one place and hence, the idea of Central Instrumentation Facility (CIF) came up. This, again, was a novel concept in educational institutions. Based on this, a university-level central facility (AIRF) came up much later which is functional even now and, as VC, I made sure it got enough financial support. At the faculty meetings within the School, we differed in our approach on various academic issues; on the kind of courses that we need to teach; and the frontier areas we need to nurture. However, these sharp differences stayed only till the meetings lasted.

The SLS has, during these fifty years, nurtured excellent research, and produced publications of high quality. Our students have been of exceptionally high calibre, with many receiving prestigious awards and occupying high positions in Indian and foreign institutes and universities. Many faculty members have received Bhatnagar awards, and quite a few became the presidents or vice presidents of various national academies. Some also took over important administrative responsibilities, three served as VC at JNU, while others moved to different universities.

The story I have described for SLS, is similar to that of other Schools. I realized this even more after becoming the VC.

As the Vice Chancellor

After taking over as the JNU Vice Chancellor, I decided not to physically occupy the chair meant for the VC. I sat on a chair and table on one side of the room to perform my duties as a teacher, and to attend to the genuine problems of one and all, even of those who did not agree with my viewpoints.

As VC, I learned to see the University from a larger perspective, and benefitted from interactions with all the members of the university community. I got a chance, not only to familiarize myself with the academic profile and achievements of the faculty, but also of their wider needs. The same was true of my interactions with students.

Despite student demonstrations and slogan-shouting in front of the administrative building, I found that most students—I would say 95 per cent—were very serious about learning and completing their studies. I remember an incident in this regard. A student, who was very vocal during demonstrations, came to meet me. I had even fined him on one occasion for his unacceptable behaviour with one of our officers. During my discussions, I tried to find out about his PhD topic and insisted that he should attend to his studies, besides his other activities, and try to successfully complete his research. Thereafter, whenever I met him, I would always remind him about his thesis. After a year or so, he called me on a weekend and expressed his desire to meet me. Thinking he might have some urgent work, I invited him home. He came with his PhD thesis, where he'd acknowledged me as a teacher who motivated him to finish his work. At present, he is a teacher in a university and is still in touch with me. There were many such interactions which helped me understand the inner desires and talents of students, even those who appeared to outsiders as involved only in extracurricular activities. I found that more than being an efficient administrator, the VC of a university has to be a friend, a teacher, and most importantly, the head of 'one family'. He must show no bias and maintain a peaceful milieu for everyone to perform to the best of their abilities. It is equally important to be in touch with the personal problems of individuals within the university community and provide necessary help.

What Does JNU Stand for: My Views

JNU is an institution of excellence, comprising people from all parts of the country and harbouring opinions of all shades: where academic discourse does not end with the finishing of a class or a course; where subject boundaries are blurred and new ideas emerge at the crossroads of interdisciplinary and transdisciplinary research; where you prepare students to become leaders in their chosen fields and careers to serve the nation; where we differ, discuss, debate, demonstrate and yet, come to a decision that is best for the institution and move on to live peacefully and with respect for the divergent views; where decision-making is through a bottom-up approach in which everyone participates; where helping hands are provided to the disadvantaged; where we believe education is empowerment and every mind is important for nation-building, and no able person should be denied this opportunity due to his or her economic, physical or social conditions.

13

SCIENCE AT JNU: THE EARLY YEARS

ALOK BHATTACHARYA

The School of Life Sciences was the first school of science to be set up at JNU. It initially offered MPhil/PhD programmes and began admitting students from 1972. I was one of the students of the first batch. I had a master's degree in chemistry from the Indian Institute of Technology, Kanpur, and was keen to pursue research in biology. At the time, only two universities admitted a non-biology student to a PhD programme in biology: the Tata Institute of Fundamental Research and the Indian Institute of Science. Since I had missed the last date for applying to both of them, I realized I would have to lose a year before fulfilling my dream of learning about New Biology (as molecular biology was called then).

However, a chance meeting with the late Professor O. Siddiqui (Tata Institute of Fundamental Research, Mumbai), a pioneer in the area of new biology, changed that. He told me about a new programme that JNU was planning to start on interdisciplinary biology, to which students from chemistry or physics were encouraged to apply. I took his advice and applied to JNU's School of Life Sciences. Nearly 40 per cent of the first batch of MPhil/PhD students had training in physical sciences. The diverse peer group helped in cross-fertilization of ideas and fostered a collective attitude of problem-solving, which was hitherto unseen in Indian universities.

The university had planned the science departments in the form of four different schools: Life Sciences (SLS, unified Biology), Physical Sciences (SPS, Chemistry, Physics, and Maths), Environmental Sciences (SES) and Computer and Systems Sciences (SCSS). The establishment of the Environmental and Computer Science schools in the seventies was path-breaking, especially when both these programmes were relatively unknown and long before terms such as global warming, sustainable development, the internet, and big data were coined. SCSS was more than a computer science school, as the concept was to combine system sciences and large-scale modelling with computer sciences. The vision of all the four schools and its programmes were novel in the Indian higher education system. The vision outline of SLS's formation and development was drawn up by Professor Siddiqui and other leading scientists of the country. This document remains relevant today, having laid the foundation for interdisciplinary teaching and research in biology.

Teaching science and research requires laboratories and other infrastructure including computation facilities. Initially, the labs were in the buildings (in the old campus) that are now known as ISSTM. The buildings were designed to provide training to administrative staff of the government and not meant for laboratories. When we entered the laboratories for the first time, all we could find were empty lab benches made of concrete. We were not disheartened as we were told that equipment would arrive in due course. Unfortunately, when none of the promised equipment arrived for the next few months, we had to approach the Vice Chancellor, Mr G. Parthasarathi. We convinced him to equip labs with necessary instruments and to get chemicals and reagents requisite for our research. Back then it was possible for a group of students to directly walk up to the VC to air their grievances.

As it turned out, funds are not the only thing required for procuring equipment and chemicals from outside India. There were serious bureaucratic hurdles, partly due to strict foreign exchange regulations, and getting even simple reagents from outside, particularly the US or European countries required significant effort. Since most of our material and instruments had to be imported, the university tried to find other ways of providing the necessary facilities. This included buying equipment from countries belonging to the Soviet bloc, where they could use Indian rupees instead of foreign currency. While we largely settled for second-rate instruments, in some instances we obtained world-class products. We were lucky to get a spectrophotometer with world-class optics from Carl Zeiss, East Germany, that performed with full efficiency for decades. The school had only one such machine and most students used it for their research work. Since we had only a few instruments, and only one of each kind, a reservation system was developed and all of us staggered our work, spanning the entire day. Though there were occasional fights since some wanted to jump the queue, and others were not ready to accommodate them, all problems were eventually sorted out. The scientific output of SLS was high, with a number of publications out within the first few years. Today, although we have most of the instruments in multiple copies, productivity has sadly not gone up.

In general, there was a tendency to design and build small add-on or accessory systems that were needed to get better measurements. Many students were working in the (rudimentary but very helpful) workshop and with outside vendors to develop and make these small devices. There were also heroic efforts to develop major instruments which were either not available or difficult to procure, to carry out a specific line of experiments. One such attempt was at building a highly sensitive spectrofluorimeter with high spectral resolution. Arindam Sen, who had a background in physics, sourced the components from various places including the India International Trade Fair. He got a free hand from his supervisor and the school and eventually managed to build a fully functional machine. A lot of students owed their PhD research to this spectrofluorimeter. He also built equipment needed to study black lipid membranes (BLM), an artificial membrane system used as a model for studying plasma membrane. It was the first such attempt in India and many investigators around the country visited JNU to learn about the system. Facilities were created and instruments were built if required, rather than waiting for someone to do it for you. One should also thank the faculty who supported this attitude of the students and provided the necessary ecosystem for students.

In those days, JNU was one of the newest universities in Delhi. There were other universities as well as research institutes, not too far from the campus. Right from the beginning there were working linkages with some of these institutes that allowed our students to interact as well as use instruments and facilities in these places. In particular, the All India Institute of Medical Sciences (AIIMS) and the Indian Agricultural Research Institute (IARI), Pusa, not only provided us laboratory access, but also access to libraries. It was a familiar sight to see a student carrying an ice bucket of perishable biological material, looking for an autorickshaw on hot days to go to these institutes. I never heard anyone complaining about these hardships.

Research at that time was based more on ideas and not as much on technology and materials. There was much collaboration among students resulting in publications. Though most of the students were bubbling with ideas, it was not always possible to attempt some projects due to lack of tools or funding, so many students took up theoretical projects. A group on theoretical biology emerged in the School of Environmental Sciences. Similarly, a number of strong groups on theoretical sciences also developed in the School of Physical Sciences.

In later years, research infrastructure at JNU improved and it became possible to execute a range of projects. Many instruments were bought and housed in a common facility maintained by technical officers so that all students and faculty have equal access. Setting up a 'common instrumentation facility' or CIF was a pioneering decision that maintained the character of JNU. First started by SLS, the system was adopted by many other schools to set up their own CIFs. This was in stark contrast to other universities where instruments were kept under supervision, restricting free use. Currently, CIF in SLS has all the standard instruments which allow any new faculty to start research work without waiting to set up a new lab.

In the early days of JNU's history, the university played a major role in teaching science and research in India. Interdisciplinary teaching programmes founded here were replicated across the country. With greater funding in the late '80s, new scientific institutions were created and the scientific landscape changed, and JNU suddenly found itself competing with these new institutes for students and faculty. The university lost its interdisciplinary culture and the number of cross-disciplinary students in our programmes dropped. For example, SLS stopped receiving applications from physical science students in their programmes. I believe that lack of cross-disciplinary ideas has changed the quality and the nature of the research being carried out at JNU now.

In summary, I feel that the founding concepts for setting up scientific schools at JNU were well ahead of the times. However, it required faculty as well as an administrative structure to implement those concepts in the right spirit. Unfortunately, over the years, there was no special effort to recruit faculty or admit students from other disciplines and eventually, the interdisciplinarity the university once celebrated was forced to become part of the research culture, rather than organically imbibed.

14

PHYSICAL SCIENCES AT JNU: THE FIRST TWENTY-FIVE YEARS

RAM RAMASWAMY

Why did it take JNU more than fifteen years to set up a school of study in the natural sciences, especially when schools of study in the biological and environmental sciences had been established quite early on? G. Parthasarathi, whom I had met in the early 1990s, mentioned in conversation that he had been thinking of inviting the physicist E. C. George Sudarshan to the proposed School of Environmental and Theoretical Sciences when JNU was founded. For some reason, that idea did not fructify, and 'theoretical' was dropped from the School's name. It would take until 1986 before the University, under the Vice Chancellorship of P. N. Srivastava, would initiate the formation of the School of Physical Sciences.

In keeping with the multidisciplinary character of the other Schools of JNU, it was hoped that 'physical sciences' would encompass the disciplines of physics and chemistry at the very least. Therefore, initially seven or eight persons were selected from across the world, and in keeping with these ideas regarding the need for a School of Physical Sciences (SPS), appointments were offered to both physicists and chemists. There had also been some prior discussion with the Tata Institute of Fundamental Research (TIFR), Mumbai, about the possibility of having an independently funded School of Mathematics located on the JNU campus. So, the hope was to have the disciplines of physics, chemistry, and mathematics at JNU, to complement the existing Schools of Life Sciences and Environmental Sciences.

In the event, this was not to happen for another twenty years. Of those selected in 1986, only three joined. Baidyanath Misra, a distinguished mathematical physicist who had worked closely with Sudarshan and also with the Nobel Laureate Ilya Prigogine in Brussels, was to be the first

Dean of the School. Sushanta Dattagupta, a condensed matter physicist, moved from the University of Hyderabad, while I, nominally a chemist, migrated here from the TIFR. We tried to persuade some of the others who had been offered positions at the SPS, but no one else from the first appointments joined JNU.

The School was given four rooms in Block-III of the JNU Old Campus, one for each of the faculty, and one for the school office. Four of the adjacent rooms were occupied by the School of Arts and Aesthetics, and the remaining rooms on the floor were used for faculty transit housing. Most of the centres and schools of JNU had moved by that time (late 1986) to the New Campus, so there was a sense of isolation. In the early days, there were no students, no courses to teach, but one of the first things we started with the help of colleagues at the Indian Statistical Institute, Delhi, was a seminar series. In addition to our own lectures, we slowly started inviting colleagues from other institutes and universities and would hold the talks in the School of Life Sciences building. There were other physicists in the School of Environmental Sciences—Lalit Pande, J. Subba Rao, and Gulshan Malik—who were a great support.

This was the time when the New Campus of JNU was getting populated, the Central Library had been completed and books were shifted there from the School of Computer and Systems Sciences (SC & SS) building. A part of that space—dark, airless, and somewhat depressing—was refashioned into offices for SPS and we moved there sometime in 1987. By that time some more appointments had been made, and given the asymmetry in the initial group, the next set of colleagues were all physicists. Deepak Kumar, Akhilesh Pandey, Subir Sarkar, Debashish Chowdhury, and Sanjay Puri joined us in 1987 and 1988, by which time the first set of PhD students had also been admitted.

One of the unexpected bonuses of being in the SC & SS building, though, was the proximity to the (also newly founded) Centre for Biotechnology. It somehow happened that we had one available telephone line as well as one of the few PCs on campus (strange as that seems today!) and these were integral to setting up the JNU email system—jnuniv.ernet.in. Standing in line to use that one computer to send emails, one got to meet faculty from other schools and centres, and this was the beginning of many good collaborations.

In our second year we already had four students in the PhD

programme, three from the physics stream and one from chemistry—all admitted for the PhD in Physical Sciences. We were to keep this openness for a few years, allowing students to cross over these barriers, and indeed some of our brightest and most successful students have been those who crossed disciplinary boundaries. An engineer who is now a Professor of physics at an IIT, a chemistry MSc who became a tenured Professor at a major US university, or an MSc in physics who is today a Professor in biology. JNU, unlike most institutions in India, allowed for this 'change of stream' and we greatly benefitted from this unwritten policy.

As the School expanded, we needed more space for offices and laboratories and this was found for us in the old Centre for Russian Studies mini-campus at the edge of JNU. SPS moved there in 1990, and for the next twenty years, this was our home, as we struggled to establish ourselves in a university that was so well known in the social sciences and humanities. In the early days, the confusion was whether we were a School of Physical Sciences or a School of Physical Education! Then there was a long period when few people (including the security staff) seemed to know that there was a physics school at JNU. Given the statutes of the university, even though we were much smaller than School of International Studies (SIS), School of Social Sciences (SSS) or School of Language, Literature and Culture Studies (SLLCS), we were well represented in the Academic Council and other decision-making bodies.

By 1991, the faculty strength had grown to thirteen, and we launched our master's programme—an MSc in physics. This increased our footprint on campus somewhat. We also started having visitors from the leading centres of physics in India, as well as from across the world. When we turned 10, in 1996, I had produced a leaflet to hand out (*Times of JNU*) on which we noted that visitors to the school in the preceding ten years had included Vladimir Arnold (Moscow), Sam Edwards (Cambridge), Michael Berry (Bristol), Gerard 't Hooft, Roman Jackiw (MIT), Deepak Dhar (TIFR), Tony Leggett (Illinois), Leonard Mandel (Rochester), N. Mukunda (IISc), Volker Heine (Cambridge), Itamar Procaccia (Rehovot), Per Bak (Brookhaven) and Ian Percival (Queen Mary). The faculty had also started organizing winter and summer schools and topical conferences, both at JNU and outside, and we also started what has now become an annual feature, the SPS March meeting. This is a two-day event each year,

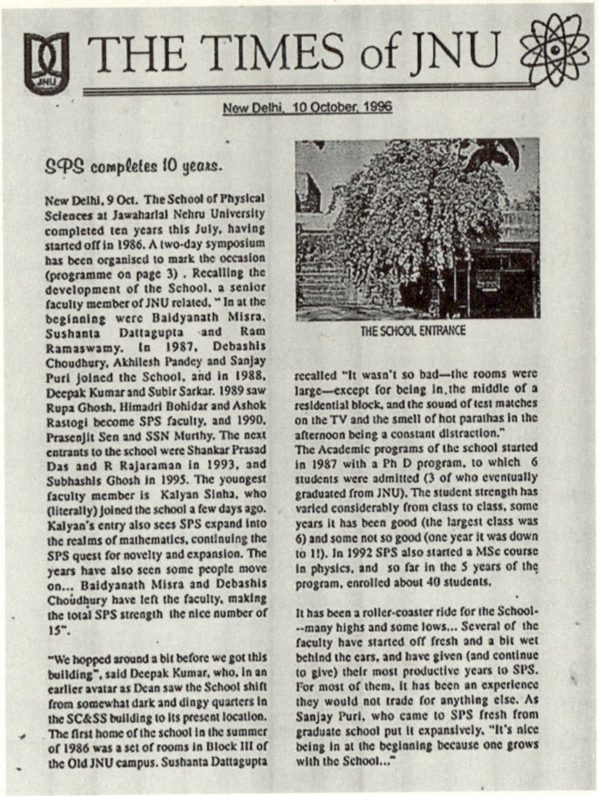

THE TIMES of JNU

New Delhi, 10 October, 1996

SPS completes 10 years.

New Delhi, 9 Oct. The School of Physical Sciences at Jawaharlal Nehru University completed ten years this July, having started off in 1986. A two-day symposium has been organised to mark the occasion (programme on page 3) . Recalling the development of the School, a senior faculty member of JNU related, " In at the beginning were Baidyanath Misra, Sushanta Dattagupta and Ram Ramaswamy. In 1987, Debashis Choudhury, Akhilesh Pandey and Sanjay Puri joined the School, and in 1988, Deepak Kumar and Subir Sarkar. 1989 saw Rupa Ghosh, Himadri Bohidar and Ashok Rastogi become SPS faculty, and 1990, Prasenjit Sen and SSN Murthy. The next entrants to the school were Shankar Prasad Das and R Rajaraman in 1993, and Subhashis Ghosh in 1995. The youngest faculty member is Kalyan Sinha, who (literally) joined the school a few days ago. Kalyan's entry also sees SPS expand into the realms of mathematics, continuing the SPS quest for novelty and expansion. The years have also seen some people move on... Baidyanath Misra and Debashis Choudhury have left the faculty, making the total SPS strength the nice number of 15".

"We hopped around a bit before we got this building", said Deepak Kumar, who, in an earlier avatar as Dean saw the School shift from somewhat dark and dingy quarters in the SC&SS building to its present location. The first home of the school in the summer of 1986 was a set of rooms in Block III of the Old JNU campus. Sushanta Dattagupta recalled "It wasn't so bad—the rooms were large—except for being in the middle of a residential block, and the sound of test matches on the TV and the smell of hot parathas in the afternoon being a constant distraction."

THE SCHOOL ENTRANCE

The Academic programs of the school started in 1987 with a Ph D program, to which 6 students were admitted (3 of who eventually graduated from JNU). The student strength has varied considerably from class to class, some years it has been good (the largest class was 6) and some not so good (one year it was down to 1!). In 1992 SPS also started a MSc course in physics, and so far in the 5 years of the program, enrolled about 40 students.

It has been a roller-coaster ride for the School--many highs and some lows... Several of the faculty have started off fresh and a bit wet behind the ears, and have given (and continue to give) their most productive years to SPS. For most of them, it has been an experience they would not trade for anything else. As Sanjay Puri, who came to SPS fresh from graduate school put it expansively, "It's nice being in at the beginning because one grows with the School..."

III.7. The first (and only) issue of the *Times of JNU*, brought out on 10 October 1996, marking ten years of School of Physical Sciences. A two-day conference was held on the occasion.
Photo courtesy: Ram Ramaswamy

centered on the research interest of one or more of the SPS faculty, but with speakers drawn from all across the country.

Within the broad area of physics, our initial decision had been to concentrate on the relatively focused area of condensed matter and statistical physics. This strategy had been moderately successful in terms of the quality of the work that had been done at SPS and the kind of students that had been trained, both for the PhD, and increasingly for the MSc programme (Physics). Over the years, there was a steady stream of students from JNU into other research departments, and today, after some thirty-two years, one can find SPS alumni in many departments of physics across the country, in the Central University system, IITs, the new IISERs, TIFR, IISc, and other institutes. The faculty were also recognized by national and international awards, most notably the Shanti Swarup Bhatnagar prizes to Deepak Kumar and to Sanjay Puri.

With the passage of time and as the faculty strength increased further, there was serious discussion in the School as to whether and how we should expand into mathematics and chemistry. There was no doubt in our minds that we needed to do this, and space was also beginning to become a constraint. Around 2005 we seriously contemplated moving back into the main Academic Complex in the middle of the JNU campus. The initial appointments in mathematics and chemistry were also done a couple of years later, and we eventually moved to our present location on the JNU campus in 2009.

SPS@twenty-five

The move to the Academic Complex integrated us fully into the university, in contrast to the relative isolation of our old premises at the edge of the campus. There was more sense of participation, both for the faculty as well as for the students, as well as more acknowledgement by the rest of the campus community.

Our March meeting in 2011 gave us a chance to take stock of twenty-five years of SPS. The meeting, aptly titled 'SPS@25: Looking Forward' brought back a number of alumni who had gone on to careers in research and teaching all across the country, and, in fact, across the world. In addition, we had a number of distinguished speakers—including the Chancellor of JNU at the time, Yash Pal—who spoke about the challenges in the fields of mathematics, chemistry, and physics.

With the current faculty strength of about thirty and the number of students nearing two hundred, SPS has by now carved out a distinctive space for itself in the landscape of the university. The present phase is largely one of consolidation, starting new master's programmes and fashioning the growth of the School in the changing circumstances. While the focus on research and the strong commitment to graduate education has paid dividends, maintaining the academic standards that have been gradually internalized over the years remains a challenge, but one that is worth the effort.

15

THE CULTURE OF CULTIVATING BIOLOGICAL SCIENCE TEACHING AND RESEARCH AT JNU

BIRENDRA N. MALLICK

The School of Life Sciences (SLS) was the first among the Science Schools at JNU. It started in 1970–71 in the Old Campus and then moved to the present campus. Among the natural science subjects, the School of Environmental Sciences (SES) and the School of Computer and System Sciences started soon after. In the new campus, the latter had its separate building, while the former was housed in the upper two floors of the award-winning inverted pyramid SLS building.

The initial faculty recruitment continued until the latter part of the 1970s. The faculty members appointed in the early days set the ball rolling and laid the foundation of basic biology teaching and research at JNU. The foresight and hard work of those academicians following the vision document of the empowered committee laid the foundation for the culture and spirit of conducting research in biological and biomedical sciences. It was for the first time in the country that JNU initiated research and teaching in biology in a comprehensive and integrated manner, almost on a par with other progressive academic institutions in the world. It was realized that well-trained human resources as well as good research in biology could only be produced if biology was not viewed in isolation; rather, it had to be studied as well as taught by people trained in classical biology as well as non-biology subjects. So the SLS and the SES inducted faculty members with expertise not only in classical biology subjects (e.g. Zoology and Botany), but in non-biology subjects as well.

Students from all classical science disciplines could be inducted in the MSc and PhD programmes, which paid off in terms of the quality of human resource generated. Semester system teaching was started and the students could choose to study subjects of their interest. Further, they were offered remedial and bridge courses i.e. those joining from classical biology subjects could study basics of natural science subjects (Physics, Chemistry, and Mathematics), while those joining from non-biology backgrounds could study basic biology subjects (Zoology, Botany, and Physiology). The interdisciplinary ethos of the SLS attracted faculty members from diverse academic backgrounds; their expertise in different subjects, and their drive to deliver even in trying conditions with limited resources was very inspiring. The establishment of a Central Instrumentation Facility (CIF) at the SLS was yet another important initiative and still continues to be the lifeline for conducting research and training in the SLS. The CIF concept has since been emulated by many organizations in the country. The CIF at SLS serves not only its students/researchers, but has supported students and researchers from other Schools at JNU, neighbouring academic institutions and many from outside Delhi as well.

It is necessary to highlight the culture of conducting academics and biology research at JNU. Would natural science studies have survived and prospered if the then overall academic and administrative culture was not favourable? The credit goes to the leadership of the formative years that brought even the humanities schools under the umbrella of 'sciences' e.g. the School of Social Sciences. In the humanities schools, teachers and students were inducted both from within and outside the classical disciplines, and this trend and spirit continues. These time-tested ideas and cultures may appear trivial in today's context, but have been implemented in other leading academic and research institutions in the country, even those established before JNU. It is equally important to highlight that such an ethos and spirit have not only been maintained in SLS, but necessary modifications have been integrated through the five decades, to preserve its unique character. In my opinion, those steps in the seventies were nothing short of revolutionary.

During Professor P. N. Srivastava's term as Vice Chancellor, I was among the second batch of faculty recruited to SLS. I am tempted to narrate my personal experience that speaks volumes of JNU's culture, which, to a large extent, was responsible for my joining the university. Although I was completing my PhD at AIIMS (geographically close to JNU), I never had any occasion to visit the campus; I had, however, heard that it was a progressive university. In late September 1985, I was busy submitting my thesis and had missed the JNU advertisement for the teaching post. By the time my thesis submission was completed, the last date to apply for the post was over. The late Dr Jayaraman, a PhD student at JNU at the time and frequent visitor to my hostel at AIIMS, told me about the position and advised me to apply anyway. I ignored him thinking that someone who had just submitted his PhD thesis would not be considered.

Jayaraman visited my neighbour again the following week and enquired about my application. On hearing of my inhibitions, he fixed an appointment for me with the VC (P. N. Srivastava) and I was left with no other option but to meet him. I had no idea why I should meet him and what to say, except to vaguely beg him to allow me to apply. I had mentally prepared myself to be scolded by the man. On the appointed day, I entered the VC's chamber with trepidation. PNS came up to me, shook my hand, and made me sit comfortably before occupying his seat: unbelievable! That was JNU's culture. I spent no more than fifteen minutes with PNS; he took my CV, scribbled something on it and told me to show that to his PS, to collect a form and apply through the proper channels (i.e. my HOD/Director, AIIMS). The rest is history: on a later occasion PNS remarked that he did what a VC should do in the academic interest and as permitted within the rules.

After I joined SLS, following the award of my PhD degree and ignoring the USA-post-doc offer in hand, I asked the then Dean about my reporting time and the duty hours. I was told to take the classes as per the time table and then do research for the rest of the time! An ambiguous statement at best, it could have been interpreted in many ways. To me, it allowed great freedom with utmost responsibility and made me feel respected by the university. It also encouraged me to resolve that I must reciprocate in terms of academic spirit and output.

The faculty colleagues were very supportive: Professor Rameshwar Singh shared the spare keys to his laboratory for my use, and my students and animals were accommodated there.

Despite colleagues from various backgrounds, the academic culture was so cordial I could gradually develop the common surgery room and the common lab-space to temporarily house experimental animals brought from the Central Animal House Facility (CAHF) where one could work during off-hours. The then Rector, Professor S. Saberwal, personally came down to carve a bit more space for me by reorienting the door of my makeshift wood-partitioned office room. On another occasion, he personally intervened to reorganize space in the CAHF to accommodate larger experimental animals (cats) for the first time at JNU. Also, I remember Professor Anil Bhatti taking personal interest in resolving the administrative bottlenecks while approving purchase of an equipment. Though neither Professor Saberwal nor Professor Bhatti belonged to the science stream there was a collegial spirit which reflected the JNU culture. In those days, one had to obtain a 'not-manufactured in India' (NMI) certificate from the Government of India before buying any equipment from abroad. The procedures for procuring chemicals, spending foreign exchange, e.g. Sigma chemicals, were extremely cumbersome and time consuming. Later, many of the purchase rules and processes were streamlined during Professor Asis Datta's tenure as VC. The VCs, Rectors, etc., who occupied the highest chairs were easily accessible and commanded respect for their academic achievements.

The SLS building was never completely dark, except during power failures (scheduled or unscheduled), which were almost routine. Transit house accommodation on the campus helped me reach the lab by 8 a.m.; several other colleagues also used to reach by then. In the early days, I often visited the SLS Lab past midnight to standardize experiments (along with my students) for data collection, to use my computer or to take care of my operated cats. In the late eighties, mine was perhaps the first personal computer in the SLS bought from the US with significant investment. Professor J. Siegel had kindly shared software with me such as Word Perfect, Statistical software package, Ref11, which I shared with other colleagues and their research scholars.

During my late-hour visit, I often encountered students and scholars from different labs. There was a regular flow and exchange of information among the members of various labs, which is crucial for learning, developing newer ideas, and diversification of research. This culture has led to developing newer methods, interdisciplinary research, and appreciation of each other. As such, many switched their subject of research during their PhD or postdoctoral period. I could freely discuss and work with colleagues of SLS as well as other schools at JNU who were knowledgeable about different domains. There was no restriction on having an IIT Delhi professor deliver a few lectures in my course and vice versa. I took classes for a section of students from the School of Languages, and non-biology and engineering students worked with me.

Measured freedom is necessary for the mind to explore the unknown and to nurture excellence and produce knowledge.

The research and academic culture has paid off in terms of excellent researchers that JNU has produced within the short span of its existence. Among the SLS alumni are heads of organizations, professors—in India and abroad—many have won high research awards in the country and abroad, and have made excellent contributions in their field of research. Faculty members of the science schools at JNU have received high accolades and honours, e.g., S. S. Bhatnagar Award, President of the Indian Science Congress, President of the National Science Academy, Padma Awards, President's Award, and so on.

In addition to the teaching community, the students and the non-teaching communities are equally important to the academic and research culture of a university. In JNU, students have always been selected through a national entrance test. Socially and culturally, it was unique to have students' hostels interspersed with the family accommodation and women's and men's hostels unsegregated. However, gradually JNU's stakeholders could not face up to the evolving challenges and the focus started drifting. In my view, an important factor for this drift was the selection of people with compromised credibility and vision in decision-making positions, undermining those with proven ability to face the challenges better. This was further aggravated by the lack of commensurate financial and material support.

The workforce of research is students. However, not enough has been done to protect students' interests. For example, they do not get their salary/fellowships on time, though all other stakeholders get their salaries on time. Scholars' working conditions and accommodation have worsened. Also, with several national institutes with better all-round facilities as well as support coming up in the country, JNU has lost its charm for many students. It is not the quantity of funds spent; it is the priority of causes on which funds are spent at JNU that undermines the respect and dignity of the stakeholders directly responsible for delivering academics and research. Students run around in an undignified manner to get their reasonable dues, to have their papers processed correctly, on time and so on. Similarly, for one's research as well as administrative support, the teachers and the students must bring funds through competition; hardly any money is provided by the university, not even from the corpus funds.

Unlike sectors such as the railways, defence, judiciary, health, business, administration, finance, etc., personnel with proven domain-specific administrative and financial knowledge and training do not handle the education sector, particularly in higher education. Every move of teachers and students is continuously monitored and evaluated by the administration as every paper must be routed through them. Although the teaching and research by students and teachers are continuously monitored by independent peers, as well as by the end users, the administration continues merrily without any peer evaluation of any sort!

When there are audits, neither the teachers nor the students (the end users or the beneficiaries) have any say nor do the auditors care for their comments/feedback.

Despite serious limitations, the academic-oriented farsightedness of the founding faculty members and the policymakers created a unique culture and ambience of cultivating biological science teaching and research at JNU. We must not forget that institutions of higher learning are known by the eminence of their teachers and their research. I sincerely hope that the focus of academic excellence is revived in this university so that we fulfil our all-round responsibilities before we reach the point of no return.

*I would like to thank my students, associates and some colleagues with whom I discussed issues while writing this article.

16

SETTING UP THE SCHOOL OF ARTS AND AESTHETICS

JYOTINDRA JAIN

The very first schedule of the Jawaharlal Nehru University Act, 1966, and the Statute of the University mentions that the university shall 'foster the composite culture of India and establish such departments or institutions...for the study and development of the languages, arts and culture of India'.

The School of Creative Arts was supposed to be one of the first seven schools of study envisaged in the JNU Act to be made functional by the early 1970s. Apparently the present School of Arts and Aesthetics (SAA) had its roots in this idea of the School of Creative Arts. Yet the idea of such a school remained latent until 2001, despite at least two previous attempts to establish it. It was only in 2001 that the present School of Arts and Aesthetics ultimately came into being.

As the first Professor and Founder Dean of the present school, I would like to tell the fascinating story of the setting up of SAA and how it eventually and indisputably became one of the premier centres for the study of the arts in post-Independence India.[1] From the beginning, our mandate was clear: teaching and research in the arts was to be contextualized in their historical as well as contemporary perspectives, and was to be understood within a broader critical, aesthetic, social, and political framework. It was decided to develop a composite and interdisciplinary approach towards the arts and, more importantly, the arts themselves would be viewed not merely as an insulated aesthetic genre, but from the vantage point of broader socio-historical and cultural processes. The divisive colonial

[1]Another such centre is the Faculty of Fine Arts at the Maharaja Sayaji Rao University of Baroda, which became a pioneering centre for the study of Art History as well as for modern and contemporary art practices.

classificatory categories, 'classical' and 'folk', 'fine' and 'commercial', or 'structural' and 'decorative' arts, were questioned while preparing the syllabi of the new school. Similarly, the three major streams of the arts—the visual, performative, and cinematic—were identified as flowing side by side, entwined with each other. Interdisciplinarity was therefore seen as important for critical insights on any particular art form.

The Story

As I reminisce, eighteen years after the establishment of the SAA, an ocean of anecdotes and memories flood my mind. The present SAA, which has now attained global reputation as one of the preeminent centres of learning and higher research in the field, began in a small room—Room no 109—on the first floor of the Administration Block. It was here that the first batch of five teachers, Dr Shiva Prakash, the renowned Kannada writer and theatre scholar, Dr Bishnupriya Dutt, a specialist of colonial and modern Bengali theatre, Dr Kavita Singh, an authority on Rajasthani and Mughal painting as well as on New Museum Studies, Shukla Sawant, a practising artist and specialist of materials and techniques of the visual arts as well as local histories of modernity, and myself, a scholar of the Indian vernacular arts as well as of Indian popular visual culture and photography, began brainstorming on how the budding school should develop new perspectives on its objectives and on the academic and pedagogic concepts underlying it. We aspired to become a pioneering modern institution which would approach the traditional arts of India from a critical vantage point, while focusing on developments in modern and contemporary practices in the visual, performative, and cinematic arts as well as the simultaneous growth of their theoretical framework in academia. We reflected on the way strategies of visual representation had confronted issues of gender, race and community violence, along with questions of social marginalization and colonization, and negotiated our post-colonial predicament. This also became instrumental in developing a contemporary and wide-ranging understanding of concepts of aesthetics.

It was against this background that we replaced the nomenclatures of the disciplines of Art History with Visual Studies, Theatre Studies with Performance Studies, and Film Studies with Cinema Studies. As we expanded the orbit of 'Art History' to 'Visual Studies', we were able to introduce new courses, such as 'Indian Popular Visual Culture', which covered the recent histories of art as well as the critical framework around photography, mass-culture, fashion, advertising, urbanism, etc.

In the spirit of tapping into the potential of an unanticipated and unbiased approach to studying, we also did away with conventional admission requirements, such as having a previous degree in art history or any related discipline. We prioritized written statements from the applicants about their aptitude for studying at SAA, and gave tremendous importance to student interviews rather than focusing on their past degrees. This invited a whole new spectrum of applications. For example, one student had a medical background, and had already done his MBBS degree. Later, he went on to write an insightful term paper entitled 'The Medical Body'. I also remember that some students, whose English was not so good, asked to be allowed to write their exam paper in Hindi, which we agreed to, and which resulted in one student from Bihar writing a brilliant paper on Bhojpuri cinema in Hindi.

Our dream of adding a department of Cinema Studies was yet unfulfilled. Provisions were made for starting it but by the time the faculty appointments were made, Vice Chancellor G. K. Chadha had retired. Posts were advertised and interviews were conducted. There were conflicting views about the selection of the candidates: The selection committee, the then Vice Chancellor, and I disagreed on our choices. Even though the Vice Chancellor could veto my recommendations, he refrained from doing so, letting my views prevail. It was during this period that Ira Bhaskar and Ranjani Mazumdar joined as Associate Professors for Cinema Studies. Their hard work, knowledge, and commitment made the department one of the best of its kind in the country. We also needed faculty to teach aesthetics and at least one or two more for ancient Indian art. The University facilitated these appointments and we were fortunate to have Professor Parul Dave Mukherji for aesthetics; and Dr Naman Ahuja, and Dr Y. S. Alone for ancient Indian art and architecture. After my retirement from JNU in 2008, the school expanded multifold. Today, the school has grown to nineteen faculty members, and approximately 175 students, enrolled for MA, MPhil and PhD degrees.

In the initial two years, as our vision for SAA evolved, and the first five members of the faculty continued to plan courses, the work on the construction of the building was progressing at a pace that would have exasperated a snail. Let me record a couple of anecdotes about how we navigated our paths to get our own building(s).

We were all rather excited that a separate small plot of land was allotted for the construction of a building for the school. We made regular visits to the site of construction and, with every foot that the walls rose, we dreamt about the classrooms, faculty rooms, exhibition, and interactive spaces. As the small building neared completion of the ground floor, I was shocked to see that entering the building meant facing the toilet block located right at the centre, just 10 feet away, almost like a sanctum sanctorum, with faculty rooms situated on the circumambulatory path around it. I went to the Vice Chancellor to plead with him to get the toilet block relocated outside the building. The architects, the engineers and the finance departments of the university unanimously rejected the proposal on the ground that such alterations would cause infructuous expenditure and endless delay in completing the building. After a great deal of negotiations and a delay of over four months, to my great relief, the 'sanctum' was relocated behind the building.

Over the next couple of years, the school grew in student and faculty strength. There weren't enough funds for furnishing the faculty offices and the classrooms, nor were there funds to establish a specialized departmental library or to acquire audio-visual equipment. We began to look for funding to meet some of these requirements. The Ford Foundation came up with an offer of a major grant. We discussed the proposal among the faculty and after ensuring that there were no conditions attached to the grant, we accepted it. This led to the establishment of a specialized departmental library as well as classrooms with adequate furniture and modern audio-visual equipment.

As the student and faculty strength increased, we needed more space. I recollect an unforgettable story of how smoothly the school was granted an additional plot of land and funds for a new building just in front of the existing one. This story is set in an atmosphere of positivity, freedom, and support to the new School. The then Vice Chancellor, Professor Chadha, had developed a great regard for the school on account of its rapid progress. The school had open access to him, and as the Dean, I routinely visited him every week to impress on him our need for additional space. One day, just before lunch, I went to his office to reiterate the matter. He got up from his chair and asked me to accompany him to a vacant plot just in front of our existing building. With a flick of his wrist he called over one of the karmacharis standing nearby and gave him a fifty-rupee note asking him to get a coconut from the JNU market. Until the karmachari returned, he discussed with us the activities of the school and enquired if all was well. When the coconut arrived, Professor Chadha broke it on a boulder nearby and said 'This land where we are standing is granted to you for the construction of an additional building for the school.' He also added that he had put a plan in place for funding the construction. To my utter surprise, he fast-tracked the project and within a year the building was ready and handed over to us. In my nearly twenty-year career at the government-run Crafts Museum in Delhi and as the Dean of the SAA, I've never come across such zeal and commitment as shown by him. The school's success is also owed to this positive support of the then JNU management.

While initially the regular faculty strength and our areas of study were limited, 'We the Five' established a norm of inviting visiting faculty to offer new courses. Besides others, Geeta Kapur taught a workshop course on curating practices, and Christopher Pinney taught a course of Indian popular visual culture jointly with me. Similarly, Samik Bandopadhyay's presence as Visiting Professor brought strength to the field of Performance Studies. The well-established JNU culture of academic honesty, 'political' scrutiny of issues, freedom of thought and expression, and acute concern for social justice constituted the intellectual setting in which the newly established School of Arts and Aesthetics was moulded and from there, found its own individual path. Personally, I gained immensely from this intellectual environment, both as a scholar and as a teacher.

III. 8. Students receiving a lesson at a weaver's workshop to understand the intricacies of the loom and weaving. Bhujodi village, Kutch, 2008.
Photo courtesy: Jyotindra Jain

III.9. A student explaining in English the lessons the group got in a lac turnery in Kutchi–Gujarati–Hindi. Nirona village, Kutch, 2008.
Photo courtesy: Jyotindra Jain

17

WOMEN'S STUDIES AT JNU: OR, A SHORT STORY ABOUT FEMINISM AND THE UNIVERSITY

G. ARUNIMA

Feminists across disciplinary boundaries have produced some of the most challenging and exciting scholarship in the past few decades. Indeed, much of this has contested conventional notions of disciplinarity and critiqued the foundations of established disciplines. Women's Studies, as an academic area, emerged in response to these kinds of disciplinary contestations. It also reflected the political mood within women's movements that demanded an alternate discipline to the study of women's issues and questions of gender. The birth story of Women's Studies in India, however, is normally narrated as an outcome of the confluence of women's movement and a liberal state response. Within this narrative, a policy intervention in the form of the 1975 'Toward Equality' or the Committee on Status of Women of India report is understood as a means of sensitizing the liberal state, which, under the aegis of the University Grants Commission (UGC) in the 1980s, led to the establishment of Women's Studies centres in universities.

In other words, the entry of Women's Studies into university spaces in India is always held up as being distinct from many other instances in the global south which appear to have been influenced far more by international concerns of gender governance. Despite the story of an enabling state and its institutions, the reality of Women's Studies programmes in the country belies this narrative. And, in spite of more than three decades of state funding, and the steady introduction of programmes and courses within the university framework, there are very few universities where Women's/ Gender Studies have acquired the status of fully-fledged departments. This has implications for everything: from the creation of faculty positions and hiring, to the development of curricula, offering degrees, and on pedagogic practices generally. More importantly, it also has a very serious impact on the question of 'knowledge production', and the manner in which Women's Studies has been perceived generally.

The story of the early years of Women's Studies at JNU, therefore, needs to be understood within this context, where its entry into the university in the late nineties was as a part of the UGC's scheme for establishing outreach programmes in universities and colleges that would 'sensitize' the academic community about gender issues. Predictably, the university had little or no expectations of Women's Studies, least of all as an academic field. And therefore, the programme was dispatched to the top floor of the SSS-II building, and loaned three rooms (of which one doubled as an office and a library-cum-reading room) by the Centre for Economic Studies and Planning (CESP), no credible faculty strength and certainly no infrastructure until 2013 when, after years of meetings, lobbying, and strategizing the programme became a Centre of the School of Social Sciences.

My own association with Women's Studies at JNU began in 2006. At this time, it was still a UGC-sponsored outreach programme. It was funded by the UGC and the programme was directly answerable to it. An annual audit was conducted to check if a sufficient amount of outreach activities had been carried out by the programme. It just had one permanent faculty position, two contractual posts tied to the five-year plans, and a couple of optional courses, one each for MA and MPhil/PhD students from across the university. It offered no degrees, and thus had no students of its own. The years between 2006 and 2013 were spent in convincing the university that Women's Studies was an academic field, that this meant a variety of things, including developing degree-granting programmes of study and research, evolving new courses, and strengthening infrastructure, which meant at the very least being given more rooms, books and computers. Today, the Centre has finally found its feet, and most of the students admitted to its direct PhD programme launched a decade ago in 2009, and four batches of those admitted to the combined MPhil/PhD programme that was started in 2014, have successfully defended their degrees.

However hard it may be to believe, the truth is that Women's Studies at JNU has faced everything from benign indifference to active hostility, apart from being repeatedly reminded by some colleagues at the university that 'everyone does gender'. As the number of courses on offer increased in the last decade, matched by the footfall of students from across the university opting for them, it became increasingly clear that despite the supposed engagement with questions of gender 'everywhere', very few centres offered stand-alone courses with gender as the entry point of intellectual enquiry. That apart, in the early years, it was also always assumed that Women's Studies must shoulder the administrative burden of running GSCASH, despite constant reminders to the university that this was their mandatory responsibility. Well-meaning students, including, on one occasion, office bearers of the Students' Union, would ask slightly reproachfully why the Women's Studies Programme did not conduct gender sensitization workshops.

In other words, there was no intuitive understanding about Women's Studies being an academic field, either at JNU or elsewhere—a problem that was frequently addressed in Women's Studies seminars and workshops organized by UGC programmes across the country. Other than the oft-mentioned lack of support, from financial to infrastructural, Women's Studies also had to face a frequently articulated critique that highlighted an absence of disciplinary focus; this was matched by frequent acts of self-flagellation by feminists who felt that disciplining gender would take away its radical, 'movement-inspired' edge. It is unsurprising then that institutional spaces, including JNU, showed neither initiative nor imagination in strengthening Women's Studies academically.

The eventual upgrading of Women's Studies from programme to department status in 2013 happened only because of the constant support of feminist colleagues in different Centres of the university. Some were ready to step in as directors and frontally engage administrative challenges; others gave good institutional advice, tea and sympathy; allies and supporters within, and outside, the university pulled their weight by being part of statutory committees of the programme; and, finally, a feminist Dean of the School of Social Sciences ensured that Women's Studies would be a full Centre, and an integral part of the academic life of the university. This shift made Women's Studies not just acceptable, but also gave it a legitimacy that it had hitherto been denied. It meant an expansion of its faculty strength, some infrastructure, including a separate room to house its small, but excellent, library, and a routinized intake of students into its MPhil and PhD programmes. The non-teaching staff who

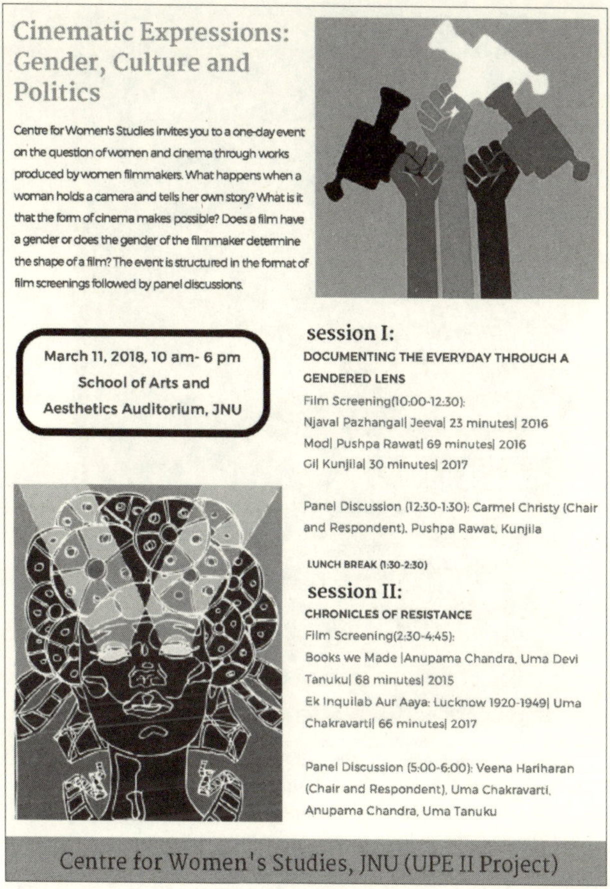

III.10. Of films, books and histories women make: a discussion about cinematic choices, agency, and women filmmakers.

constitute the backbone of the Centre, have unfortunately continued to struggle in precarious contractual positions.

At present the biggest strength of the CWS is its interdisciplinary MPhil/PhD programme in Women's Studies. This can be gauged from both the large numbers of applicants who wrote the entrance tests in all these years, and also the large numbers of non-CWS students who have both credited and audited our courses. It is one of the few research courses in the country that frames questions about gender by simultaneously addressing sexuality, political violence, labour, caste, and religion. Other

III.11. Of documentary photography and the Depression: Linda Gordon's talk opened up new ways of thinking about Dorothea Lange's documentary photography that challenged the politics of the American New Deal.

than exposing students to a wide variety of primary and secondary texts on these themes, the programme encourages them to critically engage theory even as they are made to constantly think about the methodological challenges in doing interdisciplinary research. Other than the mandatory requirements of coursework, term papers, presentations, and a thesis, students are encouraged to work on projects that help them refine their research and writing skills.

So what does the future hold for Women's Studies at JNU and elsewhere? This is a particularly difficult question, given the rapidly changing context of higher education in India that is accompanied by a no-less-dangerous cultural nationalism of the Hindu right. Neoliberalism entails an obvious and rather tedious market orientation in its relationship with the intellect, including new forms of commodifying knowledge, and a smug desire for producing 'deliverables'. The Hindu Right on the other hand is far more direct in wielding its ideological hatchet, as is obvious from many of the smaller universities where UGC-sponsored Women's Studies programmes are steadily mobilized for monitoring state-sponsored projects. Gender as a political and an analytical category is extremely threatening to many forms of patriarchies, and especially so to right-wing movements and governments. The question therefore is whether the myriad kinds of critical knowledge generated by the women's movements and feminisms that resonate in different intellectual and political contexts can produce new forms of resistance that can sustain Women's Studies at JNU, and in other Indian universities.

Hence, I want to end this piece by reflecting briefly on feminism and pedagogy. In his famous text, 'The Ignorant Schoolmaster', Jacques Rancière argues that the task of the emancipatory teacher is not to replace false with true consciousness, but to put one's knowledge at the other's disposal, without assuming this is what will 'emancipate'. To be 'emancipated' is not something that requires learning, but 'using one's intelligence under the assumption of equality'; this enables a person to inscribe themselves in the political project of equality. Alongside, he also stresses that the emancipatory teacher's role towards students who may refuse to emancipate themselves is to deny them this option. In other words, not permitting students to remain objects of study is the only way of making them into subjects. In these increasingly difficult and challenging times, it is perhaps this radical project of emancipation that the feminist pedagogue must recover. If conformity and commodification are all that are on offer from cultural nationalist projects, then forms of educated dissent alone can lead to emancipation.[1]

[1]I wish to acknowledge here the immense institutional and intellectual support I received from Maitrayee Choudhury, Kumkum Roy, and Saraswati Raju, the three directors of the Women's Studies programme with whom I worked very closely during 2006–13. Mary John, Jayati Ghosh, and Tanika Sarkar had helped build the programme's foundations from 2002–06. This helped give form to Women's Studies at JNU. The conversion of the programme to the Centre for Women's Studies would not have happened without Zoya Hasan's commitment and resolve.

18

AN EXPERIMENT IN INTERDISCIPLINARITY: FOUNDING AND EVOLUTION OF CSLG

NIRAJA GOPAL JAYAL

The story of the founding and evolution of the Centre for the Study of Law and Governance (CSLG) exemplifies a quality that is quintessentially JNU: the chronic tension between an intellectual instinct that is progressive and experimental, and an institutional instinct that is preservationist and even conservative. CSLG is by no means unique in this respect; the fifty-year history of JNU is replete with examples of such institutional conservatism combined with intellectual progressivism.

In 2002, these tendencies were first expressed as resistance to the founding of the CSLG. The first objection centred on the disciplinary ambitions of the new Centre, signified by its name, 'Law and Governance'. It has rightly been an article of faith at JNU (only recently violated) that professional education—law, medicine, engineering, and management—is not part of the original mandate of the university. The only extant recognition of law as an object of study at JNU was the field of international law in the School of International Studies. The name provoked unmerited apprehension of a taint, by putative association, with the World Bank's contemporaneous use of 'Good Governance' as the handmaiden of structural adjustment policies. Scholarship at the intersection of law *and* governance was simply unintelligible to its critics.

There was also dismay about the proposed institutional form—of a 'Special Centre'—despite being specifically recognized in the Jawaharlal Nehru Act, 1966, and in the Ordinances of the university. Historically, the idea of the School—the paradigmatic institutional form at JNU, equivalent to faculties in other universities—has run so deep as to foster a suspicion of the idea that a plurality of institutional forms can subsist within the structure of a university. This has persisted even when expansion within schools has manifestly hampered functional efficiency.

To further its interdisciplinary ambitions, CSLG was initially conceptualized as a site where faculty from other Centres and Schools could spend research time. This is not an uncommon model in other leading universities, which have Centres populated by multiple members from different 'core' disciplinary faculties. However, this was jettisoned in part because seven faculty positions were sanctioned by the UGC under the Ninth Plan.

The reluctance to think creatively about institutional design has seldom inhibited the incredible intellectual creativity for which JNU is deservedly known. Within CSLG too, notwithstanding the scepticism, the originary moment was one of excitement. Former JNU Rector, Professor Kuldeep Mathur was the first Academic Director of the Centre and, by the end of the first round of recruitment, five disciplines were represented by seven faculty members (including the two concurrent Professors, Kuldeep Mathur of the Centre for Political Studies and Pratap Bhanu Mehta of the Centre for Philosophy). In its very first year, the Centre attracted ten doctoral candidates, who were taught by every faculty member. Some of these were mature students, practitioners in fields as diverse as the law, the civil services and even the military. Right from its inception, the Centre was multidisciplinary, a quality that has since been productively sustained in ways that may not be possible in mainstream social science departments.

When the Centre was formed, Vice Chancellor Asis Datta convened agenda-setting meetings with senior faculty from the School of International Studies and the School of Social Sciences. Later, we organized a series of similar meetings to craft the syllabus, with helpful inputs from colleagues across JNU. An ambitious interdisciplinary MPhil/PhD programme, with higher than usual credit requirements, was presented to and approved by the Academic Council, and innovative interdisciplinary courses were introduced for the first batch of MPhil/PhD students in 2004.

The institutional antipathy about the Centre, sadly, did not abate, nor did the baseless rumours about it being a creation of the Ford Foundation. While the foundation did give a grant to the CSLG to fund conferences, workshops, and visiting fellowships, it gave similar support to the School of Arts and Aesthetics, apart from supporting projects of several faculty members in SIS and SSS. At CSLG, the Foundation additionally endowed a fiftieth anniversary Chair for a Visiting Professorial Fellowship, identical to its endowments for the Rajni Kothari Chair at the Centre for the Study of Developing Societies and the R. K. Hegde Chair at the Institute of Social and Economic Change, Bengaluru. The Sir Dorabji Tata Education Trust also gave the Centre a grant to set up a departmental library. These resources enabled essential academic infrastructure to be put in place, some of it—like the multi-year subscription to the Supreme Court Cases Online—benefiting all JNU library users.

As a Centre for graduate research, CSLG from the start distanced itself from the doctrinal black-letter approach to the study of law typically associated with professional law schools. It thus became the first academic space in India to direct intellectual energy to the task of bringing an interdisciplinary focus to bear on the relationship between law and governance, and to interrogate the socio-legal processes that embed practices of governance. It quickly became the originator and the fulcrum of law and society scholarship in India. This interdisciplinary imagination found expression in the LASSnet collective, a virtual network of law and society scholarship on South Asia, with about 500 members worldwide. Over a thousand people attended its first major conference at JNU in January 2009, followed by three magnificent editions in Pune, Kandy and back to Delhi in 2016. Today, the Centre is an academic niche for scholars who wish to pursue interdisciplinary research on law, and do not find the space to do so in Indian law schools.

On governance, the Centre had adopted a critical approach to the conception of governance associated with neoliberal thinking and championed by multilateral economic institutions. Moving gradually towards critical governance studies, the Centre has sought to embed conceptions of constitutional governance; to explore the dispersal of governance practices over various sites from the family and community to government and market; and to analyse notions of governmentality, sovereignty, and rights. At the intersection of law and governance, the objective has been to examine how practices of governance get stabilized through law and how these practices open law to further contestation. The study of marginality in many forms, including caste and gender, has been located as a core issue at this intersection. For example, a CSLG working paper was published on judicial narratives of sexual governance as early as 2009.

It is tempting to think that CSLG inadvertently became an exemplar for several academic programmes linking law and governance that came up in Indian universities in subsequent years. These include the School of Law, Governance and Citizenship at the Ambedkar University, Delhi and the Law, Governance and Development Initiative at the Azim Premji University, Bengaluru (now the School of Policy and Governance).

A more appropriate gauge of its intellectual achievements would be the range and diversity of the research done by the Centre's students, including cross-disciplinary explorations of the concept of rights, with multiple perspectives from philosophy, economics, and politics, being brought to bear on economic rights, water rights, the right to food, property rights, and intellectual property rights. Our students have researched and written theses on topics ranging from judicial iconography, ethnographies of stamp paper; alternative dispute resolution mechanisms in multiple social and regional contexts; DNA as a technology of justice; sexual citizenship and asylum; and the housing struggles of the urban poor. More recently, there has been much interest in issues like green tribunals and environmental justice or the political economy of global public goods like climate; as also in the digital economy and algorithms as a tool of governance. While some have deployed narrative policy analysis to study social movements against Special Economic Zones, others have used policy discourse analysis to study the MNREGA, and yet others have applied the lens of governmentality to study conflict in areas affected by Maoist insurgency.

Just a few examples illustrate the range of faculty research: critical engagement with governance indicators as a policy tool; law and economics perspectives on the separation of powers and the right to property; administrative accountability through e-governance; picturing law, reform and social violence; the impact on capital accumulation of the Hindu Undivided Family as a socio-legal entity at the intersection of corporate and personal law; the materialist logic underpinning the spatial segregation of Muslims in the context of globalization and the disciplinary state; privacy, citizenship and constitutional morality in the internet era; judicial review of legislation by tribunals; social justice in Maharashtra through an empirical analysis of the Dalit condition; the Look East policy and the Northeast.

Looking back at the significant intellectual achievements of CSLG, it has accomplished an enviable degree of diversity and interdisciplinarity.

The Centre's record on constitutionally mandated social diversity as well as gender diversity amongst faculty and students is impeccable. The third and fourth wave of recruitment introduced greater disciplinary diversity—currently representing the disciplines of economics, political economy, law, social and legal anthropology, social work, political science, political theory, and public administration—and also brought different visions and energies. This has meant productive debates and disagreements, and a plurality of approaches and voices being articulated on the very fundamentals of the idea of law and governance. Though the Centre does not offer an MA programme, it has very recently put on offer a range of master's courses for students from other Centres and Schools at JNU.

However, sustaining interdisciplinarity in the classroom has not been without its challenges. A typical classroom is populated by students holding master's degrees in a range of subjects—law, economics, political science, sociology, social work, development studies, and public administration—who often find themselves intimidated by their encounter with disciplines to which they have had no prior exposure. Yet this frequently turns out to be intellectually exciting, firing imaginations, provoking new research questions and opening up new fields of enquiry.

CSLG is situated on the picturesque edge of a ridge in the Aravallis, overlooking a forest. Its physical location could be seen as a metaphor for its institutional isolation. That was certainly how it seemed in the early years when 'building' CSLG was also *literally* about building it. For the first year or so, we functioned out of makeshift cubicles accommodated in one large hall in one of the science schools in the heart of the campus, so that visiting the construction site of the new building was a veritable expedition. The faculty were not consulted in the design of the building, which resulted in disappointing tiny faculty rooms alongside aggravatingly wasteful lobby and corridor spaces. In pre-GeM (government e-marketplace) times, however, we made up by designing our own furniture with a pair of talented young NID graduates, leading to space-maximization and aesthetic desks and bookshelves at a much lower budget. We also reclaimed the wasteland in front of our building, planted trees, grass, and flowers, with the garden winning the first prize in a competition run by the Pusa Institute.

Today, CSLG is less isolated, not just physically and institutionally, but within the JNU community. In 2013, CSLG successfully pioneered an initiative for Special Centres to get representation, by rotation, on the Executive Council. Until then, Special Centres had remained systemically unrepresented on the highest executive body of the university.

It is unfortunate that it took an externally induced crisis at JNU for the Centre to lose its isolated status. It was through the solidarities forged in the wake of the attack on JNU from 2016 onwards that CSLG finally found acceptance in the fold of the university mainstream. As it moves closer to completing the second decade of its existence, CSLG is happily no longer a space of exception within the larger space of exception that is JNU.

III.12. Centre for the Study of Law and Governance—the building is located on the picturesque edge of a ridge in the Aravallis.
Photo courtesy: Samim Asgor Ali

19

SETTING UP NORTHEAST STUDIES AT JNU

TIPLUT NONGBRI

One of the most memorable and challenging parts of my career at JNU was my association with the North East India Studies Programme (NEISP), established vide Academic Council resolution dated 21 April 2006 to promote teaching and research on the Northeast region. How this programme came about is a long story, involving a large number of players and configuration of forces, to which a brief narrative like this piece cannot do justice. Suffice it to say that NEISP is a unique institutional space catering to five schools, namely, School of Social Sciences (SSS), School of Language, Literature and Culture Studies (SLL & CS), School of Environmental Sciences (SES), School of Arts and Aesthetics (SAA), and School of International Studies (SIS). Based on an interdisciplinary framework, the NEISP was intended to serve as a platform where students and teachers from the different Schools and Centres pursuing research on the region could come together to share their ideas and flag new areas of research in a spirit of cooperation and dialogue.

The main thrust of the NEISP is to undertake critical research and build a body of scholarly works on the region. It aims not only to introduce students to the diverse and complex problems of the Northeast, but also to equip them with appropriate skills necessary to carry out research on social, cultural, political, economic, and environmental issues salient to the region. Further, the attempt is to inculcate multidisciplinary perspectives by exposing them to different theories and approaches utilized by scholars in understanding the region. It seeks to infuse elements of criticality in the students in their approach, particularly towards policies and laws applied to the region across time and space, so as to stimulate debate and search for solutions to the multifaceted problems that afflict the region.

As part of its strategy to bridge the gap between the Northeast and the rest of the country, the NEISP promotes active interaction between

JNU and universities operating across the country and the northeastern region. This is done through the exchange of scholars, as well as workshops, seminars, symposia on themes pertinent to the region. The ultimate goal is to develop it into a Centre of excellence which would serve as a resource base for scholars from different parts of India and abroad, and a platform that brings together academics, administrators, policy makers, civil society actors, and activists interested in the region to engage in objective and constructive dialogues on the problems and prospects of the Northeast.

To run the programme, an Advisory Committee comprising Rector-1 and the Deans of the five participating schools was constituted, with the Dean, School of Language, Literature and Culture Studies acting as the first Coordinator, a position to be rotated among the Deans of the five schools every two years. However, a year later, in March 2007, the coordinatorship of the programme was passed on to Dean, School of Social Sciences, and a Professor from the Centre for the Study of Social Systems was appointed as the Director, to carry out the day-to-day activities. To maintain the interdisciplinary thrust of the programme, a Steering Committee, comprising representatives from the different participating Schools and Centres, was constituted. However, servicing the programme was by no means an easy task. With no office space, secretarial staff or regular budget, we were able to sail through the initial years largely because of the selfless cooperation and support extended by the School and Centre representatives in various committees set up for the purpose. The fortnightly seminars and the national and international seminars and conferences organized by the NEISP in the early years of its existence owe much to this collective effort.

Why the Northeast?

The adoption of the Northeast as a special area of study not only illustrates JNU's democratic and inclusive character but also its commitment to creative and innovative research. Prior to the establishment of the NEISP, teachers from the SLL & CS had evinced keen interest in the wide variety of languages and linguistic forms spoken in the region, some by a minuscule number of speakers. To deepen the understanding of the rich cultural resource, a proposal was submitted to the university for the incorporation of languages from the Northeast in its teaching and research agenda. The Northeast's social, cultural, and biological diversity along with its distinctiveness from mainland India had also attracted the attention of scholars in the School of Social Sciences. Further, the region's growing economic disparity, regional imbalance, ethnic unrest, and social and emotional distance from the dominant population had been a matter of serious concern and called for close and systematic scrutiny.

The fast pace of change that erupted in the Northeast both as a consequence of endogenous and exogenous forces made the region an interesting field of enquiry. The process of colonization and conceptualization of the region as a 'frontier' that called for special laws and regulation has not only reduced it into a 'state of exception' but also raised serious questions for its understanding. Further, the Northeast's strategic geopolitical location with 98 per cent of its borders linked to neighbouring countries—Bangladesh, Bhutan, China, Myanmar, and Nepal—and its proximity to the ASEAN bloc of countries, one of the world's fastest growing economies, not only makes the region a critical element in India's Look/Act East policy, but also for international relations and diplomacy. For a university that is firmly committed to innovative research and to progress and development of the individual and the nation, the Northeast's complex and multifaceted character makes it an ideal site for study.

The large influx of Northeast migrants into metropolitan areas for education and employment, and the associated rise in the rate of crime and violence against them has added a new dimension to Northeast studies. Though the primary focus remains the northeastern region, the scope of enquiry extends to the large Northeast diasporic communities settled in mainland cities, which some commentators described as the 'ninth state' of Northeast India. A project entitled 'Other in the City', was undertaken in the early phase of the programme, and extended into a book, *Identity, Migration and Conflict: Lived experience of Northeasterners in Delhi.*

The NEISP also serves as a platform for social and personal interaction. On a personal note, one of the things I cherish in my association with it was the opportunity to interact with teachers and students from different parts of the country and different disciplinary backgrounds. The knowledge and understanding I gained through those interactions went beyond what one could gather from books and classrooms. While I am indebted to my colleagues and office staff at CSSS for their continuous support, I recall with nostalgia the collegiality and solidarity I experienced with the School representatives and members of the Steering Committee whose tacit support and personal commitment to the cause played a significant role in taking the programme forward.

The Current Scenario: Institutional Constraints and Challenges

Much water has flowed down the Brahmaputra and its tributaries since the NEISP was established. The Centre now has its own faculty in place (four Assistant Professors and one Associate Professor) drawn from different disciplines, giving the programme a new synergy. The MA (optional), MPhil and PhD courses, seminars and projects started by the young team have won wide admiration not only from scholars at JNU but outside as well. However, all is not well in the NEISP. The failure of the administration to appoint a Director after the term of the last incumbent ended in July 2016 has hampered the daily functioning as the faculty had to await clearance of the Coordinator for all matters generally handled by the Director. Instead of appointing a new Director, the administration placed the additional charge of looking after the everyday running of the NEISP on the Coordinator, who as Dean is burdened with the affairs of his own school as well. What was perceived to be an interim arrangement carried on for two long years. While the incumbent in question is a highly competent person and his commitment to the task cannot be doubted, the arrangement has taken a toll on the programme, as delay in the movement of files and other matters became inevitable.

While the administration may have its own reasons for making the arrangement it did, the act has left many wondering why the practice of appointing the most senior (Professor or Associate Professor) from the ranks of the faculty was not followed. This is a widely prevalent practice at JNU. In the absence of a Professor, the most senior Associate Professor was appointed as Director and even Chairperson of Centres in the past. Why this was not followed in the context of the NEISP defies logic. This would not only have avoided the constraints faced, it would also have acted as a boost to the morale of the faculty attached to the Centre. Experience reveals that active involvement of the faculty in the affairs of the programme or centre is critical for the success of the institution. The faculty constitutes the backbone of the institution; any arrangement that marginalizes the members from its affairs can only have a disastrous effect. No institution can hope to survive or flourish on the diktats from above or on the strength of a single personality.

The administration needs to recognize that the system of appointing adjunct faculties, as Director or Chair of Programmes and Centres, is a temporary arrangement adopted in the absence of faculty eligible to hold the position. It goes without saying that once the faculty is in place it is only logical that the responsibility is handed over to the internal member/s who, as the permanent constituents of the entity have the highest stake in its success. This is not to suggest we dilute the interdisciplinary framework on which the programme is based, but vesting headship in adjunct faculty or rotating it among schools is not the best way forward. A system of representation from different schools in committees set up at the level of the programme/centre where all stakeholders can meet and interact in a spirit of cooperation and dialogue, such as the one in the Steering Committee during the NEISP's formative stage, could be a better way of realizing the goal of interdisciplinarity.

Recently, the NEISP has been elevated and renamed into a 'Special Centre for the Study of North East India'. On the face of it, this is a welcome step and an answer to the proposal submitted way back in early 2010. According to a statement issued by the university:

> A committee will be formed comprising professors of different schools and then the Centre will be given a shape. *The courses will be decided and it will then be approved by the Academic Council.* (italics added)

Strangely, no mention was made about the existing courses that are being run successfully by the NEISP faculty or the various projects of the past and present. While a Professor from one of the Centres in SSS, an old hand on the NEISP affairs, has been appointed as Chairperson of the Special Centre for a period of two years, what remains unclear are the administrative structure and the modality of its constitution. Given the stalemate within the NEISP, it remains to be seen what measures the newly appointed Chairperson and the university administration will take to save the Special Centre from meeting the same fate as its earlier avatar.

IV

SITES OF LEARNING

20

CHS TUTORIALS

ROMILA THAPAR

When the Centre for Historical Studies (CHS) was started in 1971, it was associated with a number of innovations unfamiliar to the departments of history in other Indian universities, even the best of them. Our courses were different as they focused on social and economic history that was not being taught elsewhere, and were structured around problems and perspectives rather than chronologically arranged narratives. The emphasis was a little less on the narrative of history and more on ways of analysing and explaining the past. Our approach, therefore, had to be interdisciplinary. By this, we did not mean a jumble of disciplines, but rather a focus on the one discipline namely, history, but inducting into the analysis the methods and information from other disciplines where relevant. This meant reading much more widely on those disciplines and ferreting out the relevance of their analyses to history. In working out a method of analysing a topic we moved towards defining what we called the historical method.

The major innovations were the four compulsory courses that were strongly problem- and concept-oriented. These were quite unheard of and when we made our syllabus public, our friends from the universities across the city predicted that we would not get students to take the courses as they sounded too unfamiliar. Yet that is precisely what attracted a large number of bright and interested students, as also did our methods of teaching.

So the problem was how were we to introduce these innovative ideas and methods of studying history to a student who had been through a BA-level degree in the manner of the usual undergraduate university courses. The students we admitted, even the best of them, were trained in the traditional way of gathering information, making notes for answering a question, and laying out the opinions of established historians. The onus on the student to think through the topic was relatively unknown. We decided then to introduce tutorials as a requirement of taking the course concluding with an end-semester exam. The system was entirely new to Indian universities. We had to first clarify our own thoughts on how it was to be run and this meant modifications in the first couple of semesters and sorting out a few of the glitches.

Why did we adopt the tutorial system? It was not that some of us had been through this system in our own training, but because we had debated its advantages and disadvantages rather thoroughly before deciding to implement it. Pedagogically it was undoubtedly a superior way of teaching in the pre-research stage. It required the student to think intensively about the topic, to read as extensively as possible given the time constraints, in order to gather information and perspectives, to organize the information so collected to help formulate questions about the material, to learn to marshal data and to discuss the possible perspectives from arguments about alternative explanations. It required the faculty to be up-to-date in their readings on the courses they were teaching and it required students to be alert.

Writing tutorials meant the faculty had to suggest thoughtfully argued questions on seminal topics; and students had to get to grips with the topic. The questions tested the ability of students to collect information, familiarize themselves with the problem implicit in the question, and attempt an answer. It tested the ability of the students to read on the topic and understand its relevance. This encouraged the habit of reading, investigating and questioning the information before pronouncing on the topic.

The initial approach to knowledge means learning to ask questions that are relevant to the investigation of a topic. In learning history there has to be an awareness of the role of a hypothesis, of how to consult sources that are of entirely different kinds, and how to arrive at generalizations. There has to be a recognition and control over causal connections. In this, something of a small imaginative leap may be permitted as a forerunner to a generalization but the necessity of giving objectivity a central place is constant. Generalizations have to be rationally viable.

The tutorial system also provided an opportunity to explain historical method to the students and get them to apply it in their essays. This involved not only gathering evidence but learning how to assess it and test its reliability before making causal connections. Evidence required consulting a range of sources and for students of Ancient India the range was almost endless—texts, inscriptions, artefacts from excavations, objects from museums, architectural monuments, knowledge of the methods used in related disciplines such as social anthropology, religious studies, demography, and these days, genetics as well. An argument could not be taken for granted merely by quoting earlier 'authorities'. Students were encouraged not to chase after grades but try and understand the subject. This has changed somewhat in present times.

However, there were some problems. One was the necessity of the easy availability of books and readings in sufficient numbers to enable all the class to go through the readings. If a few students borrowed the books then they would not be available to all. This meant stocking the library. So that took us to bookshops that sold old books to purchase what we needed, which we did with much enthusiasm. We enquired about and purchased some private collections of which the best was the library of D. D. Kosambi. It was also decided to give specific readings from a range of books so that there would be a wider spread of readings. It was then that we worked out that a separate section of the library would be reserved as a reference section where the books could not be removed. That was also where the particular sections of the books that we wanted students to consult could be photocopied and these copies again placed for reference.

The other problem was the ability of the students to read regularly when they were not used to this system. For some this was a problem of being unfamiliar with the system, but for others it was also a problem of not being sufficiently familiar with the language. Students from metropolitan areas had little problem with English as the medium, but those from suburban and rural areas did have a problem. We were anxious to retain the latter category of students so the faculty had to make a special effort with their tutorials in the first two semesters. It was impressive how quickly the majority of them came on par with the others.

My big disappointment, however, was that Satish Saberwal and I had worked out a one-year course for any student who wished to take it, but hoped that the students that did not have prior training would do so. However, it was rejected by the students. The course focused on improving their use of English, that being the language of teaching, as well as learning methods of critical thinking. The Vice Chancellor who approved of the idea was willing to consider that the university help finance those students who opted for this extra year prior to the MA. But the students did not wish to spend three years on an MA. We could not convince them that the quality of their education would be greatly improved if they took such a course. Since the course was rejected we dropped the idea. Much of the discussion about this course took place after the tutorial sessions.

The tutorial system works best of course if the number of students at each session are few, around five or so. This would allow a careful discussion of each essay. With increased numbers it is not always possible to give a fuller scope to the discussion. This leaves the purpose of the tutorial somewhat incomplete.

The tutorials also became a way for the faculty to get to know students. This form of friendliness once established, persists into later life as many of us have found when we come across our students from earlier times. It is taxing to think up questions that are relevant, namely, where the answers will not only explain but also extend the scope of the subject. It was not just a one-way process. In order to have a worthwhile dialogue with students, the faculty had also to be not only knowledgeable but open to some of these discussions, suggesting areas of exploration to both faculty and subsequent research students.

The system also encouraged the exchange of ideas among students themselves, as also among faculty. Starting from the age-old problem of the first-year students 'borrowing' tutorials from their seniors, an activity that had to be controlled by keeping a record of earlier questions and essays by the faculty, the discussion of problems among the faculty helped both in clarifying questions and establishing procedures. This did not mean complete agreement on every issue, not at all, but thrashing it out with others was always helpful and somehow a way was found of resolving issues, and often one learnt from the experience of the other. We tried, for instance, in the Historical Methods course to make it a joint effort of the faculty. In the beginning each of us gave one lecture and all the others attended—a brave attempt to make it a cooperative effort. But gradually the person giving the lecture was left alone to cope with whatever subject he or she was speaking on. And by and by, it became another course given by just one faculty member.

With all the new ideas with which we presented history and the methods through which we taught it, we did contribute to the great change that the discipline of history in India underwent in the latter half of the twentieth century: the change from being a subject of Indology to becoming a discipline in the social sciences.

21

THE CLASSROOM

UDAYA KUMAR

My earliest memories of a JNU classroom go back to the early eighties, when I joined a class of five students for the MPhil programme in English at JNU. I had done all my studies until then in Kerala, and had travelled outside the state only once. I had come to JNU with a foolishly ambitious proposal to write an MPhil thesis on the entire oeuvre of James Joyce. In those days, the Centre for Linguistics and English did not have much room for literary studies; its focus was mainly on language and linguistics. However, with a generosity and flexibility which I have encountered time and again at JNU, I was permitted to go ahead with my project even though it was not quite clear how the designated scope of an MPhil in English Language allowed it. I remember being struck by the friendly informality of the campus, although for someone who was new to Delhi and to a 'cosmopolitan' campus, this was somewhat intimidating as well. Since classes involved considerable discussion and presentations by students, I was forced for the first time to speak mostly in English. In Kerala, I had bunked classes in order to avoid this frightening challenge; here there was no easy escape.

For someone who had stayed away from many lectures during undergraduate and postgraduate years, I was surprised to find myself attending most of my classes at JNU. I don't think this was simply because my new teachers were more scholarly or eloquent, or the topics of lectures more riveting. It may have been prompted more by the ways in which the air and ease of animated conversations on the JNU campus seeped into classes and set their tenor. The classroom was just one among the many live communities of conversation on campus. In a friend's hostel room where I stayed until I got my accommodation, in teashops, hostel messes, on the lawn, on the street or in buses on the way back from music concerts or film screenings in town, such communities—small and large—flourished.

Sometimes a reading group, sometimes a casual exchange on a film or a book or an idea, sometimes a heated debate on a political issue—their shapes kept shifting. Like most JNU students, I learned more from such groups than from my 'official' classroom. Classes, in fact, manifested their best energies when they approximated the unofficial. My time as a student at JNU was hugely enriching, even though I did not finish the course I was enrolled in.

Decades later, when I returned to JNU as a teacher, much had changed in my former Centre, as well as in me. The School had moved to the New Campus long ago, and the Centre had bifurcated into Linguistics and English Studies. The English centre, which I joined, had become a more confident and full-fledged intellectual space, with a wonderful set of students. In comparison to Delhi University, where I taught for several years, the MA classes at JNU were clearly smaller in student size. In DU, there was a huge mismatch—sometimes as large as three to one—between the number of students admitted and the seating capacity of the lecture hall. Finding it impossible to enter, many students used to give up on lectures after the first few weeks. In JNU, it was possible to get to know most of your students. But this was not because of small numbers alone; the main difference lay in the readiness of students to participate in any discussion that would open up. Neither competence over the English language, nor—sometimes—command over the text or the issues being discussed, really stood in the way. Many students were ready to jump in and wager their ideas and see how and where they would go. It is possible to run master's courses entirely in a participatory workshop mode at JNU, as many teachers do, where discussions develop a rhythm, tempo, and destination all on their own, exceeding the limits of pre-meditation.

I did run a course on Joyce's writings—including a close reading of all chapters in the somewhat difficult *Ulysses* over six or seven weeks—mostly in that mode, in which initial inputs from students determined the agenda of the class and the path we followed. This course was offered during a semester in which the university went through considerable turbulence. There was authoritarian action, unrelenting resistance, lockdown, and boycott of the classroom. The same students and teachers who were at the forefront of protests also met for their classes, which took place outside the building in protest mode, on the lawns, in the car park, or on the staircase which doubled as a gallery. These classes were difficult: the tense, uncertain

IV.1. Open-air classes were regularly held during the prolonged students' strike of 2018.
Photo courtesy: Samim Asgor Ali

IV.2. Raising questions: a class in progress in SSS-III.
Photo courtesy: Samim Asgor Ali

atmosphere had depleted the intellectual concentration of students and teachers, and the strike and protests had affected the preparation required for close textual work. Nonetheless, there was a different sort of intensity, propelled partly by the determination to hold classes as an essential component of the plan to boycott official classrooms, and partly by the sheer intellectual pleasure of collective work in politically charged times. The students who worked hardest and participated most actively in that course, interestingly, did not always have strong language skills or a prior track record in academic achievement. This was an interesting feature I learned to recognize: grades across the semesters were not consistently loaded in favour of some students as against some others. In this inconsistency there was a creative possibility; it was possible to be affected intensely by a course, a theme, or an issue, which could alter not just the graph of performance but a student's relationship to knowledge, ideas, and the world. Not that this always happened, but the existence of that possibility—increasingly rare in our times—has to be noted.

This account should not mislead us to think that the JNU classroom is an ideal, utopian space. It cannot obviously be; how can it? The reality of the world and of life breaks in, in refracted and at times skewed ways. Universities are strange places; their existence is predicated on a putative lease of protection, a tentative deferral of the 'payback' time, the erosion of which has been all too palpable in recent years. Higher education has been a hard-won opportunity and privilege for many. At the same time, the peculiar position occupied by the university in relation to other spheres of life can easily lead to a sense of self-enclosedness among the university community. This is perhaps more evident at JNU than in many other public universities in India. The ease and friendliness of the residential campus are sometimes intermeshed with a reluctance or an incapacity to move out of one's comfort zone. This is a complex matter: I remember being grateful as a student that JNU was a sort of bubble, protected from the abrasive texture of interactions in the city. However, the protective warmth of a community with its rituals and conversations can imperceptibly lead to a loss in mobility and openness. Forms of self-involved campus identification, I feel, might be seen in many of us in the faculty too. This is not solely a matter of those teachers who were students of JNU and have continued their lives on campus as faculty; those who join the university later in life as teachers can also acquire these habits quickly. The enclosed nature of the campus is not the only reason for this; I have wondered sometimes if there is perhaps not an exaggerated sense of comfort, bordering on self-satisfaction, which lowers our ability to appreciate and engage other spaces closely, and to recognize and respond to what the university and the classroom, as they evolved over the years, have rendered invisible.

The most noteworthy change in central university campuses over the past two decades has been in their demography. Increased diversity in caste and religious backgrounds is clearly visible at JNU over this period, even against the background of the social justice measures the university has had in admissions for a longer time. The classroom in which I teach now is considerably different as compared to my student years, yet it is possible to miss what is at stake. Around twenty-five years ago, Aniket Jaaware, who taught in Pune, drew attention to the silence and the invisibility of the subaltern student in the English classroom. The readiness for discussion I encountered at JNU is not equally available to all. A space like JNU, with its self-perception of inclusiveness, may make it easier to miss such silences. It remains a challenge for our classroom communities to evolve ways of being together that draw in and engage all without placing anyone under obligation. But the classroom does not exist in isolation; it is a part of several spaces of togetherness among students, and among teachers and students. Silence may not be a purely territorial effect, and engaging it means changing the dynamic of those spaces as well.

As for the classroom, it remains a challenge to develop idioms of discussion free from rewarded performances and humiliating senses of inadequacy. It is easier to notice students who speak in class, ask 'intelligent' questions, and students who 'progress' and achieve greater articulateness and facility with academic protocols of expression and argumentation. As teachers we often tend to see our work as involving the inculcation of knowledge and skills and, consciously or unconsciously, the grooming of a 'certain kind of academic subject'. Ethical dimensions of the classroom in our present may demand a modification or even an interruption of this project and a willingness to see the province of the university as located in a larger landscape of difficult human togetherness. It is not perhaps solely a matter of drawing the silent student into the protocols of academic exchange, but of modifying these protocols to recover the meaningful connection between the academic, the intellectual and the ethical. The question posed by the classroom now concerns that 'certain kind' that has defined the normative horizon of our pedagogy. What new figures of academic subjectivity might define the potentialities opened by our present? We may not—and perhaps should not—engage this in terms of concessions and adjustments to an external world; it is a matter of whether we can imagine and reconceive practices in higher education, recognizing the new possibilities manifested in silences or in 'unreasonable' demands in our campus and the classroom.

As a student or as a teacher, I do not recall a period when there was as intense and widespread a sense of precarity in our university campuses as at the present moment. I am speaking about a widely shared experience, knowing well this may not at all be new for the unprivileged. The situation is now widespread, with the destruction of any real sense of academic autonomy in public universities and, along with it, erosion of the sense of protection and shelter that the campus offered. There is a palpable sense of fragility among students, with little institutional support in ensuring adequate academic infrastructure and living spaces, and mental healthcare and support systems—we seem not to have adequately understood the scale of this need. What would be the shape of a pedagogy, or an idiom of classroom interaction, that recognizes the fragility and precariousness of the student? The teacher might easily miss, as I sometimes have, what the student may intend as a sign or manifest as a symptom. How do we learn to forge connections based on recognition of vulnerabilities? There is a need to create ways of working together as teachers and students without wishing away the lines of power that connect us, even through their division and separation. How does one work with humility—admitting one's limits—with and against the inequalities without wishing them away? These challenges are not unique to the JNU classroom, but they seem to define a core segment of the place we inhabit now as an institution and as a community.

22

PHILOSOPHY AT NIGHT

SUDIPTA KAVIRAJ

Writing about events experienced half a century earlier contains evident risks of simplification and romanticization. A college or a university is a complex thing. It is true that it provides a space where learning takes place; but sometimes the learning process is more complicated than appears at first sight. My education at Presidency College, Kolkata, was a complex process of curricular training in political science through syllabi that were partly obsolete, partly unrelated to my history, and mostly delivered with a deadly dullness. Despite the dreary curricula, Presidency College was an exciting place. It wasn't just the inside of the classrooms: it was a name for a far more complex combination of settings—which included its classrooms, the lawns, the streets in front where college railings were covered with second-hand books, the adjacent coffee house, and the most intangible yet forceful web of personal interrelations with teachers, friends, booksellers, and political activists.

I had a dual experience at JNU. In those easier times, it was possible to start as a teacher right after our MA. When I began to teach, I was also doing my PhD: so I was both a teacher and a student. In my experience, students at JNU in the early decades fashioned a space of learning about the world that was similar in its intellectual scope, making JNU a leading higher-education institution in the country in an astonishingly short time. The Presidency College had a history stretching back more than a century. JNU was the newest university in the 1970s. As spaces, the two were vastly different: in Kolkata those influences were scattered across different types of places around College Street and College Square—from the classrooms to the pavements with second-hand books to the dark eating places to the benches in College Square. In the case of JNU, these were all concentrated in an intensely isolated space—a large, mostly empty campus of shrubs and rocks with brand-new buildings—teaching blocks, faculty houses, student

IV.3. A post-dinner public talk in a hostel.
Photo courtesy: Samim Asgor Ali

residences, a tiny shopping centre. Few buses connected this isolated place on a hill with the neighbouring city, imparting to the life inside an unusual inward-looking intensity.

JNU was partly a residential university—with much of the student population living on campus with the faculty. This made it possible for formal lectures to spill over into informal discussions which could unfold endlessly, such that it became a *long* conversation in the true sense—without a clear start or a clear end. Of course this absorbed a great deal of time, and encouraged sceptics to criticize it but clearly this could not have happened if the lectures did not ignite in the students some indefinable spark of real cognitive curiosity.

The spaces that played the most surprising role in this story were the food halls in student residential blocks—the hostels. Called 'the mess'—after some arcane ancient English linguistic usage—these were vast cavernous halls filled with cheap metal dining tables and chairs in which usually unedifying 'mess' was served every day for lunch and dinner. But often, in the evening, after the dinner was over at 8 p.m., these were transformed into strange amphitheatres of ideas. Initially, the variety in these ideas was somewhat limited: but the debates were real nonetheless. JNU was primarily known as a social science institution—with a vibrant tradition of student politics. Natural science research usually does not involve large political questions. It is not true that most of the JNU faculty were leftists: scholars without pronounced political loyalty or of different political views were certainly more in number than left-wing members of the faculty. The leftists were characteristically voluble, and they had a large student following, due to various strands of the left-dominated student politics at the time.

In any other university, as a young teacher, I would have been compelled to teach syllabi devised by forgotten ancestors, with which I felt no intellectual connection. JNU gave us the freedom to devise our own courses, and teach the way we wanted. Left syllabi could have meant offerings of dull dialectical materialism. Instead, we were allowed to reflect in our courses the deep churning taking place in Indian Marxist thought: replacing older Comintern Marxism with texts from Lukács, Gramsci, and Althusser. Teaching Marx could be transformed by introducing his early humanist writings—particularly the suggestively incomplete fragments of the *Economic and Philosophical Manuscripts*. Not everyone was happy about reopening the fundamental questions of Marxist thought, and revisiting those decisive moments where it reached a fork of philosophical or historical decisions. Some thought students were attracted more to Althusser and Gramsci than to Marx—which was partly true. Only partly, because this was also a time of internal differentiation within Indian radical thought. In reading Western Marxism we were seeking an escape from the stony certainties of the Comintern that Indian Marxist parties had turned into religious faith. Eventually, for many, conventional Stalinist certitudes triumphed: they found the burden of independent thinking unbearable and took shelter, as long as its comforts lasted, under the shadow of the amazing innovation of Indian politics—leftist parties with Stalinist organization which nevertheless proved invincible in electoral politics. But I cannot imagine that the intense and enjoyable discussions about abstruse questions of radical political theory—mainly about Hegel and Marx—were meaningless, or that these did not bear fruit. The students gradually developed an intensely intellectual political culture. All students were not leftists or Marxists: there was spirited opposition to left-wing parties, but the debates were of remarkable quality and maturity.

The dining halls were usually the spaces for political debates. In the evenings, after the tables were cleared, these spaces were transformed into strange stadia of argumentative tournaments. Intense debates were not unexpected—either at the time of general elections in the country, after significant political events, or before the student elections at the university. But these were not the only subjects for the dining hall discourses—where speakers spoke, the audience asked questions and made comments—leading to debates of astonishing intensity. I was always surprised by the number of students who attended these discussions: the halls at nights were full to bursting. What amazed me were the subjects that attracted such interest: sometimes these were on analyses of the 'Indian state'—for mundane elections had to be elevated into spectacles of contest between large historic forces of revolution and reaction. At other times, themes were complex and scholarly disputations about the exact arguments between Trotsky and Lenin regarding the colonial question, or even more surprising, deep textual disputations about either the foundations of modern radicalism in Hegel and Marx or contemporary interventions by Althusser or Gramsci. To sceptics who would say that there was hardly anything 'Indian' in these discussions, it needs to be pointed out that this was happening in India, in the heart of Delhi, and not in a small, smoky basement in Oxford. What was remarkable about this circulation of ideas was that it turned the usual conventions of university life upside down. Normally, students would be relieved after classes are done: abstruse questions of political theory do not usually enliven their spare time. Here, in the JNU dining halls, surprisingly, what was discussed within more rigid limits of time in class were taken up again for much more elaborate examination which students evidently enjoyed. Remarkably, the initiative for these extensions of intellectual debate came from the students. This was primarily a celebration of youthful enthusiasm for ideas—turning the university into a genuine space for learning. In the early years of JNU, these nocturnal discussions on political philosophy brought some strange and unusual excitement to them. It is hard to explain what caused that unusual excitement—except that the young usually respond to new ideas with an excitement.

Compared to my college culture at Presidency College a decade earlier, JNU's intellectual culture was less focused on literature, more on questions of political philosophy—though I am sure privately students must have been avid readers of literature from other Indian and European cultures. I sometimes wonder what they could have learnt from these intense discussions which made it appear that their entire lives depended on understanding concepts like 'value' or 'overdetermination'. Perhaps the answer lies in the idea that these discussions opened to them a world of new ideas—attractive, intricate, challenging. In the newly created physical space of JNU there was a new space of thinking as well—where tired truths of more conventional Marxist thinking were being made fresh again. We should appreciate the many layers of newness involved in this experience. Of course JNU was a new university—better funded than many others in India's public university system. It was established with some hype about its quality even before it was tested; but it certainly allowed unusual experimentation in teaching and learning.

There were two respects in which this experience of ideas was new to the people who came as students. First, lest we forget, it was new to them as individuals. At the end of adolescence, at the point of their first contact with serious theoretical ideas, they encountered these arguments—which of course contained within them a claim to newness because they appeared to be part of a process of social renewal. Second, many of these students, who had done their undergraduate study in good institutions, must have been introduced in a conventional way to the ideas of Marx and other Western thinkers. Repetition of those truths they would have found dull. But the infusion of structuralism, Hegelianism, existentialism etc. into it made them encounter a new Marx. Or rather they encountered the idea that an old thinker can become new again through critical reading, and that reading was a creative, meaning-conferring activity—distinct from writing, because writing, or rather the written word, depended so heavily on the historically situated activity of reading.

Young people are always in search of the new: they refuse to live in the world soiled by the use of their elders. In the case of ideas, this means finding new ways of relating to concepts and arguments that are familiar. By the time JNU came up, a certain form of Marxism, inherited from the Comintern, heavily laden with lines of thinking drawn from Russian radicalism and later Chinese communism, was already so familiar as to become dull. In JNU young minds encountered Marxism again—renewed by infusions of Hegel, Heidegger, and structuralism it was virtually a new doctrine of history. Afterwards, I am sure some of these students may have relapsed into entirely wooden formulaic thinking about Marx and the world. But during this formative period of their life, they participated in the thrill of thinking and argumentation, a transient life of ideas—which is what a good university is meant to provide to its entrants. I assume many of the people who passed through JNU then might not be able to remember exactly what those ideas were. But I think JNU gave them a taste of a life of thought, and hope they continued to live their lives thoughtfully ever after.

23

LEARNING OUTSIDE THE CLASSROOM

D. RAGHUNANDAN

The gods I don't believe in must have ordained it, because joining JNU was a strange and life-changing event for me, and also perhaps rare in Indian academia in the mid-1970s. I was an engineer, sorely disappointed by the work I was not doing but would have loved to do in the Indian aviation industry. My interests had gradually veered towards social anthropology, which I had spent a lot of time reading in an otherwise dull industrial experience. I wandered from one university to another but the most that any were willing to do was consider me for admission to the master's course. JNU was the sole exception.

One of the most senior faculty members I met for advice never questioned my choice but only recommended I take up economics, a subject I could 'sink my teeth into' rather than 'woolly sociology' that bordered on philosophy. An economics professor I next met told me he was himself considering a shift to botany. I was clearly in the right place! An ex-Oxford professor at the poorly named Centre for the Study of Social Systems didn't bat an eyelid telling me to apply for admission to its MPhil/PhD programme, arguing that five years after school studying engineering was equivalent to an MA, but of course I must make the cut-off in the written admissions test and interviews, and have a good tentative research proposal in hand. That is all the chance I had ever wanted and grabbed it with both hands. Such cross-disciplinary transitions were extremely rare in India, but those were heady days at JNU, perhaps as much for the faculty as for the students. Sadly, I believe I could not repeat this feat today, even at JNU. Academia in the country is slipping backwards, whereas elsewhere researchers are traversing disciplinary boundaries or working in teams across them.... But that's another story.

So there I was in this brave new world where seemingly anything was possible. There were myriad things to learn, and campus life to experience

IV.4. Time for a break: the passage to the library in the Old Campus—a space where students sat around, discussing and chatting over cups of tea when taking a break from their studies. *Photo courtesy: Anwar Huda, 1977*

which, to my deep regret I had never done until then, having studied engineering in a provincial college in England sandwiched between weeks in the factory of M/S Rolls Royce (Aero-Engines). In 1975 campus life at JNU meant a heady intellectual and political-ideological ferment, despite the Emergency ban on anything remotely resembling political activity. There was never an idle moment, and everything sparked intense discussions, inside classrooms and outside.

I audited as many courses as I could in sociology and in other disciplines, wanting to soak up as much as possible, requiring only a nod from the concerned faculty. Classrooms teemed with debates, lectures were often punctuated by students challenging the professor or one another, especially on political-ideological implications. These debates and positions expressed who we were, or aspiring to be, and often took on partisan colours along lines of student organizations one was affiliated to; but there was also much debate between members of the same organization. These were great learning experiences, often requiring study, preparing for the next round. Intense discussions were always on, in the canteen, in the lawns, outside the library, and in hostel rooms.

Lectures by visiting scholars especially from abroad drew immense interest. I particularly recall a series by historian E. P. Thompson where the lecture gallery was chock-full on each of the four days with faculty and students of all hues and disciplines sitting or standing in every available inch of space inside the hall and outside the various windows.

It was not all about books either. I teamed up with a sophomore friend from Bangalore to pursue a common interest in cinema and helped him run the JNU Film Society. We screened films at the Centre for Russian Studies (CRS) auditorium in glorious 16mm. Films were sourced from embassies and cultural centres in Delhi but also from the National Film Archives. Week-long film appreciation courses were organized, in part to tap into the extensive NFAI catalogue. The shows were often packed for screenings of classics by European masters, the great early Soviet masters like Sergei Eisenstein, and Indian alternative cinema. Unfortunately, my friend had to quit JNU due to a disruptive family bereavement, and I picked up the baton.

Many screenings were followed by discussion, sometimes with the filmmaker. Mrinal Sen, Kumar Shahani, and Mani Kaul led discussions with reasonable audiences. Raising the Film Society annual fee from five to ten rupees squeaked through the society's General Body but not without a debate on whether culture was being commercialized. Eisenstein's *October* celebrating the eponymous Soviet revolution, screened during the Emergency on the Nilgiri Dhaba lawns sparked another debate. A scene depicting Leon Trotsky looking around the table rather sneakily and hesitantly raising his hand in support of the proposal to launch the Revolution triggered anger in some students. Trotsky was always a hot-button topic at JNU.

A particularly memorable screening was of the award-winning Cuban film *Memories of Underdevelopment* (1968) by Tomás Gutiérrez Alea, an amazingly portrayed story of a bourgeois property owner in Havana completely out of place in socialist Cuba and told from the protagonist's viewpoint. CRS was jam-packed, and several repeat screenings had to be held on popular demand. Many a student received an unexpected and rich cultural education at JNU, at least in cinema.

With the lifting of the Emergency, JNU burst into intellectual ferment, mostly outside the classroom, and especially in the famous post-dinner hostel meetings. I remember an extraordinary period of extra-mural teach-ins by students during a student movement. Soon after the Emergency, the JNU Students' Union (JNUSU) charged the Vice Chancellor with having collaborated with the Emergency regime, and prohibited his entry into the campus. The authorities responded by closing the university, and the students 'took over' the hostels and messes, and conducted informal classes. I was assigned to take some classes for new entrants to MA sociology, and did so on the lawns near the library. I must have done a good job, for one young lady met me many years later at a seminar and thanked me for having inspired her to pursue an academic career in sociology.

After the end of the Emergency, and the release of the arrested JNU students including the incumbent JNUSU President, there was a popular demand that the JNUSU seek a fresh mandate. My organization, the Students Federation of India (SFI) which had held the JNUSU presidency when Emergency was declared, preferred to wait till the normal elections due in October. But the pent-up desire among students for open political activity and a renewal of the representative character of the JNUSU could not be contained. This position was given powerful voice by a JNU student and well-known leftist scholar who was on the campus, and shook up the student body. His speeches covered much ground about radical politics and democratic organization, what he considered to be flaws of the traditional Left, and the role of spontaneity in socio-political movements, all targeting the then dominant SFI and rallying all those who for whatever reason revelled in this demolition job. I am sure there are differing interpretations as to who prevailed in this prolonged debate: the SFI lost the University General Body Meeting (UGBM) which decided to hold elections immediately, but won the actual elections that followed.

Wherever one's judgement lies, those debates were brilliant, illuminating and thoroughly enjoyable for students. A large part of the debate revolved around Stalin, sometimes Lenin, and Trotsky, and their respective ideas and historical roles in conceptualizing and building socialism and related political organizations: 'Socialism in one country' versus permanent revolution, the early history of the Soviet revolution, the Leninist organization versus the tendency to bureaucratism, the Third versus the Fourth International. Speakers on both sides would come to the post-dinner hostel meetings with armfuls of books with flagged pages for reference. Besides the usual seating, students sat on the floor many rows deep, eagerly taking notes. Were these debates relevant to the 'election-no election' issue? Who cared? Students learned a lot over those weeks. Perhaps more importantly, they learned a great deal about how to review and critically understand political ideas and practice.

I recall meetings on Afghanistan after the Soviet armed forces rolled across the Amu Darya. I had myself returned from Kabul a few weeks back after visiting my mother who was working there with UNICEF. A cartoon poster pasted on the hostel walls after an earlier visit had shown me through an aircraft window flying above JNU with hostels burning, with the caption 'Bhaagegabhai Kabul-London/D. Raghunandan, D. Raghunandan,' lampooning one of my election campaign slogans 'Aam chhatron ka abhinandan/D. Raghunandan.' I was the JNUSU President, but my organization did not have a majority in the students' council. It took tough filibustering in the council and much debating in hostel meetings to hold back a JNUSU demonstration against the Soviet action.

The Solidarity movement in Poland led by Lech Walesa, mounting a serious challenge to the Polish government with ripple effects across Eastern Europe, prompted heated discussions on campus, with the organized Left on one side and some other left-wing individuals or groups on the other. An all-organization meeting was held in Periyar hostel by supporters of Solidarity. There were always divided opinions about the advantages or otherwise of speaking first or last at JNU meetings, the latter being generally preferred. In this meeting, the organizers preferred that I speak first. The organizers opened with a reading of the long list of Solidarity's demands, hoping to underline its radical character. I followed by questioning Solidarity's charter for not having a single demand advancing the socialist cause, and attacking support for the movement by the US and the Pope, while conceding that the movement itself was a response to the lack of internal democracy in the Polish Workers Party and in Polish society. That triggered such a prolonged and fierce debate that there were no other speakers that night!

The debates on such issues were highly educative for JNU students and confirmed that, despite frequent arguments that JNU discussions be restricted to campus life, JNU students were hugely interested in, and gained much from, discussions on national and international events and issues. Two other features of these debates were noteworthy. First, the participation of many international students. Whereas most tended to support the organized Left at JNU, some of them specifically expressed their unhappiness to me over my critical position vis-à-vis the government in Poland and wanted me to take a more unyielding position against Solidarity. Second, no political party in India had yet taken a position on these issues and we at JNU were really thinking on our feet, and were ahead of the curve.

Ah, nostalgia, they don't make it like they used to!

24

AN ACCIDENTAL EDUCATION

ABHIJIT BANERJEE

I ended up at JNU trying to escape my destiny. I had applied for a master's in Economics at both JNU and the Delhi School of Economics (DSE), trying to decide between the two. At DSE, a brash young faculty member told me it was the royal road to PhD programmes in the US. That made up my mind.

I went to JNU with the idea I would somehow break loose. Economics at Presidency College, Kolkata, was very well taught, and for that reason perhaps, I thought it was ho hum. What you expected, mostly happened. When the price went up supply went up, demand went down. The market cleared. Unless for some reason it didn't; then things got a little more interesting, as we descended into the spicier geography of the Keynesian model. But even that took a couple of days of getting used to and then it was all rather predictable. I was twenty, I wanted philosophical depth—insights that would make me wake up shivering with excitement and entirely new ways of thinking about the world.

JNU failed me. Or more plausibly, I failed JNU. The insights that would change my life never came to me, probably because I did not know what to look for. I still don't.

There were moments when I thought I had it. Drowning in Piero Sraffa's *Production of Commodities with the Means of Commodities*, I thought I saw glimpses of the deep, but Krishna Bharadwaj, who taught us Sraffa and deeply admired him (as did most of the JNU faculty), quickly pulled me out of the water. She explained that Sraffa was demonstrating a result followed from applying the Perron Frobenius Theorem without using any math, just verbal logic, which she thought was remarkable (which it indeed was). And that ruined it for me. I wanted a conceptual leap, not calisthenics. Anjan Mukherji, one of my favourite teachers of all time, delivered the coup de grâce by explaining why Sraffa's assumptions, in his view, were too extreme to be of general interest.

I was ready to immerse myself in Marx, who was the talisman of the JNU economics department. I was (and remain) a firm believer in the fact that there is oppression in the world and that it is aided and abetted by the concentrated private ownership of capital (who, looking at the United States today, could disagree?). I had tried to read *Das Kapital* as an undergraduate, encouraged by the fact that with the subsidy from the Soviet Union it might have been the best deal per page of book material in history, but it was not a great success. Every page was littered with baffling sentences, which, I gathered, were comments on scholars who I had mostly never heard of, making it slow going at best.

In my courses at JNU, Marx showed up often, but the emphasis was on the many ways in which conventional economics was wrong, not because it told the wrong story about the world but because of some relatively obscure (to me) quasi-logical flaws. The labour theory of value baffled me. As a descriptive theory of what determines prices, it seemed plain wrong and, as a normative view of how we ought to value production, it seemed bizarrely indifferent to the contributions of mother earth. If I wanted to see the world in a new light, that was not where I was going to get it.

While waiting fruitlessly for that signal moment of illumination, JNU transformed my entire sense of what it meant to be Indian. In the particular enclave of Bengalidom where I grew up, the RSS did not exist. At JNU they were a tiny minority, but a distinct one, keen to engage in debates about liberal positions that many of us took for granted, yet always polite, if slightly formal. Hearing the shrill right-wing brigades of today, I cannot help wondering where that stream ended up.

Literature in Indian languages other than Bangla mostly didn't exist for us in Kolkata, the combined result of unselfconscious Bengali chauvinism and a clear emphasis on English as the one other valid cultural space. We knew a smattering of names: Ghalib may be, Harivansh Rai Bachchan for the obvious reason, Premchand, because of Satyajit Ray, and Kabir, going back a few centuries, but that was it. The presumption was there was not much else to find. JNU fixed that, though I remain a slow and diffident reader of Hindi.

And then there was caste. In the world I grew up in, caste was this atavistic thing that occasionally showed up in conversations about parental disapprobation of coupling plans. My parents were from different castes;

their parents had ignored that; we were past caste. It was only after being at JNU that I began to understand why caste played so little a role in my life until then. The eclipse of the lower castes in Bengal was so complete that they had no voice in state politics; I wondered if this was a direct result of the fact that the upper and middle castes had managed to reach an amicable compromise among themselves, which made it easier to exclude the rest.

Caste was very real at JNU. It was used to understand, explain, categorize, occasionally to disparage (usually upper castes from particular states were the targets). At Presidency College, the reservations based on caste were mostly honoured in the breach. There were apparently no qualified candidates. At JNU, a clever system of points-based admission, which gave applicants extra credit not only for being from previously discriminated castes, but also for being poor and going to a rural school, both of which went hand in hand with being from one of those castes, meaning many more of them made it in. It was striking how quickly so many of them caught up, despite their initial disadvantages. It made me a life-long fan of affirmative action.

This was hotly debated at JNU at the time. There was a general concern with discrimination against 'meritorious' students—as usual without recognizing the circularity of an argument that starts by measuring merit through test scores. But the argument also had its local Marxist variant, in which there was an underlying worry about students who carried too much baggage from their backgrounds. If you are so obsessed with caste, the concern seemed to be, are you ready to lead the revolution? I recall many conversations about whether caste should be a legitimate concern for left-wing politics; or was it just the last vestige of false consciousness, soon to be washed away by the rationalizing torrent of proper class feeling? 'You cannot spend your life looking backwards', I heard someone once pronounce, 'these personal bonds just get in the way of the revolution.'

Indeed, the personal was another space where the revolution was coming. Liberation from the structures of patriarchy, it seemed, was being used as a code-word for resisting the kind of sticky, sentimental, monogamy that we (or may be just I) practised in Kolkata. In some circles, multiple partners (in modern parlance) were the aspirational goal. The rest just gawped and gossiped. And teased each other for being jealous.

Above all, JNU framed for me what it is to be a friend in India. It is to be nosy, intrusive, and giving, to tease often, to laugh easily, to not worry about over-stepping. It is unique, in my experience, and it is what I miss the most when I am elsewhere.

It took destiny two years to catch up with me. I went straight from my masters at JNU to a PhD programme in the US which, even by the standards of the time, was relatively conventional. And there I remain, an economics professor married to another economics professor, exactly what, I guess, as a child of two economics professors, I was meant to be. Destiny had its revenge.

25

THE SENSORY ARCHIVE'S ANALYSIS (SAA): MANNER & MEANS

NAMAN P. AHUJA

It has been a hard battle to make the public realize that the faculty at the School of Arts and Aesthetics (SAA) were not hired *because* they made art, performances or films. That they do so privately is the bonus on which they base their research. They each do, however, have a profound engagement with performances, films, sculpture, painting, photography, print culture, and new media practices which they use to construct history, ethnography, debate institutional politics and their instrumental role in nationalism, propaganda, and Indian identity, and so on. This makes the events organized at SAA straddle a balance between showcasing an art form by practitioners and inviting a variety of researchers to analyse it. It takes teaching beyond the classroom in a way that is as educative for the art practitioner as it is necessary for the research itself.

Thus, while performances and exhibitions continue apace through other auspices at the university and SAA studies them, when they are hosted by SAA, they tend to be more experimental and participatory. Several practitioners have welcomed the opportunity to bring a historical context to their work and explore avenues for critically framing it through the research at the school.

In 2001, when SAA was set up, Dayanita Singh, a photographer, sent postcard versions of her now-famous pictures of survivors of the 1984 riots, a wedding tent in the Kargil War, family portraits, and Goa to a random selection of JNU employees (including faculty) asking them to record their responses to the picture and send them back to SAA through the university's internal mail. Thinking back on that now, eighteen years later, she says it transformed her way of thinking about photography, forcing her to realize how different people view the same image, and how differently they read them compared to her intention while recording them. Each reading was as true and as correct.

In 2010, hot on the heels of having won the Skoda Prize for contemporary art, the artist Mithu Sen exhibited her provocative paintings and collages at the SAA gallery in a show called: 'Black Candy' [iforgotmypenisathome]. The exhibition explored homosexual love, and paid homage to Bhupen Khakhar, coinciding with a major three-day conference on the 'Architectures of Erotica: Political, Social, Ritual' which attracted an extraordinary array of speakers from all over the world. The school's administrative staff and others were startled by Sen's paintings, and asked how art that looked like 'graffiti in a public toilet in its subject matter' could be appropriate for our gallery walls? This led to six marvellous weeks of discussions about what allows a citizen to claim the right to publicly show what's suppressed and innate.

The conference on erotica as well as another called 'Circuits of the Popular' were created with an interdisciplinary focus, funded by the Tata Social Welfare Trust which enabled a four-year grant for the development of the school. Events, workshops and the opportunity to invite visiting faculty directly fed into the school's research profile. Two previous grants from the Ford Foundation had been similarly utilized. A major grant from the Getty Foundation supported a Distinguished Visiting Professor Programme (2009–13). A collaboration with the University of Warwick developed co-teaching and supported a UGC-UKIERI research project on gendered citizenship. An active student exchange programme with Freie University, Berlin, and Cologne University's summer school and faculty exchange with King's College, London, is ongoing. A British Academy Grant supported projects on 'Political Theatre and the Cultures of the Left' and the provocative conference 'What's Left of the Left?', and a grant from the Inlaks Foundation allowed the school to run curatorial programmes for three years. Such grants continue to fund visiting faculty, allow travel for students, support faculty and student exchange, research, salaries for technical staff, library development, conferences, exhibitions, and seminars.

The gallery has showcased photographs by the Alkazi Foundation for the Arts twice: once from the albums of John Marshall, former director of the ASI, reminding us how the photographed site or artefact forms the basis of the pedagogy of art history, and how this reportage is never unbiased or unmediated. Their second collaboration with us was with

IV.5. Naman P. Ahuja and Parul D. Mukherji with SAA students on a field trip to Khajuraho in 2007.
Photo courtesy: Naman Ahuja

the artist Pushpamala N. in a practical workshop called the 'Archive of "Indian" Gestures' in 2009. The artist created a theatre set with the students against which she invited them to perform and photograph themselves, in order to bring home how the photographed source is revealing of the projection, adoption and thus, formation of identity.

These projects have each questioned our role as documenters and archivists, matters that Jyotindra Jain was always attentive to at the inception of the school. Yet, we also live in times of archive-fever: suffering the burden of the responsibility of archiving and museumising too much in the new millennium. Dayanita Singh recalls that she did not know what to do with all the pictures she displayed at JNU and begged the school to take them. Without a museum or archive space to keep them, the school refused, and thus cast away, students took whatever they wanted for their hostel rooms. Yet cast away photographs and prints themselves become a major subject of study. Jyotindra once lent the school an extraordinary exhibition from his private collection called 'The conquest of the world as picture'. Displayed worldwide, this exhibition was largely made up of ephemera of the twentieth century to tell an extraordinary history of modern India through household objects—calendars, toys, matchboxes—

each of which used to carry 'sceneries' and pictures of peoples' changing hopes and aspirations.

Moving from everyday art, to what is now regarded 'high' art: unpublished pictures and sculptures worth crores of rupees by Ramkinkar Baij were exhibited in the SAA gallery in 2007. Petrified about the security, the curatorial team installed our first CCTV cameras and asked for round-the-clock security guards, quickly realizing how the same space became a case study for our opposition to surveillance! At any rate, confident that the artworks were safe, we kept the exhibition open till 11 p.m. every night because that's when the magic happened. Families with children would come after dinner to see an important art exhibition rather than watch television. Ramkinkar elicited a serious conference alongside. Art critic Geeta Kapur used the opportunity to invoke Gayatri Spivak's 'Can the Subaltern Speak?' and the students learned, by example, how to handle all aspects of pitching an exhibition to diverse constituencies of viewership. The exhibition had a dual focus. It was as much about Ramkinkar as it was about archiving his work and its documentation by the artist Devi Prasad.

Each of these projects brought home how cinema and the camera have become the most significant historical sources for studying the twentieth century, forcing us to examine critical apparatuses for the handling of these sources. In 2014, a massive four-day international conference on 'visible evidence', looked at non-fiction media culture with powerful projects such as Decolonizing Architecture Art Residency (DAAR) from Palestine, and the premiere of *The Look of Silence* by renowned documentary filmmaker, Joshua Oppenheimer. He had already stunned the world with his award-winning *Act of Killing* on the Indonesian genocide of 1965–66. The screening of its sequel, *The Look of Silence,* followed by a conversation with the director, was one of the most riveting exchanges we have had on the capacity of non-fiction cinema to interrogate themes of genocide, witnessing, and memory. Over 250 participants from all over the world participated in this conference that was held for the first time in Delhi.

This was followed by 'The Music Box and its Reverberations: Technology and Music in India', which forged a collaboration between the SAA and the Music Digitization Mediation project based at the University of Oxford. If ways of studying the recorded image have been the concern of cinema and visual studies, this paid particular attention to the explosion of audio technologies in the past two decades and examined the particular materialities of digital circulation, reproduction, and storage of audio that has simultaneously impacted established music industry norms and subjective engagements of listeners with music. It brought together academics from different disciplinary orientations, practitioners, and performers to reflect on questions of music and technology in India. Complementing the debates during the day were musical concerts—classical, popular, and folk—which drew in wider audiences and were much appreciated.

During 2008–12, teaching at the school also underwent a change, from 35mm slide projections to a dependence on digital projection and PowerPoint, from VHS and analog tapes to digitally equipped rooms for teaching, and the teachers too realized how their pedagogic tools and archives were now to be archived.

As the accelerated pace of change triggered by digital technology unfolds in the twenty-first century, our courses continue to be structured to expose students to a wide range of issues such as moving image technologies, the stylistic and aesthetic dimension of diverse media forms, the political and cultural evaluation of audio-visual representations, and the infrastructures of media production, circulation, and exhibition. In January 2013, a conference to mark the centenary year of Indian cinema attracted academicians from across the world. The interrogation of the idea of '*a*' national cinema led to research on cinema cultures from Assam, Manipur, and Nagaland; Bhojpuri cinema, Bengali cinema, Tamil, and Malayalam cinema. South Asian arts exist in a variety of languages and this has been showcased through festivals of regional cinema, various talks and conferences in theatre and performance studies on 'Regional and Local Performance Histories of Manipur' (2013) which was complemented by the close documentation of the Lai Haraoba from four locales of Manipur. During 2016–18, we documented the unique Dussehra at Kullu, the practices of devadasi dedication at the Soundatti Yallamma temple, Karnataka, and the Chhau and Naachni performances of Purulia, Bengal.

A project called 'Art and Politics of the IPTA' (enabled by a grant through the Ministry of Culture) studied the progressive amateur theatre movement. Original documents were sourced and archived digitally for future references and teaching. The second phase of the IPTA (1951–54), saw the emergence of the regional, the subaltern and even the later cultural

IV.6. Public participation was explored in the exhibition Self X Social, co-curated by art critic Geeta Kapur and the students, 2005.
Photo courtesy: Naman Ahuja

policy of exploring roots. H. S. Shivaprakash, who developed points of departure from classical traditions through the varieties of regional Bhakti practices, provided a firm foundation for the history of the regional. The history of ideas of pluralism emerged in his courses on aesthetics which revealed differences between Sanskrit and Dravidian aesthetics.

How all this plurality construes ideas of the nation is a theme SAA has explored year after year. While the exhibition on popular culture by Jyotindra Jain exhibited the variety and change in images of Bharat Mata, in another exhibition (Self X Social: 2005), an ironic display of a sheet of revenue stamps with the image of Gandhi revealed, if looked at from the other side, cut-outs of pigs. The environment of vigorous debates has made institutional politics and political representation major themes in what is exhibited and researched. Issues around the study of sacred texts and the possibilities of their misuse for caste and communal politics continue to be analysed. The inner workings and the state of our institutions for the preservation and dissemination of the arts (museums, the states' 'akademis', and the private sector) have become the subject of entire courses and seminars. In 2014, Rajeev Sethi, a noted art curator who had just made Mumbai's Terminal-2 double-up as a museum, came to speak on how public spaces need to address a changing Indian viewership.

Over the years, the school has tried to provide a strong foundation to reflect on the many kinds of impetus for making art and its consumption. Many students now work as curators and critics, academics and historians, and some infuse their art practice with the theoretical knowledge they have gained. In turn, these activities have brought the school accolades and its faculty organizes film and theatre festivals and curates exhibitions at the most prestigious venues in India and abroad.

26

THE LIBRARY AT THE CROSSROADS*

GIRIJA KUMAR

Sapru House was the intellectual centre of the metropolis in the 1950s and 1960s. A whole generation of political leaders, media persons, academicians, civil servants, and a spectrum of intellectuals of all hues had their baptism on the lawns and in the canteen, classroom, and library of Sapru House. The library was indeed the natural centre. I had a great sense of pride in being associated with the structuring of the library, brick by brick, since its inception in October 1947. It was difficult for me to break the long-standing bond—a love affair lasting more than two decades. There were, however, other challenges in the offing.

It must have been late 1970 or early 1971 when I received a call from G. Parthasarathi. We had a pleasant chat, in which he outlined his plans for the university and said he would like me to work as his deputy in structuring the university.

I assumed the offer was in respect of the university library, but, to my great surprise, he made it clear that he wanted me to take up a much larger role. I then asked him to send me a formal offer. This never came. Instead, after several months, Moonis Raza was appointed to the position. I did not care. After all, the Sapru House Library meant the whole world to me.

It was sheer coincidence that led to my association with JNU as its University Librarian. In early 1972, the Indian School of International Studies (which administered the Sapru House Library with its parent body—the Indian Council of World Affairs) decided to merge with Jawaharlal Nehru University. Consequently, the Sapru House Library was split into two parts. The study of international relations and regional

*From Kanjiv Lochan (ed.), *JNU: The Years*, Bombay: Popular Prakashan, 1996, pp. 77–82. The essay has been edited for this volume.

studies have suffered considerably on account of this decision. But I was not conscious about this then. I felt excited at the prospect of laying the foundations of a truly national university library and dealing with academicians and young scholars from a wide range of disciplines. The world was young and I was excited at the idea of contributing to strengthening the foundations of intellectual India. Looking back after a close association of thirteen years with the university, I have a feeling of great satisfaction. I do, however, regret that the potential of the library has not been fully explored by the university community and, indeed, the situation has deteriorated in recent years.

The library is expected to be a democratic organization. The barometer of the success of a library lies in its democratic functioning within the organization, and through equal participation by its users (clientele) in the governance of the organization. The students are the lifeline of any academic institution. I had decided that the primacy ought to be given to the students, and then to the teachers of the university. There is a dialectical situation inherent in such a policy decision. To favour have-nots (students) over haves (the faculty) held potential risks for the successful running of the library.

The doors of the librarian's office were always open to the students of the university. A continuing dialogue took place with them and attempts were assiduously made not only to identify their needs but also to anticipate and, above all, to meet them to the extent possible. After all, the students constituted the majority of the university community and they were the future of the country. The result was one of the best-equipped textbook libraries in the country. In my association with the university there was hardly an occasion when the students created trouble for me. My only regret was that knowledge for its own sake came to be downgraded in the overall scheme of things.

I had come to realize very early on that my expectations of building a national university library on the JNU campus could not be met for a variety of reasons, the most important being the university's academic structure, which was a product of lopsided, and juvenile thinking. Imagine a university of national status without departments of studies in Sanskrit, Greek, Latin, philosophy, logic, law, English literature, astronomy, medicine, physics, chemistry, and mathematics. The result reflected in the equally lopsided growth of collections at the university library. The founders must not have realized the simple fact that it is not possible to delink medicine from life sciences and social medicine. Basic research and research in interdisciplinary areas are not possible without a complete overview of the whole spectrum of intellectual knowledge ranging from basic and applied sciences to the humanities, the arts, and the social sciences.

There was another basic lacuna that prevented the development of a comprehensive collection on various disciplines in the library. This was a skewed book selection policy passed down from the bureaucratic practices prevailing in the university system of our country. The selection of new books and retrospective literature was the prerogative of the head of each Centre. He or she could be a first-rate scholar, but without an interest in the overall development of collections in the discipline. There were instances when the incumbent head of a Centre was hidebound by ideological constraints. Books not in line with their ideological tastes did not find a place on the shelves. Feudal practices thus prevailed in the 'progressive' environment of the university.

Two fundamental issues have bothered me about Jawaharlal [Nehru] University from the first day I began my association with it. I discovered to my horror that it was essentially a bureaucratic organization with a veneer of democracy. Surface-thin democratic functioning had in fact deteriorated into populism and opportunism of the lowest order. The library was not spared in this malaise, which started in the 1970s during the best years of stewardship of the university by G. Parthasarathi.

Who dominates the university? It is neither the students, nor the administrative staff, nor the academic community. Library professionals don't have a worthy position in the scheme of things either. As the university librarian, I have been an ex officio member of the Academic Council for the entire period of thirteen years. During this time, hundreds of committees have been appointed by the Council yet I am unable to recall a single instance when I was invited to be a member of any of the committees. The university librarian is almost never consulted when new courses are introduced. The librarian also has to face the mortification of expressing helplessness when students approach the library enthusiastically for readings on revised or new courses. The basic dichotomy arises from the ill-defined status of professional librarians in the university hierarchy.

There has certainly been a downslide in the last decade or so.

Professional librarians are nowhere to be found. The university library is now being run at the behest of university bureaucracy as a minor department of the Registrar's office. The library was bound to get caught in the crossfire when subjected to the tyranny of the Administrative Registrar, Academic Registrar, and the Finance Officer, with the Vice Chancellor. It would be interesting to keep a record of the number of hours spent by the head of the university browsing through the reading rooms and stacks of the library; and the results ought to be published for the public. The neglect is evident in the maintenance of the library building. Look at the manner in which the Nehru Memorial Museum and Library are maintained. It is high time we redress the situation. It is not mere hyperbole to assert that the library is a barometer of the health of the university. It will require a lot of effort to reverse the damage done but I am confident the situation can be improved.

The bureaucratic stranglehold translates into acts of populism. Universities in India are publicly funded. The bureaucracy of the university does not have the slightest squeamishness in pandering to the pressures of populism. Quality has been so compromised that it is not possible to introduce high standards at all in any department of the university. The Central Library is the prime victim of this mindless policy of adopting Gresham's law as the norm for the functioning of the university. Professional, academic, and managerial qualities are no longer the criteria in awarding promotion in the library. The senility principle (seniority) is the only criterion. The standards of service in the library have fallen abysmally and may continue to fall in the years to come. The channels of communication with the faculty and students of the university have also begun to clog. The professionals working in the library should be subjected to the strictest appraisal on a continuing basis.

This is the situation at the top echelons, and things are no better at the lower rungs. The university bureaucracy has also played havoc with the lower strata of library administration through a cleverly designed university-wide promotion policy, whereby posts become interchangeable at many levels. The registrar's office manipulates the transfer games cleverly so as to turn the library into the dumping ground of the university. These follies are compounded by intense trade union activity which has replaced genuine professional and non-professional work in the library. In light of these realities, it may not be justifiable to grant academic status to professional librarians working at the university library without ensuring certain qualitative improvements.

The university library needs to be run as a managerial organization in this age of Quality Revolution. The basic principle of Quality Revolution is to give recognition to the information needs of its clientele. 'The user is king' is the maxim that needs to be adopted in the functioning of the university library. User satisfaction is thus the basic criterion. Quality presumes the adoption of democratic norms at all levels—university administration, academic departments, the student community and, above all, inner democracy within the library organization. There is considerable potential for improvement and much latent goodwill among the academic community for the library. It has to be tapped to its full potential. Several collections and services of the library are of excellent standard and indeed unique, which only need the fullest utilization. Democracy in the real sense of the term needs to be introduced at all levels. Let the library be made a laboratory within the university organization in order to upgrade itself and set standards at the national level.[1]

[1]Editors' note: Girija Kumar's article was written in 1996, before certain Centres and Schools—listed as essential to a university—were started at JNU. Even the library, about which he expresses considerable anguish, received a major facelift and boost, establishing a cyber library, acquiring many important digital resources, and systematizing online access to the rich pool of MPhils and PhDs of JNU.

27

JAWAHARLAL NEHRU UNIVERSITY LIBRARY—SOME REMINISCENCES

L. N. MALIK

My stint in the Modern European Languages Department in Delhi University served as a springboard for my appointment at the JNU library in 1971. I joined the library when the library started functioning in the Old Campus. The initial years were crucial for its growth. Enormous funds were available for purchasing books and journals and the library also received donations of scholarly books from eminent personalities. When the Indian School of International Studies was amalgamated with JNU in 1970, the library was also transferred to JNU. The embassies of Germany, France, Spain, Japan, China, Portugal, etc., generously donated books to the library in order to enable students to carry on studies and research in their respective literature, language, and cultures. It was a big challenge for the library staff to organize these books in a systematic manner by classifying, indexing, and stacking them in a helpful sequence. As the library was at a formative stage, hundreds of books were added to the stacks every day and strict supervision was enforced to ensure the books were accurately indexed. It was a golden period in the history of the JNU library under the inspiring and dynamic leadership of Mr Girija Kumar, the first university librarian.

During the 1970s and 1980s, computers were not available in the library and photocopying facilities were also very limited. The library timings were from 9 a.m. to 10 p.m., but students lined up even before the opening time to get books from the textbook section. Sometimes there was a scuffle amongst students over getting hold of a particular recommended book. The library was always overcrowded. Sometimes the seating capacity was not sufficient and students did not mind sitting on the floor.

The JNU library has always remained a hub of academic activity and the nerve centre of the university. From its inception, the library laid the foundation for various services to the students to enable them to pursue their studies and research without any hassles. These services included current awareness services in the form of a monthly list of newly acquired books, a list of articles in periodicals, and press clippings catering to the needs of area studies. The library also used to bring out a list of dissertations and theses submitted by the students in their respective centres. These documents were widely consulted not only by the students of JNU but also by those of other universities. The reference section of the library maintained the interest profiles of the research scholars and faculty and brought to their notice the latest information in their field of interest. Now all these facilities are provided through online computer-based services.

The library is a growing organism and every year thousands of books and other reading materials are added to its collection. On entering the library a newly admitted student is often baffled and confused. In order to enable students to use the library collection efficiently and effectively, user education programmes are organized at the beginning of each academic year. The library staff explains to the students how to use the computer for retrieval of books, periodicals, press clippings, and theses. A conducted tour of the library is organized to familiarize the students with the location of books and other documents. The organizational set up of the library is also explained to students, and they are introduced to the library staff posted in various sections of the library.

The university community is diverse. Students and staff are drawn from all parts of India, from different castes, religions, linguistic communities, and with different traditions. A substantial number of students hail from regions where adequate educational facilities are not available. Some of them have pursued their studies in their regional languages and are not fluent in English or Hindi. After spending a couple of years at the university, they acquire a fair command in both spoken and written English and complete their studies with good grades. We, in the library, direct our special efforts to ensure the successful completion of their studies by rendering all possible assistance. One invariably finds comments about the library staff in the acknowledgement pages of their dissertations and theses. In one instance, a student from a less-privileged economic background completed his studies at the university with laurels and appeared for the IAS examination. After passing the written examination, he went for the interview wearing slippers. When a member of the interview board asked him why he had come in chappals, he replied that he did not have money to buy a pair of shoes. He was selected and offered a responsible post. A number of visually impaired students are admitted every year in various courses and the library has provisions to facilitate their studies through computer-based devices.

The university students, faculty and non-teaching staff have always lived in harmony. One could not fail to observe the enthusiasm and fervour which the students exhibited in the pursuit of their studies, and this in turn spurred on most of us to do our utmost to help them achieve their goals. It was also rumoured that most students were inspired to take their work seriously by observing our selfless and dedicated devotion to our duties. In one of the classes of the School of Language, Literature and Culture Studies, students had to write a composition about their favourite personality. One of them chose to write about me. This was a source of encouragement for me to discharge my duties more effectively. I am not married and used to work in the library on all the seven days of the week, as I did not have any family obligations. Observing my presence in the library for most of the time, a group of students enquired about my family and when I replied that I was not married, one of the students remarked: 'You do not know that he is married to the library.' Whether I deserved it or not, the university thought it fit to honour me with an award for lifelong service to the library at a function held on the occasion of Jawaharlal Nehru's birth anniversary. When I was receiving the award, one of my colleagues who attended the function told me that a student sitting beside him shed tears of joy. This reflected the affection and empathy students had for me.

The faculty of the university also took keen interest in the development of the library. Most of the teachers were regular visitors to the library and kept track of the newly acquired books. It was amazing to see that they had perfect bibliographic control over the library collection. A faculty member wanted a particular book and it was discovered that the index entry for that book was missing in the catalogue and hence it was reported that the book was not available. But the professor had once borrowed the book from the library. So efforts were made to trace the book and ultimately it was located. One could always spot teachers in the periodicals section of the library, perusing articles in the journals of their interest.

Their contribution to the periodical literature was also noteworthy. Most of the faculty had written books and these were displayed separately. Some teachers had a great attachment to the library and donated a large number of books from their personal collection. Though most of them were scholars of great repute, they interacted with the library staff very cordially as if they were one of them. On all special occasions, ranging from the organisation of seminars, interactions with national and international scholars to solemnizing the marriage of their wards, they ensured we were present during these events.

Cordiality also marked the relationship amongst the non-teaching staff of the university. Though we came from diverse linguistic and cultural backgrounds, our relations with one another were like a big big family. We were always prepared to stand by one another in good and bad times. We collectively celebrated festivals such as Eid, Christmas, Diwali, Holi, etc. with great enthusiasm by exchanging gifts and feasts of the choicest food. Some of us were not destined to be married, but living amongst our colleagues, we never felt like we were living a solitary life. We shared enormous love and affection. It was a painful experience to get separated from them at the time of retirement.

The non-teaching staff was mostly satisfied with the prevailing working environment and well-defined rules for their promotion and career advancement. Practically all the employees got at least three promotions before attaining the age of superannuation. Employees were financially secure and the majority of them were allotted university accommodation, as there was an acute problem of finding accommodation outside the campus. On the sad demise of any employee, the authorities were kind enough to offer employment and allot some accommodation to their wards. This benign gesture of the authorities proved a boon for the bereaved family members to sustain their existence. Whenever any employee was ill or seriously injured in any accident and hospitalized, the authorities along with the Vice Chancellor invariably visited the hospital to enquire about the well-being of the employee. When I was in service, I once met with an accident and seriously fractured my leg. After resting for a few days, I started coming to the library with my plastered leg to discharge my duties. Somehow, Dr G. Parthasarathi, the first Vice Chancellor of the university, got to know about my injuries and came to the library to enquire about my health. In those days the bus service was not reliable

IV.8. Inside the library: the usual sight in the reading room of the Dr B. R. Ambedkar Central Library—packed at all hours of the day and night.
Photo courtesy: Samim Asgor Ali.

and I had to travel a distance of 20 kilometres to reach JNU. Without my asking, the Vice Chancellor was kind enough to sanction the allotment of university accommodation for me through his discretionary powers. Is it possible to forget the humanitarian outlook on the part of the authorities?

Pursuing serious study and research work for a considerable period of time in a day requires some sort of break in order to invigorate oneself for the job. One requires stimulus such as coffee, tea, and good snacks. Though all the Schools of Studies have canteens, the one in the central library is the main attraction for students. It remains open the whole day from 9 a.m. to 10 p.m. and serves a variety of snacks and inexpensive and good lunch and dinner. Mr Gopalan and his son, Ajay, take every care to provide hygienic food with healthy and fresh ingredients. Both father and son have a pleasing personality, and always receive students with a smiling face.

After attaining the age of superannuation, some kind of musings over the past events in one's life is soothing and removes the monotony of everyday life. Some of us who have retired from service are in constant contact with one another and keep meeting to refresh our memories of the time spent together at the university. We follow with keen interest the innovations and development initiatives undertaken by the university to fulfil its obligations to the society at large. After completing their studies,

IV.9. The Cyber Library on the ground floor of Dr B. R. Ambedkar Central Library at JNU.
Photo courtesy: Samim Asgor Ali

JNU students settle down in life, but they are nostalgic about their stay in the university. One often hears that whenever they visit the university or happen to meet outside the campus, they anxiously enquire about the well-being of the teaching and non-teaching staff. Our bonds with the university are absolute and we pray that it may attain the height of glory and fame for all time to come.

28

A PHOTOSTAT SHOP AT JNU*

ASHISH DAS

In 2001, I opened my photostat shop on the ground floor of the old building of the School of Social Sciences (SSS-I). Though I did not choose the venue, I was told that the students required a photostat shop in this building. In fact, it had been demanded by the students' union. At the time, I was working on a project with Professor Ashwini Ray of the Centre for Political Studies (CPS) and hence also knew other members of the faculty. Professor Ray, along with Professors Kuldeep Mathur and Niraja Gopal of CPS, recommended my name to the then chairperson of the Campus Development Committee (CDC), Professor Mridula Mukherjee. However, I had to fill out an application and appear for an interview. There were nearly 250 applicants, but as I was the only graduate among them, I was awarded the shop.

The same building also houses the Centre for Historical Studies (CHS) on the ground floor. Having studied history during my undergraduate days, I thought that this opportunity would allow me to remain in touch with the subject. The CHS recommends readings for each course. I photocopy all the materials relevant to the courses and compile them into separate sets of readings for the students. I was the one who started the system of handing out 'course readers'. The advantage of this system is that I don't have to do it afresh every year and the students get ready-made reading materials at the beginning of every semester. My primary aim is to help the students. For example, I don't have the licence to stock stationery goods in bulk, but I do keep some day-to-day stationery materials in my shop to cater to the urgent needs of students. If any of them suddenly needs a pen or a CD, they simply come down to my shop.

---

*As told to Kunal Chakrabarti.

My services mostly benefit the students of history and geography, the two Centres originally located in SSS-I. When they shifted to the new SSS-III building, I moved along with them. Even though CPS is housed in another building, I frequently get some work from them because they know me. The students of the other Centres of the School, the Economics Centre, for instance, do not come here. They prefer to go to the photostat shop in their respective buildings.

I usually photocopy course-wise readings for students and reading materials for researchers. I also photocopy class notes, particularly for those students who are irregular in attending classes. Students also come to get their documents, such as marksheets copied.

But with the advent of the internet, the nature of my work has changed. Almost everything is available on the internet now and most students have taken to reading softcopies. As a result, demand for photocopies has considerably diminished. Only a small section of the students, who cannot read soft copies, buy printouts from my shop. Since they cost more than photocopies, it partially compensates for the loss I incur due to the fall in demand of photocopied materials. On the whole, my income has declined.

There is another reason for the drop. The cost of raw materials, manpower and electricity charges has gone up, but, unlike the photostat shops outside the university campus, we cannot increase our charges. It has remained more or less fixed for many years. For example, earlier I used to buy a ream of paper for Rs 120; after the introduction of GST it has gone up to Rs 190. Since my turnover is less than 30 lakhs per year, I do not fall under the GST bracket. But, as a result, I have to purchase raw materials at a higher rate. GST has definitely adversely affected my business.

The new technologies have brought about another perceptible change. Earlier, from the photocopies, I could have some idea of what the students were reading. Now most students read softcopies. They do not even come to my shop for syllabus or course-contents. Either these are available on the website or the teachers provide these to them via email. They take photos on their mobile phones of those materials which do not have softcopies. Thus now there are many students who I do not know at all. I have been serving this university for nearly two decades, but I cannot make out whether, and if so how, the reading habits of students have changed over the years.

IV.10. The photostat shop in SSS-III. Ashish at the computer, taking a printout of reading material for a course.
Photo courtesy: Samim Asgor Ali

The only change that I have noticed is that earlier those who sat for competitive examinations would come to me to photocopy UPSC materials, but they would do so surreptitiously, as if committing a crime. Their supervisors would discourage them from spending time on preparing for the UPSC examinations while enjoying a research fellowship or holding on to a hostel room. Now they do it openly because the teachers do not seem to mind any more. Teaching jobs are becoming scarce and the supervisors have lost the moral authority to admonish those who seek alternative employment. These days, students who have obtained their PhD degree from JNU often come to me to enquire if a continuing student would require his/her dissertation copyedited for a small fee. There are no jobs in the market.

I keep my shop open even during the vacations, but for a shorter duration, because the workload gets reduced. Perhaps eight to ten out of twenty MPhil students of the CHS ask for printouts of the drafts of their chapters because their supervisors insist on reading hardcopies. But increasingly a greater number of teachers prefer to make their corrections on the softcopies of the students. Towards the end of the summer vacation, when it is submission time for the students, we have to work hard. At times my assistants and I work through the night. But I do not have binding facilities in my shop and I have to outsource it. Thus the profit margin is not as high as it could have been. Since the CHS did not admit any MPhil student year before last (2017), there will be no submission this year and I will have very little work during the vacation.

Earlier I used to get a lot of work when academic conferences were organized. Nowadays, only the programme and the abstracts of papers are photocopied, not the conference papers. And even then, if it is a well-funded large conference, they get their abstracts and other materials printed rather than photocopied. We do not benefit from the conferences any longer.

As a photostat shop owner at JNU, I have had a few bizarre experiences. Once I received a fantastic proposal from a college teacher from the south who I got to know when he had come for a refresher course in the Academic Staff College of JNU. He was a serious scholar and used to take a lot of photocopied materials from me. He had come during the peak season when the MPhil/PhD submissions were on. He offered me fifty thousand rupees in return for all the MPhil/PhD drafts of that year. Ostensibly he wanted to read these to have a feel of what kind of work was being done. I begged his forgiveness and told him that I could not do that. I would rather retain the trust the students have reposed on me.

Even more shocking was a proposal I once received from a total stranger. He introduced himself as a PhD scholar from a university in Haryana and told me that he was working on aspects of Mauryan economy. He had six months before his registration would expire. He had heard the names of Professor Kunal Chakrabarti and Professor Ranabir Chakravarti of the CHS. He wanted either of them to write the thesis for him. Money was no consideration. I was supposed to liaise with them on his behalf. I told him such proposals are not entertained at JNU. He could try his luck in Ber Sarai where, I had heard, there were takers for such proposals. He told me that someone in Ber Sarai had suggested he approach me. Since both the professors are Bengali and I am a Bengali too, I was supposed to clinch the deal for him. I simply asked him to leave. I did not have the courage to mention this to either of the professors even later.

Many people have asked me whether the changes that I have witnessed at the university in recent years are good for the institution or not. I do not know the answer to this question; I think only time will tell. All that I can say is that I was used to the old ways and was comfortable with them.

V

LIVING AND LOVING

29

RECOLLECTIONS OF JNU

PRABHAT PATNAIK

As I write this, I hear of Namwar Singh's passing away, and am deluged by a flood of memories: G. P. Deshpande, Anil Bhatti, and I, who spent all our evenings together, would drop in on Namwar, and sip tea under a large photograph of Hazari Prasad Dwivedi whom he called his guru. The three of them would talk about Bakhtin; I would only listen. Sometimes Namwar would drop in at GPD's place, or Moonis (then the Rector) would drop in at Anil's, where we would have gathered earlier, for a chat.

The university was a small and sociable place. The authorities were not aloof; they were our friends and acquaintances. (I cannot forget Moonis's tearful speech at the condolence meeting for Ashok Lata Jain, who had been a student leader from CSRD.) One confronted them directly over grievances: if there was no water supply (which often happened), we angrily marched to Moonis's house and he would pacify us with tea and snacks.

But the university was not just full of warmth and conviviality; it was marked by an intense intellectual engagement. A friend of mine, later a Professor at SOAS, London, told me that when he first visited JNU, he was amazed that a place with such intellectual intensity existed anywhere in the world. But this intensity was not just for academic self-promotion; it was motivated by an ideological passion, which, though not identical in its texture for all, can nonetheless be captured, rather broadly, under the rubric of 'anti-imperialism'. The mood of the nation in the wake of the Bangladesh War had been anti-imperialist. Non-alignment was the dominant theme (though Castro's enfolding Indira Gandhi in a warm embrace came a little later, at the Delhi NAM summit); and JNU symbolized this ethos, taking on the dominant Western academic traditions with gusto, which gave it intellectual vigour.

The CHS, led by three eminent Professors: S. Gopal, Romila Thapar and Bipan Chandra (Satish Chandra had left to become the chairman of UGC by the time I joined), and with the support of other scholars like Suvira Jaiswal, R. Champakalakshmi, Sabyasachi Bhattacharya, Brajadulal Chattopadhyaya, and Harbans Mukhia, had made a name for itself with its critique of the Cambridge School, and of the colonial periodization of Indian history, lapped up by the Indian communalists, into the Hindu, Muslim and British periods. The CESP, which had a younger faculty of which I was a member (alongside Sunanda, Anjan, and Utsa), was led by Krishna Bharadwaj and Amit Bhaduri, into producing a critique of neo-classical economics. And much the same was true of other Centres.

Nothing like this had ever happened in any Indian university before. In fact, the trend earlier had been to replicate as faithfully as possible the curricula and syllabi of universities like Oxford and Cambridge, and thereby to create among the students awe about those universities and the metropolis in general; its consequence had been a perennial sense of intellectual inferiority. JNU broke that; and its excellence flowed from this fact.

Notwithstanding other differences, the whole JNU community more or less converged on one issue: the issue of imperialism; and this was most evident on the afternoon of 30 April 1975, the day of the Vietnamese victory against American imperialism, when the Old Campus saw an impromptu demonstration of teachers and students to celebrate that event. That night we congregated on the lawns of the first quadrangle in the New Campus, where K. Seshadri of the CPS regaled us with Makhdoom Mohiuddin's 'Yeh Jung Hai Jung-e-Azadi' at the request of P. C. Joshi, one time General Secretary of the CPI, who was then engaged in a history project that happened to be located at JNU.

There is a pervasive belief that the academic excellence of an institution can be bought with money. Several private universities in the country today are aspiring to achieve excellence by spending large amounts of money. And the government, even as it starves higher education of funds, substituting tenured faculty by temporary teachers who are paid a pittance, devotes crores of rupees to select private and public universities to make them shine. This is a chimera.

Universities starved of funds will languish because the abysmally paid temporary faculty will lack motivation; universities endowed with funds to make them clones of Harvard, Oxford or Cambridge, will also languish because intrinsic to this perception is a sense of inferiority: to imitate another is to accept one's inferiority vis-à-vis that other. And a sense of inferiority produces no excellence.

JNU, instead of imitating, engaged in critiquing the dominant ideas developed in metropolitan institutions. It was imbued with an intellectual passion for doing so; and that was the source of its excellence. There was always a sense that something big was happening here; *not* getting into the top 100 or 200 universities of the country in the *Times Higher Educational Supplement*'s annual list was ironically symptomatic of exactly that. JNU could not care less about *THES*-type rankings.

In fact there was an occasion when some foreign funding agency came to offer money to JNU and a meeting of senior professors was held in the VC's Committee Room along with the potential donors. I was not senior enough to attend it but I have heard from C. P. Bhambhri that several senior professors told the agency that if the people of India wanted JNU to have more money, then they would have made more money available; JNU therefore had simply to make do with whatever they had made available to it.

This sense of being engaged in something big existed even among the students, which is why despite numerous strikes, dharnas, and gheraos, there was never any incident of violence against teachers or the authorities despite teachers and students living cheek by jowl with one another. The students' union had several run-ins with the CHS those days on the question of reservations, accusing it of an 'elitist' bias; but the very students spearheading the agitation, would hold Bipan, Romila, and Sabyasachi in high esteem for their scholarship (I know this for a fact); and scholarship was something which mattered to *everybody*. Likewise, notwithstanding serious differences among teachers, matters never got out of hand; the university continued functioning with a sense of purpose.

Scholarship, not just for academic self-promotion but in the interest of the people, no doubt in some vague sense, was what JNU valued; and G. Parthasarathi used to articulate it explicitly. Whenever new members were recruited to the JNU faculty, GP would make it a point to meet them. I remember one day being told by Romila who had just met GP that he would like to meet Utsa and me. We went along to his office (we were then in the Old Campus). GP, who, to my surprise, had read an article of mine just published in the *EPW*, told us: 'I have no doubt you will make names for yourselves; but always ask what you are doing for the people of the country.'

Despite our living in close proximity with students, and indeed because of it, Utsa and I made it a point not to encourage students to visit us at home. The exception was Holi which was celebrated in the New Campus with great gusto irrespective of religion. Gujiyas and namkeens had to be bought in adequate quantities beforehand for students who would come to visit us at home in several groups. The Bengali students who dominated CESP would make it a point to touch our feet when they dropped in for Holi, despite our best efforts, much to the amusement, and I suspect envy, of Anil Bhatti.

Likewise, Eid was great fun, when one had kababs and sewaiyan at several houses, notably Zoya's, Atiya's and Imrana's (Moonis's leaving the campus to become the Delhi University Vice Chancellor had meant one less house to visit). Imrana and Zoya were close friends. Imrana was our neighbour, and the heroine of a play, Mohit Chattopadhyay's *Barricade,* that GPD had staged for the faculty to soothe nerves after a showdown between students and the administration under B. D. Nag Chaudhury, that had also divided the faculty.

Since the health centre, just set up, was not accessible at all hours, Imrana was the informal physician to the entire campus, having been an AIIMS doctor before joining the CSMCH at JNU, and she cheerfully accepted the demands on her time even at odd hours.

One of the nicest things about living on the campus was the bonding among the campus children. Even though their careers and paths diverged later on, the camaraderie formed among them during their childhood, I have found, survived. And they also came to imbibe, quite spontaneously, the secular, progressive, and democratic ethos of the campus, totally oblivious of any caste or communal differences amongst them.

Before I came to JNU, I had been teaching at the Faculty of Economics and Politics at Cambridge, and had a Fellowship at Clare College. Life there was cushy. By contrast, when I first taught at JNU during the monsoon semester of 1973 on a sabbatical from Cambridge, life here was extremely tough. We got quarters in the Old Campus and help from our old friend Sajni, then at JNU, but the sheer logistics of living were difficult.

A poor crop and the first OPEC-administered oil shock had pushed

V.1. The canteen in the Old Campus, 1978. (Sohail Hashmi [standing], D. Raghunandan, Prabir Purkayastha, Ashok Lata Jain, and C. Raja Mohan [all seated]).
Photo courtesy: Anwar Huda

inflation to 30 per cent (and we had to live only on Utsa's salary). Gas connection was difficult to get (as were telephone connections because of which we used Imrana's telephone for years); so cooking had to be done on a kerosene stove. But kerosene itself was not easy to get. One would suddenly hear that the petrol pump near Priya Cinema had got hold of some kerosene and was selling it. So one had to literally trudge there with a can along a winding footpath, as there was no road link those days and we had no cars anyway.

From the Old Campus where we lived, there was only one bus, 45E, starting at IIT hostel which linked us to the city, but that was so infrequent one hardly bothered to use it. (A minibus to ISBT from IIT hostel via Connaught Place started sometime later). Taxis were available at the IIT hostel but were expensive. One was literally cooped up in a life that was quite miserable in material terms. But the intellectual excitement and vigour of the place more than made up for it.

Vivan Sundaram's painting exhibitions were a source of excitement. Ashok Mitra visited CESP in spring 1975 to give a set of hugely-attended public lectures on his then forthcoming book, *Terms of Trade and Class*

Relations. There were also interesting casual visitors of whom I remember two in particular, the poet Nabarun Bhattacharya, Sudipta's friend, and Hemanga Biswas of IPTA.

There was even a Marx Club whose meetings, though infrequent, were well attended by faculty members, not because they were all Marxists but from intellectual curiosity. I remember Anil Bhatti expounding at one such meeting on how Hegel had put the 'Absolute' in the place of the old Christian notion of God. And there were innumerable lectures and discussions organized by students where political leaders spoke. Raj Narain was one such speaker after the Emergency. The Emergency itself had seen a three-day strike by students, and arrests of several student leaders, including Prabir Purkayastha and the JNUSU President, D. P. Tripathi, who remained incarcerated for months.

For me, the transition from Cambridge became manageable because of the intellectual excitement of JNU and the hope of a revolutionary transformation in India. Such a transformation seemed round the corner not just before the Emergency, but also afterwards. It all appears unbelievable today when the country is in the midst of a veritable social counter-revolution, and JNU itself is fighting for survival. But, as they say, this too shall pass.

30

RESIDING IN JNU

IMRANA QADEER

The JNU campus today is recognized by its red-brick structures scattered amongst the lush greenery and ancient rocks at the end of the Aravalli ranges. For me, however, it all started when one day P. C. Joshi took me to his house where we talked until late at night about what I could possibly do after completing my residency at the All India Institute of Medical Sciences. I was looking for something different and exciting, as the routine research in medical schools did not interest me. PC told me about a new university where research was going to be geared towards contributing to the challenges of building a vision of development grounded in Indian reality. My experience was of institutions that kept back rare and incurable patients for long periods of research and teaching, ignoring the ordinary illnesses that caused the major load of morbidity. Or otherwise, they focused on newsworthy surgeries which, even when successful, ended in deaths of small children as the families were too poor to afford the required care after going home. He convinced me that being a good doctor was not enough. The option of experimenting with a new path was exciting and I found myself facing G. Parathasarathi and Debabar Banerji in a selection committee. I joined the Centre of Social Medicine and Community Health in the School of Social Sciences that was mandated to make health services meaningful for the people of this country and that, over the years, changed the concept of the Hippocratic Oath for me.

The early seventies were stimulating and new for me in every sense. The residences and the university administration, hostels, and the various schools were housed in the blocks of what is today the police academy. Our lives flowed from one block to another without any distinction in the architecture and status. Whatever rules for segregation had been framed generated protest, as students demanded freedom and the recognition of

V.2. Old Campus, 1978. School of Languages was in the building in front, now taken over by the police academy. Next to this were three similar blocks housing all the other Schools as well as some faculty flats and students' rooms.
Photo courtesy: Anwar Huda

their responsible selves. A sensitive administration reached out to discuss and change the rules, keeping every one's comfort in mind. Differences were always handled amicably and the residential issues of the university community were attended to by the Rector Moonis sahib, the Registrar Murthy sahib, and P. N Sharma (the academic coordinator), all of whom lived in our residential block. I remember waking up at midnight on the day I shifted to the campus, with my room on the third floor shaking like a leaf and loud voices calling us to come down. We all rushed down to find a worried Rector herding his brood. The tension dissipated and transformed into laughter and relief when we realized it was not a geological calamity, only a huge plane passing by—a phenomenon that became a part of our lives and forced theatre lovers to innovate and accept suitable pauses in the plays they staged at the open-air theatre near the Parthasarathi Rocks—a space which, like many others, has now been closed.

Murthy sahib and Moonis sahib were two refined human beings whose intellect, warmth, and openness were visible in all their activities. They participated in and supported a wide range of interests, from responsible academics and political thought to music, poetry, cinema, drama,

V.3. The open-air theatre at Parthasarathi Rocks. Until recently, many performances were staged here.
Photo courtesy: Joy L. K. Pachuau

literature, and sports. This gave the young university campus a flavour of diversity, freedom, and responsibility. The campus, though small, had big dreams and beautiful people among the students, faculty, and the staff. The administration was perceived as a partner in a creative experiment of building alternatives to meaningful higher education, not tuned to turnkey programmes of study. It was on the lawns of the Old Campus that the first (and the last) convocation was addressed by Balraj Sahni, the guest of honour. It was Moonis sahib's idea to celebrate Independence Day for the first time on the campus by asking the young son of Gopal (who ran the dhaba near SSS) to unfurl the national flag. We often congregated at Gopal's dhaba to satiate our hunger for dosas and exchange ideas. One cup of chai could hold you for hours, as conversations crossed disciplinary boundaries to address contemporary challenges. Suneet Chopra frequently visited this joint, even after leaving the university, to assure us that revolution was around the corner. Even if that promise has not materialized, his warmth and friendship remains.

This initial tradition of living close to each other and having dialogues, even across balconies and between all hues of thought became a way of life that the campus carried forward when we moved to its new location in the Aravallis. We knew not only colleagues but also their families and having Boudhayan da, Murthy sahib, Atiya, Mahale sahib and his family, Sharma ji and Nasira and their two adorable kids as my immediate neighbours gave me—a person from a small town—the feeling of living in one large family. My sister and brother-in-law, Tahera Hasan and Zia-ul-Hasan and their children, who stayed with me, became a part of this larger family which continued to grow to include GPD (G. P. Deshpande), Kalindi, Utsa, Prabhat, Anil, Heidi, SK (S. K. Rao), and many others. For me, work and living were all mixed up and I was often called to attend to pediatric emergencies and, at times, non-pediatric emergencies. I still remember the day when we had gone to see a film and, as we came out, I found a worried Talageri standing on the stairs of the auditorium waiting to take us home (I had no car then), as his little daughter was not well and it was too late to take her anywhere. Many of my colleagues sympathized with me for having left the practice of pediatrics and were not convinced that I could be happy. It must be granted however that these demands helped me transition from a life where one is constantly handling disease and death to one from where you can see how the system never works to root out ill health.

The departments shifted first to the New Campus, so we used to commute from our residences to the departments crossing the field where the Central School stands today. Finally, we were allotted our respective residences as well. That was a memorable experience. As we were packing to move to 117 Uttarakhand, a young boy came with a slip of a paper given to him by the students of JNU (who had been arrested and kept in Tihar jail during the Emergency). Put in jail for petty theft and allotted to them as a cook, he spent some months in their company and learned not only to read and draw but also about the unjust world he lived in. When freed, he had nowhere to go, so he was given the address of JNU. Armed with a list of names of faculty members who could be of use to him, he knocked on my door. Without hesitation, he was adopted and put to work handling the daunting task of shifting. He stayed with us and taught us a lot about the life of those living at the margins and in jail. He had perfected various skills, so losing a key was never a problem since Bir could undo the lock or climb the wall to open the door from inside. He was so convinced of the coming of the promised revolution that he would make it a point to attend political meetings of the students. Over time, he opened his own dhaba which became one of the popular joints in the New Campus—one life that was transformed by the sheer force of dreaming.

Those spacious houses of the New Campus were wonderful but located in a totally barren terrain among impressive rocks. The university helped by putting truckloads of earth into depressions meant to be our lawns and all of us busied ourselves with planting saplings in our free time. Banyan, peepul, mango, lemon, sheoli, bougainvillea, champa, neem, gulmohar, laburnum, and jacaranda were my favourites; others had their own choices; and in ten years the campus could barely be recognized. Moonis Raza was responsible for choosing bougainvillea as the signature flowering bush for JNU as it did not need much water; his resolve not to interfere with the wilderness and let the natural shrubs, the kikar trees and the terrain remain as it was, paid dividends and gave JNU its riot of colours. The campus acquired yet another type of diversity in its natural resources, which was a heaven to grow up in for the children who were lucky to be born and nurtured on the campus. It was safe for them to explore the wilderness and see and learn about the plants, the water bodies and the wildlife—nilgai, deer, foxes, rabbits, ant eaters, snakes and mongooses together with the civet cats who often visited our houses. The campus was a bird watcher's delight and a home to almost all varieties of birds of North India who visited it at one time or the other. Very often we discovered new things on the JNU campus through the explorations of our children. There was one wild, inconsequential bush that flowered in the summer, its small white flowers filling the air with their exhilarating scent. To me, that heady smell is strongly associated with the memory of JNU campus—a campus which has gradually been manicured into straitjacket order: broad motorable roads, manicured lawns, and iron railings to protect the administration. I hope that flowering bush continues to grow and spread its rich scent.

My small-town habits were preserved by the privilege of having Atiya and Habib, and Utsa, and Prabhat in the same residential quadrangle, from whom I could always borrow a cup of sugar or a bit of curd to set my own. There were no time limits as work meant being a teacher and a student, together learning the value of social sciences in meeting the challenges of public health. To have a community of supportive neighbours was therefore a privilege. The campus was designed for close living of the faculty, staff and the students. Often my PhD students, who needed to spread their papers and were short of space, came home to occupy some corner of the large living space and became part of the disorder of my house. This architectural imagination provided enough opportunities for participation in activities—cultural, political or social. The collective celebration of Holi, Eid, the post-dinner debates in the hostels, and the resistance put up during the Emergency by the students and supported by a significant number of teachers was possible because of this close relationship between different sections of the university community.

This bonhomie however got a jolt in 1983 when a protest turned violent, shattering not just the window panes of the very residences that we thought we were safe behind, but also some of our confidence. It led to a sine die suspension of classes and a prolonged period of gloom and rethinking beyond debate and dialogue about the essentials of building trust and re-establishing roles, responsibilities and communication. The 1984 anti-Sikh violence in Delhi saw the campus revitalizing its collective spirit and the residents (all sections of the JNU community) were not only actively engaged in protecting their own campus but also reached out to families and engaged in relief work. I remember Professor Phadnis of the School of International Studies drove alone to rescue a family from an unsafe locality, hiding them in her van, and bringing them to her residence where they could feel safe and cared for. The Bhopal gas tragedy in the same year, and the destruction of Babri Masjid in 1992, continued to teach the residents to reach out and to remember that violence is not a resolution of problems, but relating and sharing ideas and differences is. Living in JNU with that small shrub of white flowers whose smell intoxicated me, but whose name I did not know, was just the opposite of my present; now I live in the real world of this largest democracy whose name I know but the exuberance is missing.

31

TWO VIEWS OF THE PERIYAR HOSTEL

KUNAL CHAKRABARTI

I

Rudrangshu Mukherjee, my friend and classmate from Presidency College, Kolkata, and I entered the Periyar hostel for the first time on an August afternoon in 1974. One wing of the hostel was still not officially handed over to the university, and we were made to enter through the backdoor into Room 005. Rudrangshu moved to another room the next semester, and I had 005 to myself for the remainder of my MA days. Yes, in that golden period, even MA students were allotted single rooms. The room was sufficiently large, with a bed, a small study table and a chair, a bookcase, and a cupboard—all that a student would require. There was a balcony to the east and a long spacious corridor to the west. When my father came to visit me that October, he looked at the room and at the palm trees outside swaying in the wind, nodded disapprovingly and said, 'too good'.

Our entry into the hostel was, however, completely unceremonious. When the warden ushered us into the room we discovered that it had only one bed. We required another and were told that there was a spare one on the third floor. There was no caretaker or any other help in sight. After some hesitation, we brought it down ourselves. Nobody noticed that two new residents had moved in. We found our way to the mess, ate dinner, made our beds and turned in. This may appear surprising in view of the horrific stories one hears and reads in the newspapers about ragging of new entrants to educational institutions and hostels. We were not ragged; as a matter of fact, we were completely ignored. I must say I prefer indifference any day to ragging, a cowardly sadistic act that, in extreme cases, even takes lives. There are more civilized ways of being friends. JNU has an extremely good track record in this regard—when I was a warden, I did not receive a single complaint of ragging from a resident.

V.4. Periyar Hostel, 1977. One of the three hostels to come up in the first phase of JNU campus development
Photo courtesy: Antony Thomas

But, of course, there can be no unalloyed happiness. The mess food was not to my liking. Obviously, I did not expect home-cooked comfort food in the hostel, but neither could I anticipate that north Indian food would be so disagreeable to my Bengali palate. An oily concoction of onion, garlic, and tomato paste was put into every dish. Some vegetables were unfamiliar to me, and I took an instant dislike to tinda and arbi. Breakfast was the best meal of the day because there was little to cook in bread and butter, egg and half a glass of milk. The variety in the mess food that I hear about nowadays was unheard of in our times. But the food was hot and adequate in quantity. I gradually got used to it and, during my five years at JNU hostels, I never suffered from stomach ailments. The mess bill in the mid-seventies did not exceed Rs 120 a month which came to a little over one rupee per meal. I later wondered how the food could be any better for the money that we paid.

During my MPhil, I shifted to the brand new Sutlej hostel, and I was one of its first inmates. My three years in Sutlej were as uneventful as my stay in Periyar. A lot was happening in the outside world—the Emergency years, for instance—that deeply impacted the student community, but the hostel moved in its own tranquil rhythm, except for one or two stray incidents. The wardens were faculty members and occupied the four corners of the hostel; an occasional meeting with them was unavoidable. In Periyar, I lived in a room adjacent to a warden's quarters. On a summer day our door was open, and Rudrangshu and I were laughing uproariously over a joke. The warden, a gentle and soft-spoken person, was passing by. He peeped in and asked if he could join in the mirth. We welcomed him warmly. He smiled and moved on. I remember this insignificant incident so vividly possibly because this was my only encounter with a warden during my entire stay in the JNU hostels. I was inducted into the faculty in early 1979 and moved out of Sutlej immediately after.

II

I joined as a warden of the Periyar hostel in January 1982 and was immediately thrown into the deep end of the pool. I was made the Mess Warden, the most difficult of the four 'portfolios' (that is what it was actually called). I was out of touch with the JNU hostels for three years and soon discovered that things had worsened. Residents' dissatisfaction with the quality of mess food had grown sharper. The mess managers were clearly less than competent and indifferent to their duties. The cooks were no culinary experts. A seemingly new problem was the increasing number of defaulters who did not pay their dues but continued to eat in the mess. The infrastructure was provided and the workers' salaries were paid by the university, and the messes were to run on a no-profit-no-loss basis. The non-payment of dues created pressure on the limited resources, and often daily necessities, such as rice and dal, had to be purchased in small quantities. This was hardly the state of affairs in which the functioning of the mess could improve.

We smarted under the tag, but technically the students were correct in viewing us as representatives of the 'authorities'. However, there was little a warden could do to solve the mess problems. As a warden who was a student just a few years back, I was caught in a dilemma. How could I perform the duties as a warden yet be sensitive to the problems of students? I was supposed to check defaulters eating in the mess, persuade them to pay up, ensure that unpaid balances did not accumulate. But I was aware that many students came to study at JNU against parental wishes, and had no financial support from the family. I was aware too that a large number of students did not have the money to pay the mess dues—even though it was not exorbitant. JNU had already created an intellectual culture where social justice and equity were valued ideals. The admission policy, with its innovative use of deprivation points, enabled the underprivileged to study at JNU. Since the scholarship was not adequate to pay for all expenses, many had to borrow from those who could afford to lend. Perhaps the use of the term 'loan' would be incorrect in this context. For it was almost taken for granted that the needy could not repay back. When loans mounted and the sources dried up, students could not easily pay hostel dues. In this situation, how could a warden possibly solve the problem of unpaid bills? What was necessary was larger scholarships, and increased state support for education. Not surprisingly, even the students who regularly paid their dues did not support the wardens' initiative to make the defaulters pay. They empathized with the problem their friends faced, and were unwilling to break students' solidarity.

Students inevitably protested against high hostel dues, and demanded increase of scholarship money. As a warden, the symbol of administrative authority in the hostel, I often felt the heat of demonstrating students. How could I not? After all I had chosen to be a warden. No one forced me. One gain from this perennially stressful situation was that many of the leaders of these demonstrations later became my friends. They were usually gentle, polite, and amenable to reason when individually spoken to, and I often engaged them in conversation. A leader of the first demonstration I had faced finished his PhD and was going to the US on a postdoctoral fellowship. In the rush of things he could not meet me earlier, but made it a point to say goodbye to me before leaving for the airport. He was not obliged to do so, and I was touched. In fact, the students also knew that the wardens could do very little. All that students wanted was a sympathetic ear to their often justified demands, and I lent them one, being always open to dialogue. Another student, a bright, lanky fellow from the life sciences, always assumed a militant posture and would tell us that unless steps were taken to remedy the situation, things would blow up. I developed a genuine fondness for him. He completed his PhD and moved out. Some years later, I ran into him, and he informed me that he was teaching in a university and was the warden of a hostel. I could not resist the temptation of asking him what steps he was taking to solve all the students' problems, and prevent things from blowing up.

There were a few other issues as well. By the early 1980s, the ground-floor rooms had become double-seaters. Thus the number of residents increased, but the infrastructure remained the same. Back then, water was supplied to the hostels three times a day. By the time I was a warden, the mid-day supply was stopped, and the hostels received water for about an hour and a half in the morning and evening. Understandably, the cleanliness of the toilets and the mess utensils left much to be desired.

This could not go on for long, and the crisis came in 1983. It began with a demonstration against a warden of the Jhelum hostel, and soon took an unfortunate turn. Some window panes of wardens' houses were pelted and the Vice Chancellor was gheraoed. On the third day, the police lifted the gherao and arrested hundreds of students. Many of them stayed in Tihar jail for a fortnight, and cases were lodged against them.

The university felt that the hostels needed large-scale reform. The academic life of the university continued to function, but fresh admission of students into the university was suspended for a year, and committees were set up to look into the problem and frame new hostel rules. However, this did not mean that the hostels became completely trouble-free and that there was no further cause for complaint on either side. The authorities issued instructions from time to time that appeared unreasonable to students and, on occasion, even to me. When we were students, at first there was no restriction on the entry of girls into boys' hostels. After a few years, we were told that girls could only enter until ten o'clock at night. I remember that one faculty member laughed and said that he failed to understand why the authorities believed that certain biological functions could be performed only at night. I repeatedly told my superiors that JNU was a postgraduate university, the students were all adults and we should not assume the role of their moral guardians. Besides, there were many points of entry into each hostel and this rule could not be effectively implemented. But the authorities stuck to their position. Therefore, roughly once every two months, the wardens had to conduct 'raids' under the observing eye of the provost. Most of us were unwilling, but we had no option as wardens. Some provosts, however, clearly relished their job. Once, we reported to the provost, who was standing in the courtyard to prevent escapes through the main gate, that we did not find any girl or unauthorized guest in any of the rooms. He was deeply disappointed and said, 'ek bhi shikar nahi mila?' Decades later, I still retain my sense of shock as the words keep ringing in my ears.

In our times, wardenship was a trying job. (It may still be so.) The students were politically sensitive and the authorities demanding. We were not allowed leave for more than three months at a time, and only once in the tenure. Thus, during the first fifteen years of my career, I could not take up a fellowship or go abroad for an extended period of time. We felt genuinely constrained. While the Poorvanchal flats were constructed, I went to the site once every month to check their progress. Finally, with a huge sigh of relief, I gained my freedom. But I discovered soon after that this freedom, like so many others of its kind, was short-term and elusive.

32

SABARMATI HOSTEL

Z. BHATIA NÉE HAUHNAR

The Sabarmati hostel at JNU had a tumultuous beginning. The east wing of the hostel was constructed in the early 1990s and its first occupants were female students. A year later, the west wing was completed and the male students moved in. The mess fees suddenly shot up and the women protested about having to shell out another two to three hundred rupees, a considerable sum of money twenty-five years ago. Men eat more, and we have to pay—was their complaint.

The protests had hardly died down when a male resident was seen looking at the east wing with a pair of binoculars! He claimed he was 'just looking at things' but the women were livid. One evening, a dozen or so women met in one of the rooms, hurriedly chalked out a plan, called the other women to join them, and then marched down to the dining hall. A GBM was hastily organized and the man with the binoculars, whose leg was in a plaster cast, was carried in.

There were angry raised voices, accusations, counter-accusations, discussions on the culture of voyeurism—and all the signs of an energetic healthy democracy. When one of the women was shouted down by the men, LP, a six-foot-tall Czech student banged her fist on the table and shouted 'Let her to speak!' And so, they let her speak.

It is in the everyday life of the hostels that embedded ideas and prejudices are most visible. It is here that entrenched attitudes and practices of students—voyeurism, sexism, misogyny, male chauvinism, homophobia, casteism, racism—are collectively debated and negotiated, new selves constituted. While most students change radically over the years, it takes time to refashion oneself. And often, in the meantime, the social prejudices we share, and the stereotypes we operate with, can cause enormous individual damage and collective suffering. In a socially diverse and culturally heterogeneous space like JNU, hostels frequently are the sites where the trauma of cultural confrontation is often experienced.

The saddest incident in my life in Sabarmati hostel involved a Sudanese student called Gift Warille. He was a big friendly fellow, who always had a huge smile on his face. He was quite a proficient Bharatanatyam dancer and had even given performances at an embassy or two. One day he found a paper filled with racist and sexual expletives pinned on his door. Deeply affected, Gift had a mental breakdown. His friends and teachers tried to help him—listening and talking to him, empathising with his feelings, affirming their concern and friendship; but eventually Gift had to be admitted to the psychiatric wing of Safdarjung hospital. At that time, in the early 1990s, Sudan was witnessing immense political upheaval and this must have weighed heavily on Gift's mind. Life on JNU campus in India must have brought him some peace, until this ugly incident took place.

Even at JNU the battle against embedded racist ideas has never been as strong as the fight against casteism and sexism. Perhaps no one recognises racism as a major issue, perhaps everyone feels there are bigger battles to wage. As the incident revealed, these are flawed notions. Racist ideas are deeply ingrained within the collective consciousness of a large section of Indians. JNU community cannot afford to ignore this fact.

V.5. Sabarmati Hostel. Girls and boys stay in the same hostel in two separate wings. *Photo courtesy: Samim Asgor Ali*

While preparing this short piece, I searched the internet for 'Gift Warille' and this is what I found on a website:

> Gift Matayo Warille, a southern Sudanese student recently returned from India, was arrested on 1 January 1995 in Khartoum. As far as his family was concerned he simply 'disappeared'. In May 1995 he was found in a military barrack in Khartoum. Torture had paralysed the right side of his body. Within a month he was dead. His family was not even officially told of his arrest, let alone his death. His crime: attending a public meeting addressed by SPLA leader John Garang de Mabior while overseas.[1]

This paragraph was part of a long report by Amnesty International that recounted horrific tales of human rights violations in Sudan: the systematic persecution of young people who dared to be political. Many were regularly beaten up, tortured, maimed and killed for attending political meetings. For their families: they 'disappear'.

The chilling lines of the Amnesty report made me remember Gift Warille with immense sadness. I wish we could have made him feel at home at JNU, and protected him from the violence the young students were facing in Sudan. In India, at least, such violence is not part of the experience of the young.

As I read the proof of the typeset essay, I am no longer sure of the last line. After 5 January 2020, Sabarmati Hostel has acquired a new image in the public imagination.

[1]Amnesty International, *Progress or Public Relations?*, 29 May 1996, AFR/54/06/96, available at <https://www.refworld.org/docid/3ae6a9b58.html> [accessed: 10 February 2020].

33

THE HEAT OF A THOUSAND SUNS: JNU IN THE LATE SEVENTIES

MUKUL MANGALIK

'I am damned critical—for it's the only thing to be, and all else is damned humbug.'—Henry James, in a letter dated 19 July 1909.

Summer, in the late 1970s, would hit JNU with ruthless intensity. Rocks would spit fire, the uneven path connecting the 'up' and 'down' campuses would feel like a string of blazing bricks, the red-brick hostel buildings appearing like six tongues of flame leaping into the sky through swirls of heat and dust. We thirsted for water, for greenery, for shade in that scorched landscape of burning boulders and stony outcrops, but all we got were tantalizing mirages. Nothing, it seemed, could survive the summer heat; everything, we felt, would be laid to waste. And yet we stayed, and in staying, we thrived.

1

Summer upon summer break we stayed back because we simply could not bear to tear ourselves away from burning in the heat of another furnace, the heat and glare from a thousand suns. This was unique to JNU, making the scorching summer feel almost cool in comparison. Flames leapt up, sparks flew, there was crackle and boom, but no scorched undergrowth, or wood-ash. Instead, without a hint of personal or abusive thrusts, intimidation or violence, ideas crackled, brains sparked, arguments flew, graffiti flashed, and questions exploded—questions about everything that had been taken for granted and considered 'natural', everything that was not meant to be questioned because to ask 'why' would have been either embarrassing or sacrilegious.

It was as if Diderot and Voltaire had descended amongst us, daring us to take risks and know: 'Everything must be examined, everything must

V.6. Ganga Dhaba at night. This fabled site—where students chat, discuss, and commune over cups of hot tea—has acquired an iconic status among the young of Delhi.
Photo courtesy: Samim Asgor Ali

be shaken up, without exception and without circumspection'. It was as if Simon Rodriguez, teacher to Simon Bolivar was in our midst—personified in teachers and students alike—with his exhortations, 'Instruction is not education.... To order recital from memory of what is not understood, is to make parrots.... If you accustom students always to see reason...they miss it when they do not see it, and ask for it, saying, 'Why?'.... They learn to obey reason, not authority like limited people, nor custom like stupid people.'

From books and articles to films, everything under the sun was avidly devoured and discussed in exhaustive detail. Often, just a phrase or a single word could become the reason for brainstorming inside classrooms and outside, along walks under starlit skies or in groups collected outside the library or at the dhabas, in tutorial discussions, study circles, pamphlets at breakfast, or at intellectually and politically charged post-dinner public meetings, our unforgettable 9.30 p.m. dates with hostel messes at JNU.

Eloquence erupted. Ideas grew luxuriantly in sharp arguments between people, seducing minds, and igniting passions. Colours, figures, and slogans rioted on walls in stunning poster art that announced, with grand flourish, neither the '68 protesters in France nor the grand trio of Mexican muralists, Diego Rivera, David Alfaro Siqueiros, and José

Clemente Orozco, would be forgotten.

Elections to the students' union were classroom, library, tutorial discussions, and theatre rolled into one, intense exercises in participatory democracy, and open invitations to public lessons in economics, history, political science, and sociology. Annual feasts of informed, high voltage oratory and debates, election campaigns compelled students and teachers to think seriously as much about everyday material concerns on campus, as about wider problems of exploitation, inequality, humiliation, injustice, and authoritarianism, in the past and in the present. They forced us to think of the many ways in which inegalitarian practices seep into societies, threatening to overwhelm civil liberties and human rights. They forced us to understand that a threat to freedom and rights anywhere was a threat to freedom and rights everywhere; that the notion of anything being 'apolitical' was a complete illusion, and that individual and collective struggles were absolutely central to the preservation of rights to freedom.

Syllabi, reading lists, and lectures—whether the L-3 tornadoes or the regular classroom ones—were like gusts of fresh air blowing through the dusty corridors of academic and political orthodoxies—including most of all, Left orthodoxies—loosening up hierarchies between teachers and students, teaching us the value of reading, writing, thinking, and speaking *critically*, independently, thoughtfully, fearlessly, and as equals, *about everything*, introducing us to the rigorous ways of reasoned critique, acquainting us with questions of disciplinary methods and challenging us to pose new questions and break new ground. Rigid boundaries were dissolved, as much between disciplines as between the classroom and the outside. Each flowed and fed into the other, this porosity allowing for a richness and depth of understanding that brought with it a profound sense of emancipation.

The ground shook beneath our feet. Everything that had seemed permanent, melted, appearing suddenly to be vulnerable and malleable. Old certainties came crashing down. It felt simultaneously frightening and exciting to experience freedom emancipating itself from the clutches of fear, turning our lives upside down, opening up hitherto unimagined possibilities for ways of living and for imbuing our lives with inspired meaning and fresh purpose. JNU rocked to the music born of the heat of its 'incredible furnace' and the reverberations were felt across the country. Radith Geismar could well have been speaking of JNU while remembering May 1968 in France: 'The real sense of '68 was a tremendous sense of liberation...of people talking.... It was much more than throwing stones.... A whole system...of authority and tradition was swept away. Much of the freedom of today began in '68.'

This freedom demanded, in turn, that JNU remain self-critical, committed to principles but open to reframing intellectual concerns and to re-inventing itself, a demand to which JNU *continues to respond splendidly.*

2

Contours softened as the sun set on each passing day. At twilight, the Parthasarathi plateau, that intoxicating mélange of ancient rock and babool, made for love if ever there was such a place, from where the eye could range over all of Delhi, and which, on a misty winter's night could well appear to a stoned imagination to be floating atop the waters of the Tethys Sea, would don mellow colours. *Yet* JNU shone with greatest intensity after dark. Nights were darker here than perhaps over any other part of the city, but like the heat of the furnace, the stark darkness of the nights, far from being scary, drew us in, urging us to reach for the star-spangled sky.

This was when freedom reigned in as absolute a measure as possible, when the stars we were reaching for, seemed to descend into, and illuminate our own beings. JNU poured out of hostel rooms, demonstrated, held hands, courted, fell in love and walked into the dawn. Shanney Naqvi, JNU's beloved 'wandering minstrel', sang at all times of day, but it was at night that his singing and full-throated, uninhibited laughter, like the music from Louis Armstrong's trumpet, stretched out and out, *incredibly*, to greet infinity. It could hardly have been otherwise. The night after all, was when, with minds keener and hearts more open, with rebellion and radicalism—in the sense of questioning and seeking to understand by getting to the root of things—at their most intense, we were willing to give and receive like we could never have done during any other time of day.

It was no less incredible that the darkness as much as JNU's extraordinary furnace were kept alight by the passions and intellectual energies of the small number of teachers and students that constituted JNU at that time. They came from all over the land, each student marked by distinct or shared histories of privilege, deprivation, marginalization, and struggles. Speaking languages, talking of things, inventing slogans, reciting poetry, and singing songs that none had heard before, they found themselves—in rivalry and in love, in the thirst for knowledge and in the throes of despair, in anger and meanness but also in generosity and solidarity—thrown together in a university that was trying to put down roots in inhospitable terrain, *but* at a time that 'comes but rarely in history'.

For all its inner contradictions and limitations, it was a time when hope came easy. It was a time when, to be a realist meant demanding the impossible by imagining 'all the people sharing all the world', by striving to move *beyond* political equality towards a world in which 'all belongs to all', by struggling to create a world not only free of want and inequality, but also of alienation, so that human beings, *freed from objectification and their immediate identities*, might begin to feel themselves 'at home' at work as much as outside it, 'glorious things', in the words of Rohith Vemula, 'made up of stardust'. It was a time when:

> Bliss was it in that dawn to be alive,
> But to be young was very heaven!
> When Reason seemed the most to assert her rights...
> Not in Utopia...
> But in...the world
> Of all of us...!

3

'A University', Nehru had hoped, would stand 'for humanism, for tolerance, for reason, for the adventure of ideas and the search for truth...for the onward march of the human race toward ever higher objectives.' The Kothari Commission Report, 1966, had envisioned 'the pursuit of truth and excellence in all its diversity' as being the true concern of universities, a pursuit that, according to the earlier Radhakrishnan Report, in turn requires 'an atmosphere of freedom' in which 'teachers...be as free to speak on controversial issues as any other citizens of a free country'. The Kothari Commission Report was equally clear that 'universities are pre-eminently the forum for a critical assessment of society—sympathetic, objective, unafraid' whose 'business is not primarily to give society what it *wants* but what it *needs*.... It is not a community service station, passively responding to popular demands and thereby endangering its intellectual integrity. Nor is it an ivory tower into which students and teachers can withdraw...accepting no responsibility for the improvement of society. It has to maintain an ambivalent position, balancing itself carefully between commitment and detachment—commitment in action, detachment in thought.'

Born at a rare historical conjuncture, it was perhaps not altogether surprising, though nonetheless amazing, that JNU, more than any other university, came to embody these ideals in all their fullness, as it did Gandhi's idea of knowledge as freedom, Aurobindo's idea of knowledge as a search for a greater truth, and Tagore's understanding of knowledge as a process of realization. It was these ideals that had allowed the three thinkers to dream of universities as institutions that could help people transcend the boundaries of nations, make the universe their true concern, and cultivate sensibilities free of any shades of otherness.

It was equally remarkable that true to the iconoclasm and critical commentary, the distinctive hallmark of any university, JNU, while staying clear of deification or purely symbolic representation, embraced the substance of these visions. It combined them, in course of time, with Ambedkar's pitch for not just creating physical space for those whom Indian knowledge systems never accepted in the past, but, as G. N. Devy puts it, '[for] making their life experiences, their dreams and aspirations the substance of education.' It transformed Gandhi, Aurobindo, Tagore, Nehru, Radhakrishnan, Kothari, and Ambedkar into living breathing entities, allowing us an electrifying brush with the incomplete, tentative, irresistible textures of a peoples' university in the making.

4

'Anyone who hasn't been in the Chilean forest doesn't know this planet. I have come out of that landscape, that mud, that silence, to roam, to go singing through the world.' Anyone who has been touched by it could so easily say of JNU what Neruda wrote about the Chilean forest. This perhaps is the reason why the ruthless siege of JNU that began in 2016, also gave birth to the magnificent struggle that students and teachers, drawing upon the invaluable energy from JNU's furnace of a thousand suns, continue to wage to this day. They have in fact, done much more than simply defend their university.

This is a history that nobody can snatch from them. It is for us now, those who are no longer at JNU, to take inspiration from this, remember afresh the heat and nights of JNU, continue to 'Stand With JNU' and wherever we happen to be, to keep 'asking questions...and walking to the left where the heart resides'.

Like Majaz's 'Nazr-e-Aligarh', this can be *our* tribute to JNU, among the finest tributes that anyone might offer to any university.

34

AFTER THE PLAGUE, THE PARIS COMMUNE OF PEACOCKS

AMIT SENGUPTA

'*On the shore of a dead river, a frog is dancing on the head of a snake...*'—an old Baul song

This winter did not remind me of JNU. It did not fill me with longing for my Old Campus which comes back to me like black-and-white cinema in slow motion: the sensuous fog in the twilight zones of street lamps moving into an eternity of desire. The presence and absence of love. The slow unfolding of nocturnal insomnia, with a postcard pushed inside the little red letterbox outside Kamal Complex opposite Sutlej Hostel. A post-midnight letter to an unknown lover. Or, perhaps, to a patient, humble, peasant mother in a distant village, waiting for her son to return by the first train in summer.

This winter in Delhi reminded me of *The Plague* by Albert Camus. The enclosed town plagued and trapped within a fatal epidemic, the metaphor of fascism as an inevitable and slow holocaust, and the looming landmarks and milestones like the freedom of choices people stare at. Only survivors will live to tell the tale of this tragic and brave magical realist story. Only those who fight back and don't run away must find redemption. Only those who walked the by-lanes of death and dying will find the first glimpse of life.

It also reminded me of a hand-written poster drawn by a first-year MA student in CPS/SSS after sine die was declared at JNU in the turbulent summer of 1983. We had returned from Tihar Jail to the campus under siege. The hostels and streets were empty. The students had been forced to vacate. The poster said: *Where do we go from here?*

This summer, where do we go from here, as we remember the by-lanes and lanes of JNU where we walked in our Hawai chappals with such freedom and passion, our faded cotton shirts blowing in the wind, our jholas full of idealism and dreams?

Indeed, this was an Indian winter in 2019 that rewrote the epical return of the epidemic. I can't think or write about JNU as memory without this darkness at noon stalking my political unconscious. The slow, vicious, soul-shattering illness which stalked the land and the landscape, ravaged the body and mind, hiding in crevices in this dry, infinite cold like a concealed epidemic which would come back and again even when we all thought, oh, now it seems to be going! It does not. It will not. It is relentless, and it is deathly. It is the plague.

The plague of fascism looms, inside and outside the classroom, while walking the streets, on television and social media, and across footpaths. It is in text, word, violence, imprisonment, image, silences, syllabus, and sedition—tacit and deliberate, open and transparent. Mass phobia becomes patriotism, jingoism is collective catharsis, mob-lynching is instant justice, a clear message and a public spectacle of organized polarization, and the doublespeak of ultra-nationalism and hate politics is war. You just can't escape it.

To be romantic is to be radical, we used to believe at JNU. Now, we struggle with both romance and radicalism, as waves of counter-cultures and protracted struggles by the students, teachers, and sections of the alumni return to the streets, on the campus and across the barricades, even as the repressive machinery moves, unrepentant and relentless, and the tyranny of mediocrity rules supreme. This winter, it was a monster and his barbarians who stalked the land—like a grotesque horror film. Hence, the birds sounded blue and the blues became icy with disgust, and hate was so tangible that you could touch it with your hand, like a knife cutting a slab of ice.

This is like a pamphlet of passion which we wrote in our fantasies of student days at JNU, walking in the eternal nights of the campus between ancient rocks and trees, reading Pablo Neruda.

On the rocks near Godavari Hostel, after midnight, a young couple is hanging out. Winter, 1989–90. I walk by. They are shy. I stop by. I tell them, there are twenty demands we have inherited from the earlier students' unions. We will fight for them. However, we have already fulfilled one demand: the right to love. The campus is open and free for lovers—this is a students' union decision.

Next day, the story flies like wildfire. The JNUSU President has declared at midnight on a street that lovers are free on the campus. No restrictions, no fines, no searchlights, no double-locks, no ban on entries, no ban on free movement, no searches in the hostels, no fear or threat.

The JNU Students' Union of 1989 was led by a collective front called Solidarity. The name was inspired from 'Solidarnosc' which led the Gdansk Shipyard Uprising against the military dictatorship in Poland, then backed by Soviet Russia. Solidarity comprised of independents, socialists, radical left and liberal free thinkers. It was born from the protests on the campus against the Tiananmen Square massacre in Beijing, June 1989. The Solidarity-led union was based on the non-dogmatic principles of learning and unlearning, total and transparent democracy, the union as a living stream of consciousness comprising all students—elected or not elected, the union as not the leader but a catalyst, a participant, a cathartic moment of continuous revelation. It also stood for universal justice, freedom, socialism, non-violence and against oppression and exploitation across caste, religion and gender.

That is why we succeeded in creating a campus where free movement of men and women in hostels and messes became a priority, and also managed to turn the library into our main scaffolding of collective consciousness, getting the exorbitant fines reduced for late return of books, including new editions in social sciences and literature, getting the science

V.7. Parthasarathi Rocks: a view from below.
Photo courtesy: Joy L. K. Pachuau

V.8. Picnic at Parthasarathi Rocks. From the late 1970s this has been a place to which students escape—to socialize, romance, meditate.
Photo courtesy: Cherian Samuel

schools involved in both politics and in understanding knowledge systems, and ushering in a realm of free debate and discussion.

The JNUSU organized a three-day seminar at the School of Social Sciences auditorium on 'Marxism and Freedom', even while the Soviet Union and East Europe were breaking up. Professor Sudipta Kaviraj spoke on Euro-Communism and Freedom in East Europe. We pushed up the SC/ST quota of reservation in admission from an abjectly low percentage to the maximum possible. We aligned with ecological people's movements across India—from the Narmada Bachao Andolan to the Gandhian anti-dam struggle in Tehri Garhwal, Uttarakhand. We walked from Gangotri to Rishikesh for the preservation of 'jal, jungle, zameen'. We fought for the dignity of the construction workers at JNU, organizing ration cards, voting rights and health camps for them and their children. When they were not paid, we went to the labour court and fought their cases. From Bolivia to Beijing, we joined in solidarity struggles with people fighting for justice all over the world.

Most crucially, this highly popular Union, resigned in support of affirmative action and the historic Mandal Commission report. We also affirmed that reservations should be aligned with land reforms for the landless, the right to education and work, and scholarships for Dalits, OBCs, Adivasis, minorities and women, among other radical reforms. We were the first Union to come out in total support of reservations and the Mandal Commission. Our stand was later vindicated by the Supreme Court, and Indian politics changed forever.

Indeed, JNU is eternal. It is eternal in its quest for social justice and the liberation of the mind. They can try to bring in tanks, but JNU will never be defeated. It will fight with the wings of desire and defiance. It has not succumbed in the past and it will never succumb in the future.

Life is like this only at JNU. It was always like this. Its golden periods are etched on its walls, rocks, classrooms and corridors. They reverberate in the calls of longing of the 'Paris Commune of Peacocks' in its forests. Behind young eyes and fingers, and inside clenched fists.

In the ideas which bloomed here once like one hundred flowers, JNU will live and outlive itself in its dogged resistance, in the brilliant graffiti, in the revolutionary slogans and songs, in the unity of beauty and rebellion, in the synthesis of theory and praxis, in the books and the placards, in solidarity against injustice, and in the by-lanes of this great zone of possibilities. The zigzag journey of knowledge, love and liberation, which is its destiny—is JNU.

35

MAIN SARAK SE AAYA THA*

LATEEF

I came to JNU in 1992. My family lived in Kasba Mafiat, a small village in Sultanpur, Uttar Pradesh. My father was a labourer, who usually drove tractors for village landlords. We were eight brothers and a sister. All eleven of us lived in a mud hut about 10' x 10'. There was a pond next to the hut. During the rain, water entered the hut. Living was tough and we could not meet the expenses of the family. So in 1990, when I was nine, I began to work in a hotel near home for Rs 70 a month. After working there for some months, I began looking for other jobs, to earn a little more. My brother-in-law (jija-ji) took me to Lucknow, where I got a job in a biscuit factory in Phoolbagh, Hazrat Ganj. That was 1991. I began to get Rs 150 as salary. I worked there for a year and a half. Then in early 1993, my jija-ji got me to Delhi. His son, my cousin, Shafiq Ahmed, used to work with Mr Rao at JNU.

Mr Rao agreed to pay me Rs 300. I was delighted since this was double of what I earned at that time. I agreed to work for Mr Rao. But he got into trouble for hiring me. Employing anyone below eighteen years of age was illegal, and I was only eleven years old. He had to pay a penalty to the university. Mr Rao did not dismiss me from service but transferred me to a small canteen next to the SBI office in the Old Campus. I kept working there for several years. My salary increased from 300 to 400 and then slowly to 1,200. In 1996, he refused to increase my salary any further. I told him that I could not possibly live on the salary I was getting and would have to leave. Then he agreed to an increase. When I was eighteen, I started working in SSS-I. Initially I used to wash plates and utensils; later I did room service, taking tea, coffee, and food to the faculty rooms. All the canteen workers used to stay in Munirka. Mr Rao had arranged for our

---

*As told to Neeladri Bhattacharya.

stay. We used to eat our meals in the canteen and return to our rooms only at night. Finally in 2013, I left work in the SSS-I canteen.

At that time a new building, SSS-III, was coming up. The CHS and CSRD, the two departments in SSS-I, were shifting to this building. Some teachers told me to apply for permission to run a canteen in the new building. They asked me to meet the Dean, Mridula madam. I hesitated but then picked up the courage to go and talk. I said to madam, 'I have been serving the university for twenty to twenty-two years, ab mujhe bhi kuch diya jaye. I want to run a canteen in SSS-III.' Mridula madam was sympathetic. She said, 'we will consider your name.'

I am told that my name was entered in the minutes of the very first meeting held to discuss the question of the canteen in SSS-III. After that there was another meeting. My name was there in the minutes of that meeting too. But then Mridula madam had an accident. I was very upset, wondering what would happen now. I thought I would no longer get a chance to run a canteen. Then when Aditya Sir became the Dean, I went to meet him. Though he could not give me permission directly, he asked me to check with the Chairpersons of the departments in SSS-III. So I met the Chairpersons. Amaresh ji, who was the Chairperson of CSRD, told me I had to take a risk since there would be no permission to cook in the building. I could only sell tea and coffee. I had already left my job with Mr Rao. So I said 'risk le lete hai' (let me take the risk).

Initially I bought small quantities of provisions to run the canteen. I used to heat milk on a small stove and make tea and coffee. Then the administration declared that no stove would be permitted. So I got an electric kettle. But my kettles kept busting. I was heating milk in a kettle meant for boiling water. What could I do? I had no option. I wasted so many thousands of rupees replacing my electric kettles. The kettle cost Rs 3,000 and every third day it would collapse. How could I earn anything? The milk would congeal in the bottom of the kettle. How could it possibly work? The shopkeeper selling the kettles was frustrated, pareshan. He told me I could not possibly go on buying kettles and destroying them. He said: 'Why are you bothering yourself and troubling me?'

He then suggested that I buy an induction heater. So I invested in an induction heater. After that I could make a few more things to sell. But the sale was still not enough to pay for the salaries of three helpers and their place of stay. So I started catering on a very small scale. If the catering was for 100-150 people then I got the food cooked in one of the rooms I had hired in Munirka. If the numbers were more, then I set up angithis in a tent at the site where the lunch or dinner was held. Catering allowed me to earn enough to pay for the people who worked for me. Without catering, I could not meet my expenses, pay the salaries and the room rentals. I have to pay for three rooms in Munirka: in one I live with my family, in another my four helpers stay, and the third is used as a kitchen. I have to pay 16,000 for three rooms and 5,000 to 8,000 each to the workers. I also have to pay for their stay and their food. How can I manage everything by selling tea for Rs 5 and samosas for Rs 5? How many samosas can I sell in a day? How many cups of tea? One packet of biscuits brings me only 50 paise. How many packets of biscuits can I sell and how much can I possibly earn by selling biscuits? You just calculate how much I can earn in a month.

We have to all find ways to survive. Two of my assistants are now working in the hostel. They stay with me and make the samosas in the morning. I pay for their food. But the salary comes from the hostel. This arrangement helps all. I don't pay their wages but look after them, and they

V.9. 'I work along with my boys': Lateef in his canteen at SSS-III.
Photo courtesy: Samim Asgor Ali

don't have to spend on their stay and food, and can save their wages for the family. This is the only way we can all survive. What is the way out?

Now I am in trouble. Last month I had gone home. On 31 May a letter arrived at the canteen. My brother rang and told me about the letter. I was anxious, so I rushed back. I found that the university was asking me to pay Rs 11,06,380. They are charging Rs 24,000 per month, from August 2014 for this small canteen which does not even pay for the salaries of my workers. Initially when I started the canteen, I had no investment apart from the kettles that I had to keep buying. So if I was asked to leave then I would not have lost a huge amount of money. Now I have invested 4 to 5 lakhs on utensils, plates, and cups. Where will I go with all this? I am ready to pay a fair charge for the rental and electricity, but my position should be regularised. If I borrow a huge amount to pay what the university is now demanding then I may be bonded for life. There is no guarantee that I will be allowed to run the canteen.

I do not know what life will be like in the future. The mahaul (atmosphere) here at the university is no longer good. Earlier teachers would help us in our troubles. Once a boy from our gaon (village) had come. He had some problem in the family and needed money. The teachers collected the money and gave him. Now even the teachers do not know what might happen to them. How can they help me in this troubled time?

'Main kahan se gyarah lakh university ko dun? Lag raha hai gaon wapas jana hi padega, koi chara nahi hai.' (How will I give the university 11 lakhs of rupees? It seems I have to return to my village. There is no way out.) I had a dream that I would support the education of my brothers. I did not want them to labour like me. But they had to drop out of school. One of them works with me now. I pay him a worker's wage. Now my kids' lives will be ruined too. Here they study in the Sarvoday School in Munirka. In the village schooling is not as good as here. And in the village, you do not get good teachers for extra tuition. 'Yahaan tuition accha mil jata hai.'

'Hum log to sarak se aye the aur phir sarak par chale jayenge.' I came from the streets, and will have to return to the streets again.

36

ON COMMITTEES, DOGS, AND TOILETS AT JNU

MOHAN RAO

What, one might wonder, is the link between committees, toilets, and dogs at JNU?

I am, of course, talking about a JNU we all loved. It was mystifying to me why some people were on influential committees and others were not. It was mystifying then, but today it has become very clear.

I did occasionally, very occasionally, want to be part of a committee! It was dreadful never to be on one. Was I not asked because I did not speak Hindi? Did not know how to kowtow to the powers that be?

What happened in committees? Did they gossip? Eat cashew nuts and kebabs? Did they seriously discuss issues at hand, or call for data? Or did they openly fight? Friends regaled me with wonderful stories of those who wielded shoes and ashtrays. What passion! I wanted to see this, and duck, should a shoe be thrown my way.

Some of us at the Centre of Social Medicine and Community Health including myself, have been on various advisory bodies of the Government of India on health. These engagements have been reluctant on both sides: governments considered our Centre difficult in its early days; we did not want to touch the government with even a barge pole. But yes, I was a member of the National Commission on Population during the UPA-I, which was then discontinued. I was also on various committees of the National Rural Health Mission which abruptly dissolved under both the UPA-2 and BJP.

What was mystifying to me was that for most of my life at JNU, CSMCH was not consulted on the public health issues of the campus. We wrote, as a Centre, on the widespread incidence of dog bites and what ought to be done, but our advice was ignored, and all our science schools were silent.

My visually challenged students told me that when they complained they were getting disproportionately bitten, they were advised not to use the white cane since dogs felt threatened and attacked the users.

But the dogs on the JNU campus attack not just blind students, and we, as a Centre, did work on a system to reduce dog bites, and provide the requisite treatment within JNU, instead of sending the afflicted people to Safdarjung hospital. None of this was even considered. It is amazing that animal lovers privilege dogs over nilgais or peacocks or other animals on campus. I have seen nilgais with flesh hanging loose after dog attacks. And I know there is a report about dogs attacking peahen nests. Therefore, my involvement at JNU as a public health worker came to nought. As indeed our Centre's considered suggestions.

My second involvement came from being a member of our School's Library Committee. I was astonished when I was appointed the Chair. I convened regular meetings of all Centres in our School, but there seemed to be a block in the Library. Something was not right there. On looking into it, we discovered evidence of substantial corruption. For instance, we found that several lakhs of rupees were being wasted on ordering multiple copies of a nondescript encyclopaedia, from an agency run by the then officer's son. There was an official enquiry, but the man was let off with premature retirement.

The outcome of all this was that I was not appointed on any other committees since I stirred things up. I was not called urban Naxal or anti-national but just a troublemaker.

My third involvement was with the appalling state of toilets at JNU. The journalist Anjali Mody, who covered Gujarat 2002 brilliantly, was a friend. And in those days, journalists used to come and interview people face to face, spend time talking to people.

She called me up one day, angrily saying she was on campus to interview someone, but that she could not possibly use the toilets that were shabby, ill-maintained, and stinking. She threatened to write a piece in *The Hindu* about the dreadful state of toilets at JNU. 'You teachers go home, so you don't care for the shocking state of facilities', she said.

I took her home for coffee and told her some of us had indeed been working to clean up JNU's toilets. I suggested instead that she write a piece on the fact that the Indian Railways was the biggest faecal polluter in India. In doing so, I was able to save JNU's reputation.

When I told Professor Dipankar Gupta this story, he was motivated to get the Dean to set up a School of Social Science toilet committee and we recommended substantial modifications to the toilets we had. On each floor of the SSS-II we had four small toilets, segregated by gender. They were small, dank and full of fungus. We recommended breaking down walls, making them the large restrooms that we now have.

The big airy toilets we have today were the result. Instead of two for ladies and two for gents on each floor, we have one large stall each for men and women, though usually not maintained. A toilet for differently abled people was also to be provided on the ground floor of each building but that never materialized.

Before the transformation happened, I went to check the washroom on my floor and saw a large number of young men furtively hanging around. I wondered what I had walked into. From the small, dark, fungus-ridden WC emanated a voice 'Samuelson bolche...' and a whole lot about what Samuelson had 'bolched', in Bangla of course.

I found out that an examination was going on in the Centre for Economic Studies and Planning. These students were, uncommonly for JNU, cheating! I said loudly, 'say what Samuelson bolche in English, otherwise I will report this to your Centre.' The young men went quiet and slipped away, one after another. I was tempted to stay on and see the last young man emerging from the black hole with his books and notes but decided not to embarrass him.

My experience of committees is therefore limited. But who would have imagined the farcical state to which all committees have been reduced?

Committees can make, but can also unmake JNU. RIP.

LANDSCAPES OF JNU-I
An early photograph of Kaveri Hostel (to the left) and Sutlej Hostel (to the right, in the back ground) that came up in 1972–73. In the foreground, we can see the ancient metamorphic rocks of the quartzite variety that form the Aravalli terrain, rounded over centuries by weathering.
Photo courtesy: Antony Thomas

LANDSCAPES OF JNU-II
From the 1930s, large parts of Delhi ridge were slowly colonized by the vilaiti keekar (*prosopis juliflora*) trees that can be seen in this picture. Introduced by the British in the aforestation drive of the 1930s, the vilaiti keekar, with its crooked branches and feathery top, has now become an ecological threat, depleting the soil of moisture, rapidly displacing native varieties, and invading the landscape. Old ronjh trees (*acacia leucophloea*) are still found in large numbers in JNU, but babool (*acacia nilotica*) can be seen only in the low-lying parts of JNU.
Photo courtesy: Samim Asgor Ali

LANDSCAPES OF JNU-III
Parthasarathi Rocks loom over the thorn-forest landscape of JNU. The rounded boulders that cap the ridge, formed by the weathering of ancient rocks, are a great example of 'tor' formation.
Photo courtesy: Joy L. K. Pachuau

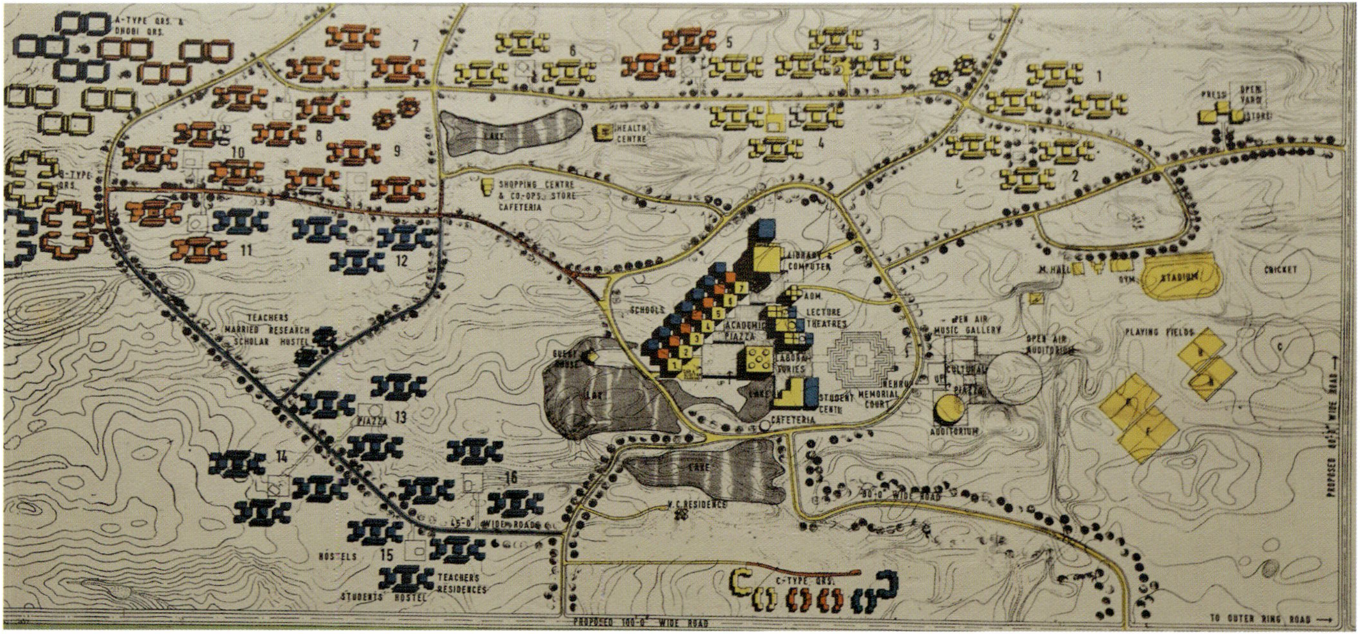

LANDSCAPES OF JNU-IV

Master plan of JNU indicating stages of development: the first stage is marked in yellow, the second in blue, and the third in red.

Source: A Study in Campus Designs, p. 36.

LANDSCAPES OF JNU-V

Over the last fifty years, the landscape of JNU has been dramatically transformed. When the buildings of the School of Life Sciences (on the right) and School of Social Sciences–I (second from right) were built in the late 1970s, you could see only bare rocks and thorn bushes around (see III.5, p. 80). Now the building complexes are thickly honeycombed with trees.

Photo courtesy: Samim Asgor Ali

SEASONS IN JNU-I
Deciduous trees shed their leaves in winter—minimizing water use in the dry months. Champa (in the foreground) remains bare from December to March. After May they are covered with clusters of scented pink and white flowers.
Photo courtesy: Samim Asgor Ali

SEASONS IN JNU-II
By March fallen leaves cover the ground.
Photo courtesy: Samim Asgor Ali

SEASONS IN JNU-III
In April you can see the new leaves sprout, with bougainvillea adding its splash of colour all around.
Photo courtesy: Samim Asgor Ali

SEASONS IN JNU-IV
In spring, bougainvillea paints JNU in colour. Originally from South America, this hardy flowering plant was introduced into Europe in the early nineteenth century, and later Kew Gardens propagated it all over the colonies.
Photo courtesy: Samim Asgor Ali

SEASONS IN JNU-V
In May and June amaltas blooms in full glory, with its yellow showers drooping elegantly, and their blazing colour bringing cheer in the summer heat. Native to India and much of Southeast Asia, amaltas is a fast-growing deciduous tree that survives well on poor and rocky soils. Its pods are used for herbal medicines and its flowers for ritual offerings.
Photo courtesy: Devayani Prasad

SEASONS IN JNU-VI
When monsoon comes in July–August even the dry thorny trees turn deep green.
Photo courtesy: Samim Asgor Ali

BIRDS IN JNU-I
The peacock symbolizes JNU. At night they retreat into the forest, and roost on the trees, but in the day—from early morning—they roam the open spaces in the residential areas looking for plant feed and insects.
Photo courtesy: Samim Asgor Ali

BIRDS IN JNU-II
Red Munia
Photo courtesy: Surya Prakash

BIRDS IN JNU-III
White-breasted Kingfisher
Photo courtesy: Surya Prakash

BIRDS IN JNU-IV
Rose-ringed Parakeets: the ring around the neck distinguishes the male (left) from the female (right). The Alexandrine Parakeet looks similar, but has dark red shoulder patches and a larger bill.
Photo courtesy: Samim Asgor Ali

BIRDS IN JNU-V
Yellow-footed Green Pigeon
Photo courtesy: Surya Prakash

ANIMALS IN JNU-I
Among the largest of Asian antelopes, nilgai can live in dry areas. The males of the species can be distinguished by their bluish-grey fur and horns—as in this image—while the females are usually yellowish-brown and hornless. Nilgais have good eyesight and hearing but not a great sense of smell, and can run up to 46 km per hour when chased.
Photo courtesy: Surya Prakash

ANIMALS IN JNU-II
Capable of living in a wide variety of environments, the golden jackal can tolerate the dry rocky habitat of the Aravalli terrain. It feeds on fruits, insects, small ungulates, and garbage dumps, and scavenges on dead animal carcasses. The fur of the Indian golden jackal is a mixture of black and white, with buff on the shoulders, ears and legs, and black predominating on the back.
Photo courtesy: Surya Prakash

ANIMALS IN JNU-III
Loved by some and feared by others, dogs are an integral part of JNU life.
Photo courtesy: Vidur Krishnan

REPTILES IN JNU-I

The Aravalli region is home to many rare lizard species. Monitor lizards (in the image) survive well on dry scrublands, conserving their energy in dry seasons by staying still. They can attack the enemy with their powerful tail, grip rocks with their strong claws, and smell food with their flicking tongue (yes, their power of smell is in the tongue).

Photo courtesy: Surya Prakash

REPTILES IN JNU-II

There are about 40 species of snakes in the forests of JNU, some venomous others not. The saw-scaled Viper (in this image) is a deadly venomous snake with haemo-toxins in its venom. This is one of the 'Big-Four' category of snakes in India.

Photo courtesy: Surya Prakash

NIGHTS IN JNU-I

As darkness descends, the forested campus looks magical. Turning southeast you can see the Qutab Minar looming high in the distance over the forest.

Photo courtesy: Samim Asgor Ali

NIGHTS IN JNU-II
Time for a stroll: the lanes and bylanes in JNU look enchantingly different at night.
Photo courtesy: Samim Asgor Ali

NIGHTS IN JNU-III
Often crowded, Parthasarathi Rocks continues to be a space for intimacy even today.
Photo courtesy: Samim Asgor Ali

NIGHTS IN JNU-IV
The academic blocks are deserted as students leave for the library, hostels, and dhabas.
Photo courtesy: Samim Asgor Ali

NIGHTS IN JNU-V
For many JNUites, Ganga Dhaba at night continues to be the site of nostalgic memories.
Photo courtesy: Samim Asgor Ali

NIGHTS IN JNU-VI

While old timers romanticize Ganga Dhaba, the younger generations flock to the new dhabas for a break from the hostel food. The open-air food court 24/7—famous for its puri bhaji, parathas and Afghani chicken, as well as tandoori momos and chicken rolls—used to be open day and night. In the last few years it has been forced to close at 11 p.m.

Photo courtesy: Samim Asgor Ali

NIGHTS IN JNU-VII
Located opposite Lohit Hostel, Mughal Darbar claims to offer genuine Mughlai cuisine. Students come here at night for its succulent kababs and spicy kormas.
Photo courtesy: Samim Asgor Ali

NIGHTS IN JNU-VIII
At night, the banyan tree that connects the academic blocks to the library looks picturesque, invoking both temporal depth and Orientalist imagination.
Photo courtesy: Samim Asgor Ali

NIGHTS IN JNU-IX
The preferred hour for intellectual labour—the library at night.
Photo courtesy: Samim Asgor Ali

BUILDINGS OF JNU-I
The early buildings in the academic complex had the shape of an inverted pyramid, with each ascending floor extending outward.
Photo courtesy: Samim Asgor Ali

BUILDINGS OF JNU-II
The newer buildings, such as SSS–III (in this picture), have departed significantly from the way the academic blocks were imagined as inverted pyramids in the original campus design.
Photo courtesy: Samim Asgor Ali

BUILDINGS OF JNU-III
The School of Social Sciences—JNU's largest School—now occupies three buildings.
Photo courtesy: Samim Asgor Ali

BUILDINGS OF JNU-IV
The Administrative Building popularly known as the Pink Palace
Photo courtesy: Samim Asgor Ali

BUILDINGS OF JNU-V
The formal splendour of the Convention Centre—where special lectures, workshops, conferences, and performances are held—is a contrast to the informal busyness of the Academic Blocks.
Photo courtesy: Samim Asgor Ali

BUILDINGS OF JNU-VI
The distinct pyramidal tapering structure of the early hostel buildings can be seen in the design of Godavari Hostel—the first women's hostel in the new campus, built by end-1973.
Photo courtesy: Samim Asgor Ali

BUILDINGS OF JNU-VII
Though also in red brick, vertical straight lines define the new hostels in contrast to the pyramidal structure of the original master design.
Photo courtesy: Samim Asgor Ali

BUILDINGS OF JNU-VIII
The student union office, a badminton court, and a student canteen are located in TEFLAS—the student activity centre—situated opposite Narmada Hostel.
Photo courtesy: Samim Asgor Ali

LEISURE IN JNU-I
More than any other sport, football symbolizes JNU. Much through the year, the sports stadium is crowded with enthusiastic footballers carving out the ground into many mini-football fields. The stadium, until recently, was a community space used by people from the neighbourhoods around JNU, not just by the residents of the university.

LEISURE IN JNU-II
Cricket amidst the keekar trees
Photo courtesy: Samim Asgor Ali

LEISURE IN JNU-III
The carnival of holi in JNU has been customarily and uniquely celebrated in ways that allow women to participate with a sense of comfort and safety.
Photo courtesy: Chandrashekhar Tibrewal Collection

LEISURE IN JNU-IV
The Korean Counter at the International Food Festival, JNU, 26 January 2019.
Photo courtesy: Samim Asgor Ali

LEISURE IN JNU-V
Satyabhama and Krishna, in an episode from the Mahabharata ('Shreekrishna Parijata') performed by a Yakshagana Troupe from Karnataka, organized by the Kannada Language Chair of JNU on 26 January 2019.
Photo courtesy: P. Bilimale

LEISURE IN JNU-VI
A leather puppet show by Belagal Veeranna and troupe organized by the Kannada Language Chair of JNU on 16 August 2017.
Photo courtesy: P. Bilimale

POLITICS IN JNU-I
The SFI-AISF desk during the JNUSU election of October 1979 in which D. Raghunandan, the left-front presidential candidate, won. Sitting on the right of the desk is V. Bhaskar who became the JNUSU President in the subsequent year.
Photo courtesy: Nirmala George

POLITICS IN JNU-II

An eagerly awaited event before the JNUSU election—when the presidential candidates display their rhetorical skills. The meeting continues till the late hours of the night.

POLITICS IN JNU-III
The famous poster politics of JNU began on a small scale in the 1970s with A3-size posters, before the large murals began to appear.
Photo courtesy: Nirmala George

POLITICS IN JNU-IV
AISA—All India Students' Association—protests against the politics of repression that lies behind the rhetoric of development. This left-wing organization was formed in August 1990 and has a strong presence in several states of India.
Photo courtesy: Sthira Bhattacharya

POLITICS IN JNU-V

Birsa, Ambedkar, Phule, Students' Association (BAPSA) was formed on 15 November 2014 at Jawaharlal Nehru University on the birth anniversary of Birsa Munda—an iconic tribal leader. Critical of both left- and right-wing student organizations, BAPSA seeks to foreground the issue of caste discrimination and work for the rights of Dalits, Adivasis, and other minorities.

Photo courtesy: Sthira Bhattacharya

POLITICS IN JNU-VI

Reclaiming the walls: after the JNU administration stripped the walls of posters, students decided to once more occupy these spaces.

Photo courtesy: Samim Asgor Ali

POLITICS IN JNU-VII
A protest on JNU campus when the GSCASH, which had won national and international acclaim, was revoked in September 2017 and replaced by a nominated, rather than elected, Internal Complaints Committee. Students and faculty, feminists in particular, felt that such a nominated committee could not be fully trusted, and cases of sexual harassment by teachers would not be properly and seriously investigated under ICC.
Photo courtesy: Samim Asgor Ali

POLITICS IN JNU-VIII
Teachers on a silent march through the campus.
Photo courtesy: Samim Asgor Ali

POLITICS IN JNU-IX
Since 2016, JNU has witnessed protests on an unprecedented scale against the systematic attack on its norms, statutes, and values.
Photo courtesy: Samim Asgor Ali

VI

POLITICS, POSTERS, PERFORMANCES

37

'STUDY AND STRUGGLE': A FRAGMENT FROM JNU (1988–98)

ROHAN D'SOUZA

The first time I found myself at JNU was in 1986, sometime in early October when campaigning for the students' union election was at its peak. As a visitor/understudy, I was part of a merry band of impressionable members from the Delhi University (DU) unit of the All India Students' Federation (AISF), who were keen for a ring-side view of the political action that we had heard so much about.

To get to JNU from Delhi University's North Campus, however, was a small journey in itself. We first made our way to what was then a distant Connaught Place, before catching the famous 615 bus. On the bus we patiently held on as it huffed, wheezed, and meandered for nearly an hour before arriving at JNU's famed Ganga stop. The 615 and the 666 shuttle, to this day, remain the stuff of legends, as these raggedy buses were for many decades the only affordable transport for getting people in or out of the campus. And in all likelihood, I suspect, the emotional trials from the eternal waits at the bus stop must have fuelled those apocryphal stories about JNU's 'eternal wanderer'. In these richly told and retold improbable tales, there is a chance meeting of a freshly arrived JNU student who cheerily asks a bedraggled aged man for directions. The eternal wanderer then soulfully opens up, about how he so sincerely and genuinely wished he could actually help. But alas, despite having submitted his PhD ages ago, he was still turning circles on the campus in search of the road that would lead him out of the place. His predicament is best concluded, with the haunting refrain of the American rock band, the Eagles, in their classic 'Hotel California': 'you can check out any time you like but you can never leave.'

I joined the AISF in 1986 and was still making sense of the world with newly gained political convictions. That year at JNU, the AISF had

VI.1. Election time: volunteers wait for voters (1982). Second from the right is young Nirmala Sitharaman.
Photo courtesy: Chandrashekhar Tibrewal Collection

VI.2. After the vote: the tense wait at night for the election results
Photo courtesy: Samim Asgor Ali.

broken its electoral alliance with the formidable and better organized Students Federation of India (SFI). Though the decision to fight alone seemed daring, it still could not hide the palpable fact that the AISF was woefully short on both membership and finance. And logistically speaking, a total mess.

In the long night during which the election results were hand counted and announced at regular intervals—school by school, candidate by candidate, and for each individual office bearer of the central panel—the atmosphere for us DU understudies appeared festive rather than edgy. The withering dry lawns in what was then called 'down campus', now Institute of Secretariat Training and Management, was divided up between different organizations and their crudely marked sections were messily settled in by clumps of enthusiasts who shouted slogans, sang or made relaxed conversation. When the Election Commission's loudspeaker crackled to life to announce another counting round, everyone, as if on cue, immediately froze. The silence snuffed out even the faintest buzz in the air. But once the latest numbers were declared it seemed as if a dam had just burst with a huge wild roar of drums, cymbals, full throated slogans and ringing calls for the JNUSU to 'march on'.

As the night progressed from its inky depths to the violet hues of early dawn, a sequence played out: every announcement causing people to freeze, likeable to the childhood game of statue, then followed by an explosive revelry—similar to those atonal blaring bands in a Punjabi marriage party in Delhi.

But the loudspeaker was not the only show in town either. There was a picnic mix of women and men or, put differently, young students, research scholars, and some very seasoned-looking PhDs milling about, drinking tea, warming themselves around tiny smouldering fires and in various knots of casual banter, animated discussion or idle talk.

In later years, as an AISF candidate and regular political activist on campus, I increasingly came to believe that the JNU students' election was, in essence, an open-ended interdisciplinary, trans-disciplinary and multidisciplinary symposium. It was a deep learning process and the campus's primary academic melting pot moment. The innumerable speeches, the presidential debates and the countless meetings all added up such that the collected sap and distillate of theories, ideas, concepts, and facts that were otherwise bottled up within specialized academic thinking was now flung upon the student community to unsettle existing opinions and question beliefs. The election, in other words, was a festival in which classroom abstraction sought to come to grips with the concrete realities of living worlds—the moment when the tree of knowledge reached out and tangoed with the tree of life.

In the final results for 1986, the AISF squeaked in a Joint Secretary (later to become a Principal Economic Advisor to the Government of India) and two councillors in the School of Languages (one of whom is now a faculty member at JNU and the other either got elected or ran for a position in a village panchayat in Himachal Pradesh).

In the early hours of the morning, a victory procession was taken out and we sloganeered across all the hostels and thanked the electorate, who were still bleary-eyed and in breakfast mode. Interestingly enough, for our little ginger group of understudies from DU, the bad press about JNU being full of sour and grim comrades proved entirely untrue. If anything, JNUites were witty, good-humoured, and even gave us a take-home message to chew on: 'Comrade, your poverty and the mess that your life may be in is not entirely of your own making. Your mistakes come from larger economic structures, deeper political histories and the "impossible cards" that society has dealt you without permission.' The solution: study, struggle, and organize. All terribly inspiring stuff, and into this wide basket of thoughts were added other ripened words: 'sectarian', 'revisionist', 'Stalinist', 'Trotskyite', 'bourgeois', 'class conflict', 'historical materialism', 'comprador', and the signature term for verbal duelling—'reactionary'.

On being admitted to the MA programme at the Centre for Historical Studies in 1988, JNU's colourful political culture still continued to surprise me. For one, though political talk and talk about politics did suffuse everyday discussions and interactions, political activity per se was decidedly seasonal.

The electioneering phase/season stretched roughly from August to the last week of October. November to mid-December was the time to desperately catch up on finishing delayed tutorials, term paper submissions, and exam preparations. In fact, if by some special 'correlation of forces' the great Indian proletariat staged a revolution and overthrew the bourgeoisie in those critical weeks, rest assured that there would be near zero participation from JNU. The month of February, on the other hand, was specially marked for feisty agitations and movements and March was sweetened with Hostel celebrations. In April–May, heads were down once again, followed by the annual homeward bound migrations of the MA and BA crowd.

It was the month of June, however, that stood out entirely by itself and for itself. It was the month in which the campus was roasted on either side by the unforgiving pre-monsoon sun. JNU is strewn with 'tors'—huge lumpy rocks scattered about as the pre-historic Tethys Sea gradually drained when the supercontinents Laurasia and Gondwana smashed into each other. Geologically speaking, the JNU campus—the hilly undulations on the edge of the Aravalli range—was for millions of years under salty water. The most spectacular formation of tors on campus, in fact, are the Parthasarathi Rocks—also the stony backdrop to innumerable JNU romance stories.

In June's elongated day, these tors along with every red brick and cemented surface ravenously drank up the molten sun. And in the evenings, the punishing hot breath from this day long consumption of lava steadily radiated outwards from every cooked wall, charbroiled building, flamed tor and burnt strip of concrete.

Only two student constituencies remained on campus under these near hellish conditions: those submitting their MPhil dissertations and a determined lot taking the preliminaries for the civil services exams (UPSC). Both these groups were on the edge, but for different reasons. While the dissertation submitters suffered to craft original arguments for situating their facts, the UPSC exam-takers, in contrast, would be painfully grinding away at accumulating facts so that they could weigh-in on either side of any argument. Psychologically, in this yin and yang circuit, the former was required to handle the stress that emerged from the need to be creative, while, for the latter, it was about the urgency for sustaining the mental stamina for rote and memory.

Meanwhile, as the summer heightened and inched towards its monsoon denouement, the swathes of bougainvillea that curtain JNU would have exploded into their primal colours of pink, orange, deep red, and vanilla white. This was also the time for the migratory return of the koel, (a genus of the cuckoo bird), who from the early light of day would saturate the air with their rhythmic hoots. And if you were amongst the despairing who were writing dissertation chapters and had lost all sense of day and night while cursing yourself for leaving everything to the last minute, there might be the occasional wake-up startle from the manic drill of the brain fever bird (hawk-cuckoo) or the ugly screech from one of the countless peacocks on campus.

Research writing actually entails the stapling of two otherwise unconnected psychological dispositions. The first requires the capacity for solitude: the ability to commune with yourself in order to think and write. Solitude is very different from being lonely, which is the inability to understand or be curious enough about the other. The second requirement is about evoking the unhesitating generosity of friends.

Decades later while teaching at JNU and supervising MPhils and PhDs, I would always underline the necessity for friends over family during dissertation or thesis submission. And, for me at least, acknowledgements (the sources and causes for intellectual debts) are crucial for understanding the research story. Good scholarship is thus not about cutting a lonely furrow but really about creating community.

In my case, the entire supporting weight for writing up the dissertation was borne by my roommate of many years, comrade from DU and one time AISF councillor from the School of Social Sciences—Rajesh Mahapatra (who later became the executive editor of the *Hindustan Times*). Though Rajesh and I were batchmates when we joined in 1988, we both lost our admission and then secured re-admission into JNU in different years. For my submission, Rajesh, consequently, was ideally placed for unstinted support; except, as we both found out the hard way, he had also made similar commitments to several other equally frantic dissertation desperadoes. His tasks, hence, not only multiplied by X, but he had to be the only calm head in a boiling ocean of urgent needs and deadlines. Drafts had to be edited, bibliographies compiled, footnotes checked, chapters keyed into computers (this was the early 1990s), printouts taken and the dissertation bound. Then there were dramas, when the old file was copied onto the corrected version or a diskette (today's pen drive) got 'corrupted' or someone broke down because they had no argument. But the rains came on time that late July and all the dissertations under his weary watch were submitted and Rajesh, somehow, emerged very much alive.

Having thus survived the dissertation, the next few months as a senior is when political activism becomes therapeutic. As the campus fills up with the newest batch, this is the semester that you give generously back to the campus and nurture the next generation with your time, learning, and patience. The moment kept aside for you to polish and shine JNU's legacy: 'when politics decides your future then decide what your politics should be.'

38

RESHAPING POLITICAL CULTURE ON THE CAMPUS

JAIRUS BANAJI

I arrived at JNU from England in September 1972, with my wife and one-year-old daughter. I had written to Romila Thapar asking if I could study Ancient History with her as I had just finished a thesis at Oxford on Inner Asian colour symbolism and its possible relation to the caste system. Romila agreed and started me off on a UGC scholarship of just under Rs 400 a month, just enough to keep a young family going in those days. (Since accommodation was scarce, we were housed in Class-IV quarters at the edge of what was later called the Old Campus.) But the political atmosphere in India at the time, and at JNU especially, was so intense and vibrant I soon decided I couldn't bury myself in antiquity when so much was happening around us. Within two weeks I had moved, first to Medieval History, then rapidly, in another two weeks, to Modern History, which is where I first encountered Bipan Chandra.

What struck me most about Bipan was his capacity to learn from history and to make that learning an instrument of both political and theoretical clarification. He had an astonishing flexibility which I later realized stemmed from an absolute lack of dogmatism. It was said on campus that Bipan was close to the CPI(M); I have no idea if that was ever true but in the way he taught us and the history he wrote there was no trace of any affiliation of that sort. Bipan was, in the tradition of E. P. Thompson, someone who made theory work, not someone who applied ready-made schemas to its complex tapestry.

The Centre for Historical Studies had a remarkable collection of historians straddling the main periods of Indian history and, when I recently finished writing a short history of commercial capitalism, I realized just how much my ideas and approach had been shaped during those formative days at JNU thanks to teachers like Saugata Mukherji and

Sabyasachi Bhattacharya, as also (from the Centre for Economic Studies and Planning) Krishna Bharadwaj and to some degree Amit Bhaduri. What made the political life of the campus so vibrant was that underlying it and supporting it was a striking intellectual base of teachers, distinctly left-wing but not dogmatically so. The approach to politics was creative and flexible; none of our teachers ever sought to discourage students or shy them away from it, but they did insist on intellectual integrity as vital to both academic work and political involvement. Madhavan Palat was an invaluable source of books that were otherwise impossible to find. I recall how carefully I read his copy of Michael Confino's magnificent book on the Russian landowners of the eighteenth century. I would buy hardbound exercise books from the stationers in the market at RK Puram in Sector 3 and carefully compile notes into those. I still have a collection of these notebooks, the earliest in the series I accumulated over the decades that followed.

The landscape of student politics was largely dominated by the two main (and rival) student organizations of Left parties that had parted ways barely ten years earlier when the Communist Party split. They exerted a virtual domination, but nothing vaguely close to hegemony, that is, the power to persuade students by the sheer force of ideas, to win them over by demonstrating why Marxist theory and politics were so exciting, not least here in India where the late sixties had had its own version of the radicalization that swept through large parts of the world. But this was something the leaders of the student Left simply could not do, because they were reluctant to engage with the richness of the Marxist theoretical tradition. Between them and both these exigencies (the need for theoretical debate as well as a wider political activism), stood the inflexible screen of the Party, that is, of their respective parties. The party imposed a division of labour that must have been, to the average student in those organizations, stultifying both intellectually and in terms of any wider political involvement not directly mediated through its hierarchy.

It was also a fiercely sectarian landscape that resented any intrusion into what the main student bodies saw as carefully nurtured monopolies. Thus any tendency to raise issues about why the Russian Revolution had failed and what had happened to account for its defeat or degeneration was viewed as a pure interloper. The first thing any tendency of this kind would have to do was break the artificial monopoly of ideas and politics. That happened over the course of the mid-seventies, both before and soon after the Emergency, in a series of sharp confrontations played out in various public meetings and forums on the campus. To me, it was impossible to imagine that the Left tradition could ever be rebuilt from the ashes of its defeat during the inter-war decades without making the issue of Stalinism central to debates on the Left. And this presupposed that Marxist theory itself would have to be taken more seriously and restated in more creative ways. One upshot of this was a circle of students that began to look at the Russian revolution through texts such as Isaac Deutscher's biography of Leon Trotsky and E. H. Carr's magisterial history; another was the labour of translation that some of us undertook both at JNU and later in trying to make still untranslated Marxist works in German accessible to a wider student audience. I remember translating the French translation of Kautsky's classic on the agrarian question, if only because so many of the debates on the Indian Left were about the peasantry, about agrarian capitalism, and about whether and in what ways capitalism was developing in Indian agriculture.

The great exception to the normal pattern of the stultified intellectual culture of the party was K. Damodaran. A long-standing Left intellectual who was now with the more liberal CPI, he was in the process of building up and managing the P. C. Joshi archive, then housed in the ground floor of the Old Campus not far from where the student cafeteria was. Damodaran had no hesitation in associating with students who were generally (and abusively) labelled Trotskyites, left-wing opponents of Stalinism, and in his own way reflected the same lack of dogmatism, indeed hostility to it, that characterized Bipan Chandra. One of the things we jointly did was select a whole range of titles from the New Left Books (NLB) catalogue which he could order. When these finally arrived (a mass of Western Marxist literature that NLB had been publishing in the early seventies), it was a major intellectual watershed both for Damodaran personally and for many of us who saw ourselves reviving the richness of the Marxist tradition as part of a wider renewal of the left.

Debate was the unwritten rule on this more radical, less party-oriented Left. The JNU student circle expanded into a wider group that included Left-radicals from other parts of Delhi. We met regularly, studied and debated collectively, and contributed to a collective self-formation that sought to escape the tightly controlled political space on the campus.

Two legacies of the JNU days that carried over into this wider political association were the continued emphasis on theory (but now with much less reverence for the Bolshevik tradition) and a more durable orientation to the working class. The first of these led to the rediscovery of political traditions on the Left that were less obsessed with party-building (less vanguardist) and more rooted in traditions of worker activism, while the second led to the emergence of groupings that started to work with actual groups of workers, notably, the Union Research Group (URG) which was formed in Bombay at the end of the seventies to help the employees' unions there with their bargaining needs.

39

MY STORY OF JNUTA

KAMAL MITRA CHENOY

From the beginning, JNU was established as a liberal arts university even when various science schools were an integral part of the institution. Unexpectedly, a large number of distinguished faculty from across the globe joined the university. Within a few years, with the rapid increase in faculty strength there was a growing feeling that teachers should have a forum to discuss various issues.

By the time the first MA batch of students joined, the need for a forum of the JNU teachers was beginning to solidify. By 1974, a faculty club was established and the Emergency of 1975–77 was a trigger for the faculty to face the challenges of the time and its control over educational institutions. In 1972, the veteran diplomat G. Parthasarathi had put various eminent scholars into positions of decision-making. One who became very important with each passing year was Professor Moonis Raza: he was both a builder of the university as well as an activist, virtually the main mover and shaker of the administration and a support to the JNU administration. Later Professor Raza became the VC of Delhi University. It was in this atmosphere that the JNU Teachers' Association (JNUTA) had its beginnings.

However, the JNUTA was forced to play a major role in the making of the university. Discussions amongst the faculty were useful in protecting students opposed to the Emergency. After those exceptional years there was no looking back for JNUTA. Teachers now had their own forum and rules which were always democratic and fiercely protective of the academic excellence of the university.

In 1972 I joined JNU as a student of MA in political studies in the School of Social Sciences. Within days I began to understand and learn from my teachers. Professor Rasheeduddin Khan, a Rajya Sabha member, nominated by Indira Gandhi was one of my earliest guides to JNU and social science. At that stage, the JNUTA was not particularly active.

By 1975, things changed rapidly. Prabir Purkayastha, a computer sciences student, was arrested from the campus along with two others: notably, D. P. Tripathi, the JNUSU President, from my Centre.[1] With the changed situation, the JNUTA had had enough. My teacher Professor C. P. Bhambhri, a Left-Congress supporter along with Professor Yogendra Singh, a prominent sociologist, Professor Ram Rattan Sharma of the Centre for Russian Studies, Professor K. J. Mahale a prominent French language teacher, and Professor Bipan Chandra of the Centre for Historical Studies, among many others stood up to protect the students and JNU.

When I was suspended from the university, Professor Khan warned me that it was because of my political activities. But the faculty, without any qualms, tried to cheer me up. My suspension, and later my removal from JNU began. Even then the JNUTA stalwarts ensured that I could join the post graduate JNU Centre at Imphal, Manipur, with the army kindly providing a residence for my wife, Anuradha, and me. By now everyone knew my story, and some colleagues of the Manipur JNUTA sent occasional letters or postcards to their students in Delhi, keeping them informed of how I was doing.

Later in March 1977, I suffered from a severe attack of cerebral malaria. The Imphal CRPF gave me constant attention and when Professor Raza was informed about my condition, he told the JNU Centre to get me back to Delhi as soon as possible. When I arrived at JNU the thirty-odd JNUTA faculty members were shocked to see me so ill. They cheered me up by saying that Prabir Purkayastha was well and out of jail. Professor Khan had played a role in his release. Throughout the Emergency, JNUTA played a significant role keeping track of arrested students, and offering moral support to others who were in trouble. This is how the JNUTA was with their students!

There were also other instances, both good and bad. After some time, I was offered a position in the Indian Institute of Public Administration (IIPA) in 1980–81. Since that was a full-time job, I had little time to meet with the faculty at JNU, but I usually got to know what was happening in JNUTA. The impact of the Emergency was over. But in 1983–84, there was a breakdown of student-teacher relationships at JNU, over a

[1]For D. P. Tripathi's account, see '"Ideas replaced by the market"', *Deccan Herald*, 16 September 2012.

fairly trifling matter of the change of a hostel room. Students ransacked some hostel rooms and broke window panes in faculty houses. Professor M. S. Agwani, the Rector-1, and Professor P. N. Shrivastava, the Vice Chancellor, were not allowed to leave their quarters. When I went to the VC's residence I was visibly shaken. Such an incident was unheard of. Some teachers were abused, atrocious slogans were shouted against the VC and the Rector. Most within the faculty were aghast and shaken by what had happened in May 1983. Seeing me woebegone, Professor G. S. Bhalla (CSRD) along with Professors C. P. Bhambhri and R. R. Sharma called me over, and we discussed guidelines to tackle such an event, if it ever arose again.

Since 2016, the political scenario on the campus has changed. Saffron consolidation within the faculty and the actions of the current Vice Chancellor have forced JNUTA to refigure itself, and adopt a more militant posture.[2] In the past the JNUTA was rarely, if ever, involved in any prolonged confrontation with the administration. Issues concerning teachers and the university were discussed and negotiated with the authorities, mostly amicably. But now JNUTA has an embattled relationship with the Vice Chancellor. It has been engaged in protecting university norms which are being violated daily, offering support to the innumerable court cases which teachers are being forced to file against administrative orders, unifying the academic community against the onslaught of the administration. This is not a role the old JNUTA could have effectively discharged. JNUTA has had to reinvent itself.

After the 1986 Pay Commission, the central universities' teachers felt betrayed by the All India Federation of University and College Teacher Organisation (AIFUCTO). This created a furore amongst the central universities' teachers' associations who felt let down. It became clear that the AIFUCTO could not represent all teachers of central universities, since their strength was amongst the colleges and state universities. A number of JNUTA members, including Professor Jaishekhar of SIS, Girijesh Pant and I, among others, decided along with DUTA to form a new federation to be called the Federation of Central Universities Teachers' Association (FEDCUTA). This association was committed to the welfare of all the

---

[2]See Fareeha Iftikhar, 'JNU's VC tweaked rules, got loyalists on key posts', *Hindustan Times*, 25 August 2020; Vakasha Sachdev, 'The Case Against JNU VC Mamidala Jagadesh Kumar', *The Quint*, 8 January 2020.

central universities that were willing to join. Since then, FEDCUTA has flourished and incorporates almost all of the forty-three central universities' teachers. Because of travel difficulties, FEDCUTA meetings are held in the Delhi-based central universities.

If one looks at the development and esprit de corps, JNUTA has continuously risen to its challenges. The faculty and students have come together now to form a 'historic bloc', which is increasingly well known and respected. The resistance to the creeping authoritarianism on the campus put up by JNUTA along with JNUSU shows what a challenge a left-liberal campus can build and achieve.

It is typical of JNU that a number of students go on to become teachers, and what's more, become presidents and activists of JNUTA. Professor Anand Kumar, who was earlier the President of the JNU Students' Union was twice elected as the JNUTA President. Several other JNUTA presidents were student leaders, like Professor Ajay Patnaik, Sachidanand Sinha, and others. JNU teachers and students, JNUTA and JNUSU, together continue to fight with passion to protect the academic, democratic, and inclusive traditions of JNU.

40

THE JNU STUDENT MOVEMENT DURING NDA-I

ALBEENA SHAKIL

It is both ironic and befitting that the Jawaharlal Nehru University is entering its fiftieth year at a time of relentless attack from the ruling regime. Unjust arrests, court cases, disciplinary actions, vilification campaigns and brazen high-handedness have ensured that the entire JNU community has had to revisit the fundamentals of every institutional practice and norm. The hostilities testify to the fact that the university has remained true to its character and has not kowtowed to the powers that be. Consequently, instead of ceremonial golden jubilee celebrations that would have otherwise come to pass, both past and present generations of the university community are poised to observe this momentous occasion with deeper conviction, resolve, and regard for everything they cherish about JNU.

I joined the university in 1997 for an MA in English at the School of Languages (later renamed as School of Languages, Literature and Culture Studies) and passed out in 2005 after completing my PhD. By that time, the new battle lines in JNU politics were clearly drawn—on the one hand was the ABVP, the right-wing group motivated by the rapid growth of the NDA at the Centre, and on the other were left, democratic, secular forces, committed to defending the democratic and peaceful ethos of the JNU campus. This was also the year when the Supreme Court issued the Vishaka guidelines against sexual harassment at the workplace. I was drawn into student politics by the struggle to implement these guidelines. In the same year, I was elected to the JNUSU council from the combined Left platform of the SFI-AISF; thereafter, I held the posts of the Joint Secretary, Vice President (twice) and of the JNUSU President. During those five years, the university faced major challenges arising from attempts to privatize education, contending with tensions arising from India–Pakistan cricket matches, non-vegetarian food in hostel messes and the celebration of religious festivals. There were attempts to subvert and deny democratic rights of students, and numerous incidents of violence took place on the campus. Efforts were afoot to alter the system of education at JNU. The BJP-led NDA government exerted continuous pressure on the JNU administration to reorient the university's functioning towards its ideological moorings.

The sustained unity of students, teachers and karamcharis was instrumental in saving us from difficult situations like the arrest of sixty-three JNU students on 2 October 1999, followed by the imposition and withdrawal of sine die at JNU. The infamous Justice P. K. Bahri Commission of Inquiry was formed to investigate an incident of violence triggered by two gun-wielding men during an Indo-Pak mushaira held in the KC open-air theatre on 29 April 2000.[1] Sensational allegations of ISI-backed anti-national activities at the university soon ensued. Justice Bahri spent a couple of unsuccessful months at JNU looking for ISI agents, after which he exited hastily. The two men subsequently turned out to be soldiers and their actions were widely criticised.[2] In the same year, there was an attempt to impose a code of conduct upon JNU students through a High Court injunction that sought to prohibit democratic protests.[3] By 2001, the notorious Xth Plan proposals were prepared, which, in the eyes of many, aimed at the saffronization and privatization of education at JNU.[4]

Not only were these moves resisted, but several advances were also made by the JNUSU in areas affecting students' day-to-day lives. Five new hostels were built in the era of budget cuts; library facilities were improved, including the right of students to select books for annual purchase; free internet-with-computer facilities were added. JNUSU protested (to demand more hostels) against the then human resource minister, Murli Manohar Joshi, who had come to campus on the invitation of the Vivekananda Vichar Manch to commemorate the Pokhran-II nuclear tests. The limitations of the proctorial inquiry were soon exposed—it could investigate violence but not targeted caste violence against a Dalit student. This resulted in a long drawn JNUSU struggle that culminated in the formation of the Dalit Advisory

[1]UNI, 'Pak poet's take on Pokhran angers audience', *Rediff.com*, 30 April 2000.

[2]V. Gangadhar, 'Jingoism at the JNU', *Rediff.com*.

[3]'Code book burnt on JNU campus', *Times of India*, 2 August 2000.

[4]Sanjog Gupta, 'JNUSU joins clamour against "saffronisation"', *The Tribune*, 14 September 2002.

Committee (later renamed as the Equal Opportunity Office) in 1999.

The formation of the Gender Sensitization Committee against Sexual Harassment (GSCASH), also in 1999, after nearly two years of struggle, was historic. The first committee of its kind in the country, it inaugurated a substantive change at JNU's student politics, with gender issues becoming an integral part of mainstream student discourse. The demand for a representative and democratically elected GSCASH was first expressed to the JNU administration during a student-teacher JNUSU Convention held on 8 March 1998 and was simply dismissed as 'shameful'. 'Gender' was a new concept making its entry into JNU, as was 'sexual harassment'. The struggle was not easy and continued well after the formation of the GSCASH in order to first get policy, then the body and its decisions ratified, followed by its rules and procedures. All this was done while the ABVP relentlessly prescribed moral policing and dress codes for women. The GSCASH also faced periodic cycles of backlash by the university administration every time a 'senior' in the university hierarchy faced inquiries.

A historic university general body meeting of students was held in 1999 to amend the JNUSU constitution and include elected GSCASH student representatives as invitees to the JNUSU council. This prolonged gender sensitization of the student community was instrumental in later paving the way for the election of a woman to the post of JNUSU President. The constitution of a committee consisting of elected representatives of students, teachers, staff and karamcharis, whose decisions would be binding on the administration, had far-reaching effects on democratic institution building. Despite this pioneering achievement, the fight against entrenched patriarchy and sexism remained one of the toughest challenges, as successive complainants had to leave the university owing to inadequate community support, in spite of getting their grievances redressed by GSCASH. That took more than a decade to change.

The JNU students' movement was in shock following the election of a JNUSU President from the ABVP in 2000–01 by a narrow margin of one vote. This followed a split in the SFI on the eve of the elections. However, this difficult defeat was accepted by student organizations without raising a finger of doubt against the JNUSU election committee. (This was in complete contrast to ABVP's behaviour during close contests). In the same year, the JNU administration introduced the controversial 'self-financing' courses in the newly formed School of Information Technology.

The courses were withdrawn only after stiff protests, albeit by a deeply divided JNUSU. Memorably, the JNUSU also organized a massive people-to-people contact programme in 2001 to emphasize the importance of unity during the Vajpayee-Musharraf talks in Agra, despite the ABVP remaining lukewarm. Nearly thirty delegates arrived from Pakistan instead of just the invited few, with the swelling crowds requiring a change in venue.

The next round of JNUSU elections were held against the backdrop of the September 11 terror attacks in the US. Students voted against terror and war-mongering, and the one-vote defeat of the previous elections was reversed in favour of the SFI–AISF combine for all the four office bearer posts. The same result was repeated the next year. The social profile of successive JNUSU Presidents during those five years—Dalit, Muslim, OBC and woman—also exemplified the wider social coalition that formed the backbone of the JNU progressive student movement.

The tenure of the new JNUSU 2001–02 started with agitations. The five-year term of the previous Vice Chancellor was being deliberately prolonged by the NDA regime. During the winter vacations, JNU's Xth Plan proposals were suddenly prepared and sent to the University Grants Commission (UGC). The proposals exemplified the full extent of the RSS-BJP's designs for JNU, including the introduction of subjects like 'Human Consciousness' or the study of water as a source of ritual purity.[5] Despite the unified opposition of the JNUTA and the JNUSU, and a prolonged agitation involving a rare four-day university-wide strike, the administration remained unaccountable.

On 27 February 2002, during a UGBM of students, news reached us of the death of fifty-nine karsevaks in a fire inside the Sabarmati Express train near Godhra, Gujarat. The JNUSU UGBM passed a unanimous resolution and took out a silent march condoling the tragic deaths. Instead of joining the march, the ABVP later took out a separate procession that was provocative towards faculty members from the minority community. Students of JNU mobilized on an unprecedented scale against such a display of hateful communalism. With Vishwa Hindu Parishad (VHP)'s shila daan programme in Ayodhya just round the corner, students, teachers and karmacharis of JNU formed a huge human chain on 14 March 2002 to send an unequivocal message that peace and harmony must prevail in

[5]Gupta, 'JNUSU joins clamour against "saffronisation"'.

our country. Students and teachers of the university marched day after day for nearly two months across the streets of Delhi, went on fact-finding missions to Gujarat, and extended legal aid and relief to victims in relief camps. In fact, the response from JNU against the communal carnage in Gujarat was so emphatic that leaders of the VHP started demanding the closure of JNU. *Panchjanya*, the official mouthpiece of the RSS, also vilified JNU as a den of 'Marx-Macaulay-Madarsa'.[6]

Students soon resumed the ongoing Xth Plan agitation against an unaccountable and absentee administration, which had shifted base for occasional work to the Aravalli guest house on the campus. For a while, it seemed as if the NDA government would triumph. The JNUSU decided

VI.3. Marching in line: Students march from Ganga Dhaba to the Parliament, carrying banners 'Save Public Education', 'Fees Must Fall', 'Ensure Affordable Hostel for All', 18 November 2019.
Photo courtesy: Samim Asgor Ali

to lay siege at the Vice Chancellor's office. A memorandum was sent to the President of India, K. R. Narayanan, appealing for help and for

[6]The attack repeated a charge that was more widely made against liberals and left-leaning intellectuals. See <https://archives.panchjanya.com/arch/2002/3/3/index.htm>; also Mridula Mukherjee and Aditya Mukherjee , 'Communalisation of Education', *Outlook*, 13 February 2002; 'New RSS target : JNU home to anti-national forces, says Panchjanya', *Firstpost*, 3 November 2015.

VI.4. Students sit peacefully on the road near the INA bus stop when prevented from marching to Shastri Bhavan. Later that evening, 18 November 2019, students were lathi charged by the police.
Photo courtesy: Samim Asgor Ali.

the immediate appointment of a new VC. The office of the President responded and heard our grievances. It was rumoured that the President broke protocol to summon the file for the appointment of the JNU VC from the HRD ministry. Within a week, Professor G. K. Chadha was appointed as the new VC of JNU. The agitation against the controversial Xth Plan proposals resumed and successfully concluded under the term of the new Vice Chancellor, when the academic council rejected all the dubious courses and proposals.

The current script unfolding at JNU under NDA-II is uncannily similar to the one that unfolded under NDA-I, with a majority BJP government in office and the appointment of a pro-regime Vice Chancellor to JNU in January 2016. Since February 2016, JNU has been in constant ferment. The historic GSCASH has been dissolved and replaced by a mockery of a committee. JNUSU has been constrained in its functioning. But the determination of JNU to safeguard freedom, dignity, research, secularism, and democracy at the university is exemplary. A large painting inside the JNUSU office carries the only slogan to be ever passed by a JNUSU UGBM. It declares: 'Oppression is your Privilege, Protest is our Right!' As long as JNU continues to speak truth to power, there is always hope for its future.

41

JNU'S LASTING GIFTS TO ME

KAVITA KRISHNAN

I was moving to a new home in March 2019, and had to sort out the bits and pieces of my JNU life. Rummaging through an envelope of old papers, I came across a leaf from a film-festival brochure: one side announced that two Federico Fellini films would be screened on Saturday, 18 February (no year), and the other had a colour photograph of a clown. A small hand-written note in the corner noted that it was a shot from *The Clowns*, Fellini's 1970 film. The familiar hand took me back two decades, to March 1997—the momentous month when our friend and comrade Chandu was killed in Siwan. Just before he left for Siwan, to become a full-time activist of the CPI(ML), he had given me his papers: his identity cards, his school and college certificates, a letter to an old love that was never mailed, and various little hand-written notes and reports that he had preserved in his JNU years. I still have those papers with me—a friend's little treasures kept safe when the friend himself is not.

In those days, we wrote leaflets by hand, and had them typed, cyclostyled and printed. Notorious for my bad handwriting, I was forced to write legibly so that someone could typeset and cyclostyle the leaflets I wrote. Chandu had a neat and distinctive hand; his writing was never any trouble to read. I found a leaflet he was working on in the bundle of his stuff, asking JNU students to join the CPI(ML) election campaign in Bihar between 7–26 November 1995, which said that 'with pressure from the communal fascists there is a BJP-ization of the Congress'. And I thought about how this continues to resonate today, with the Congress under pressure to demonstrate its Hindu-ness, Brahmin-ness, and even to book Muslims under NSA for 'cow slaughter' in Madhya Pradesh.[1]

[1]Milind Ghatwai, 'In MP, this time under Congress, three held under NSA for cow slaughter', *Indian Express*, 6 February 2019.

The other old leaflets I found were mostly ones I myself had drafted. I would sit in the SIS canteen or the library canteen, drinking coffee and drafting leaflets in breaks between classes or class campaigns, so that the leaflet could go to press in the evening on time to be distributed at hostel dinner tables. I learned, then, to write fairly lucid polemics under virtually any condition. Late nights were the norm, because those were the only times available to write term papers and assignments. Reading happened at libraries, in hostel rooms late at night fortified with coffee from the dhaba in flasks, at the JNUSU office, and when needed even at dharna sites.

In the 1990s, AISA women were profiled as hedonistic 'free sex' types (just as all JNU women are now, for instance, by Gyandev Ahuja of the BJP[2]) I wondered then, as I do now, to whom I should complain that no free sex orgies ever happened as advertised! Instead, there we were: packing in impossible schedules of room-to-room and class campaigns, leaflet-writing, term papers, assignments, classes, course-readings, visiting the British Council and Sahitya Academy libraries, night-time public meetings, and fairly mundane loves and heartbreaks into twenty-four-hour days.

I found one leaflet with a poem copied from an even older AISA leaflet that I was told was dashed off by the first JNUSU General Secretary from AISA, Prathama Banerjee: 'You're your country's lost property/With no office to claim you back.'

A leaflet from 6 December 1996 that I must have helped draft, noted that just four years after the Babri Masjid demolition, BJP leader K. R. Malkani had written an op-ed in the *Times of India* dated 22 July 1996, which described the demolition as 'a mystery wrapped in a riddle inside an enigma' and tried to remake the very memory of the demolition conducted in public view by kar sevaks of the Sangh Parivar egged on by the top BJP leadership. Malkani suggested that 'Pakistan,' possibly with 'other accomplices, local and/or foreign' might have committed the act! 'Obviously,' he wrote, the demolition 'was the handiwork of forces that wanted to destabilise India.' He was right about that last bit, of course, except that the 'forces out to destabilise India' are India's own, not Pakistan's!

I found a 1995 leaflet entitled 'Towards a Feminised Marxism', I

[2] '"3000 condoms, 2000 liquor bottles at JNU": This BJP MLA is keeping count', *The Hindu*, 24 February 2016.

recall helping to write this along with some other women comrades. We wanted the leaflet published in the name of AISA's office bearers including myself, so that it would be carried as the organization's position and not of some individuals alone. We were reassured when the organization's then General Secretary signed the leaflet along with me, though he said its formulations did not line up entirely with the 'official' position of either AISA or the CPI(ML). The leaflet began with the statement, 'It is a welcome phenomenon that feminism, after much effort, is being discussed as a legitimate subject of political practice on this campus.' It ended with, 'AISA believes that one day Marxism and Feminism will be synonymous words and that today is the first day of the long life before it.' I feel a certain affection for that leaflet, in spite of its awkward formulations, because it kindles memories of the heated arguments and meetings which spelled democratic comradeship, taught us that a left-wing organization need not be doctrinaire, and made us feminists confident we were right at home where we belonged.

An AISA leaflet dated 19 July 1996—a year before the Vishakha judgment—proposed a 'gender-sensitive enquiry committee' to encourage women to report sexual harassment; a 'body that is independent of both the Administration as well as other pressure groups...that is unbiased and has the specific function of advising on all matters relating to gender'. The leaflet asked the campus community, the JNUSU and students to 'come forward with suggestions on how to make such a body viable and effective'. That proposal, I recall, was discussed in meetings we organized in hostel messes, which were attended by faculty members as well as by feminist lawyers from whom we learned about the ongoing Vishakha case.

An important piece of history from Chandu's cache is a five-page document of the 1993–94 JNUSU (the first one to be led by office-bearers elected from AISA), signed by the then JNUSU President, Pranay, and General Secretary, Prathama. It is entitled: 'A "New" Old Admission Policy: Justifying JNU.' It began with these words: 'JNU, situated in the capital, metropolitan in all the political-economic senses of the term, is far distanced from the entire mass of our population—both geographically as well as socially. In view of this, the sole purpose of a JNU community that looks for a justification of its own existence, must be to make JNU accessible to all sections of our society.' The document is a spirited and rigorously argued call to revive the 'Old Admission Policy' (which had been scrapped in 1983 amidst a landmark student struggle) and for deprivation points to be credited to the admission-seeker 'according to her social, economic, gender and regional deprivation'. The rest of the document outlines a detailed plan and proposal for awarding the deprivation points: in its attention to detail and its rigour, it is an excellent example of how JNU students used their academic training for social justice.

I remember JNU for a lot other than academics and politics, of course. There are smells which can still conjure up specific moments and emotions of JNU of the 1990s for me: the spicy night-time smell of the saptaparni evokes the onset of winter and the peculiarly bitter-sweet tensions of the JNUSU elections; the wild lemony smell of the shirish at Ganga bus stop at night heralds the JNU spring; and the heady scent of the wild karonda flowers on thorny bushes means the summer walks through the shortcuts towards the school buildings for exams. JNU spring-summer is also the bright red of the bougainvillea spilling in cascades from tall trellises far above, right down to the ground; the orange splash of palash; the glorious golden festoons of amaltas; the tart taste of the shehtoot plucked from trees on the way back from classes or the library.

My hostel rooms at JNU were always home to cats. On our very first visit to Ganga hostel, Parnal and I went in to check out our room, while my dad waited in the visitor's room outside. We came back to find him cosying up to a black cat. We later learned she was the inimitable Spike, who had many batches of kittens in our rooms. Our neighbour on the third floor, Huma, once said to us 'Cats can't know their names—she just responds to you because you feed her.' So I told her, 'You don't feed her, do you, so try calling her by her name and see what happens.' Huma replied by calling out 'Spike!' And Spike promptly turned right around with an enquiring 'Miaow?' And Huma just sat down where she was in utter shock, saying 'She asked me what I wanted!!'

JNU was the place where I made some of my most lasting friendships, especially with women. JNU is Tithi singing out-of-tune revolutionary songs even as the Jugnu comrades sang them in perfect tune. JNU is spending a full night in Shubhra's room in Godavari, perfectly sober, being introduced to the music of Dylan and Joan Baez, and greeting the dawn together. JNU is hanging out with Parnal and K. Kalpana on Holi, the time for bhang and colours and song. JNU was hearing the poems of Hindi and Urdu Marxists—Faiz, Muktibodh, Dhoomil, Gorakh—brought alive by friends. JNU is the public art on the wall posters, full of poetry and passion and politics. JNU is learning the comforts of comradeship—that meant sharing one's strengths, compensating for one's weaknesses, caring for each other in sickness, watching out for each other, learning to work with our differences, learning to lose elections and other battles without losing hope and will, learning to win without arrogance....

I am amused now to see the administration attempt to impose compulsory attendance registers on students (and teachers). As I remember it, it killed us to miss the classes we loved. Turning up for class was not a chore we did for credits. The teachers and students turned up for class, which could easily last well past the allotted two hours, because we loved how it challenged us.

JNU's greatest gift to me was to break me out of my protective shell of privacy. The loss of privacy was what made me try to run from public life in my first year and a half at JNU. We could feel the sour breath of fascism in the celebrations of the Babri demolition and the speeches telling us free women must be jailed—and that filled us with an urgent sense of duty that we *must* do what we could to resist it. In Ganga hostel one night in 1995, I walked into the mess to fill water, to see K. R. Malkani addressing an ABVP meeting on 'Uniform Civil Code' and Shah Bano. I went back to my room, 27 Ganga, and came back armed with readings on the UCC. I questioned him on why Hindu women were denied the right to inherit ancestral property—and he dug his own grave, replying that 'Hindu women do not need property because their families care for them.' He was promptly booed by the mess full of women students, and left in a hurry.

Although contesting an election was very far from my mind, I was persuaded by Chandu, who helped me overcome my dismay at the fact that public life as an activist meant you had to be available for anyone in need of anything, big or small—any time of day or night!

42

PEACE IN MIZORAM AND THE ROLE OF JNU STUDENTS

LALTHUAMLIANA

In the summer of 1979, much like the sweltering Delhi heat, the political scenario in the country was boiling hot. At the Centre, there was rising discontent in the reigning Janata Party against Prime Minister Morarji Desai. In Mizoram, the Mizo National Front (MNF) had issued a Quit Mizoram order against non-Mizos.

These events coincided with the arrest of Laldenga, a Mizo leader and founder of the MNF, on 8 July 1979. The leader had come to Delhi from London in January 1976 for peace talks with the Government of India with assurances of peaceful conduct back in case the talks failed. After protracted negotiations for more than three years, the talks did not make much headway. The dialogue broke off as Charan Singh, the then Home Minister, refused to talk to him, and Laldenga was sent off to Tihar jail.

Soon after his arrest, a couple of Mizo students from JNU including myself turned up at the family residence of Laldenga at Gulmohar Park, Delhi. The news of our visit reached the media and the *Indian Express* even falsely implicated us of having discussions to strategize the underground movement in Mizoram. This report came as a surprise to us as these visits were merely friendly calls to the family of an incarcerated fellow-Mizo, albeit a rather well-known one.

When Laldenga was arrested, the army prepared for military operations. As Mizoram was under Armed Forces (Special Powers) Act (AFSPA), the military had the right to kill anybody who was suspected of supporting the underground movement and the same could not be challenged in a court of law. Mizoram had enjoyed more than three years of relatively uneasy peace during the negotiations; the resumption of army operations in the state would have been too much to bear. It was clear that innocent people would be subjected to arrest, torture, and killings on mere pretexts of wrongdoing if the military operations resumed as even friendly visits could be misconstrued.

Some of the Mizo students of the university decided to approach Professor Dhirendra Sharma, an activist of the People's Union of Civil Liberties (PUCL), to help arrange a good lawyer for Laldenga. Professor Sharma, a teacher at the Centre for Political Studies, had also been involved in anti-apartheid, anti-nuclear, and anti-Vietnam war protests. He was quite sympathetic and told us he would be willing to help but on the condition that Laldenga would agree to talk within the framework of the Indian Constitution. The next day, we learned that Swaraj Kaushal, husband of Sushma Swaraj, subsequent governor of Mizoram, had volunteered to take up the case of Laldenga. Kaushal was a well-known lawyer who had also pleaded the case of George Fernandes in the Baroda Dynamite case.

The arrest of Laldenga brought renewed gloom in Mizoram and, considering the circumstances, engendered a spectre of fear and anxiety. In Mizoram, nobody dared speak out nor protest against Laldenga's arrest. In JNU, however, some Mizo students, Jack L. Darkim, Laldena, Thangkhangin Ngaihte, S. Ngiahu, Flora Zothanpari and I, decided to approach the leaders of various parties on campus to help us protest against Laldenga's arrest. We approached the JNU Students Union (JNUSU), Students' Federation of India (SFI), All India Students Federation (AISF), Free Thinkers, and other party leaders and all of them agreed to help. Initially, it was agreed by all parties to hold demonstrations headed by JNUSU in front of Parliament House to protest against the arrest of Laldenga. Fortunately, the President of the JNUSU, David B. K. Thomas, Free Thinkers, a close friend and a classmate in the Centre for Historical Studies, was very helpful in organizing the protest movement against the government's actions. Thomas had a B.Tech degree from IIT Kanpur, but having had a keen interest in history, had enrolled for an MA in history (Ancient) at JNU.

We soon found out that it was a huge surprise to the people and politicians in Mizoram that they were receiving the support of non-Mizo students, and that these students were willing to organize demonstrations against the government for the Mizos. To my mind, it pricked their conscience and even made the political parties bolder in their support of our cause. Meanwhile, the JNUSU had second thoughts about the proposed demonstrations at Parliament Street as the Morarji Desai government was falling and, instead, decided to hold a public meeting on the JNU campus. Unfortunately, many of the people we had decided to call, such as Justice Tarkunde from the People's Union of Civil Liberties, George Fernandes, and Madhu Limaye were eventually unable to participate due to prior appointments and, finally, it was the MPs from the Northeast who came and attended the meeting.

The public meeting was to be held in the afternoon at the JNU hall in the Old Campus; this was sometime in the third week of July 1979 and the topic was 'Current Political Situation in Mizoram'. We put up posters with slogans like 'Condemn Laldenga's arrest', 'Release Laldenga', and 'Resume peace talks in Mizoram' all around the campus on the eve of the meeting. Later, I even read a *Times of India* column about our posters. An uncle of one of the students who visited the campus was surprised when he came across posters supporting Laldenga, a 'rebel' leader. His nephew explained to him that all the important issues prevailing in the country as well as abroad were discussed at the university, which was why the issues in Mizoram were also being raised here and the government's actions being objected to. His uncle was taken aback and commented that older people would never understand what the young generation was thinking about.

I was provided a car to pick up the MPs invited for the meeting. Dr Rothuama (Mizoram), Rano Shaiza (Nagaland), Lalsawia (Mizoram), were the MPs who addressed the meeting. I still remember the whole event vividly. The meeting was chaired by David Thomas, the then JNUSU President. After Flora Zothanpari, a student from Mizoram, made some introductory remarks, David Thomas went on to narrate the army atrocities in Mizoram that violated human rights—the villages that were grouped together under the sham category of 'Protected Progressive Villages (PPVs)'. The villagers, in the name of protection, were not even allowed to work freely which had resulted in starvation. He stated that Laldenga had been invited for peace talks from abroad with the promise of safe conduct in case the talks failed. But, instead of sending him back, the government had arrested him. He boldly stated that no country had ever arrested peace negotiators except in this country and the home ministry officials had given India a bad name. They, therefore, were enemies of the country who chose to make war instead of peace, advocated disintegration instead of unity. It was time for the good citizens of the country to rise up and expose their misdeeds. David Thomas condemned strongly what the home ministry had done to Laldenga and urged that he be released immediately and peace talks resumed. D. P. Tripathi, speaking on behalf of the SFI, raised the issue of army atrocities and how army operations impoverished the Mizos resulting in the untold sufferings of the people of Mizoram. He highlighted that the longest curfew in the world was declared and imposed in Mizoram. He, too, strongly condemned Laldenga's arrest and army atrocities in Mizoram, demanding Laldenga's immediate release and the resumption of peace talks. Tripathi, a good orator, was the JNUSU President during the Emergency and was jailed during that time. He subsequently became a member and leader in the Nationalist Congress Party (NCP). The other MPs from the Northeast also stressed the need for creating a stable environment for peaceful negotiations. Speakers from other students' bodies too condemned Laldenga's arrest and demanded his immediate release and the resumption of talks.

Perhaps because of the bold stand taken by the JNU students during the crucial time of the peace talks, the home ministry was hesitant to further pursue its high-handed treatment of Laldenga, who, after some litigation, was given first-class treatment in jail, later released on bail and, finally, military operations were abandoned. Seven years after Laldenga's arrest, the Government of India and the Mizo National Front signed the historic Peace Accord on 30 June 1986. We are the children of war and we know the sufferings, and difficulties of war and revolution. We also know the value of peace.

During our JNU days, our friend Labu Sakhrie, a Naga scholar, used to sing an old fifties song called 'Last Night I had the Strangest Dream', composed by Ed McCurdy, an American musician. It was the most popular song amongst the anti-war groups for half a century. The song was recorded in seventy-six languages. When the Berlin wall was demolished in 1989, the East German children too sang this song. It goes like this:

Last night I had the strangest dream
I'd ever dreamed before
I dreamed the world had all agreed
To put an end to war
I dreamed I saw a mighty room
Filled with women and men

VI.5. Students from the Northeast in front of Chandrabhaga Hostel, organizing against sexual harassment, August 2018.
Photo courtesy: Samim Asgor Ali

And the paper they were signing said
They'd never fight again.

Peace remains elusive in Nagaland. How long will Labu Sakhrie sing McCurdy's song which he used to sing thirty-nine years back? We are extremely privileged to have peace in Mizoram today. I thank and salute all those who worked and sacrificed for peace in Mizoram. Let us dedicate ourselves today to protect the peace which was achieved with great difficulties along with sweat, tears, and sacrifices.

43

PINK AMONG THE REDS

ROHIT AZAD

The Pink Palace stands out at JNU

Buildings of similar vintage at JNU are red-brick styled structures and have an old world charm about them but the same can't be said about the Pink Palace. The fact that it has always been known to be a palace instead of the Administration Block or Ad Block, gives it the negative connotation it deserves, at least among the students. I first saw it closely during a hunger strike at JNU led by the JNUSU in the monsoon semester of 1999 on the issue of lack of hostels, among other things. That was during my first year of MA. I had to pass the litmus test of sitting on at least a relay hunger strike to become a political activist.

The Pink Palace for us was the place from which our 'class enemy' ruled and our entire purpose was to delegitimize that space politically. The contest always was whether Teflas (where the JNUSU is located) is the power centre of the university or the Pink Palace, and we were proud to say that whenever there was a contest between the two, Teflas won hands down.

As part of the popular mobilization during the agitation I am referring to, Satyajit Ray's *Hirok Rajar Deshe* (1980) was screened, since the Vice Chancellor was unwilling to come to the discussion table with the JNUSU. To us, the film represented the dethronement of an authoritarian Vice Chancellor. In this context, the first Bangla slogan I was introduced to was 'dori dhore maro taan, VC hobe khan khan', in which I gleefully participated since my mother tongue, Magahi, has some overlaps with Bangla. However, one fateful morning, the police arrested people sitting on the hunger strike and some bystanders. I felt bad for the bystanders since they had come just to see if we were doing okay. Within no time, the Pink

Palace was cordoned off by the police who appeared from nowhere in the wee hours of the morning. Senior student leaders of different organizations were sent to Tihar jail for the weekend whereas we were kept in the police station for the day. The VC had called the police fearing a confrontation with the students even though there was no sign of violence. This made the students furious and a very large number gathered in different hostels protesting against the high-handedness of the JNU administration. As a response to this arrest, the students took out marches where the slogan which reverberated on the walls of the JNU hostels was 'gher lo bhai gher lo, Pink Palace ko gher lo'.

The Pink Palace for us that year was also the place where we prepared for our first mid-semester exams at JNU while being on hunger strike. After an intimidating undergraduate exam structure in DU, JNU was a welcome change, and sitting at the site of the strike and reading for the exam made that space quite personal and at the same time collaborative since classmates were often found discussing their term papers and syllabus interspersed with sloganeering.

The Pink Palace interestingly had two contrasting images, one that was synonymous with authority and the other where admissions used to take place. The same student leaders who would deride the Pink Palace always had a soft corner for the other side of the Ad Block. So much so, even though they are two parts of the same building, we never identified the admission side to be part of the Pink Palace. The contrast between the two sides was such that we used to consider the admission staff to be our allies against the administrative staff on the other side of the building. In fact, the bridge on the second floor which connects the two sides was the Lakshman Rekha between the good and the evil. We expected problems to arise from one side while the other side would help us find solutions.

During those days, one couldn't imagine a place for student protests other than the Pink Palace. And for us, the stairs, which have become popular in the post-2016 days, were not the site of student activity. It was the front entrance of the Pink Palace, now a gated space, where we used to sit on hunger strikes with rival organizations often taking the two sides of that space. All the meetings during the agitations used to take place at the front door and since that would block the entrance, the administration used to cry hoarse that the students had blockaded the Ad

Block while we claimed otherwise. We used to derive vicarious pleasure out of such protests since it would force the administration to use the backdoor to enter their own offices. In my seven years (1999–2006) of student politics, I can say with pride that there was not even a single act of violence despite sharp differences with the administration as well as among the student organizations. I had been a student of Delhi University where political violence was pretty normal. I was, therefore, always amazed at the maturity of student politics at JNU. Under certain circumstances, for example, when one of our comrades had sat on a fourteen-day long hunger strike to no avail, it would have been completely impossible to maintain that tranquillity and calm, but somehow we never let that anger turn into violence. Despite raging anger against the palace and the kingdom inside, it was never vandalized.

I remember one particular instance of a somewhat naughty and thoroughly entertaining plan we made. The university, under its Xth Plan proposals, decided to introduce some commercial courses along with others with dubious academic credentials; one of these was called 'Yogic Sciences'. An entry of such courses would have opened the floodgates to commercialization and communal propaganda. We tried every trick in the book—UGBMs, public meetings, human chains, relay hunger strikes, hunger strikes, even a longish university strike—but to no avail. It was one of the toughest political movements I have been a part of at JNU, as a student. Since our futures were at stake, we were desperate and the patience of students started running thin. Our plan was to move the protest upstairs but we didn't know how to do that since the hunger strike was taking place at the Pink Palace entrance and the front gates were always closed from inside. Of course we had the option of vandalizing the building but that was a strict no-no for us. No violence under any circumstances was the mantra. So, we came up with a plan. The bridge between the two buildings of the Pink Palace was never closed, so we decided that a few of us would sneak in from the other 'friendly' entrance, cross the Lakshman Rekha in the dead of the night and hide ourselves. I was one of them. We slept inside the building that night, and the plan was when our student mobilization outside the Pink Palace would reach its peak, we would open the main entrance door from the inside. Since the guards had no clue that we were inside the building, they were busy chatting with the door bolted. Once we got the green signal from the pitch of sloganeering outside, we appeared from nowhere and opened the door. We all went up the stairs and the students entered the VC's office, only to find that he was not there. Entering the VC's office was pretty normal those days; it was just that the numbers were big that day. The students decided to wait for him in his office in protest. People started singing songs; some made cartoons of the VC and put it on his chair. We won that battle eventually after the Vice Chancellor was changed with Dr K. R. Narayanan's intervention at the request of the JNUSU and the controversial tenth plan proposals were withdrawn.

After that experience, my own interaction with the building and the later occupants became relaxed. The new Vice Chancellor would easily give you time to meet. Not just the office bearers but also the entire union! He would come down to meet us whenever we sat on a strike. The Rectors would always make it a point to listen to what we were saying. It was another matter that they didn't necessarily agree with what we were saying but the process of dialogue had opened up. We were still bitterly fighting for our rights and demands but at least we were being acknowledged. All

VI.6. The Administrative Block: the space in front of the building was named 'Freedom Square' when it became the site of the protest movement of 2016. The administration has now placed pots of plants on the stairs to prevent protesting students from sitting there. *Photo courtesy: Samim Asgor Ali*

our negotiations used to happen in the committee room on the top floor. In those days, after successful negotiations, joint statements signed by the VC/Rector and Union office bearers were released, after which agitations would be formally called off.

The Pink Palace of our student days has today transformed into a space of resistance against the authoritarian regime both inside and outside JNU. One of the reasons it shot into prominence is that universities and other academic spaces have become sites of resistance in the absence of an effective political opposition by the mainstream parties. It was here that the lectures on nationalism and azadi in 2016 were held. It was here that Kanhaiya, Umar, and Anirban gave their speeches on being released from jail after their prolonged illegal detention by the police based on fabricated videos. Instead of being a symbol of power for the administration, the space now symbolized resistance. From an obscure pink-coloured building, it was transformed into one which the country, for good or bad, identifies with JNU. It is no wonder then there is a contest between the administration and the academic community of JNU whether to allow it to go back to its earlier avatar of being a

VI.7. Bounding protest: in 2017 the JNU Administration marked the boundaries within which demonstrations and meetings were disallowed.
Photo courtesy: Samim Asgor Ali

citadel of the powers that be or a site of resistance. Every agitation, whether of students or teachers, has been an effort to reclaim it, and reclaim it, we will!

44

SOUNDS OF SILENCE

SUMANGALA DAMODARAN

Picture a scene from the early 1980s: a group of students standing around the entrance to Sutlej hostel on the JNU campus at midnight. It is late summer and there is a slight drizzle. As they begin walking towards the area where the Ganga Dhaba later came up and then down through the rocky areas towards the karamchari quarters, a voice wafts through the night, growing louder one moment and fading away in the next. These are the strains of the Lata Mangeshkar song 'O Sajna Barkha Bahar Aayi', sung in an unusually different way. As they move closer towards the voice, they realize that it belongs to Shanney Naqvi, the fabled singer, who is sitting with a few friends several hundred metres away from them.

I heard several stories about Shanney when I took admission to JNU in 1987. He sang ghazals, Hindi film songs from the Roshan–Madan Mohan–Salil Chowdhury era, and popular English songs; he could also recite the poetry of a wide range of Urdu poets. It was a common occurrence for those on campus to hear his booming voice as he frequently broke into song.

The other senior student whom I heard about, but never met, was Gorakh Pande, the moody and intense poet whose 'Samaajwaad, Babua, Dheere Dheere aayi' was being sung by groups outside JNU, including by Parcham, the group to which I belonged. The song parodied the socialist vision of the Indian State, describing the slow yet certain arrival of socialism, 'Dheere Dheere Aayi, Chhup Chhup ke Aayi, Angrezi Baaja Bajaayi'. When I joined the campus, I heard that he rarely emerged from his room. One afternoon, we heard that he had taken his life in his hostel room. Among the hundreds of students who gathered outside the hostel were many of his close friends and associates, grief-stricken at what he had done to himself. His mourning turned into a celebration of his long presence on the campus, his participation in political events of various kinds and, above all, how influential his poetry had become.

Two songs came to my mind that day, a Bhojpuri Biraha or song of separation describing, in a woman's voice, the travails that she had to suffer after being left alone due to her husband's migration to the city. The second, 'Hillele Jhakjor Duniya', a radical call to shake up the world and usher in a new order, was very popular within and outside the campus and was picked up and performed by the band Indian Ocean, in turn becoming one of its most popular songs. Created in the ethos of JNU, these songs continue to live on.

My song group, Parcham, used to perform regularly on many occasions at JNU from the early 1980s. I joined the group in 1983 and remember the late-night political meetings in the messes of the hostels, preceded or followed by our songs. 'Samaajwaad Babua', 'Tu Zinda Hai Tu Zindagi ki Jeet Mein Yakeen Kar', 'Jaane Waale Sipahi Se Poochho', 'Hum Mehnatkash Jagwaalon Se' and the Bengali anti-war song 'Juddho Noi, Juddho Noi, Tolo Awaaj' were always in great demand as students joined us in singing along. The atmosphere was always charged, and for me, a young undergraduate day-scholar from Delhi University, JNU appeared the ideal place to seek admission to. Parcham performed well into the 1990s, at mess meetings and especially during the counting of votes after the JNUSU elections.

Between 1987 and 1991 when I lived in JNU, there was a lot of singing on the campus. The Pratidhwani collective which had created a fabulous corpus of resistance songs from different parts of India, had gone past its most vibrant phase by 1987. Many key people had left the campus, but their songs were sung on various occasions. Shubhendu Ghosh, who composed songs based on the poems of Gorakh Pande, Faiz Ahmed Faiz and Nazim Hikmet, had started teaching in Delhi University's Department of Biotechnology and he would visit the campus a few times a year, having composed new stuff and singing at specially organized events.

Pratidhwani's songs got a fresh lease of life in the JNU Music Club, which was formed to bring students with musical talent together. Debu, a member of the Pratidhwani, sang the collective's songs, of which I remember two distinctly. The first is 'Ajadiya Hamra Ke Bhaavele', composed from one of Gorakh Pande's poems and 'Tumhare Haath Pattharon ki Tarah Sangeen Hai', from Nazim Hikmet's 'I kneel Down and Look at Your Hands'. Akin to what I'd heard about Shanney Naqvi's voice, Debu had an astounding range. His full-throated rendering of the refrain 'Ajadiya Hamra Ke Bhaavele', an octave higher than others, wafted out of the room where the music club met, and could be heard a good 200 metres away. He also sang Baul songs from the repertoire of Lalon Fakir, the Baul philosopher and poet from Bengal, of which 'Mohammader Naam Neete Neete' was a favourite, picked up by others and sung regularly in the club.

The music club's repertoire was wide-ranging due to the diversity of the students who came to JNU. It was remarkable how singing songs in different languages, learning different accents and listening to various songs turned JNU into a microcosm of the whole country. I heard the Rajasthani song 'Challa Challa re Dilaiwar Gaadi Haule Haule' from Mahendra Sisodia and Sanjay Chauhan, two active members of the club, as well as several Assamese Bihu songs from Debu.

One of the high points every year was the night when votes were counted after the students' union elections. Singing and sloganeering went together with high levels of excitement and anxiety all night. The venues were the open spaces outside the School of Social Sciences buildings or outside the School of International Studies. Almost all political groups performed, accompanied by the daphli, and sometimes the harmonium,

VI.8. Students perform a play during the hunger strike organized by JNUSU, March 2019. *Photo courtesy: Samim Asgor Ali*

other times, joined by a guitar. Typically, songs from the peace movement like 'Aman Ke Hum Rakhwaale' or 'Hum Sab Is Jahaan Mein Zindagi Ke Geet Gaaye' or 'Jaane Waale Sipahi Se Poochho' would be sung every year, and folk songs like 'Jogi Ra Saara Raara' adapted to the political issues at each election. Singing would be punctuated with sloganeering, accompanied by percussion and clapping, to be then followed by more singing. As Brecht had it: 'Will there be singing in the dark times? Yes, there will be singing, of the dark times!' This appeared on posters around the campus and invariably, singing would reach a crescendo as results came in and groups broke into either jubilation or silence, depending on the result!

The JNU ethos left an indelible imprint on me as it did on several generations of students before and after me. Apart from the academic training and exposure to many brilliant minds at the Centre for Economic Studies and Planning, where I completed three degrees over the years, were the kinds of political and cultural engagements of which singing formed a crucial part. This made JNU a rare university space indeed.

45

WALLS THAT SPEAK: THE MURAL TRADITION OF JNU

AKASH BHATTACHARYA

Walking through the JNU campus, it is hard to miss the vast murals that adorn its faded red-brick walls.[1] A fine example of university graffiti, they look down at passers-by and speak to them in a language that parallels political speeches and academic lectures. In its form, content, and making, the mural tradition of JNU is a spectacular and artful statement of its campus-based student politics.

The colourful murals, alongside black-and-white posters, coalesce into a wonderful collage that greet people at every school, at the canteens and in parts of the administrative building. The larger ones, visible from a distance, loom over the landscape of the campus.

The mural tradition was initially popularized at the university by the left-wing groups, primarily the Students' Federation of India (SFI)—the student wing of the Communist Party of India (Marxist) (CPI [M]) and the All India Students' Association (AISA)—the student wing of the Communist Party of India (Marxist-Leninist) (CPI [ML] Liberation). Over the years, these murals have increased in both size and grandeur and are now used by organizations across the political spectrum, including the Rashtriya Swayamsevak Sangh (RSS)-affiliated Akhil Bharatiya Vidyarthi Parishad (ABVP), the Indian National Congress (INC)-affiliated National Students' Union of India (NSUI) and the Birsa Ambedkar Phule Students' Association (BAPSA).

These are usually created by student organizations that participate in everyday campus politics and contest the students' union elections.

[1]This piece was written before the JNU administration decided, at the start of the academic year July 2019, that the walls of JNU had to be 'cleaned' of all posters, citing the Delhi Defacement Act, 2017.

VI.9. The battle for wall space: Left student organizations defend the right to dissent and protest against repressive laws.
Photo courtesy: Sthira Bhattacharya, 2018

VI.10. NSUI criticizes the rewriting of Indian history by the RSS.
Photo courtesy: Sthira Bhattacharya, 2018

VI.11. Gorkha students on campus have been increasingly vocal about their identity since the 2017 Gorkhaland agitation that followed the West Bengal government's decision to make Bengali compulsory in schools across the state.
Photo courtesy: Sthira Bhattacharya, 2018.

Occasionally, organizations such as 'Gorkha Students', which are relatively amorphous at the university, also put up one or two murals.

Student organizations often use this art form to express political positions, pose provocative questions and address problems in the light of their ideologies. The murals usually have a year-long existence. While these help set the broad ideological tone of the student organizations, the black-and-white posters carry notifications for upcoming events and immediate demands. These have a more transient existence of a week to ten days.

The spaces for murals are divided in a democratic manner. Every year towards the end of April, on a specific date decided in coordination by the organizations, the spaces for murals are claimed on a first come, first served basis. Often, there is a pre-existing understanding between organizations regarding wall allocation. The number of walls that each organization is allowed to claim is a function of its numerical and electoral strength on campus.

The murals are usually made by the students themselves. However, some organizations designate artists from within their ranks (not necessarily JNU students) for this purpose. Colours, brushes, and paper

VI.12. In the lead up to the JNUSU election in 2016, BAPSA stated that both the Left and the RSS/ABVP-led Hindu right wing seemed to practise caste discrimination and violence with equal vehemence.
Photo courtesy: Sthira Bhattacharya, 2018

VI.13. AISA raises questions about the political economy of the Commonwealth Games hosted in Delhi in 2010.
Photo courtesy: Akash Bhattacharya, 2011

VI.14. Students' Islamic Organization (SIO) translates the Palestinian Intifada for JNU students.
Photo courtesy: Sthira Bhattacharya, 2018

VI.15. AISF protests against the stereotyping of all Muslims as terrorists.
Photo courtesy: Sthira Bhattacharya, 2018

are purchased from Chandni Chowk over the summer break. Every poster is painted and cut into squares. The final product emerges out of a fine placement of the squares on the walls. Most of the murals are ready by the end of August in time for a new batch of students.

These murals have stood witness to the changes in the landscape of campus politics over time which, in turn, is connected to the ebb and flow of national politics, institutional transformations, as well as the changing values and aspirations of young people. For instance, the partial democratization of access to higher education through reservation and deprivation points has not only altered the student composition of JNU but also made social justice a key issue in campus politics. Debates between organizations on the meaning and implementation of social justice have spilled on to the walls in the form of iconographic contests.

As far as political forms go, the murals occupy a unique position. On the one hand they are part of the spectacular, alongside the long (often) aggressive speeches, noisy marches and intensive sloganeering and on the other, unlike the speeches, marches and slogans, the murals are less

VI.16. ABVP campaigns for the idea of a strong, united nation.
Photo courtesy: Sthira Bhattacharya, 2018

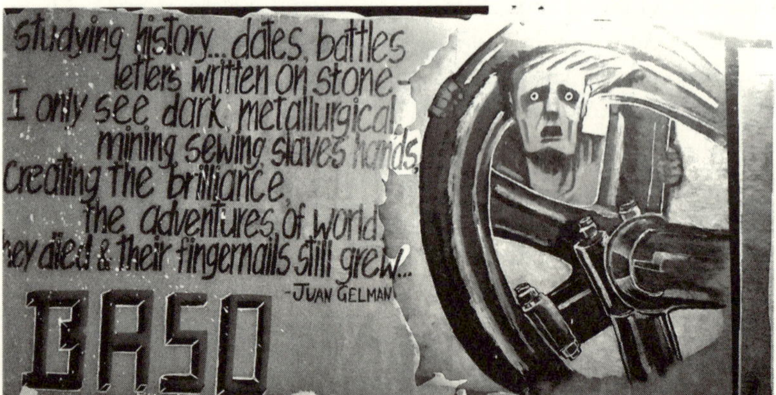

VI.17. The Bhagat Singh Ambedkar Students' Organization (BASO) underlines the need to recover the unknown histories of working people.
Photo courtesy: Sthira Bhattacharya, 2018

VI.18: Connecting art and politics.
Photo courtesy: Sthira Bhattacharya, 2018

ephemeral in character and seldom carry the burden of the tedium and ritualism often associated with the former. The enduring presence of a mural throughout an academic year allows it to become part of everyday conversations on campus in a way that a speech or a protest demonstration often cannot.

Conversations surrounding the murals range from the abrupt to the sustained, from the bristly to the friendly. One day, as I stood at the entrance to the School of Social Sciences, a professor walked in and had a long look at the AISA mural which said: 'Until deer have their own historians, histories of the hunt will always glorify the hunter' (see p. 294 below). I had known and respected the professor as a sincere scholar with a deep commitment to archival research but her apparent lack of sympathy for campus politics had always upset me a bit. As she was walking away, an activist from AISA entered the building and asked her, with a hint of sarcasm, what she thought of it. We geared for a debate on politics and history-writing when, to our bafflement, she asked, 'Why aren't these archived regularly?' and walked away. Was that counter-sarcasm? We were left to wonder.

There are other conversations or instances that are more sustained and substantive.

12 April 2005: A young man stepped into JNU for the first time to attend an academic seminar. He could not help but feel overwhelmed and confused by the sight that greeted him when he got off the Blue line 615 at the Ganga Dhaba. Staring at him was the huge face of Karl Marx painted in white against a black background. Marx looked sideways with one of his oft-quoted lines filling the space below: 'The philosophers have only interpreted the world in various ways, the point, however, is to change it.' The young man suddenly sensed a huge burden on his shoulders.

This is the story of a friend, who hailed from a village in West Bengal and was studying in Delhi University during his first visit to JNU. He would subsequently join JNU for his MA, MPhil, and PhD degrees. He recounted his first encounter with the university and with Karl Marx on the day he left the campus after submitting his PhD thesis in 2014. He said, 'Over all these years on campus, the spectacle of that mural grew on me much more than that quote did.' But what about that quote? I asked him recently. Never a big supporter of left-wing politics, he replied, 'I am still wondering about it.' It was clear from his tone that indeed he was.

Although work has taken him far away from the world of JNU, the

VI.19. When what disturbs power is reframed as defacement: in 2019 the JNU administration decided to strip the walls of JNU of its iconic murals.
Photo courtesy: Samim Asgor Ali

connection between politics and art remains an important question for him, as do the ways and means of changing the world, and the murals remain a point of reference. Those walls continue to speak to him, as they do to all of us who have sat in their shadows at some point of time, whether as a student or as a passer-by.

46

JNU SATYAGRAHA MOVEMENT, 2018

SONAJHARIA MINZ

Hailing from a humble yet conscientious Adivasi family in Jharkhand, I had the privilege of attending a Hindi-medium school at Ranchi, Jharkhand, in the seventies. I learnt the word satya rather early in life. It was part of my school motto: Satya, Premi, Shuddh (Truth, Love, Purity). These words were ingrained in us even as we sang the school song. Further, the mass recitation of the sankalp, the pledge, in Hindi, reinforced in us students a commitment to the sovereign state of India. Subsequently in my adult life, I came to realize the importance of these foundational values that had been inculcated in childhood. The moral ideals that a small-town school and my family taught me became the principles I still observe in engaging with the world around me.

Growing up during the 1970s, I experienced school as an institution that instilled love for the country. Moreover, having had teachers who had witnessed the independence movement of India, I grew up with the highest regard for the practice of satyagraha. Satya, as I see it now, has been an integral part of my evolving worldview and religious upbringing since the tender age of five. I also realize that the semantics of satya has evolved for me, from the simple idea 'not a lie' to 'what exists', 'what is and just cannot change—a constant,' and 'an absolute that prevails'. Specializing in mathematics, I did not have the opportunity to study philosophy in school or university. However, from a mathematical viewpoint a 'constant' as opposed to a 'variable' seemed to indicate the closest semblance to what I had grasped about satya.

While absorbing the idea of satya, I also saw the problems of Adivasis at home and the compelling need to address them. Values such as satya, premi, shuddh, the emotive resonance of sankalp in one's subconscious, and the issues of Adivasi life, have been, for me, an intimate part of my existence. My desire to study mathematics emerged out of a felt societal need, and the desire to address it. The underperformance of Adivasi children in science and mathematics is often correlated with the lack of Adivasi mathematics teachers. Hence I ended up focussing on mathematics for my undergraduate degree, and computer science seemed a logical path to follow later. Thus, I landed up at JNU in the summer of 1986 after qualifying in the MPhil entrance exam.

At the time of joining, other than the reputation of its academic excellence I was not really aware of all that the University stood for. I, therefore, came to be exposed to many new experiences. The small number of female students, especially in the research programmes in the science schools, forced us to interact with students from other disciplines in the hostel. It took me some time to appreciate the JNU culture of 'education beyond classroom' through post-dinner meetings, deliberations on issues of international and national concerns. I realized how these discussions nurtured the skill to argue and debate, necessary in the formation of conscientious and informed citizens. My disconnect with life outside the classroom perhaps had to do with my childhood resolve to be a maths teacher and nothing else. However, at JNU I spent time learning from the campus environment. I admired the way students participated in these intense discussions, reflecting on issues of social injustice, expressing their concern for the causes of Dalits, Adivasis and other minorities. What struck me was the way many of them voiced such views out of an intrinsic idea of justice and empathy for the struggles of weaker sections of society. Since childhood, I had only witnessed rallies of victims of injustice, demanding the rights they were denied. Thus, the idea that those not affected were willing to take up the causes of those who were affected stayed with me.

After completing my studies and a brief stint of teaching in two state universities, I came back to JNU in 1992, as an Assistant Professor. This also gave me the opportunity to observe the ethos of JNU, understand the spirit expressed in the JNU Act—its statutes, and ordinances. Above all, I imbibed a new culture, a new sensibility, one that celebrates the purpose of higher education, and fights for it as a social good. Being at JNU also gave me an opportunity to reposition my childhood values of satya, premi, shuddh while working in and with the administration led by five Vice Chancellors. Certain positions of responsibility also helped me mature in my approach to dealing with issues other than teaching and research, issues that were close to my heart.

The founding vision of JNU was to inculcate learning within an inclusive social fabric as well as a democratic culture. Over five decades of its existence, these founding principles were not challenged. However, during the past four years, the JNU community has been witness to a series of shocks, each surpassing the previous one in its form and intensity. It all began with asatya/mithya/'fiction' finding space in the system. In the minutes of the statutory bodies of the university, truth was replaced with falsehood—asatya. Legitimating and normalizing 'what does not exist' was a strategic move. A series of new ordinances were rolled out—all based on untruth, replacing truthful records of proceedings with asatya. As untruth spiralled within the system, the democratic decision-making structure within the university gave way to a dictatorial one. This deliberate misuse of power profoundly undermined the founding vision of JNU.

The impact of mithya in formal spaces came with a cost. Accepted norms were changed, conventions denied, practices thrown overboard. The ideal of social justice was subverted through changes in admissions policy (slashing the number of students to be admitted to research programmes), the statutory mechanism to ensure gender justice was dismantled, and norms of natural justice gravely undermined. The JNU community was left with no choice but to take action. Early in 2018, the teachers at JNU collectively resolved to seek the truth and hold on to it. The Satyagraha movement launched by JNUTA yearned to reclaim 'truth' in order to restore the character of JNU, and save the institution.

VI.20. Satyagraha Chowk, March 2018: The new space in front of the library building that was chosen as the site of protests after 2017.
Photo courtesy: Samim Asgor Ali

As the President of JNUTA, it was heartening for me to see that most members were committed to one idea: the need to replace untruth with truth. Reinstating satya seemed to be the only way to rescue the community from the distress we were experiencing. We recognized that this quest for truth had to be a process of reconstituting the self and transforming the other, much in line with what Martin Luther King had said: 'I can never be what I ought to be until you are what you ought to be. And you can never be what you ought to be until I am what I ought to be.' Inspired by this urge for satya, the JNUTA initiated dialogues with the administration, held press conferences, organized public programmes, and a hunger strike. This was our Satyagraha movement of March 2018. The space in front of the main library now became our Satyagraha Chowk.

To many like myself, JNU is not an employer from whom one receives a salary every month, but has been a mould that has produced what one is, a personal satya. Therefore, the Satyagraha movement was not grounded on some difference of opinion, or mere ideological conflict with the JNU administration. It expressed our affective relationship to the institution, acknowledged our gratitude to it—for all it has meant to many of us. It has been painful to witness the anguish of the university community that has suffered the spell of mithya, yet the urge to overcome that 'which does not exist', has given JNUTA the strength to pursue the truth. The history of satya, premi, shuddh is an integral part of my personal journey. My training in mathematics has deepened this commitment to truth, a desire to uphold it irrespective of the cost. In JNU, the personal and the collective social has come together in imaginative ways.

Satyameva Jayate implies 'the constant does not change'.

47

STUDENT UNION PRESIDENT'S SPEECH AT FREEDOM SQUARE

KANHAIYA KUMAR

From this platform on behalf of all of you, as the JNUSU president, I take the opportunity of the media's presence to thank and salute the people of the country. I want to thank all the people across the world, academicians, and students, who have stood with JNU. I salute them (lal salaam).

I also wish to acknowledge and thank all the people standing firm with the struggle, who are demanding justice for Rohith Vemula, whether from the media or civil society, political or non-political....

I especially wish to thank the worthies of this country sitting in the Parliament who claim it is they who decide what is right and what is wrong. My thanks to them, their police and also to the media channels... [*resounding cheers*]. In our parts they say, so what if one's name was vilified, it got one some publicity! At least they gave space to JNU on primetime even if it was to vilify it.

I have no rancour against anyone—none whatsoever against the ABVP [Akhil Bharatiya Vidyarthi Parishad, student wing of the BJP] at JNU. You know why? (*crowd roars—why?*). Because the ABVP on our campus is actually more rational than the ABVP outside the campus....

We have unstinting faith in the Constitution of this country, the laws of this country and the judicial process of this country. We also believe that the only truth is change, and we are standing here rooting for change. This change will come about, make no mistake....

I don't want to give a speech here: I want to tell you about my experience....

First things first—I don't want to say anything about the judicial process. I have said just one thing—and all the people of this country who believe in the Constitution and want to bring Babasaheb's dreams to fruition would have taken the hint. I don't want to say anything about the matter that is *sub judice*....

Truth will emerge victorious.... In my village—you have become acquainted with my family these past days—we have confidence in men at our railway stations trying to trick people into buying a 'lucky' ring that will give them anything they desire.

We have some policymakers in our country who are cast in the same mould....

If you speak out against this undemocratic regime, what will its cyber cell do? It will send a doctored video and insults, and the condoms in your dustbin will be counted too. But make no mistake, this is a critical moment and we need to understand that the attack on JNU is a planned attack because they want to delegitimize the Occupy UGC Movement. It is a planned attack because they want to discredit and destroy the struggle to get justice for Rohith Vemula....

Don't play soldiers against students

You cannot simply dilute our struggle by saying that on the other side of the picture are the country's youths who are dying on the border. I salute these heroic figures....

The thousands of farmers who are committing suicide, who grow grain for us and our youth on the border, farmers who are fathers to these youth... The farmer who works in the field is my father, and it is my brother who joins the army. [There are] those who die for the country within the country and also on the borders of this country.

Who will take responsibility for those who are dying? Those who fight are not responsible; the ones who make them fight are the ones who are accountable....

Is it wrong to seek freedom (azaadi) from the ills that plague our country today? They ask belligerently—who do you want freedom from? Has India enslaved somebody?

My answer to them is NO. So isn't it obvious that we are not seeking freedom from India? We are not seeking freedom FROM India but IN India.

What prison was like

Now I come to my experience in prison. Being a JNU student, how could I stay silent? So I struck up a conversation with a policeman and discovered he was just like me. Think—who takes up a police job inside a jail?—someone whose father is either a farmer or a labourer, someone whose father is from a disadvantaged section. I too come from one of India's backward states, Bihar. I too come from a poor family, a farmer's family...

The policeman asked me: 'Everything is very cheap for the people of JNU, right?' I asked if the same was not true for him. I asked him if he was paid overtime (he works eighteen hours a day) and he replied in the negative. When asked how he manages he replied: 'that same thing which you call corruption.'

He gets a uniform allowance of Rs 110. You can't buy even an undergarment with that amount. All this, the policeman volunteered on his own. I explained to him that it is precisely from *this*—hunger, corruption—that we seek freedom.

...I asked the policeman what he thought about reservation. 'Casteism is not a good thing at all', he replied. 'It is precisely from this casteism that we seek freedom', I told him. The policemen exclaimed: 'But there's nothing wrong with what you just said, there is nothing anti-national about it.'

Then I asked him one more question: 'who wields the maximum power in the system?'

He looked at his lathi and said 'danda' (the lathi).

'Can you wield your lathi at will?' I asked.

No, he admitted. On being asked who has the most power, his answer was, 'the ones issuing fake tweets!'

The policeman then said, 'It seems to me that you and I are on the same side'. 'Well, there's a small problem,' I replied.

So I told the policeman, 'Here you and I are having a one-to-one chat and there they screech: 'Dekhiye sansani khez' (Watch this sensational news).

'Shall I tell you something in confidence', asked the policeman. 'I decided I would beat you up when you arrived—your name was there on the FIR... but after talking to you I now feel like beating them up.' Democracy matters, as does social justice.

...This policeman, like me, comes from an ordinary family; like me,

VI.21. On the night of the return of Kanhaiya Kumar from Tihar Jail, Thursday, 3 March 2016: Kanhaiya Kumar, Shehla Rashid, and Rama Naga are at the centre.
Photo courtesy: Samim Asgor Ali

wanted to pursue studies; like me, wanted to understand the systemic ills of the country and fight against them, wanted to understand the difference between being literate and educated, yet is working as a policeman. This is where JNU comes in and that is why you want to suppress JNU's voice—to ensure that a poor marginalized individual is not able to do a PhD because it is clear as day that the poor simply cannot afford the lakhs of rupees needed to pursue a PhD in a private institution.

They want to stifle all the voices that can come together... You who don't want these voices to come together, I want to remind you of what Babasaheb said—*political democracy* is not enough. Well, we will establish *social democracy.* That is why we speak of the constitution repeatedly...

This voice of struggle they want to choke. Science says the more you press down, the more pressure builds up. But then these people have nothing to do with science for studying science is not the same as being scientific. But if a dialogue could be established with people who are engaged in the quest to build a climate of scientific temper then we will surely wrest the freedoms that we are fighting for in this very country: freedom from hunger and poverty, exploitation and injustice, and securing the rights of Dalits, Adivasis, women, and minorities. That we will secure this freedom in this country through this very Constitution, this very

Parliament and this very judicial process, is our dream. This was the dream of Babasaheb. And this was the dream that our comrade Rohith dreamed.

One more thing I want to say from my prison experience. This is my self-criticism and if you think it applies to you too, then take it in that spirit. We from JNU are refined and civilized in our speech, but we speak in heavy jargon which the common people of this country are unable to understand. It's not their fault. They are honest, straightforward and perfectly capable of understanding. It is we who are unable to explain things to them at their level....

Maa ki baat

Today, when our honourable PM...spoke about Stalin and Khruschev, I had an irresistible urge to...say, 'Modiji, why not talk a little about Hitler too? If not Hitler, then Mussolini at least—whose black cap was worn by your guruji?' Golwalkarji had gone to meet him and had been advised to fashion the definition of Indianness on the German model...

Now I come to something very personal. I spoke to my mother after three months. When I was at JNU I never kept in regular touch. After going to prison I felt one should keep in regular touch. I asked her: 'So you took a dig at Modiji?' She replied that it was not a 'dig' at him. 'To make fun of people is their prerogative. We just express our pain—those who understand, cry, and those who don't laugh.' My mother said: 'It was my pain which made me say: "Modiji is also a son to a mother, my son has been falsely accused in a sedition case. So when he talks about 'mann ki baat', why not also talk about 'Maa ki baat'(mother's plight)?'"

What words of comfort could I offer her? Whatever is happening in this country shows a dangerous pathology. Here I am not talking about one party or one media channel or only about soldiers—I am visualizing the entire country. What will be the face of this country when it is emptied of its people? That is why it is important to salute all those people who have stood up in support of JNU. They understand the importance of JNU—60 per cent of its students are women. Moreover, despite any shortcomings it may have, JNU is one of the few institutions which implements the reservation policy; where it doesn't, we fight to ensure it does so.

Also the people who come here—I have not told you until now, my family lives on 3,000 rupees. Would I be able to pursue a PhD in any big university? So when a serious offensive is mounted against JNU, the people who are standing up for it are also being tarred with the same brush... Sitaram Yechury has been charged with sedition, Rahul Gandhi, D. Raja, and Kejriwal too.[1] Even those from the media who are speaking up for JNU—actually they are not speaking up for JNU, they are stating the truth as truth and falsehood as falsehood—are being hounded and threatened.

My question is: 'Are you [those in power] able to see the difference or has your rationality been destroyed?'... Some of the people you lured with your harhar slogan can only think of the price of arhar [dal] these days.

So don't delude yourself that your victory is forever....

This is no spontaneous surge, my friends. There is but one overarching aim: wherever the voice of protest emerges in this country, choke it; whenever it seems people might start thinking about their fundamental problems, distract them, wherever the voice of protest emerges in this JNU campus, be it of Anirban [Bhattacharya] or Umar [Khalid]...brand it anti-national and delegitimize JNU.

...This is a long struggle and we have to carry it forward without stopping, without bending, without pausing for breath. We will stand against divisive forces like the ABVP on the campus or the BJP and the RSS outside the campus who are trying to bring the country to the edge of destruction. JNU will stand united against them; as history shall bear witness...

Thanking everybody who has been part of this struggle and appealing to them to walk by our side, I will end here...

Thank you

Inquilab Zindabad!

Rashtriya ekta zindabad! (Long live national unity)

Samajik nyaya zindabad! (Long live social justice)

[This piece has previously appeared as 'English Translation: Full Text of Kanhaiya Kumar's Electrifying Speech at JNU', *The Wire*, 4 March 2016. Translated from the Hindi by Chitra Padmanabhan.]

---

[1] '#JNURow: Rahul Gandhi, Arvind Kejriwal, Sitaram Yechury among nine booked for sedition', *Firstpost*, 29 February 2016.

VI.22. Students gather to welcome their President, Kanhaiya Kumar.
Photo courtesy: Samim Asgor Ali

VII

GIVING MEANING TO SOCIAL DIVERSITY

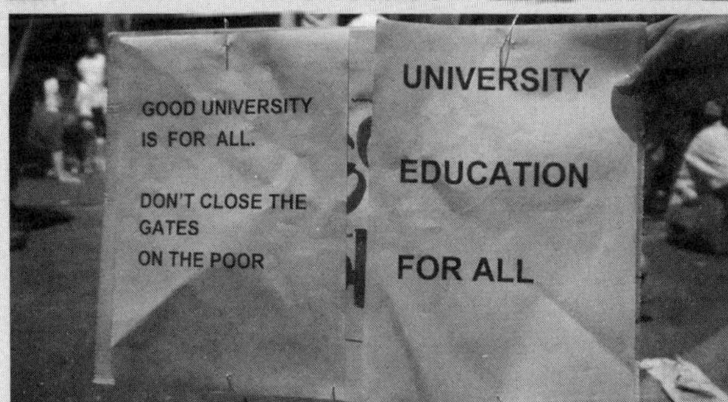

48

A TRANSFORMATIVE EXPERIENCE

KULDEEP KUMAR

I cannot imagine what would have happened to me had I not studied in Jawaharlal Nehru University. It so happened that despite my very limited ambition of becoming a college or university teacher, I became a journalist, worked in several English-language publications and wrote for Indian and foreign newspapers, magazines, and websites. However, when I joined JNU in 1973 for a master's degree in Ancient Indian History, I possessed only a rudimentary knowledge of the English language and had nearly no understanding of the discipline of history. It was JNU that enabled a small-town lad from Uttar Pradesh to overcome his circumstances and to evolve as an individual who believes in the core constitutional values of democracy and secularism.

The university was a unique experiment to introduce democracy with all its attendant grandeur into an educational institution of higher learning and it aimed at moulding its students as future citizens who would play a leading social, political, and intellectual role in nation-building that was, in those days as it is now, a work in progress. Consequently, the emphasis was not on testing the intellectual ability of students in the examination hall, but on broadening their horizons all through the year so they could devote themselves to serious study, reflection, and analysis. The effort was to hone their critical skills. In view of the state of India's education system those days, this was nothing less than an intellectual revolution as teachers themselves encouraged their students to formulate their own arguments and articulate them fearlessly even though they might have taken an intellectual position that diverged from those of the teachers. The students were not expected to learn anything by rote but to evolve as individuals who would effectively critique their times and social situations by offering new perspectives.

JNU represented the inclusive character of our freedom movement and, as an institution, tried to take the Nehruvian path by offering a democratic space to its students, teachers and non-teaching staff, and became a veritable republic of ideas. It was a place where all ideologies, schools of thought, and political tendencies interacted with one another peacefully contending for hegemony. As a university, it had a universal character. The very fact that I could get admission despite my lack of command over English and poor knowledge of history is proof enough that JNU in those days placed great emphasis on social justice, interdisciplinary approach, and inclusiveness.

I was a science student, who studied engineering for a year at the University of Roorkee (now IIT-R), and opted for Ancient Indian History in my application form for admission as I entertained vague notions about India's glorious past. I belonged to Najibabad, a small town situated at the foothills of Garhwal in UP's Bijnor district, where nobody conversed in English. As a result of the 'Angrezi Hatao' (Remove English) movement in 1967, launched by the socialist followers of Ram Manohar Lohia, the syllabus of English for science students had been considerably diluted and our ability to read and write the language was adversely affected. After the written examination, we were all to be interviewed by a panel, presided that year by Professor Romila Thapar who was Chairperson of the Centre for Historical Studies. When it was my turn to appear for the interview, sitting in the waiting room, I had eschewed all hopes of getting in. I did not know anything about Professor Thapar or the other historians on the panel. After taking my seat, I made two requests: one, that I should not be asked questions about historical events or facts, as I had never studied history, and two, I should be allowed to answer questions in Hindi.

In no other university would an interview board entertain such requests, let alone accept them. But at the Centre for Historical Studies, JNU, scholars like Sabyasachi Bhattacharya, Harbans Mukhia, R. Champakalakshmi, Suvira Jaiswal, and Muzaffar Alam had no problem agreeing. They were determined to give a chance to a candidate who suffered from disadvantages due to his social circumstances. I could never have got admission otherwise: my admission was nothing less than a miracle. And during my studies, I received constant encouragement from Professor Thapar who was always very concerned about my progress in acquiring a command over the English language as well as an understanding of history. Other teachers, too, were kind and sympathetic, as they could sense my problems.

In JNU, for the first time in my life, I came into contact with the real India as I met and made friends with students from a variety of social backgrounds—tribal and non-tribal, those from the Northeast and from South India. Like most people from the Hindi heartland, I believed Hindi to be the national language and that it was the duty of every Indian to learn it. I had no idea about south Indian languages and used to have fierce arguments with my fellow students on the issue of language. It took me almost a year to understand the linguistic diversity of our country and realize that languages such as Tamil were as old as Sanskrit, if not more, and had a rich literary tradition that could be traced back to more than two thousand years. The experience also opened my eyes to the complex process of creating a nation that would honour all its communities and citizens by integrating them into social, economic, and political structures.

I am one of those students who had lived the JNU experience through three of its most important phases—pre-Emergency, during Emergency and post-Emergency. In 1973, after the session began, elections to the Student Faculty Committee (SFC) took place and K. N. Hari Kumar won. That was when I learned that such a committee existed in every Centre and nearly all decisions concerning the Centre were democratically arrived at in its meetings.

The SFC also supervised the admission process and screened applications, besides assisting the faculty members in many other ways. It ensured the progressive admission policy was scrupulously adhered to by giving additional points to those who hailed from backward districts and depressed classes, and other disadvantaged sections of society. A substantial number of students could enter the university because of the humane admission policy that cared for social justice. The SFCs and JNU students' union (JNUSU) played a singularly important role in getting this policy formulated and implemented. The Academic Council too had student participation and in 1973, Syed Asif Ibrahim, who later retired as Director of Intelligence Bureau, was elected to it from the School of Social Sciences.

In my time, JNUSU elections took place in October. Though the Left dominated the campus's political culture, it was deeply fractured from within. The All India Students' Federation (AISF) was aligned to the pro-Congress Communist Party of India (CPI) and the Students' Federation of India (SFI) to the anti-Congress Communist Party of India (Marxist) respectively. Anand Sahay (Charlie), Gyan Prakash, and Kamal Mitra Chenoy were leaders of the AISF while the SFI was led by Prakash Karat, Ramesh Dixit, and Neelakanthan.

Devi Prasad Tripathi, who later became general secretary of the Nationalist Congress Party (NCP) and a Rajya Sabha member, joined the Centre for Political Studies in 1973. He too became a well-known face in the SFI soon. Jairus Banaji was the leader of the Trotskyites, while Anand Kumar, a national-level Lohiaite leader of the Samajwadi Yuvjan Sabha, cobbled together an umbrella organization called the Free Thinkers just before the 1973 JNUSU elections. All those who were either apolitical or critical of the traditional left joined this formation. There were a few supporters of Naxalites like Trinetra Joshi and Pankaj Singh. In short, JNU had a vibrant political culture that did not exclude any stream.

It was also a unique feature of JNU that the students themselves managed the affairs of the union without any interference from the university administration. General body meetings (GBMs) were the order of the day and all important issues were discussed, debated, and decided there. The GBMs were regularly held at every level—centre, hostel, school or union. Students would often initiate a signature campaign to requisition them. JNU was akin to a Greek city-state. Students themselves elected their election commission headed by a chief election commissioner to conduct and supervise union elections. No printed pamphlets or posters were allowed. Students would write pamphlets and make posters, cartoons and other campaign material themselves. National as well as international politics was freely discussed. If there was a dispute, recounting of votes was demanded, but never was a decision of the election commission questioned. Fierce debates took place all the time but personal relationships remained intact. Violence was unheard of, and so was eve-teasing or stalking.

In the hostels, girls were allowed into boys' rooms without any restriction. Boys could go only up to the girls' hostel mess, not into their rooms. However, for many years, one wing of a hostel was occupied by boys and the other by girls, and both ate their meals in the common dining room. To an outsider, this would have seemed like a permissive atmosphere, but it was this atmosphere that helped create a healthy ethos wherein boys and girls could freely meet, discuss, debate, make friends and, also occasionally, fall in love. As they were constantly interacting with one another, there was very little chance of objectionable or undesirable behaviour.

To a student from Uttar Pradesh, all this was a new reality. It opened my eyes to the virtues of democracy. It was also very refreshing to note that the university community was not divided into casteist or communal groups and the force of ideas was the only force that was used in daily interactions.

Teachers encouraged free exchange of ideas and a spirit of critical inquiry. Classes were an informal affair where there was no lecture from the teacher but a dialogue that helped students understand the subject much more easily and comprehensively. In most cases, politics and academic excellence did not come in each other's way. Whether it was Prakash Karat or Anand Kumar, Gyan Prakash or Devi Prasad Tripathi, Yogesh Sharma or Anand Sahay, Sitaram Yechury or Nalini Ranjan Mohanty, all of them excelled equally in politics and academics.

While JNUSU often agitated for students' demands, the relationship between students and the university administration was one of mutual faith and confidence. In the central library, needy students were given part-time jobs and they worked like any other library staff. When the university closed down on account of a month-long strike, students took over the central library and ran it themselves without any opposition from the authorities. Not one book was lost or damaged under their watch. Similarly, they also ran the hostel messes. In most cases, JNUSU enjoyed an excellent working relationship and understanding with the JNU Teachers' Association and the JNU Employees Union.

The imposition of the Emergency on 26 June 1975 ended this era. Many students were arrested, many others had to leave the university and yet many others became inactive. The university administration started flexing its muscle and Professors like Moonis Raza became ineffective. Students' participation became a thing of the past and strict rules were framed and imposed.

Admissions had to be approved by the Vice Chancellor's office and many names were removed on the recommendation of police and intelligence agencies. Regimentation and bureaucratization of the university started. In March 1977, after the Emergency was lifted, much of JNU's past glory was restored but a significant bit was irretrievably lost.

During its half-century existence, the university has faced many difficulties but has been able to invariably overcome them, acquiring the enviable reputation of being one of the top-ranking universities in India. One hopes that it will unflinchingly move ahead and play the role envisioned by its founders.

49

MY YASHODA

PURUSHOTTAM AGRAWAL

Imagine a university in North India in the seventies, where freshers are not ragged but doted upon by seniors, where women are not imprisoned in their hostel around 9 p.m., nor live under the constant dread of molestation; where you see women move around not only in busy public spaces, but also on deserted lanes in the dark of night—freedoms taken for granted by men and always denied to women; where students themselves conduct the students' union election, and election battles are fought through the power of persuasive argument, not money; where election posters are beautifully painted, not printed; where you might win the students' union election with very little money, an amount that presidential candidates in other universities spend on chai-paani for their workers; where a gentle shove or use of cuss words are seen as unacceptable violent behaviour.

Sounds like utopia? Indeed, it is, but to some fortunate people like me, it is nostalgia....

This nostalgia is also of a lived dream, and is recognition of what I owe to this institution, the acknowledgement of gratitude. I came from a university that had only one on-campus department; postgraduate classes were conducted in colleges, and students' union elections meant contests of muscle power. The gratitude is everlasting because here, at JNU, where the lingua franca was English, nobody ridiculed the twenty-two-year-old from Gwalior, Madhya Pradesh, who could somehow read but not speak English. When this boy once referred to all his female classmates as his 'girlfriends', he did not become the butt of jokes. The difference between girls who are friends and one's girlfriend was explained to him in a friendly way.

I joined JNU in 1977 for an MA in Hindi. Having completed a postgraduate degree in political science from Jiwaji University, Gwalior,

I had applied for an MPhil/PhD programme in political science as well, but there was no possibility of any scholarship, and I had no assured means to support myself. My father had passed away in 1975, the family business was in bad shape, and none of my relatives except my mother wanted me to be a scholar. I had vowed not to take any money from my family. In such a situation, I thought of registering for an MA in Hindi for I could then get a merit-cum-means scholarship. It was almost a life-or-death question for me to get into JNU, having passed the tough admission test in a subject I had not studied so far. Going back to Gwalior was out of the question, and there was no plan B at hand.

I stayed in Ali Javed's room in Ganga hostel, worked hard to study Hindi literature academically, and also tried to attain some sense of this seductive place: listening to debates at the dhabas, walking around the Kamal shopping complex, and sitting in the library reading room. It was on one such exploratory evening that Ali Javed pointed to a distant figure, someone in a dhoti-kurta and said, 'Look, there is Namwarji..., you have to face him in the interview.'

The excitement of seeing a living legend in person added to both my nervousness and resolve. Along with systematic preparation, the habit of eclectic reading picked up in early childhood helped. I was delighted to see my name at the top of the admission list.

Pleasantly surprised by the achievement, I subconsciously pledged that I would strive for excellence. Whether this was a reflection of repressed competitiveness, or the desire to acquire intellectual authority, I do not know. But I ended up with a record CGPA in my MA. I then registered for MPhil/PhD, to research on Kabir under the supervision of Professor Namwar Singh.

I did not, however, give up being an active member of the All India Students' Federation (AISF). I was a student activist even in Gwalior and was considered a 'champion' debater as well, but this 'championship' was not of much use at JNU, as addressing a public meeting here required a much higher level of preparedness. JNU was and still is a place where the excitement of serious learning is not limited to the classroom and the library. To speak even during informal discussions, I had to learn a lot, but here again, nothing in the culture of the place, nothing in the behaviour of friends, discouraged people like me. There were challenges of course, but there were reliable support systems as well. We, the new entrants, were encouraged and helped by seniors and teachers, more importantly, we were made to see this help as entitlement. There was rarely, or rather *never*, any display of condescension.

In Gwalior, my circle of friends was interestingly eclectic: there were political activists, spiritual seekers, artists, poets, painters, and even musclemen. I was actively interested in all these vocations, though I could neither paint nor aspire to be a muscleman. I think, this multidisciplinarity of interests jelled well with the interdisciplinary academic and political culture of JNU. Memories of Gwalior became endearing rather than frightening. Instead of fearing the idea of 'going back' to Gwalior, I could now love it from a safe distance. I learnt to value my past, rather than reject it.

From time to time, friends from Gwalior continued to visit me. In JNU too I formed a circle of friends: as I was reticent, it was always a small circle. This reticence was at times a problem: when I contested elections for the post of school councillor on the SFI-AISF panel, I got the lowest number of votes amongst the winners!

The interaction between my Gwalior and JNU group of friends added to the excitement and joy of my life at JNU, as also some moments of 'educative' fear. Once, at Nilgiri Dhaba, a friend from Gwalior was explaining the difference between a proper pistol and a desi katta to the ever-curious Suman. I was quietly sipping my tea and feeling a little bored. Unable to adequately explain himself through words my friend proceeded to give Suman a practical demonstration. He was about to take out his katta. I almost fainted. Terrified and shocked, I ground my teeth and told him under my breath, 'you...this is JNU not your kaalij.' Suman, being a girl from a very cultured background, was more upset at my use of hard Hindi slang in her presence than the action of my friend!

I can recall many more instances of such amusing but productive encounters between two cultural worlds, Gwalior and JNU. It is by negotiating these encounters I reconstituted myself, without erasing the past entirely, without accepting everything I saw at JNU. Such multicultural encounters created a space for the formation of new individualities.

Incidentally, Suman, a scholar of early modern poetry—a poet in her own right—expressed her gratitude to her alma mater, JNU, by editing a fascinating volume—*JNU Mein Namwar Singh*, which gives insight into the making of JNU.

The Latin phrase alma mater means 'the nourishing mother', which metaphorically speaking, every university is expected to be. But what if we recognize more than one mother? Within Hindu tradition, Lord Krishna was biologically born to Devaki, who along with her husband, was tormented and imprisoned by her brother Kamsa. The parents were forced to smuggle their baby boy to Gokul where Krishna's second mother, Yashoda, actually 'nourished' him. I cannot renounce my relationship to Gwalior. So JNU is my Yashoda, and may it be for many others.

◆

The culture of a nation, community or an institution is not to be judged by grandiose declarations but in everyday practice. In the context of individuals, being 'cultured and civilized' is particularly difficult to define, but as Jawaharlal Nehru wrote in one of the letters to his adolescent daughter, 'amongst many things it includes are certainly the restraint on oneself and consideration for others'. Within JNU culture, as I have experienced it, these two ideals—restraint and consideration for others—are both valued, at least it was in the past. Things are changing now.

This culture evolved out of conscious attempts to give the spirit of JNU Act, 1966, some tangible shape. This was a limited yet bold experiment of making an institution of excellence, which would be inclusive without compromising quality. The idea was to 'promote the study of principles for which Jawaharlal Nehru worked during his lifetime, namely national integration, social justice, secularism, democratic way of life, and scientific approach to the problems of life'.

The idea underlying the vision of JNU was to harness the youthful energy of the 'restless sixties', overflowing into the seventies, for humanistic national goals. This vision realized the importance of 'scientific approach' but more importantly knew the cardinal importance of humanities and liberal arts in the making of a humane society. The idea was to contribute to the making of a rational, communicative discourse in the wider public sphere. The vision did not suffer from high modernist myopia, of valorizing technology at the cost of humanities. It talked of a scientific approach without submitting to the terror of technology and artificial intelligence.

Indian society must be grateful to the early administrators, faculty members, and students of JNU who took the initiative to put these ideals into practise without compromising on high academic standards. JNU was conceived and created consciously as a modernist institution, yet it sat comfortably well with the traditional Indian ethos which expects even the rich and the powerful to show respect to scholars—pundits and their pupils. Hostility to scholarship, amply in evidence today, is a violation of that long tradition.

In the last four years the attack on JNU has been relentless. Kanhaiya Kumar, the JNUSU President, was murderously attacked in the premises of Delhi High Court and fake news about him and other student leaders was circulated on many TV channels. But JNU continues to symbolize the agonised conscience of India. It continues to fight injustice across international boundaries. It is at the forefront of ethical, and democratic mobilization in India.

Saba Dewan, the documentary filmmaker and organizer of the inspiring 'Not in my Name' movement wrote in a Facebook post on 25 March 2018:

> A university, its students and teachers stand up together against fascist onslaught. They resist and protest not for a month, six months or even a year. They have been doing so for over two years now in the face of tremendous pressure and terror tactics employed by the powers that be. The story of JNU is at once extremely moving and inspiring. I was never a student there but so wish now I was. Respect! Zindabaad!!

It has now been four years, not two. The vicious and persistent campaign in the Parliament and on social media against JNU has had a deleterious effect. It has created in the public mind a dislike for the university. The wider effort is clear: to destroy JNU as the site of critical thinking, as an institution that celebrates the power of deep thinking. Many were surprised when the present VC chose to invite Jaggi Vasudev and Rajiv Malhotra to lecture at JNU, and not all of these surprised souls were left-liberals. But why be surprised? Has this not become the norm today, the attack on intellectual institutions, repression of the academia?

I was visiting the University of Western Australia, Perth, with my family in May 2001 for a holiday with Suman who was pursuing an MBA degree there. One evening, we happened to reach Winthrop Hall, an impressive Gothic structure with Venetian glass windows. These windows had engravings of 'Holy Spirit's wise gifts' to man, seven in number according to the Old Testament; but we could see only five. Where were the other two?

This is the story of the missing windows engraved on the walls of the Winthrop Hall that Napier Walter designed in 1931. For many years no one bothered about the two missing windows, but in 1959, the then Vice Chancellor asked the architect to explain the mystery.

The architect replied: 'I deliberately omitted the two as these two—piety and fear of God—have nothing to do with the idea of a university.'

Reading this poignant answer brought tears to my eyes.

JNU, my Yashoda, without explicitly making any such symbolic statement, continues to nourish its students and faculty even under tremendous pressure; it continues to underline the crucial difference between a 'training' centre for imparting 'skills' (even if of the most sophisticated kind) and a university which is expected to contribute to the making of a nation 'where the mind is without fear, and head is held high/where knowledge is free/...where the words come out from the depth of truth/...where the clear stream of reason has not lost its way/into the dreary desert sand of dead habit'.

VII.1. Fighting for the histories of the historyless: Left student organizations at JNU underline the importance of social justice and social inclusivity.
Photo courtesy: Devayani Prasad

VII.2. The United Dalit Students' Front (UDSF) was formed in 1991, in the backdrop of the anti-Mandal, anti-reservation agitation in the country. Within JNU, Dalit students had for long felt overwhelmed by a Left-dominated discourse which was uncomfortable with the caste question and identity politics. Foregrounding the ideas of Jyotiba Phule and B. R. Ambedkar, and distancing itself from established political parties, UDSF has continued to organize discussions on issues of caste and help forge an identity based on the experience of being a Dalit.
Photo courtesy: Sthira Bhattacharya, 2018.

50

MY STORY OF JNU

GOPAL GURU

My story of JNU is woven around two wonderful words: fascination and fate. The word 'fascination' in the academic sense involved two intellectual trends: Marxism and post-Marxism. Marxism was integral to many courses across disciplines, and Marx as a thinker intellectually fascinated both teachers and students. The critique of foundationalism and the move towards post-Marxism—especially after the collapse of the USSR—also stirred the intellectual waters of JNU. The post-Marxist turn and the intervention of *Subaltern Studies* were felt particularly in the discipline of history, literature, and cultural studies at JNU.

At another level, what energized JNU was political activism. The two intellectual trends I refer to posed two distinct and related forms of politics: one celebrated the question of class, the other the question of 'difference'. Within the academic structure, the impact of post-Marxist trends could be seen in the intellectual fascination with a set of ideas: the state of exception (Giorgio Agamben), bio-politics (Michel Foucault), and identity politics. The political expression of this trend found its basis in the political activism of students and teachers from the Northeast and Kashmir, both regions ruled by the state of exception, the gender politics (bio-politics) of several gender activists, and the politics of Dalit and Adivasi students and faculty (identity politics).

Arguably, JNU is one of the few institutions of higher learning which did not allow intellectual solipsism. In fact, discursive conditions that continue to prevail at JNU have been such that they tend to compel scholars to participate in the collective life of the mind. I would, in fact, say that JNU is the only place in the country which provides necessary opportunities for everyone to develop and be ambitious about ideas. JNU, by and large, has encouraged every member of its academic community across disciplines to articulate their ideas with sophistication and nuance.

What is splendidly true about the university is an element of cognitive generosity amongst a large number of faculty belonging particularly to the different Centres of humanities and social sciences. This generosity has been evident in the free scholarly exchanges across these schools and Centres. One could learn and unlearn many things through the conversation of ideas. However, this much-needed sense of social generosity and the corresponding ethics of receptivity was lacking amongst some members of the faculty. This was because these academic colleagues simply resisted listening to morally disturbing realities while others made sincere efforts to compensate for this double lack.

When I joined JNU as a member of the Centre for Political Studies (CPS) faculty, political activism on the campus, as usual, was driven more by the need to be politically correct than politically conscious. Being politically correct was to stand with social and subaltern causes either through participation in protests or by signing various petitions whose flow increased particularly after the NDA came to power in the Centre in 2014. Remaining politically correct, at least in some cases, was more about endorsing established facts rather than seeking clarity about the truth. The future of this trend depended on the 'other' remaining the other, and not becoming a part of the same. To put simply, the existence of the 'other' became the precondition for a section of the academic community to express its politically correct stance and at the same time pursue research along the postmodern, post-structural lines that were a definite departure from the conventional research. Although this trend became almost an intellectual fashion, it was undoubtedly redemptive. Standing with the embattled 'other' made demands on ethical and moral resources, as well as social generosity. This was significant in a context where the modernist Left at JNU prioritized the political over the moral. This was also much required in a context where a tiny section was socially and cognitively uncomfortable with the word Dalit, even at JNU. At times, this was evident in the public utterances—such as 'I am not a Dalit'—made by some teachers.

Yes, even at JNU, one could at times hear: 'I am not a Dalit'. Such an expression was louder in conferences and seminars. One wonders whether such a performative utterance was naive or actually intended to produce a morally offensive impact on Dalits at JNU. I could not help feeling that such public expressions indicated the need on the part of the utterer to culturally/socially, if not intellectually, separate themselves from Dalits: the very word Dalit probably invoked an intense feeling of repulsion. Such a strong dissociation from the word possibly indicated that the speakers did not want the word to linger in their mouth. The word was dispelled in haste, ousted before it could pollute the mouth. For such people, the word Dalit produced a foul taste.

To hold such a position, either obliquely or openly, is to suggest that the word Dalit does not embody a changing essence; it is as if the word is frozen in time. It is as if people did not wish to utter or hear the word, nor understand how the word is mediated by time and is expressive of histories. Direct expression of certain words like Dalit disturbs many people.

Interestingly, in some Centres some teachers took a lead in introducing courses on bio-politics but without any reference to the politics of such performative utterances. The Dalit question came to be understood primarily in terms of bio-politics and was kept suspended on the fluid ground of constant meaning-making. Thus, the history of caste was treated as nothing but meaning-making, refiguration of the category over time. Intellectual persuasion takes fashionable turns where a scholar's ontological separation from the social conditions of existence allows him or her to easily shift from one intellectual trend to another.

Both these trends at JNU helped me a great deal to academically position myself differently. I was interested in making connections between concepts, institutions, and experiences. I was trying hard to delink the concept of social justice from the courses I was teaching. One was, in fact, a course on the politics of social justice, but I gave it a new spin and taught it as a course on the theory of humiliation. I tried to explore experiences as embodied in concepts, and concepts as inevitably always mediated by experiences, rather than the product of discursive relationships with other concepts. It was a difficult project. When I began to project the word Dalit as a universal abstraction, my efforts were considered by many as part of a 'hit-and-run' style of scholarship.

This description of my method created a deep confusion in my mind; but a confusion that turned out to be productive. As far as I can see, such classification has more than one intended meaning. One suggestion was that my conceptual project had an element of defiance; it refused to adequately respect the established norms that defined the syntax and structure of doing theory. In JNU, the 'hit-and-run' style of scholarship is considered to be one that subverts the rules to be followed while doing theory. Was there then a subaltern heroism in my hit-and-run style?

The second meaning of the label attached to my intellectual project was contrary to the first. It was as if my project was that of an upstart who eschewed efforts to do serious theory. 'Hit-and-run' suggested a serious lack of robustness, rigor, and necessary training in doing theory. It was as if analytical structures could be built only through standard conceptual language. The idea of a 'hit-and-run' scholarship also suggested that Dalits are not intellectually careful and have no regard for analytical rigor. This reading of Dalit proposes that they are pathologically grounded in the question of identity, and experiences related to it.

However, I was not interested in using philosophy to establish links between concepts that appeared relevant to me. I wanted to establish the relationship between concept and experience on the one hand, and concept and institutional practice on the other. My conceptualizations aimed at morally critiquing those for whom the starting point of doing theory is the available universals. Hence, my classes on humiliation explored the thick relationship between experience and concept. As a consequence, many of my students began to see the Dalit world through the mediating experience of humiliation. So the act of learning and exploring was not just intellectual play, but something that created moral turbulence among the students. This was a departure from dogmatic Marxism and inadequate liberalism. In classroom transactions, my effort was to put ethics before philosophy or treat ethics as philosophy.

As a scholar, I was thus subjected to a double reduction: first as a person who is a student of Dalit studies, then as an 'upstart scholar' who practices 'hit-and-run' theory. This led me to ask myself a question. If one is talking about Dalits, is one not talking about universal concerns? This question resonates with the question that was once posed by some scholars to one of the finest sociologists of our time—Jit Oberoi. He was asked: 'Why don't you talk about Sikhs?' To which he is said to have given the following answer: 'If I talk about the Sikhs who will talk about humanity?' Such an answer raises the broader idea of responsibility. The point is not to reduce the entire explanation to the Dalit question but to use the category Dalit as the starting point to reach broader explanations.

Reflection on the world of Dalits can be a deeper reflection of the human condition. One has to reach the universal only through the particular, whose inner dimension is universal. When I was teaching and interpreting texts in philosophy, I realized that the idea of spectre in the Communist Manifesto was used for a worker becoming a spectre for the capitalist. Drawing an analogy one could say: Dalits are becoming a spectre for those who have a Brahmanical mindset.

What is necessary is to develop an alternative theory of emancipation, a theory that would sustain itself not on the basis of already-given languages, but one that conveys a negative force. The category Dalit can be seen as embodying the premises of a universal critique, a deep power of negation. It can provide a universal category of explanation and understanding. A project in search of this idea would not only seek conceptual clarity but establish an alternate truth. This project of enquiry and reflection definitely started at JNU, through dialogic engagements in classrooms and seminars, and productive discussions with students and colleagues. This is a project I hope to finish in the future.

VIII

POLITICS OF GENDER

51

THE GSCASH MOVEMENT: A FRAGMENT (1997–98)

AYESHA KIDWAI

It is perhaps April 1997; it has just turned one o'clock. The School of Languages (SL) canteen begins to fill up. The first arrivals post the 1 p.m. class are Ritoo Jerath, Angelie Multani, and myself as we take up our positions at one of the two long tables of Madan bhai, the owner of the School of Languages canteen. Madhu Sahni and Kavita Bhatia come in soon after. The final one of the SL gang to sweep in is Ania Loomba, followed by a straggle of students with lingering questions left over from class. Ania sits down and we chat, waiting for the others from SSS—Farida Khan and Rama Baru—to arrive. They walk in shortly after, led by Mohan Rao, who has a seat at this feminist table. There is not one professor in the group, and I am the most newly minted Assistant Professor among all of them. This is a meeting of the faculty in the Gender Studies Forum.

The situation on campus had been very bad over the past year. There were innumerable incidents of 'outsiders' coming to Ganga Dhaba to harass women students. One woman had a beer bottle thrown at her from a moving car when she objected to unwelcome advances. In another instance, the perpetrators were caught at the North Gate and paid back in patriarchal coin with a severe beating, and their car torched by male students in ostensible protection of 'our JNU women'. Harassment by 'insiders' was also being increasingly met with a similarly violent response—in one instance, a student adjudicated to be a perpetrator was paraded from hostel to hostel with his face blackened. And then, there was the unnameable—what male professors can do, as teachers and supervisors. How, and to whom, does one complain when your PhD supervisor drops his pen down your shirt? Or makes sure that all consultations about your thesis happen in his campus house when his wife is away?

As the campus lurches between moral panic and violent protectionism, this 'problem with no name' remains unchristened. Most use the term 'eve-teasing', but that only undermines the complainant's testimony and smacks of patriarchal derision. Moreover, after the event, most women are silenced by the fact that the incident has no name, and there is no one to speak to about it. It is a woman's 'personal problem', and since no institutional rule relates it to the 'discipline of students' or the 'service conditions of employees', women confide in others, change their timings, their clothes, the way they hold their bags, their plans to study further, sometimes leaving the university, or their studies altogether.

Only rarely does a woman muster up the courage to speak out. Yet, each such story begins with how some university authority has discouraged the complainant from pursuing it, because every university official is male, and neither the JNUSU nor the JNUTA has ever elected a woman as president. Not that women teachers are all that helpful either, because they usually have no answer to the questions that plague complainants—'Why did he do this to me?' 'What will it take for me to forget this?', 'Can I prevent this from happening to other women?'

Until 1996, the Gender Studies Forum had held meetings with teachers and students to address this problem with no name. Women in particular are reluctant to use the term 'sexual harassment'—'I wouldn't say *sexual*, you know, because he didn't try to have sex with me'. Men are also discomfited by the new nomenclature: 'Call it discrimination, or just simple harassment, for god's sake—there is no sex involved in staring at a girl, is there?' The lexeme 'sex' invokes shame the moment it is spoken, understood as an admission of promiscuity or a proclivity to feminist hyperbole, or both.

But Ania has brought important news today that the Supreme Court of India is about to bring in guidelines mandating that sexual harassment complaints be addressed by employers. It allows the university and its institutional public culture to be fashioned anew. We begin to ask ourselves—what must change at the university for it to become a place in which 'sexual harassment' will be acknowledged and addressed? By what institutional mechanism could the Gordian knot that tied misogynistic receipt of a complaint and the asymmetries in which it took birth be unravelled?

The rest of the semester is full of conversations—with fellow teachers, students, and amongst us. Everyone is agreed that the answers lie in deepening democracy. For an anti-sexual harassment mechanism to truly work, those without institutional power must be the ones that move it—women, queer, students, employees.

By the end of July, the GSF has a draft policy against sexual harassment for JNU. The Vishakha judgment in August 1997 both uplifts and disappoints—it inscribes sexual harassment as a form of gender-based discrimination and even acknowledges the necessity of insulating the redressal mechanism from 'pressure from senior levels', but places naive faith in the employer.

In late August, a report of horrifying sexual violence reached us. A young mentally ill homeless girl, who had strayed onto the JNU campus, was lured into a JNU employee's home, held captive for two days, and repeatedly sexually violated. The employee's crime was only discovered by chance—when a JNU student saw him with her at Teflas canteen, and sensing her distress, secretly followed the employee and his captive, later alerting other students.

The JNU administration was intent on handing her over to the police, who would merely dispatch her to a Nari Niketan (the ill-reputed government home for destitute women): JNU refused to take any institutional action against the employee.

The campus is aghast. Did the university have no responsibility to the survivor at all?

A slogan that we have raised for decades—'VC teri jagir nahin, JNU hamara hai'—must now be realized. Hundreds of students and teachers gather at the Admin Block, demanding immediate suspension of the accused, and a guarantee that JNU would take responsibility for the survivor. Scores of teachers and students crowd the courtroom in which the accused and the complainant are produced to tell the judge that they do not want her to be sent to Nari Niketan, where she will not receive the care that she needs.

Surprisingly, the judge orders that she may be housed in a faculty member's house on the campus. A roster is set up by students and GSF members to sit day and night by her side, bathing her, feeding her, calming her down. No one can find out what her name actually is, because she sometimes gives herself a Muslim name, sometimes a Hindu one. We adopt the former.

The university finally orders an inquiry without which an employee cannot be suspended. The students who rescued the survivor, and her caregivers depose. But the 'inquiry' is about whether her words can be trusted given her mental state? Besides, what was the motivation of faculty like Madhu Sahni in 'supporting' her?

There is even greater outrage now and we no longer seek just a response on this case, but evidence that the JNU administration will change the system. What was once a relatively private conversation starts to become a movement, involving everyone on the campus.

The JNU administration buckles, and the employee is suspended. JNU teachers convince the court that the survivor should be handed into their care until they can make a more permanent arrangement.

The most enduring victory of this movement was the institution of the Karuna Chanana Working Group to formulate plans to combat sexual harassment on the campus. Even the composition of the committee was unthinkable just a few months earlier—a five-member committee with four women, and headed by a woman—Karuna Chanana, Sudesh Nangia, Ania Loomba, Rama Baru, with Yogesh Tyagi as the lone man. Neither Ania nor Rama was a professor at the time.

We congratulated ourselves. Within the committee, Ania and Rama insisted that experience on matters pertaining to sexual harassment lay in those sections of the JNU community that had addressed this problem when it had no name. Therefore, no action plan may be formulated without their inputs. Moreover the women's movement outside JNU had dealt with the fallout of sexual harassment for decades now. The committee agreed to consult with Lotika Sarkar and Ratna Kapur, and hold open consultations with teachers and students on the issue.

The JNUSU and GSF decided to transform the moment, by asking for much more than what the Vishakha Guidelines promised. While the Guidelines considered sexual harassment as discriminatory towards women alone, the JNU community asked for a 'gender-neutral policy'. Whereas the Guidelines were silent on how the complaints committee was to be integrated into an existing institutional framework, we asked for a standing committee that was exclusively tasked with addressing sexual harassment complaints. We also asked that even as the '50% women, and headed by a woman' composition of Vishakha be adopted, the committee must be constituted by direct election from the constituencies of teachers, students, non-teaching staff, wardens and officers, plus two external members chosen by the committee itself. Our argument was that the process of elections would enhance the credibility of candidates, and would be an awareness and consciousness-raising measure in itself, as issues pertaining to sexual harassment, gender equality, and justice would be then discussed widely, publicly.

The Guidelines vested the task of gender sensitization on the employer and focused mainly on the complaints mechanism: we asked that prevention and sensitization should be a major function. Finally, while the Guidelines did not raise the issue of how the inquiry into such complaints was to be carried out, we asked for a formal, time-bound, redressal of complaints, in which the obligations of natural justice held as much for the complainant as to the person (s)he has charged, and where interim relief and redressal are important components of the process of punishment.

The working group acknowledged the boldness of this vision—how are institutions to be built in response to discriminatory conduct?—by including what we wanted in its report submitted in October 1997. The first clash was within the committee itself, since Yogesh Tyagi submitted an alternative proposal of what was to be done. Could matters of sexual harassment be entrusted to a body comprising women students, women faculty, women karmacharis, who were both autonomous and empowered to take official cognizance of complaints and speak both for, and to, the institution? Gender justice should be discussed at most once a year, but under the watchful eye of males in institutional power. Complaints would be entertained, but at first, through an exercise of mediation. If complaints still remained, an executive committee would conduct an inquiry, but only within the framework of discipline, rather than rights and justice. There was no mention of either relief or redressal, and all the committees were to be nominated, rather than elected.

Although Tyagi's proposal was rejected by the JNU community, in May 1998, the only recommendation that was accepted from the Karuna Chanana Working Group Report was that there should be a two-member standing committee, nominated from the faculty by the Vice Chancellor with other constituents being co-opted on a case by case basis. This mechanism would make recommendations, and be accountable, to the JNU Vice Chancellor alone.

The story of how the JNU community fought for and won the Gender

Sensitisation Committee Against Sexual Harassment (GSCASH) includes the several agitations that took place between May 1997 and March 1999. In 1998, Professor Armaity Desai, Chairperson of the UGC, knocked down the last hurdle to the establishment of GSCASH: she made it clear to the JNU administration that as an autonomous institution, JNU was free to fashion Vishakha Guidelines for its own requirements. On 8 March 1999, the birth of GSCASH was announced by Professor Rehmatullah Khan, the Rector of the university.

But what happened to the survivor of the sexual violence who had sparked off this movement? Our survivor found a home in the Missionaries of Charity, and we were successful in convincing the university to take responsibility for her treatment at the Shahdara hospital. Professor Khan offered us his official car to do so for at least two years thereafter. After that, all contact melted away. All that remains at the end of two decades is the thought that, just like Bhanwari Devi, this survivor's complaint was one of rape, but as in that emblematic case, we too ended up deploying her story to make a case for the just redressal of sexual harassment.

52

QUEERING THE CAMPUS: THE ANJUMAN EXPERIENCE (2003–06)

MARIO DA PENHA

On a crisp autumn evening in 2003, a circle of friends who identified across the sexuality spectrum were sipping chai and trading banter at JNU's iconic Ganga Dhaba. As new arrivals to the university's social sciences and languages programmes, we sensed a void around conversations on queerness in an otherwise politically active and intellectually robust institution. We were all young people who had come to work in activism around sexuality either because our identities necessitated it or because of the rare, but exceptional feminist academic training in undergraduate colleges in Indian cities that existed in the early millennial years. Not long before, lesbian groups had defended the film *Fire* (1996) against violent assaults from the Shiv Sena and the Bajrang Dal. Moreover, after two years of silence, the BJP-led government had responded to Naz Foundation's petition challenging Section 377 of the Penal Code in the Delhi High Court. It declared that Indian society disapproved of homosexuality, and that alone was reason enough to retain the criminal statute.

Fired by sexuality's moment in the country's imagination, we believed it was an appropriate time to create a students' platform around queerness on campus. Gay students of generations before us noted their unwillingness to wear their sexual identities on their sleeves, for fear of peer harassment and social ridicule. Only some of us were gay or bisexual, but nevertheless, all of us knew that challenging sexual norms went beyond just how we identified. How would we go about this? What would we call ourselves? At that instant, as a cold, invigorating breeze blew by the dhaba, Parth crooned a courtesan's song from *Umrao Jaan*: 'Is Anjuman Mein Aapko Aana Hai Baar Baar.' Anjuman! A milieu, a space, a mehfil where difference was welcomed, and celebrated, without prejudice—that's what we aspired to. How appropriate it was that we had named ourselves after the words of a tawaif, a woman who skirted the edges of conformity within orthodox society. Our university's first queer collective (and India's second) had just been born.

Confronting Prejudices

During the roughly two and a half years of Anjuman's active work at JNU, challenging social biases and stereotypes around gender and sexuality remained one of our primary endeavours. At that time, many progressive students welcomed our presence, and supported our efforts at the university. However, as we soon discovered, clusters of conservatism also thrived on campus. Our introductory poster, made in both English and Hindi, tackled commonplace stereotypes of the time, such as 'women become lesbian when they can't find a man', 'homosexuals are mentally ill', and 'lesbians and gays can convert you to homosexuality if you are not careful'. We plastered these around liberally, but many posters were torn down; perhaps a sign of the entrenched prejudices we faced, and the uphill task that lay before us. Undaunted, we often made second and third posting rounds on the campus, and glued the ripped up bills back on notice boards. That November, many prejudices also found a public voice in the discussion following our screening of two films, Nishit Saran's coming out documentary, *Summer In My Veins*, and Deepa Mehta's *Fire*. Attendees queried the activist Gautam Bhan on whether homosexuality was moral, whether human beings would go extinct, and what future the family possessed if queer people were allowed to flourish. But even these partisan—and sometimes antagonistic—questions, brought us comfort, because the student community was finally speaking about sexuality in the open.

Over the next few months, we grew increasingly aware of the spatial nature of the hostility to our public discussions. Male students in and around exclusive male hostels made it progressively inconvenient for us to conduct public meetings freely. This homophobic belligerence began in minor, innocuous ways. On the eve of Holi, in 2004, at the university's annual Chaat Sammelan, the festival of humour and satire on the lawns outside Jhelum hostel, a comic asked women standing in the audience's rear to move forward. They needn't worry about the guys ahead, he quipped. 'They're all part of Anjuman.' Other humorists then mimicked two men kissing on stage, lampooning the collective. None of us were part of the crowd that evening. But we had, nevertheless, become part of the joke. In April, we organized a teatime lecture in the mess in Periyar hostel. Visiting Filipina and Thai academics, Roselle Pineda and Amporn Marddent, spoke about lesbians and sex workers organizing in Southeast Asia. Male students in the neighbouring television room raised the volume to drown out our speakers. Pineda raised her own voice in response, and spoke above the racket, but Marddent was less successful. We moved out eventually, and continued the lecture in the open at Godavari Dhaba. Both Jhelum and Periyar were men's hostels, and our claim over male spaces for gatherings, where both masculinity and patriarchy were questioned, had thrown many male students into a state of restlessness.

However, despite these ominous portents, nothing prepared us for the full force of homophobic ridicule and intimidation, which awaited us in September. That month, after the Delhi High Court dismissed Naz's petition, Anjuman organized an after-dinner public meeting in Jhelum

VIII.1. Sunandan and Padmini hold up the rainbow flag, and lead the Pink Triangle Day march through the campus, March 2005.
Photo courtesy: Mario Da Penha

hostel with two activists, Shaleen Rakesh and Pramada Menon on the anti-sodomy law, and the desideratum of decriminalizing homosexuality. On the night of the meeting, a huge mob, comprising mostly of men, welcomed our speakers with intimidating body language and mocking laughter, directing disrespectful, homophobic questions their way, speaking loudly over them and often preventing them from responding. When a student insinuated that homosexuality had a negative impact on Indian culture, Menon countered him swiftly: Was this the same Indian culture, which allowed for dowry murders, child abuse, and caste discrimination? Pandemonium ensued. Audience members shouted invectives towards the activists, and sneered at members of Anjuman. When it became clear that we had lost control of the situation, and the throng was physically closing in on us, we escorted Rakesh and Menon out, to jeers of 'Homosexuality hai hai,' and 'Gandu culture down down'. I remember my own tears that night, as Ponni and Sophia held and comforted me. Outside, two Dalit students offered solidarity to our embattled speakers; they were only too familiar with such aggression meted out viciously, they observed, whenever caste-based discrimination was discussed.

These turbulent events came as a rude awakening to the student body's self-understanding as a fulcrum for respectful debate. Until this time, party leaders on the organized Left, who were our friends, had distanced themselves organizationally from Anjuman, steering clear of our events, and looking past any conversation on sexuality, which did not encompass sexual harassment. Jhelum changed that. Within days, two parties—the DSU and AISA—publicly extended support to our collective for the first time. They decried the 'atmosphere of hatred and intolerance' and a 'sense of homophobia', which had resulted in attempts to deny democratic spaces [to] subjugated voices who have dared to question 'accepted' norms of morality'. Professors like Neeladri Bhattacharya and Purushottam Agrawal, scandalized by the violence, also stepped in, guarding future public meetings, ensuring that such overt harassment ceased. Others like Tanika Sarkar and Mary John promised assistance if future meetings were threatened. The university had intervened to protect its own.

Creating Solidarities

Increasingly after 2004, Anjuman considered it vital to build broader alliances both with student groups at JNU, and queer and feminist organizations outside it. We continued exchanges on sexuality with all students on campus, but we wished to open further channels with the organized left, which seemed the most receptive to allying with minority and marginalized struggles. In March 2005, we trooped through the university grounds, from dhaba to dhaba, along with friends and allies, behind a large rainbow flag, which Padmini and Sunandan held up. We clipped pink paper triangles to our hearts, to commemorate Pink Triangle Day in honour of the symbol used to identify and shame homosexuals in Nazi Germany, many of whom were exterminated in the Final Solution. Shipra and Ankita handed out flyers about our march to those we passed by. Joining us, among many others, were Mona Das, president of the students' union, revolutionary singers associated with the DSU, feminists from Saheli, and even Vidrohi, the university's resident poet and conscience, who recited his verse aloud. Sometime later, we also responded to a poster drawn up by the Indic Consolidation, a short-

VIII.2. Singing revolutionary songs on Pink Triangle Day, at Godavari Dhaba, March 2005. *Photo courtesy: Mario Da Penha*

lived conservative group, which argued that homosexuality was never problematic within 'Indic' traditions in the way 'Semitic' ones saw it as sinful. Our rejoinder challenged this intellectual flattening, and suggested that the experiences of Dalits and women might serve to counter such binaries. This drew cheers from many progressive quarters.

By early 2006, Anjuman joined Voices Against 377, a coalition of non-profit and progressive groups in Delhi in support of Naz's petition against the law, which the Supreme Court reinstated in the Delhi High Court. We contributed our experiences on campus in an affidavit to demonstrate the continuing presence of the anti-sodomy statute as a barrier to free expression. In March, the American president, George W. Bush, with two wars in Afghanistan and Iraq under his belt, was due to make a state visit to the national capital. Anjuman used the occasion to show how the sexual torture of detainees at Abu Ghraib, the patriarchal ideology of saving Afghan women from the Taliban, and muscular militarism remained at the heart of Bush's foreign policy. Bush's support for Christian conservatives also meant pulling federal funding from organizations that worked with sex workers abroad, or advocated the use of condoms as the primary means of preventing the spread of HIV. A group of us, along with other campaigners from Naz and Voices marched in protest against Bush's visit, carrying the rainbow flag from Ramlila Maidan to Jantar Mantar, surrounded by a sea of red, of banners and flags of trade unionists, and others from the organized left. In April, we joined sit-ins and signed a letter in support of the Narmada Bachao Andolan, which was protesting in Delhi against the raising of the height of the Sardar Sarovar Dam in Gujarat.

However, there also emerged several other moments of rupture, of the straining of solidarities, and of a failure to build alliances. During the campus-wide debates over the presence of a restaurant run by Nestlé near Tapti Hostel, Anjuman felt pulled between the reality that corporations in a liberalized India offered safe spaces—internet cafes, coffee houses, and clubs—to queer people, and the concomitant truth that many such spaces were restricted to those of specific class, linguistic, and caste backgrounds, as well as gender identities. At another time, we also drew disappointment from friends in the SFI, who discreetly reported to us that our poster on public executions for sexual crimes in Iran in 2005 (which we, and several Western queer groups misinterpreted as punishments for sodomy) had angered some of their Muslim constituents. We won no friends among

Christian students when we challenged a fundamentalist group, Exodus International, which was visiting JNU, on its history of spewing dangerous anti-gay rhetoric, with no basis in the scriptures.

But perhaps, our most glaring failure was our inability to bring caste and sexuality into an earnest dialogue with one another. By early 2006, two groups working on caste issues emerged at JNU: the United Dalit Students' Forum (UDSF), and the Ambedkar Study Circle, in addition to *Insight*, a student magazine. Bindu and I had conversations about how we might go about this. We hoped to link historical attempts to break the spatial barriers of caste, in the Temple Entry Movement, for instance, with the breaching of heterosexual male citadels across the world. However, by this time, many Anjuman members—Priya, Ponni, Padmini, Uditi, and Kalyan among them—had graduated, and left Delhi. With our dwindling numbers, and our focus on other affairs, this dialogue, sadly, remained unfulfilled.

In 2010, after many of us had left Delhi and Anjuman's activities at the university had long ceased, I jumped with joy when I read about the first openly gay candidate contesting student elections at JNU. Gourab from the SFI, was later a member of a new queer group on campus called Dhanak. In late 2018, I met Paresh, a graduate student of philosophy at JNU, at a protest against the government's new transgender bill in Mumbai. They told me about organizing a third queer collective at the university, delightfully named Hasratein. Over fifteen years after Anjuman first began, with Section 377 now confined to the dustbin of history, it fills my heart with happiness to know that the conversation on sexuality continues. Satrangi salaam!

53

PARWAAZ: REFLECTIONS ON INDEPENDENT GENDER-BASED ACTIVISM IN CAMPUS

SHIPRA NIGAM AND ANKITA PANDEY

In a fairly politicized campus like JNU, many conversations over cups of chai at the dhabas invariably centred on aspects of its vibrant and diverse student activism. The most visible and vocal activism on campus was by the organised left-wing student formations. Soon this dominant pattern became a source of dissatisfaction. In 2005–06, a bunch of like-minded people, broadly Left-oriented but unhappy with the rigidities of orthodox Marxism, were showing up for evening discussions at the dhabas to share their dissatisfaction, and a new platform was about to emerge.

Looking back, the dissatisfaction was on two counts. First, although various left parties did engage with issues of gender, these issues often became secondary to questions of class. Many of us sought a perspective that recognized the intersection between class and gender. Second, most of the gender-related awareness and sensitization was the institutional responsibility of Gender Sensitization Committee against Sexual Harassment (GSCASH). However, GSCASH was overburdened with a mandate to perform both sensitization and disciplinary functions and often found it difficult to find enough time and resources to devote to the former. We wanted to start an independent initiative to provide a platform for substantive debates over issues concerning gender on the campus. We also wanted to use the platform to connect these debates on campus with larger national issues and concerns of the autonomous women's movement. We were a heterogeneous group not bound or restricted by party affiliations and therefore had no party line to follow or justify. Parwaaz—the JNU student's gender collective—was born in 2005–06.

Over the course of the next few years, Parwaaz's engagements increased the visibility of gender issues in campus student politics but not without its highs and lows. We participated in the time-honoured JNU tradition of releasing parchas on a variety of issues that were being discussed and debated within campus. We organized public events: lectures by prominent feminists and voices from the women's movement, film screenings and workshops. We also held fortnightly public meetings. These engagements inevitably revealed the fault lines of caste, class, gender, and sexuality. We were constantly reminded of the multiple registers underlying the broad strokes of an overarching left-wing student politics. In what follows, we share our thoughts on a few of these interventions, the larger discursive contexts within which they were located, the debates they generated and lessons they brought home for us.

Most founding members of Parwaaz were also members of Anjuman (the JNU students' queer collective). The launch of the latter had met with considerable resistance from groups and individuals across the student body in those early days of queer activism. Having decided to keep the gender and queer forums separate for both normative and practical reasons, there was however a clear understanding amongst us that these were going to speak to and affirm each other wherever needed. We were convinced that gender issues could not be reduced to women's issues or sexual harassment alone. It encompassed the concerns raised by the LGBT movement. Since all parties had declared their support to women's issues in principle, we chose to negotiate with this acceptance to bring an awareness and visibility of LGBT issues through a gendered lens.

Our activities in these forums led to some very tense encounters. The very physical presence of close friends who embodied alternative sexualities brought forth sharp hostilities in the form of abusive anonymous remarks on event posters, catcalling and harassment on streets, and in public meetings organized by us. Nevertheless, the existence of a larger progressive discourse within the university enabled us to hold student political bodies accountable, take clear positions, and also build community solidarity with a wider section of students. We organized the first election meeting of its kind in 2005–06 where the Central Panel and GSCASH candidates were questioned on their views and their party's stands on gender and LGBT issues. At this meeting, Left parties on campus openly declared their support against any harassment of the LGBT community on the campus and affirmed the right of all individuals to choose their sexual orientation. ABVP candidates were widely criticized by the audience for opposing homosexuality.

There were some other encounters that brought to the fore the varying undercurrents of intersectional student politics. For instance, some politically active women went to the room of a male student in Jhelum hostel to confront him about his alleged sexist abuses. In the course of this confrontation, the women allegedly slapped him. The male student was Dalit and he filed a complaint with the university's Equal Opportunity Office. This snowballed into a messy controversy. Some saw the women's action as 'violence' and others saw it as an instance of agential 'collective action'. This created deep dilemmas for Parwaaz as a platform. We were aware of the provocations behind the incident, and the pervasive violence that politically active women often had to face on campuses. We also knew that time and again, political critique of the positions taken by politically active women was often expressed in explicitly sexist overtones; this not only deflected from the actual issues being debated upon but also highlighted their vulnerability as women. This incident raised several questions however: Did the women react with an awareness of the fact that a Dalit man was involved? Would the action taken have been different had there been Dalit women in the group? Why was there an absence of Dalit women's voices on campus? What would be a more sensitive and contextual approach to caste and gender questions from those involved with progressive politics? Could there be a nuanced position on the incident informed by both gender and caste?

Another instance that made Parwaaz reflect on the issues for gender activism came in the form of an incident which involved the targeting of a female student in a minority university allegedly for her political activities and articulations as part of a student group active there. She sought the help of JNUSU and other bodies to provide her a platform where she could present her case. Parwaaz agreed to organize a public meeting for her. During and in the aftermath of this meeting, various comments, volatile undercurrents and simmering tensions exposed to us both the presence and power of religious patriarchy as well as the vulnerabilities of minority institutions.

There were also productive and fun engagements with the campus public sphere. The GSCASH often foregrounded issues of women's safety, given the number of cases that came up before it. A popular belief amongst a large section of men on campus was that GSCASH was a weapon in the hands of women to settle scores against them. Parwaaz made its own small attempt at complementing the sensitization aspect of GSCASH. We worked in collaboration with GSCASH as a voluntary group and organised workshops, screenings, talks that disseminated information about issues of gender and patriarchy in campus. There were workshops and public meetings in hostels for information dissemination around issues of sexuality, sexual health, commonplace misconceptions about sexual health, and resources for those seeking help. The unequal power dynamic built into hierarchical relationships like that of student-professor or warden-resident or karmachari-students were also discussed during these events. We also conducted a workshop on Feminist Self-defence, or Wenlido, a technique that translates as 'Women's path of strength'. Structured with a feminist perspective, the workshop dealt with the physical safety as well as the mental and emotional health of women.

Sometimes our interventions also generated controversies on other registers. During an international film festival that we organized on the eve of Women's Day in collaboration with GSCASH, we ran into trouble while screening *Bride Kidnapping in Kyrgystan*—a documentary that followed the stories of four non-consensual weddings that came about through the custom of bride kidnapping. Some Kyrgystani students at JNU were adamant that it was not representative of Kyrgystan and showed their country in a 'bad light'. They demanded that we stop the screening. The battle lines were drawn—freedom of expression vs hurt national sentiments. We negotiated and soothed frayed tempers by inviting the students to present their point of view too before the screening.

Looking back, perhaps the real success of interventions made by Parwaaz was in re-energising the discussions around gender beyond standard concerns of Left political party engagements, while locating them firmly in their intersections within the emerging discourse on sexuality and LGBT rights. With the benefit of hindsight, our activism occurred against the backdrop of an increased visibility and political assertion of identitarian movements, and the processes of democratization and affirmative actions slowly taking root in public universities in general. Within JNU in particular, given its uniquely progressive admission policies and diverse student body, these processes of democratization have proceeded apace, even as student bodies have become more and more representative. The university's relative cosmopolitanism and broad Left legacy also continues to enable such interventions and independent

VIII.3. A feminist poster exhibition put up by Parwaaz in 2006.
Photo courtesy: Mario Da Penha

VIII.4. At a Parwaaz workshop, 2006.
Photo courtesy: Mario Da Penha

initiatives increasingly located at the interstices of caste, class, gender, and sexuality.

For many of us, JNU's unique campus milieu provided a haven and a safe academic space. Through conversations and conflicts, moral dilemmas and debates, it engendered a politically and personally transformative experience. We learned lessons in social sciences by doing politics. The intervention had a formative influence on the development of our own personal and political codes of ethical conduct. It also gave us several memorable encounters as well as companionships and bonds that have withstood the test of time.

IX

THE WAY THINGS WERE

54

JNU: FIFTY YEARS OF EXISTENCE

SOHAIL HASHMI

JNU came into existence fifty years ago, when the bill for the creation of JNU was tabled in the Rajya Sabha, by the then Education Minister M. C. Chagla, on 24 December 1964, during the tenure of Prime Minister Lal Bahadur Shastri. Two issues were raised during the discussion: the need to ensure that JNU did not become just another university and therefore the need to create new faculties. The JNU Bill was passed by the Lok Sabha on 16 November 1966 and the JNU Act came into force on 22 April 1969. Thus, on 22 April 2019, JNU completed fifty years of its existence.

Once the decision to form a university was taken, Professor Moonis Raza, the then principal of the Regional Engineering College Srinagar, was appointed an Officer on Special Duty (OSD) for JNU. A kind of camp office began to function from Vigyan Bhawan Annexe from the second half of 1969. It was here that the idea of this university began to take shape.

Quite independently of the parliamentary debates to start JNU, a decision was taken to shift the National Academy of Administration (NAA) from Mussoorie to Delhi. Land was acquired in South Delhi and four six-storey blocks that would have been used as hostels for the probationers of the Central Services were made ready. A club building, equipped with a squash court, a swimming pool, dining hall and kitchen was made ready. An administrative building, lecture halls, and a library came up at one end of the sprawling campus while housing for the administrative staff occupied another corner.

Behind the club building, extending all the way to the administrative quarters, was a large open ground where a paddock and horse-riding facilities, tennis courts, and other accoutrements befitting the NAA would come up. All this materialized with a speed as remarkable as the reversal of the decision of shifting the NAA from Mussoorie to Delhi. Perhaps to cushion the shock of asking it to stay put at Mussoorie, the academy was renamed the Lal Bahadur Shastri National Academy of Administration in 1973.

It was something of a miracle. Who knows the kind of strings the triumvirate of G. Parathasarthi—the diplomat, educationist, journalist, and first Vice Chancellor of JNU, Professor Moonis Raza, officer on special duty (OSD) and first Rector of JNU, and N. V. K. Murthy, teacher, filmmaker, administrator and first Registrar of JNU, pulled individually and collectively, but the fact remains that JNU now had a campus and the university could start.

An Institute of Russian Studies that functioned independently at IIT Delhi was transferred to JNU and became the Centre for Russian Studies in 1969. It later grew into the School of Languages in 1972 when the NAA campus was given to JNU as temporary accommodation for a period of ten years, while JNU built its campus.

There were three entries into the NAA campus, the main or the East Gate was opposite Ber Sarai, this took you directly to the four blocks and the club building and was the most used. There was an entry from the north through the outer Ring Road and this took you to the administrative block and to the lecture halls. The lecture halls were also used for hectic political debates, for seminars, and for lectures by invited speakers. For some reason Lecture Hall No III, popularly known as L-3 was the most sought after.

The third or south gate was initially used by some of the faculty and administrative staff who lived in the flats at the southern end of the campus. This was later used by those going or coming from the New Campus that was coming up to the south of the NAA campus from the very early 1970s.

Most student activities and activism were concentrated around the Schools and Centres, the lawns outside, the lecture halls and the club building. The club building also housed the university canteen and the hostel mess and, the famous presidential debates, barring one in 1972, were also organized there.

Between the canteen and the dining room was a small space marked out for day scholars' relaxation. A radiogram, a couple of chess and carrom boards and a few lounge seats were placed, but after the initial excitement, people forgot about them. In any case, JNU always had small groups who created their own music. Even though sports were never a major engagement for students of JNU, a cricket pitch and a tennis court were put together with great speed, because the VC, a former Ranji player himself, most enthusiastically supported the JNUSU demand. But the facilities remained relatively unused.

The first structure that one encountered upon entering what later came to be known as the Old Campus, through the main gate, was known as Block-I and in those days, it was the boys' hostel. Once Kaveri hostel came up in the New Campus in 1973, Block-I was allotted to SIS that now shifted from Sapru House in the same year. Two rooms on the ground floor were turned into the office of JNUSU and for years, the counting of votes used to be conducted from one of the classrooms above the office of the JNUSU.

On 25 September 1975, during a strike call given by the underground JNUSU that had begun to function as the 'Resistance', P. S. Bhinder, DIG (Range) and a close associate of Sanjay Gandhi, rushed into JNU in a black ambassador and kidnapped Prabir Purkayastha, mistaking him for D. P. Tripathi.[1] The state does not own up its silly mistakes and Prabir had to spend almost a year and a half as a Maintenance of Internal Security Act (MISA) detainee. Tripathi, the then president of JNU, was abducted a few days later by a posse of policemen, eventually placed under MISA and released only on 25 January 1977.

Behind Block-I but separated by a large open lawn was Block-III, which housed the School of Social Sciences. The Centre for Social Medicine and Community Health, Centre for the Study of Regional Development, Centre for Political Studies, Centre for the Study of Social Systems, Centre for Historical Studies, and Centre for Studies in Science Policy ran from this building.

Two other Centres of SSS, Centre for Economic Studies and Planning and the Zakir Hussain Centre for Educational Studies functioned from the ground floor of Block-IV that was located behind Block-II.

The Centre for Russian Studies grew into the School of Foreign Languages and, eventually, acquired the rather impressive moniker of School of Language, Literature and Culture Studies.

[1] 'Detained for a Year on Mistaken Identity', *Times of India*, 18 February 1978. See also, Gyan Prakash, 'A case of mistaken identity', *Emergency Chronicles*, Gurgaon: Penguin India, 2018.

A part of the first and second floor of Block-II above the passage that connected it to the other blocks was used as faculty accommodation and Professor Moonis Raza occupied one of these rooms. Initially Block-II was a multi-utility facility, with the top three or four floors being used as the girls' hostel, while different language Centres were functioning from the first two floors.

The old CRS building had a small auditorium, which was used for cultural events. It was also the site from which the JNU film society was run successfully for many years. The film society was put together by Professor Kalpana Sahni from CRS and D. Raghunandan. Raghu, as he was popularly known, was to later become the president of JNUSU. The film society was able to screen the finest of world cinema, and students were privileged when the famous filmmaker Ritwik Ghatak came and stayed at JNU for a while. He must have been surprised to see so many ardent fans of his films in this small university that had just begun to get noticed. The building is also the site from where the initial work for the South Asian University was started.

How did this handful of structures grow into one of the most remarkable institutions of higher learning?

The first idea was to create Centres and Schools instead of archaic departments and faculties. It was believed that the use of interdisciplinary studies would disrupt falsely created boundaries between streams of learning. Fulfilling the requirements of this objective became possible through the creation of an administrative structure where Centre Chairpersons and the Board of Studies at the level of the schools functioned with great autonomy and the administration worked as a facilitator, not a snooping, interfering body.

Second, the fact that JNU was able to attract some of the finest minds cutting across disciplines was due to the autonomy in selection of faculty and in administrative matters fostered by the university structure. But this was only one half of the story—the other was the rigour with which the student community engaged with and contributed to the academic and administrative life of the university.

The research scholars of ISIS—Prakash Karat, Ramesh Dixit, S. P. Tiwari, Appan Menon and O. N. Shukla, among others—were responsible for designing a students' union that would be totally independent of the university. The idea was to allow students to elect their own committee to conduct elections. Each candidate or organization would have to place a manifesto before the students, and the entire team of office bearers and the entire union could be voted out in a general body meeting. The draft was debated and approved by the student community and the university did not create obstacles in the path of the autonomy of the students. This was a unique situation, unheard of and unimaginable, but it was accepted and continued without interference from the administration except during the Emergency and now, during the undeclared Emergency, helped on its path by the provisions of the Lyngdoh Committee.

It was a union elected by the students, free of any interference from the university and accepted by the administration as the voice of the entire student community that made it possible for students to demand and eventually acquire the right to have their representatives on the student faculty committees at the Centres and to have their elected representatives be members of the Board of Studies and the Academic Council.

The objective of ensuring that JNU did not become just another Delhi-based university was achieved through the admission policy that evolved over a couple of years with constant dialogue and debate between the faculty, the administration, and the students represented by their elected union—the JNUSU. The debates were heated, sharp and at times acrimonious, leading to strikes and even a gherao of the VC and all the Deans, but ending in a mechanism that ensured the doors of the university were open to all those who wished to pursue higher education.

It was this university that first introduced the concept of quantification of backwardness and exclusion—social and economic—and created a points-based scale that would be used, overseen by student representatives, at the Centre-level student faculty committees, at the time of admissions to counter age-old instruments of marginalization.

This admission policy gave the student community its all-India inclusive character, and ensured that students excluded from education in general and higher education in particular got their fair share. These provisions were introduced much before the UGC half-heartedly thought of affirmative action in this direction. The fee structure and affordable mess bills, kept within control because elected mess committee members bought provisions and kept a check on the quality and pricing, made it possible for the economically-depressed to stay in hostels.

It was a politically aware and socially committed student community which ensured that women had as much freedom to move around the campus as men.

Much has changed in the last few years, but what has not changed is the commitment of the faculty and the students. The fight to get JNU back on its footing of eminence has to start with the kind of post-Emergency struggle that was led by the students. To begin with, the inclusive admission policy has to be brought back and the autonomy of the student union affirmed.

55

REMINISCENCES*

HARBANS MUKHIA

If there was no better reason to reminisce about JNU, the quarter-century I have spent here since around 1971 is reason enough. But almost as in a person's life, JNU's formative years have been most exciting, aesthetically satisfying and full of humour, for being experimental, exploratory, and innovative.

The very first few years were the years of the hegemony of the Marxist theoretical idiom and the dream of socialist practice. To speak in that idiom was avant-garde; any formulation minus the mode of production context was passé. There was, too, a concern for the wretched of the earth, whether in the western or in the eastern half. If this concern did not divide itself between the northern and southern halves, it is because this division itself is of later origin.

The small numbers of the three constituents of the JNU community also made possible experimentation with collective rather than representational democracy. Whenever a problem called for discussion between students and faculty, a meeting of the entire body of each Centre was convened and a long discussion, often over trivial matters, ensued; and of course no self-respecting teacher or student would complete his or her statement without placing it in the context of the appropriate mode of production and roundly denouncing the Indian bourgeoisie and, at frequent if somewhat irregular intervals, imperialism. The tradition of long discussion, especially in the GBMs, came almost from the inception. There is a good, if apocryphal, story of a thief having been caught in the act by some students who promptly proceeded to hand him over to the police. Halfway to the police station, another group of students of an alternative

*From Kanjiv Lochan (ed.), *JNU: The Years, An Anthology by the Silver Memoir Committee*, Bombay: Popular Prakashan, 1996, pp. 93–100. The essay has been edited for this volume.

political hue brought itself up-to-date on the empirical data and raised the conceptual question of whether the first group had considered the class character of the police as representative of the coercive arm of the bourgeois state before handing over the thief to it. Indeed, whether the man was a thief was itself a conceptual issue which called for discussion, for was it of choice or of the system's inability to provide him for subsistence that he committed an act that the bourgeoisie had defined as theft? The validity of the problematic was beyond contest and a GBM was promptly convened. After about eight hours of discussion and no resolution in sight, it occurred to someone to suggest that the 'thief's' own views regarding state and society may be sought, a suggestion that met with loud cheers of approval. The 'thief' came to the mike and humbly pleaded that it would be an act of great kindness if he were handed over to the police instead of being subjected to any further discussion.

The year 1977 stands out as an example of students' concerns with issues of theory, history and society. During the Students' Union elections the real contest was between two individuals, neither of them a candidate—between Jairus Banaji and Devi Prasad Tripathi. Jairus was a brilliant scholar who came as a research student (to the CHS, naturally) with an already established formidable reputation. He had spent a large part of his life in Britain, knew several languages including classical Greek fluently, was very widely read in European history and Marxist theory within which he sided with the Trostkyite version, had already published some very highly regarded pieces and was a superb speaker in English. Understandably, he was popularly nicknamed Virus Banaji, for that is how his influence spread on the campus. He also established his own non-SFI Left group, which did not long survive his departure; its name I cannot remember now. Tripathi, having been JNUSU President on behalf of the SFI, was a very good public speaker in Hindi and fairly effective in English as well; his mastery over Hindi, Bengali, and Sanskrit literature made him delightful company for conversation. He was well-grounded in the history of the communist movement in India but was somewhat at a loss in the history of Europe's Left movement.

The formal candidates in the contest were, I think, Sitaram Yechury on behalf of the SFI and Rajan James, a memorable figure of the early years, on behalf of Banaji's outfit. In the end, the SFI won the election, but like in every other contest, moral victory belonged to Jairus.

The layout of the New Campus, conceived of as the residence of a family, with interspersed faculty houses and hostels but without the exercise of parental surveillance, and the intellectual milieu of commitment to changing the world and making it a better, more egalitarian one, gave both a sense of freedom to the students denied them in their undergraduate colleges and a sense of purpose, as well as power. There was grandeur in the conceptualization of JNU which bore the mark of G. Parthasarathi's vision. Contention, dissent, and concession of the right to a different opinion formed the premise of this vision. It translated itself into heated exchanges on the streets and roads, at times turning into traffic hazards, as autumn dusks dissolved into nights; it manifested itself in some of the most aesthetically appealing posters and superb cartoons and in the coining of rhymes and phrases, especially at students' election times, but no one ever dreamt of tearing down rival posters; it came to the fore in the most uncomfortable questions put in the most polite language to celebrated speakers. If discussion in the class was less stormy, it might have been in part out of respect for teachers, but more, I suspect, because from early on, bunking classes came to be regarded as the surest sign of a student's intelligence and maturity. A sense of dignity attached to being absent from class.

The grandeur of dissent could not have expressed itself more evocatively than in 1981 when Indira Gandhi, the Prime Minister and JNU's Chancellor accepted the invitation of the School of International Studies (SIS) to inaugurate some function or other in that school. The Students' Union decided to prevent her from entering the campus, naturally following a GBM resolution, in protest against the Emergency she had imposed on the country. Y. Nayudamma was the Vice Chancellor, one of the most democratic at JNU. After a great deal of talking to and giving-in and so forth, the VC offered to the students the following formula: as a citizen of India, Mrs Gandhi had the right to visit the JNU campus, and the students, as citizens, had an equal right to protest against the visit; they could thus exercise the right to protest but not physically prevent her entry into the campus. The formula found general acceptance. Mrs Gandhi came to the Old Campus where a huge pandal had been set up for the occasion. The students had spread themselves around the pandal and simultaneously with her arrival warmed themselves up with slogan-shouting reminding her of the Emergency. The whole scene was exceptional and historic: the country's prime minister giving a speech in the precincts of the university of which she was the formal head and its students drowning her speech in a cacophony of slogans. Just then, as one of the student leaders who had smuggled himself inside the pandal to start a round of slogans right inside the den as a kind of guerrilla action, rose to enact his commission, a constable, suspicious from the start, positioning himself next to the student, caught him by the neck and dragged him outside the ceremonial site. So far the students and police were one all. But then the policemen had a perspective on the whole affair that was slightly at variance with the democratic accord between the students and the VC and they did not seem inclined to treat it as an honest difference of opinion. Instead of letting the student loose outside, a horde of policemen flashed their lathis at him. This sight did not quite meet with the approval of the student community. Thus started up a sharp contest between the police and the large student body as to who could wreck the function more effectively, and I must confess that the police won hands down. However, Dipankar Gupta and I, who were witness to the whole scene standing near the SIS building, escaped the lathi blows—I because of the streak of grey hair on my head and Dipankar because his height placed his torso beyond the reach of any of the police constables around him and they seemed loath to hit below the belt.

But what happened the next day was even more memorable. The student community was understandably livid with rage at what the police had done; teachers were divided and the VC was aghast. The atmosphere was surcharged. But one magnificent little act on Nayudamma's part diffused the entire situation within minutes: the first thing he did that day was to walk up to the JNUSU office, ironically located in the SIS building, and tender an unqualified apology to the students for the behaviour of the police. That was the end.

The idealistic vision of an egalitarian society also brought to the fore commitment on the part of some student leaders that has lasted a lifetime. Prakash Karat and Sitaram Yechury both belonged to the highest echelons of Indian society, with the best of education and family resources and support, cut out for high positions in either the bureaucracy or the managerial creamy layer. Instead, they chose to commit themselves full-time to the CPI(M). If some others did not quite go to that extent, they did, as students at JNU, undertake concerns that were unlikely to fetch them high grades in coursework. In 1981–82, on the eve of the Asian Games, a five-star hotel was under construction in the vicinity of JNU, then called Siddharth Continental (later changed to Vasant Continental to erase the memory of a devastating fire). The Government of India had prescribed obligations on the part of construction companies to pay a certain minimum wage and arrange for toilets, water, and crèches etc., for the construction workers' families, but like all laudable laws it wasn't really meant for implementation. It was the JNU students, female students in the lead, who organized the workers at the site and saw to the implementation of statutory provisions.

Even in the dark days of the Emergency the voice of dissent was not completely silenced at JNU. Even teachers, not quite renowned for taking risks anywhere and at any time, put their protest on record, if ever so mildly. At a time when the holding of any kind of meeting was under a ban, JNUTA held a GBM in which first one member, following his party's unabashed endorsement of the Emergency, moved a resolution that the JNUTA wholeheartedly supported Mrs Gandhi's action. He knew well that any voice in opposition could invite a police knock on one's door at the dead of night, which none quite looked forward to, and his resolution therefore would pass smoothly and unanimously. But the GBM nevertheless refused to oblige him on the delightful plea that any discussion of the Emergency in any form and any forum was illegal, which is indeed what the government had decreed. The member left the meeting in disgust. A while later, in the same meeting, a suggestion was mooted that teachers should stand in silence for one minute in mourning; no one asked who or what was being mourned, but all stood up nonetheless.

Students, of course, had to pay a high price for their defiance. JNUSU had called for a strike on a particular day and that day Maneka Gandhi, then a student of the German Centre and now a champion of animal rights, came all the way to defy the Union. Students pleaded with her to abide by the strike call. It was all so very surreal. But the consequence was that all hell broke loose: the next day a posse of policemen came in un-numbered cars and literally lifted Prabir Purkayastha off the ground, shoved him into one of the cars and drove away at breakneck speed in the mistaken belief that he was the JNUSU President; he remained in prison for the duration of the Emergency.

The 1990s have sadly witnessed a decline in the culture of protest and the coming of concerns such as better hostels and more promotions, etc., centre stage. This is not because the earlier generation of students and teachers were somehow superior or given to a greater degree of idealism or some such, but I believe it is so because the inspiring presence of great causes such as Vietnam and the desire to refashion the world, and of larger than life figures like Che Guevara and Ho Chi Minh have been replaced by the likes of John Major and Bill Clinton and P. V. Narasimha Rao. Even so, JNU has not completely abandoned its culture of protest. It was very heartwarming that on the evening of 6 December 1992, the fateful day when the Babri Masjid was demolished in Ayodhya, students and teachers of JNU were perhaps the first group anywhere to join hands to put their revulsion on record.

The past has not quite been erased from JNU's academic and cultural ambience; its glory is not yet history.

56

JNU UNDER EMERGENCY: THEN AND NOW

PRABIR PURKAYASTHA

Why do we need to remember the Emergency Indira Gandhi imposed on the country in 1975? Does it have a lesson for us today, or is the Emergency to remain a footnote in the history of independent India? These are the questions that come to mind when I think of JNU during the Emergency.

It is not possible to recall the past without keeping the present in mind. There was an Emergency then, in 1975. There's another one now, an undeclared one. It is tempting to look at the two Emergencies, find similarities and damn both. But that would be a caricature history, devoid of depth or real content. The more useful exercise would be to consider the ways in which the earlier Emergency challenged us as citizens; and how the present-day Emergency challenges us as citizens and as a nation.

To begin with, let's look at the past: 1975, Indira Gandhi's declared Emergency.

At that point, India had had five general elections and twenty-eight years of independence to firmly establish respect for democratic rights and values. Why then did the entire political and constitutional system collapse during the Emergency regime?

The Indian elite always had a sneaking admiration for authoritarianism and dictatorship. The veneer of modernity in a traditional caste-ridden society only reinforced their centuries-old contempt for the masses. The elite never had any deep commitment to a system in which the rulers have to seek periodic sanction from the people that they perceived as the 'herd'. The big stick for the workers and sterilization for the poor—the basic tenets of the Emergency—had social sanction in this section long before it was imposed.

The rigged elections in West Bengal in 1972 provided the template for combining state authoritarianism with the goondaism of the Youth

Congress and Chhatra Parishad—what Ashok Mitra called *The Hoodlum Years*. It is not an accident that Siddhartha Shankar Ray, the architect of this model, asked Indira Gandhi to prepare the plan for instituting the Emergency a good six months before it was actually declared. The idea of the Emergency had its origins long before its immediate cause, which was Mrs Gandhi being unseated through the Allahabad High Court verdict (*The State of Uttar Pradesh vs Raj Narain*).

How did the Emergency impact Jawaharlal Nehru University? The university was, after all, named after Nehru, Indira Gandhi's father, the patron of democracy in India; Gandhi herself was its Chancellor. JNU was a bastion of left-wing student politics with an array of other Left formations. The Emergency was a test. How would such a university stand up, as an institution, to state terror?

◆

In early 1975, I came to IIT Delhi, as it was one of the few places where computers were available for research students.[1] In those days, we had to type our programs onto punched cards, submit them for running, and wait a week for the results. So, I would spend my week's 'vacation' each time I submitted my card deck, in the JNU canteen, arguing about politics.

D. P. Tripathi was the President of the JNU Students' Union. I knew him from Allahabad where he was a student before he joined JNU. Through him, I got to know the entire SFI leadership of JNU—Ashok Lata Jain, Sitaram Yechury, Indrani Majumdar, Dinesh Abrol, Sohail Hashmi, and many others.

The students of JNU were active outside the campus as well as inside; in struggle as well as in studying and debating theory. Many evenings, days and nights, were spent in heated debates on Marxism, along with fellow Marxists belonging to different streams. It was this combination of activism and theory that made me join JNU in July 1975, a month after the declaration of the Emergency.

The declaration of the Emergency was followed by the arrest of the opposition; censorship of all newspapers and media; ban of all forms of protests. It was very clear that any resistance would be met with force and arrests. The SFI at JNU decided that it would not issue calls in its

[1]I was in Motilal Nehru Regional Engineering College and needed a computer centre for my master's thesis.

own name, but in the name of 'Resistance'.[2]

Soon after, the campus had its first taste of terror. There was a huge raid on JNU: campus hostels were cordoned off by the police at night, and there were mass arrests. Subsequently, a masked figure in the police station identified the ones to be charged and detained, while others were let off. The then President of the Students' Union, D. P. Tripathi, and many others, were denied admission. A Students' Union meeting chaired by Ashok Lata Jain, who later became the President of Delhi State SFI and the founder-President of the Janwadi Mahila Samiti (AIDWA's Delhi Unit), condemned these acts of the University administration. The University immediately expelled her. This led to the call for a three-day strike, probably the first mass action by the students of any university during the Emergency.

It was during this three-day strike that we stopped Maneka Gandhi—who, along with Sanjay Gandhi and Indira Gandhi, was associated with the excesses of the Emergency—from entering her class.[3] This is what led to my arrest. P. S. Bhinder, then D. I. G. (Range) and a part of the Sanjay Gandhi coterie which ran the Delhi administration, led a 'commando-style' raid in a black Ambassador, and kidnapped me from the campus. The action produced a sharp reaction; even those sections among the students and teachers that had supported the Emergency, condemned such a blatant act of state terror. The government responded by serving me with an order under the Maintenance of Internal Security Act (MISA), 1971, and giving me a year's 'rest' in the Tihar and Agra Central jails.

Later, the Shah Commission Report in 1977 made the reason for my imprisonment public. After I had spent six months in jail, Kasu Brahmananda Reddy, then Home Minister, had written in my MISA file that there was no reason to keep me in jail. But the Minister of State for home, Om Mehta, replied that the Prime Minister's house—read Sanjay Gandhi—was interested so the detention had to continue. Many of these and other details are recounted in *The Emergency Chronicles*, an excellent and highly readable book by Gyan Prakash, who was a fellow student at JNU and a friend.

Ashoka and I had submitted our notice for marriage before the magistrate in Tees Hazari a few days before the strike. Coincidently,

[2]A selection of these is available at JNU SFI's blog: <http://sfijnuunit.blogspot.com> [accessed: 29 September 2019].

[3]For a lucid account of these events see Prakash, 'A case of mistaken identity'.

the magistrate concerned was Prodipto Ghosh, the Additional District Magistrate (South), who was also the one that signed my MISA warrant. Ironically, he did finally officiate at our marriage, though a year later!

That was the declared Emergency. It is important to recall what happened then. But it is equally important to recall what did *not* happen then—especially today, in times of an undeclared Emergency.

Back then, in spite of some sections within JNU supporting the Emergency, the campus, as a whole had a sense of solidarity. There was no attempt—apart from the University Administration—by students or the faculty to become open agents of the police state that the country had become. There were no attacks by one section of students and teachers on other sections and collusion with the state machinery.

Contrast this with today, when a section of the students and university faculty takes pride in acting as open agents of the police and the state, and are complicit in false cases against fellow students.

During the Emergency, when freedom of speech was attacked, and open political activities were banned, it was not accompanied in the civic space with people wanting to widen the fractures within society. Yes, the Indian Youth Congress and Chhatra Parishad did use strong-arm tactics against their political opponents protected by the state. The difference was that the Congress did not have an ideology of a sectarian state, where the nation belongs to only one section of the people.

But the current undeclared Emergency has breached the concept of an Indian state that represents all its people. Whether it does so in practice is a different matter. Ideologically, the independence movement created the idea that India belonged to every section of Indians, and not just the Hindus. The RSS and its various fronts instead identified nationhood with the religious identity of the Hindus. They stayed out of the independence movement, as their battle for 'independence' was—and still is—against Muslims and Babur, not the British Raj.

The Emergency's purpose was to strengthen the state apparatus against Indians. Niren De, the then Attorney General, summed up this core tenet of Mrs Gandhi's Emergency in the famous—or infamous—ADM Jabalpur case that even if a police constable killed any citizen, there was no legal redress. The Supreme Court verdict in this case, in which I was also a co-petitioner, took forty-one years to be reversed. The people had overturned it much earlier, when they voted Indira Gandhi out in the 1977 elections.

As Sanjay's hoodlums took over, it became clear that the powers that be, extra-constitutional or otherwise, had untrammelled authority. While Sanjay Gandhi may have symbolized the worst of the Emergency, there is little doubt that the exercise of state power was capricious, if not malicious at all levels. Not just the more egregious crimes we know about, but petty everyday tyranny, from which even the privileged middle class was not exempt.

For the general public, the Emergency was even more oppressive. They became mere numbers—quotas for family planning—to be dumped at random for the beautification of the cities. People were herded like cattle, and shoved bodily behind tattered curtains, without any human dignity, to be vasectomized.

The political process in India is complex, one in which the oppression of the state is mediated through a number of political intermediaries. The mediators—bourgeois political parties—have competing structures. The radical forces provide an alternate structure of mass movements and popular resistance. The Emergency saw the complete erosion of both these structures.

The Indian people are quite often mistaken as passive. It is this apparent passivity that led Mrs Gandhi and the people around her to mistake people's apparent docility under the Emergency for approval. Therefore, the miscalculation that the Emergency could be legitimized through an election. Yet, it was this mass of 'passive' people, who routed Mrs Gandhi in 1977, asserting the primacy of India's electoral democracy.

There is a much deeper damage that Indira Gandhi's Emergency did to the nation. For the first time, it allowed the RSS and its various front organizations to don the mantle of democracy, something for which they had only shown contempt till then. When the Constituent Assembly was discussing the Constitution of independent India, they had argued that India should have a constitution based on the *Manusmriti*–India's ancient legal text of caste oppression. The RSS and the Bharatiya Jana Sangh ridiculed Ambedkar, calling him Lilliputian, while extolling Manu. The mouthpiece of the RSS, *The Organiser*, wrote in its 30 November 1949 issue:

> The worst about the new constitution of Bharat is that there is nothing Bhartiya about it.... To this day his (Manu's) laws as enunciated in the *Manusmriti* excite the admiration of the world and elicit spontaneous

> obedience and conformity. But to our constitutional pundits that means nothing.

If the Emergency allowed the RSS and the BJP to claim legitimacy for their democratic credentials, they also wounded the Congress deeply. The question today is whether the BJP is mistaking the passivity of the people as consent to its divisive politics. Or has it succeeded in cowing the Indian people with its lynch mobs, sedition charges and by disenfranchising sections of the people?

An answer either way in the 2019 elections will remain only a provisional one. Even a defeat in 2019 for the BJP will not be a defeat for its ideology of normalising hatred and its exclusionary politics.[4] The battle this time is likely to be much longer and more protracted, as the state is fusing with lynch mobs and hatred. This is our challenge today.

IX.1. Sita reads, Indira listens.
After the Emergency, in 1977, Sitaram Yechury, the President of JNU Students' Union, led a protest to Indira Gandhi's residence seeking her resignation as Chancellor of JNU. In the image Yechury can be seen reading out the demands of the students' union, while Indira Gandhi politely listens. The next day she resigned as Chancellor of JNU.
Photo courtesy: Seema Chishti

[4]This essay was written prior to the 2019 General Elections.

57

'MAY 1983': AN IRREVERENT MEMOIR*

JANAKI NAIR AND RANJAN GHOSH

I

Long before 2016, when Kanhaiya Kumar joined the list of legendary inmates at Tihar Central Jail from JNU, and well after the Emergency arrests of Prabir Purkayastha and D. P. Tripathi in 1975, was the 'ahem' moment of 1983, when about 376 students from JNU were sent to jail for two weeks. Prabir Purkayastha's arrest, we well know, was a mistake made by the police; we are yet to learn the reason for Kanhaiya Kumar's incarceration. The 1983 moment was different, a monumental farce, with bewildered students finding themselves locked up for voluntarily violating the imposition of Section 144 on campus. What should have been a heady togetherness of well over a thousand students for a few hours in the Delhi Cantonment police lockup against the police brutality on campus turned into jail for close to 400, by this time, sleepy and reluctant, students!

This 'comedy' of errors needs telling, by each in their own way. On a hot and dusty afternoon, 11 May 1983, my friend and I reached JNU, after a long day at the Nehru Memorial Museum and Library. We had to alight when the bus approached the North Gate: now closed since the campus was clearly disturbed. We learned that the police had arrived on campus to break through the student gherao of the Vice Chancellor and Rector that had gone on for two days.

The reason for the gherao had already divided the campus. The JNUSU was then headed by Nalini Ranjan Mohanty, of the non-Communist Students for Democratic Socialism. Many of us, including myself, had not supported the gherao, or even the events leading up to it. Briefly put, a student who had been transferred from his hostel room in Jhelum

*This memoir is in three small sections. I and III are written by Janaki Nair, and II by Ranjan Ghosh.

to Ganga on disciplinary grounds was led back in by a defiant President who broke the lock. When Mohanty found himself staring at a show-cause notice threatening expulsion, a university strike was called in his support. The JNUTA in protest refused to conduct exams; the student gherao of the Vice Chancellor from 9 May was to demand status quo ante. Many of us expressed vehement disapproval of the union's actions, and registered it by visiting libraries and archives off campus during the day.

On that fateful 11 May evening, we walked into campus to hear that a good friend, Abhijit, who had been among the 'encircling' students, had been whacked on the head and taken off to the police station with thirty-six others. Another had had his kneecap smashed. Section 144 had been imposed on the entire campus. The panic was palpable: it was swiftly decided to collectively and peacefully gather on Jhelum Lawns to violate that order. Not more than a few slogans about the impending revolution may have rent the air above approximately 1,200 heads (JNU had about 2,000 students in those days).

We had not reckoned with the power of the Delhi Lieutenant Governor Jagmohan, acting on the orders of no less than the Prime Minister Indira Gandhi, who was known on JNU campus only as the 'Emergency Criminal'; her address in 1981 had been continually disrupted by students who almost prevented her from entering the campus. Before we knew it, eleven buses arrived on campus to take the student protestors to Delhi Cantt Police Station. We boarded the buses in fading light, announcing the revolution.

When our details were being recorded at Delhi Cantt PS, I experienced the first jolt to my relatively poorly developed political consciousness: those before me were faking their names and their parents' names! Many claimed to be either the offspring of 'Bipan Chandra' and 'Romila Thapar', or took on the mantle of teachers themselves, 'Shereen Ratnagar', 'Majid Siddiqi.' I stuck close to Ranjan, that veteran of ten years experience with A. K. Roy in Dhanbad, who gave his own name. I did likewise. We all met up with Abhijit, who looked none the worse for the lathi blow.

A short while later, it was clear we would not return to dinner at JNU, and that Delhi Police had no budget to feed us. They generously opened the gates of the police station and allowed students to leave in search of food. About 600 simply walked away and returned to the campus, including those destined to become ministers. Some of us, having gone out to eat, returned to the police station to continue our defiance. It was late, dark, and hot, so we would make the walk back to campus in the morning.

We were rudely awakened by a midnight shake, this time to board the bus to Tihar. Not even the politically savvy among us had reckoned with Mrs Gandhi's determination to 'teach the JNU students a lesson'. Once more we lined up to provide our details, once more I followed Ranjan. But when he became 'Sukomal Sen' for the prison journey, my panic response was to assume a new name, with 'K. N. Panikkar' as parent.

As we neared Tihar, the women—exactly fifty of us—were asked to disembark. More slogans vowing never to be separated were shouted, but alas! we were dealing with the Indian state, not the tolerant JNU administration. We were taken on a long walk in the middle of that night to our 'cell'. It was a spacious one and we were not locked up: though we were surrounded by high unscalable walls, we were in our own garden of roses. What sweet irony that it had been occupied by none other than the Emergency Criminal herself! We hoped that it would be no more than a few hours before we were restored to our real names and parents.

Nothing of the kind happened, and we were in Tihar for twelve days, some for fourteen. The next morning brought fresh reminders of our new life. Being awoken at 5 a.m. for tea can be a unique form of torture for most JNU students who are accustomed to drinking it in only into the wee hours, but not at dawn. The tea was served in tall aluminum tumblers: you could risk burning your lips on the hot metal or wait until the tea was stone cold.

That was not all: we were, as C class prisoners, entitled to two meals a day, sent from the central kitchen. Our first morning meal consisted of large naan-like things with a slimy bhindi to teach us the virtues of JNU food, which we had long complained about. Worse was to come, when we mingled with our visitors at about 11 on that first day: we had nineteen charges against us, including arson, dacoity, assault, rioting, molestation, moral turpitude, and even attempt to murder—all for merely courting arrest. Even for a statistically challenged mind like mine, I could not imagine 400 students not succeeding in an attempt to murder. When the overzealous officer who wanted to throw the whole IPC at us was gently reminded that there were women among the offenders, the charges of moral turpitude and molestation were dropped. Still, arranging bail for 376 students for seventeen charges would take some time.

Our visitors, students and some teachers, anxious parents from all over the country, curious others, brought us clothes, plenty of food, and news of the outside world. Inside, it was hot and sticky, and we were informed by our SYS colleagues that we were actually on 'hunger strike' to demand higher status as 'political prisoners'. This was a little difficult to correlate with the large quantities of really good sandwiches, fruit, and biscuits that we were plied with by those who were still free.

I remember George Fernandes meeting us on the second or third day: these visits ensured that the 'hunger strike' ended successfully. The Women's Cell was now provided with two 'lifers' who would come and cook for us daily. We were warned to give them the knives *only* at the time of cooking, just in case. It was, in short, an idyllic setting: large rose garden, a tap with more water than we had at JNU, and two cooks who made the austere diet bearable. We immediately decided that the younger one, to whom the sentry outside had taken a shine, should be encouraged in this romance, if only through the window in the gate. We were good friends with our women warders as well.

'Shereen Ratnagar' meticulously collected minute-by-minute accounts of the events in a Prison Diary pace Antonio Gramsci (unfortunately lost). Others spent many pleasant hours under the flowing tap. Meanwhile, on day three or four, while mingling with our visitors, we noticed something interesting: many young men, whom we were sure were in the buses that drove us to Tihar Jail, were also among our visitors.

How was this happening? The only thing that distinguished us from our visitors was a rubber stamp on the inner forearm. In hot, sweaty, May, it was easy to transfer the imprint onto another's forearm. The numbers of young men who were had-beens at Tihar increased the next day, planting this very non-revolutionary idea among some discontented young women. When one of my classmates asked if it was all right to escape using this method, I could respond only with a scathing silence. Courting arrest, then escaping?

Nevertheless, the one-who-asked and three others left the women's cell. Since we were only fifty, and not 300 plus, like the men, it became immediately evident to the jail authorities that JNU students were escaping from Tihar Central Jail. A total of sixty-seven escaped, in a serious breach of security indeed, especially when those escaping were known as 'academics'.

II

I don't know what sort of political or social pressure was put on the jail authorities by our well wishers outside, but it must have been formidable.

For even after the famous escape of some sons and daughters of the Bipan Chandras and Romila Thapars there was no lathi charge or Pagli Ghanti. My knowledge of the jails in the coalfield made me prepared for some ugly and uncomfortable consequences after the jail break, but nothing happened, though the headcount in the evenings had begun after that. Instead, one senior officer one day begged us to reveal the identities of those jail breakers. 'You are students and your parents are big shots. Nothing will happen to you. But we will lose our jobs,' he lamented. But of course we didn't betray our comrades.

My enquiry later on revealed that the source of at least some of the sandwiches were some JNU teachers against whom the student movement was launched! I cannot vouch for the veracity of this information, but my experience at JNU made me feel that the rumour was true. I will narrate a small incident about the teacher-student relationship at JNU those days. One day I was gossiping in the canteen with some friends when a professor came along towards us. I hurriedly tried to hide the burning cigarette in my hand—smoking in front of a teacher was unimaginable for a person like me who was brought up in the semi-urban backwater of eastern India. But the professor just picked up the packet of Charminar lying on the table and said, 'Hey Ranjan, can I borrow a fag?' I was flabbergasted. How did he know my name! I had not met him more than twice before that. He was one of the seniormost professors of our department and I was one of the backbenchers in my class. He sat in the next chair and chatted with us for fifteen minutes in a way that a close friend would do. And he was not an exception. JNU teachers in those days were different.

Life in jail began to be boring after a week, in spite of all the sandwiches, volleyballs, and Pratidhwani songs. Ultimately when bail was granted, we were relieved to emerge again. Of course our exit was not as heroic as the entrance. We tamely stood in front of the camera, holding a slate on which, written in bold letters, were our REAL NAMES!

III

Our idyllic days in the rose garden came to an end; officials and warders were suspended—we realized, too late, that our own irresponsible actions had caused this. We were now checked twice a day, never mind that groups of four or five students, from Northeast to South India, claimed the same parentage. We were locked up at night, and we were no longer allowed to mingle freely with our visitors, confined instead behind a fine mesh during the visitor's hour. Among the politer things that jail officials said about these Great Escapes was 'We have housed even *** Naxals in Tihar but **** JNU students have managed to escape!' In those days, we were a tribe apart from the Naxals.

As the days turned into a long week, our despair grew. Being put behind bars produced claustrophobia, panic, and finally a full blown asthma attack, so I spent a whole night wheezing until the jail doctor arrived in the morning. He would have proceeded to jab me with a needle about the size of my thumb, but for the protection of my vigilant friends. Jail life produced new solidarities and sensibilities, and friendships deepened.

On the eighth day, a warder came to the cell and read out a list of names, mine included, and told us that our bail papers had arrived. It was about 6 in the evening; we bade long and fond farewells to take that long walk to the main gate. When we reached, we were told to return, since we had bail for only fifteen of seventeen charges! The walk back was even longer.

I cannot recall much of our actual release which happened on the twelfth day, except for the humiliating experience of being photographed like criminals, full front and profile, while we were compelled to give our real names, addresses, and parentage. SFI had arranged bail for many of us who were not in any student organization.

Since we could not return to JNU which had been closed sine die, we returned to our homes, chastened and scared. Only then did we learn of the unprecedented violence that had broken out on campus after our arrest, on some teachers' homes and properties. We took some comfort in the fact that JNU students themselves protected the teachers and brought the violence to a swift end.

France had its May '68, part of a historic wave of student protests that swept across the world, east to west, and birthed civil rights' movements. JNU had its May '83, following which many hard-won freedoms were irretrievably lost. No two events could be less similar. Though an important milestone in most of our lives and at JNU's institutional history, we need to ask: what did 1983 teach us, and what is its importance today, when farce has turned to tragedy? What did 1983 reveal about our privileges, even in jail? Was 1983 the culmination of 'a historic struggle', or a juvenile misadventure?

58

THE CUP THAT COST A PHD

NAGESH HEGDE

In February 1972, I entered the brand-new—now old—JNU campus. For a young man coming straight from the sprawling campus of IIT Kharagpur, I was puzzled by the JNU campus. All the Schools and Centres were located in four identical hostel blocks. The rooms all looked alike. The classrooms were like living rooms which in turn were like office rooms which in turn were like hostel rooms. Romila Thapar, Bipan Chandra, T. K. Oommen, Moonis Raza, and I were all operating from identical therefore truly egalitarian spaces.

There were frequent blackouts and brownouts. Bangladesh was born just a fortnight earlier and war clouds were still hovering. Pakistani fighter planes had attacked Agra and Amritsar a short while earlier, and we were all assigned to patrol the campus at night. Batches and shifts were decided by a self-styled leader called Suneet Chopra, who reminded me of Che Guevara without a gun. We students were getting to know each other more in darkness than in daylight.

I had joined the Centre for Studies in Science Policy as a research scholar. With one faculty, one clerk, one peon and one student (me), there were no classes, no assignments, and no one to talk to. I was free to explore the neighbourhood nooks and nukkads in a leisurely fashion.

On the third day, I saw a small poster near the canteen announcing an 'Intercollegiate Open-Air Art Competition' at IIT Delhi. Why not give it a try, I said to myself. After all, I did get some accolades for artistic skills during my school days. The IIT Delhi campus was just a few hundred metres away, so I just strolled across. Also, as a former IITian, I wanted to see the Delhi campus more than anything else.

There was a small commotion on a lush green lawn. People were standing in a large circle looking at what appeared to be a small tent or rather a Native American tepee. It appeared as though a shamanic ritual was about to unfold. Soon someone thrust a drawing sheet and a freshly sharpened pencil in my hand. A bell rang and the tip of the tepee slowly lifted up. It framed a haggard-looking person with a stoop, holding a stick in hand.

He was the model and we were all asked to draw his sketch. Heck, just a pencil sketch? No paint, no brush? Not even a hard pad to support the paper. I looked around for some concrete surface while others were scrambling for the heap of old newspapers stacked in the corner.

Two hours later, I was walking back to my hostel with a large shimmering trophy on my shoulder. It was nearly dark and the campus looked deserted. A tall person in pyjamas beckoned me. An off-duty chowkidar? He casually walked up to me and asked what I was carrying. I replied that I'd just won the first prize in an art competition. He asked my name, took the cup in his hand and read the inscription with admiration. 'Congratulations! This cup looks bigger than you, boy! My name is N. V. K. Murthy and I am the Registrar of this university. Come to my office tomorrow with this cup,' he said, patting my back.

The next day, he took me to the Vice Chancellor's room. The tall figure of Mr G. Parthasarathi greeted me with a smile. Known as the 'gentle giant', the VC was a test cricketer, a journalist, and a career diplomat with distinction. He had served as India's ambassador to China, Indonesia, Pakistan and until recently was India's permanent representative in the UN. I felt privileged to have tea and biscuits in his presence. He congratulated me for winning the first trophy for the university, and warmly enquired about my extracurricular interests. I bragged about my interests in photography, journalism, sports and, of course, art.

'We need to initiate some extracurricular activities on our campus too,' he said, looking at the registrar.

'Yes, we've already recruited a sports officer but are yet to make use of the indoor infrastructure for sports. There's a skating rink, a badminton court and a swimming pool but there is no facility for music and performing arts,' said Mr Murthy.

'We are still very young,' Mr Parthasarathi replied.

A small discussion ensued between the two as to where to showcase the cup in the VC's office and an administrative officer was called to execute the job. Later, Mr Murthy took me to his chamber and together we made a small list of sports and cultural activities that could be initiated immediately with some basic facilities. I suggested photography, skating, painting, and music.

That evening my trophy was displayed prominently in the dining hall with a small note from the registrar. The note, apart from the usual congratulatory message, also said that the administration would be glad to encourage recreational activities on the campus and interested students could get in touch with me.

For the next few months, I embarked on my research to scout for musical instruments, photography equipment, art materials, sports gear etc. Our small team scoured the bazaars of Chandni Chowk, Karol Bagh, and Connaught Place. Back at the campus, it was fun to watch people skidding and falling along the corridor while practising skating. A photography darkroom was set up above the girls' hostel exclusively for students. More boys were scrambling to the darkroom because the only entry to it was through the girls' hostel!

The walls started to fill with flashy posters protesting Nixon's bombing of North Vietnam. Professor K. J. Mahale started directing a street play in the foyer. Professor S. D. Muni was seen diving into the swimming pool. Amitabh Kundu single-handedly defeated me in table tennis. Sitaram Yechury was seen wielding his tennis racket on his way to political debates. Late night Marxian discourses in the hostel rooms were interspersed with rhythmic sounds of the tabla. Four-time National badminton champion Damayanti Tambay, whose husband Flt. Lt. V. V. Tambay went missing during the 1971 Indo-Pak war, gave a rare demonstration of her skills. Well-known Kuchipudi dancer Uma Rave performed Odissi in the CRS auditorium—leading to a mad rush in the darkroom the next day to develop the photographs of her dance.

Within two years, the JNU cultural team was taking part in arts and music festivals organized across different colleges of Delhi University. A bus load of students went to the Ghoomar festival in Jaipur and came back with half a dozen trophies. Sculptures and paintings sent to Bhopal for a competition fetched top prizes. Photography exhibitions were organized on the campus which was being designated as Old Campus. Our own students and research scholars inaugurated a newly built amphitheatre near (what is now known as) Parthasarathi Rocks with a Yakshagana play. JNU, known for its incessant political squabbles between the Leftists and Free Thinkers, started finding itself in the cultural pages of newspapers.

Three years later, we published a souvenir called *Memento*, showcasing the achievements of various cultural and sports clubs of the University.

To end on a personal note, I got lost in the maze of arts, sports, and other extracurricular activities, forgetting my research in science policy. My first research paper with Professor B. V. Rangarao on the economics of iron ore export (which was discussed in the Parliament) became my last. I ended up as a journalist and moved to Bengaluru.

Destiny seems preordained. The cup is the culprit! It was first sighted by the Registrar (Mr N. V. K. Murthy) who had a master's degree in journalism from the US. It was showcased by the first VC who began his career as a journalist in *The Hindu*. With hindsight it appears as though these two stalwarts conspired albeit unknowingly to change the career of a young researcher and produce a journalist instead.

59

SILVER MEMORIES

KANJIV LOCHAN

Charlie Chaplin said, 'Life seen from close up is tragedy, seen from a long shot is a comedy.' When experiencing some grave moments in life one wishes that they soon end, but we lose no opportunity sharing the unpleasant experience with near and dear ones.

Steering a project with a group of twenty-seven individuals/workers is a difficult task. Particularly so, when those workers have neither power nor money. So, as the convener of what we called our 'rainbow alliance', namely the JNU Silver Memoir Committee (SMC), I experienced some very trying and difficult circumstances. 'To fight or take flight' was always a question. Difficulties persisted until the day *JNU: The Years* was released by Professor Y. K. Alagh, the then Vice Chancellor, in a simple function sometime in April 1996.

It has been rightly observed that 'it is the success of the marriage and married life, not the pomp and splendor of the connected ceremonies, that would eventually count'. So we were content with the simple book release programme. Overwhelmed both by a sense of fulfilment and by the memory of the painful behaviour and attitude of some students, colleagues, and teachers towards the SMC, I could not speak much on the day. I only muttered that if I survived for another twenty-five years, I would jot down my experiences for JNU's Golden Jubilee volume. And I promised that, in keeping with the title of the SM Volume, I would name my article *JNU: The Tears*!

Let me begin with three points. (i) The title *JNU: The Years* was inspired by the title of the write-up authored by Dr Susan Visvanathan which was *JNU: The Days*. We remain grateful to her for permitting the title swapping, and for pardoning the omission of the last paragraph of her article, which disappeared due to the negligence of the computer operator. (ii) On the day of the book release, we realized that we had no experience of a book release function. Still we went ahead and, taking the example from photographs of such events in newspapers, we wrapped some copies of the anthology before the release. (iii) It is quite unusual for an autobiographer to reflect on the negative side of his/her life and experiences, since one prefers to foreground one's struggle, triumphs, accomplishments, and one's philanthropic activities. Therefore, someone else could be more objective about the last effort, though I have warm memories of the tireless support and help rendered by the twenty-seven friends in the SMC.

It bears repeating that the SM volume was blessed with contributions from almost all the stalwarts and teachers of the day. A significant absence was Professor Bipan Chandra, who had almost completed a write up for the anthology which did not materialize.

The list of members associated with the SMC is a remarkable one and no doubt it highlights the composite culture existing on the campus. Membership to the SMC was open, and people could associate themselves by joining any of the countless meetings which were held across the hostels, after they were duly publicized. Minutes, attendances, and proceedings of each meeting were recorded and the list of members appearing in the anthology was finalized with the consent of all those at the final meeting who had attended at least five others. Sometimes, attendance was so poor that I felt like a child playing a solo game of carrom taking positions on different sides of the board! After the book release function, we bundled the minutes of all the meetings, correspondence, copies of announcements, and appeals for papers and meetings, and draft copies of papers received by us and handed them over to the central library of JNU, requesting the librarian to preserve them for posterity.

Although all members contributed to the volume in their own ways, most of the chores were completed by those included in the working groups. Meena Gopal and I were the two coordinators. Here is a brief introduction to some of the members of SMC working groups:

Archana Upadhyaya, now teaches at the SIS, JNU.

Deepankar Sen Gupta is Professor of economics at Jammu University, Jammu.

Firoz Akhtar teaches sociology at Government College, Bharatpur, Rajasthan.

Kanjiv Lochan, teaches history in a Ranchi University College, Jharkhand.

Nabanipa Bhattacharjee teaches sociology at Sri Venkateswara

College, University of Delhi.

Rakesh Bisht teaches in a Government College in Uttarakhand.

Sanjeev Kumar Sinha is a software professional in a UK Firm.

Meena Gopal is a Professor at Tata Institute of Social Sciences, Mumbai.

It would be a sort of betrayal if I do not acknowledge the contribution of Mukul Dube, who copyedited the anthology, after charging us only a modest fee. In the editorial team, we had Susmita Sahay, the young MA student from the mainstream English studies, who completed early rounds of proofreading. Before Mukul Dube could lay his hands on the draft, the job of polishing up the language of all the articles, including mine, was done by Rakesh Bisht (from Uttarakhand) and Rona Wilson (from Kerala). Rona's inputs were very important, and we were all impressed by his lucid style.

The SMC possessed only modest resources. Only seven of us were JRF holders. None of us possessed computers. Many of us were students of MA or MSc, thus burdened with the regular semester exams and class assignments given by teachers. Many of us were affiliated to different student groups and organizations. Some of the SMC members followed ideological trajectories diametrically opposed to each other. For example, Govind Chand Mishra maintained his pre-JNU leanings towards the ABVP and was preparing the ground to claim the post of Vice President at JNUSU in the near future. Rona Wilson was very docile and hardworking. He usually remained silent and only privately talked to us about his ideological preferences. The SMC members were however able to tactfully navigate ideological contradictions without losing the moral compass.

Such diverse minds came together to form a coherent group: looking back, it seemed nearly impossible that the SMC could have accomplished its task. Looking back from a distance of twenty-five years, I may hazard certain reasons on how the task was completed.

1. Our financial beggary and poor editorial strength propelled us. Initially, we tried to get some support from the JNU administration or some reputed publishers. Their refusal fired the ambition within us. At a discussion following an unfortunate meeting with one of the Deans, we redoubled our resolve to bring out the proposed volume. I declared that the support of the JNU administration might have rendered the proposed anthology a sarkari book, now our work would

be an asarkari (that produces some effects) one! Thus our weakness was our greatest strength.

2. The second reason for the success was the fact that our group consisted of only students. We worked truly in the Gita way: put in your efforts without bothering about the results! Moreover, the SMC was organized on apolitical lines; and thus we earned the goodwill of the students and teachers cutting across diverse political spectrums. Moreover, none of us in the SMC was a known face on the campus so we were not burdened by excessive expectations. Should the effort be a failure, we would have lost nothing but some of our time. Thus there was no fear of falling.
3. There remained a sense of regard for the senior students. Meena Gopal and I were quite senior to the rest of the SMC members. At that time, I felt that the members joined us since we were able to convince them to keep aside personal and ideological differences for six months to produce something 'big and historic' for the campus to which we owed so much. We argued that merger and mixture are two different things indeed.
4. We were inspired by strong feelings of 'campus first.' Our seniors had spun an aura of awe and veneration around JNU and each of us felt like worthy legatees of a great campus tradition in South Asia. We had come to learn that there was nobody preparing to commemorate the silver jubilee anniversary of our great university. We indeed feared that if the occasion went unmarked, uncelebrated, unnoticed, what would other university people think and say? This sense of belonging and obligation kept us fired as well as united.

Finally, I must recall the generous support of those great teachers and shapers of our personalities who are in the anthology but are no longer with us. On behalf of the SMC, I pledge sincere reverence to Professors Meenakshi Mukherjee, Sabyasachi Bhattacharya, and Namwar Singh. We shall ever cherish their fond memories and will remain grateful to them for blessing our efforts. We were fortunate enough to see, interact and even share tea with the founders of a great campus!

60

जेएनयू परिसर

तमन्ना (कुसुम लता शर्मा)

विद्यार्थियों की वीरान दुनिया के रहनुमा हो तुम
अज्ञान की अंधेरी नगरी के आफताब हो तुम
तुम्हारे बुद्धिजीवियों के श्रम की शबनम ने
विद्यार्थियों की मायूसियों व अज्ञानता की
गर्द को धो डाला
अपने पुस्तकालय के सागर में
छिपे ज्ञान के रत्नों को
युवा विद्यार्थियों में बाँट डाला
जेएनयू के परिसर से
समेटकर ज्ञान के भण्डार को
कितने ही विद्यार्थियों ने विदेशों में व भारत में
जेएनयू के नाम परिचम लहराया
कोई बना प्रोफेसर-साइंटिस्ट,
कोई कंप्यूटर इंजीनियर
कोई बना डॉक्टर और
कोई आईपीएस आईएएस ऑफिसर
विदेशियों की खुल गयी मुंदी आंखें
आवाक रह गयी दुनिया
जेएनयू यह तेरे कर्मठ कुलपति कुलसचिव
प्रोफेसर एवं सहकर्मियों की निष्ठा का है प्रताप
जेएनयू का माहौल सजग व प्रगतिशील हैं
यहाँ की मिसाल खुद ही बेमिसाल हैं
अंधेरी डगर को ज्ञान के प्रकाश
से आलौकित करता यह प्यारा
जेएनयू परिसर हमारा।

61

मेरा अनुभव

विजय सिंह राठौर

जेएनयू में वैसे तो मैं 1975 में आया था, लेकिन मैंने 1980 में नियमित रूप से कार्यभार ग्रहण किया। उस समय हमारी तनख्वाह सिर्फ 6.30 पैसे प्रतिदिन होती थी। लगभग एक महीने की तनख्वाह 150/- रूपये थी। शुरुआत में जेएनयू पुराना कैम्पस में था, उसका नाम नैशनल एकेडेमिक एडमिनिस्ट्रेशन कैंपस (National Academic Administration Campus) था। उस समय एक बस चलती थी जिसका रुट नं. 666 था। ओल्ड कैंपस से पूर्वांचल तक चलती थी, फैकल्टी, स्टॉफ, स्टूडेंट्स उस बस में आया-जाया करते थे। उस समय मौहाल काफी अच्छा था। अंग्रेजी भाषा ज्यादा प्रचलित थी। उस समय भी जेएनयू में छात्र आंदोलन एक आम बात थी। एक दो बार विश्वविद्यालय अनिश्चितकाल के लिए बंद हो गया था, तत्कालीन जेएनयू में रात-दिन का अंतर है। यह जगह प्राकृतिक सौंदर्य से भरपूर है। जेएनयू जैसे बौद्धिकता वाले संस्थान ने हमें बहुत कुछ दिया है। पहले के शिक्षक व आज के शिक्षक में काफी अंतर है। जेएनयू के शिक्षक बहुत ही बुद्धिजीवी हैं। विश्व में इनकी पहचान है यहाँ शांत वातावरण था। प्रेम व भाईचारा था, लोग एक दूसरे का आपसी सहयोग करते थे। रातों को फूलों की महक से वातावरण महक उठता था। सायं काल की सैर का आनंद ही कुछ और है। रात के बारह-बारह बजे तक निडर गंगा ढाबा की ओर घूमते थे। यहाँ के विद्यार्थी हर प्रकार से सहयोग प्रदान करते थे। जेएनयू में देश-विदेश के प्रत्येक कोने से विद्यार्थी ज्ञान अर्जित करने के उद्देश्य से आया करते थे। आज भी आते हैं। यहाँ की शिक्षा का उद्देश्य विद्यार्थी में सदाचार के गुण उत्पन्न करना है। जेएनयू में आज बहुत परिवर्तन हो चुका है, काफी विकास हो चुका है, नई-नई बहुमंजिला इमारतें बन चुकीं, नए छात्रावास तथा शॉपिंग कॉम्प्लेक्स। फिर भी यदि अन्य शैक्षणिक संस्थानों से तुलना करें तो हमारा संस्थान बहुत ही अच्छा है। जेएनयू मुझे पहले भी अच्छा लगता था और आज भी अच्छा लगता है और आगे भी अच्छा लगेगा। छात्रों की संख्या में भी वृद्धि और अध्यापकों की संख्या में भी काफी इजाफा हुआ है। यह जानकर बहुत ही अच्छा लगता है और गर्व होता है कि आज यहाँ से शिक्षा पाकर निकले छात्र कई उच्च सरकारी पदों पर आसीन हैं। यह जानकर प्रसन्नता होती है कि जेएनयू का रैंक पूरे देश में प्रथम श्रेणी में है। इसकी प्रगति का श्रेय यहाँ आने वाले छात्रों, शिक्षकों, कर्मचारियों व अधिकारियों को जाता है। जेएनयू के पाठकों के लिए मेरा यह सन्देश होगा कि जेएनयू के निरंतर विकास और देश और समाज के हित में अपने नए-नए

लेख, अनुभव और सुविचार लिखते रहें ताकि हम सभी पाठकों को जो देश और समाज के प्रति समर्पित हैं, नए-नए विचारों की जानकारी का आदान-प्रदान होता रहे।

62

जेएनयू में हिन्दी*

केदारनाथ सिंह

जी, यही मेरा घर है
और शायद यही वह पत्थर जिस पर सिर रखकर सोई थी
वह पहली कुल्हाड़ी
जिसने पहले वृक्ष का शिकार किया था

इस पत्थर से आज भी
एक पसीने की गंध आती है
जो शायद उस पहले लकड़हारे के शरीर की
गंध है-

जिससे खुराक मिलती है
मेरे परिसर की सारी आधुनिकता को

इस घर से सटे हुए
बहुत-से घर हैं
जैसे एक पत्थर से सटे हुए बहुत-से पत्थर
और धूप हो की वर्षा यहाँ नियम यह
कि हर घर अपने में बंद
अपने में खुला

पर बगल के घर में अगर पकता है भात
तो उसकी खुशबू घुस आती है
मेरे किचन में
मेरी चुप्पी उधर के फूलदानों तक
साफ सुनाई पड़ती है
और सच्चाई यह है कि हम सबकी स्मृतियाँ
अपने-अपने हिस्से की बारिश से धुलकर

---

*'JNU mein Hindi', 1997

इतनी स्वच्छ और ऐसी पारदर्शी
कि यहाँ किसी का नम्बर -
किसी को याद नहीं !

विद्वानों की इस बस्ती में जहाँ फूल भी एक सवाल है
और बिच्छू भी एक सवाल
मैंने एक दिन देखा एक अधेड़-सा आदमी
जिसके कंधे पर अंगौछा था
और हाथ में एक गठरी
'अंगौछा'-इस शब्द से
लम्बे समय बाद मेरे मिलना हुआ
और वह भी जेएनयू में!

वह परेशान-सा आदमी
शायद किसी घर का नम्बर खोज रहा था
और मुझे लगा-कई दरवाजों को खटखटा चुकने के बाद
वह हो गया था निराश
और लौट रहा था धीरे-धीरे

ज्ञान की इस नगरी में
उसका इस तरह जाना मुझे ऐसा लगा
जैसे मेरी पीठ पर कुछ गिर रहा हो सपासप्
कुछ देर मैंने उसका सामना किया
और जब रहा न गया चिल्लाया फूटकर-
'विद्वान लोगो! दरवाजा खोलो
वह जा रहा है
कुछ पूछना चाहता था
कुछ जानना चाहता था वह
रोको... 'उस अंगौछे वाले आदमी को रोको...'

और यह तो बाद में मैंने जाना
उसके चले जाने के काफी देर बाद
कि जिस समय मैं चिल्ला रहा था
असल में मैं चुप था
जैसे सब चुप थे
और मेरी जगह यह मेरी हिंदी थी
जो मेरे परिसर में अकेले चिल्ला रही थी।

Yes, this is my house,
and this probably the stone against which
the axe that hunted down the first tree here
had laid its head and slept.

A smell of sweat still comes off this stone,
the smell of that first woodcutter's body—
it gives sustenance to the modernity
of my whole campus.
Close to this house
are many other houses
as there are many stones close to this stone
and whether in rain or sunshine
as a rule
each house here is closed in itself
and open to itself.

Still, when rice cooks in the house next door
its fragrance enters my kitchen.
My silence can be heard loud clear
by the flower vases over there.
The fact is, all our memories
washed clean in our own share of the rain
are so clear and so transparent
that no one can remember the number
of anyone's house.

In this township of the learned
where a flower is a query
and a scorpion a mere word
I saw one day a middle-aged man
with an angochha on his shoulder
a shapeless bundle in his hand.
'Angochha'—I met the word after long
and that too at JNU!

That perplexed man
was looking for a house with a number

and after knocking on many doors
had lost all hope
and was slowly walking back.

His returning thus
from an enclave of knowledge
I felt as a hail of whiplashes
on my back, swish-swish.
I stood facing him for a while
and when I couldn't any more
I burst out crying–
'O learned men, open your doors.
He's going back
He wanted to ask something
He wanted to find out something
Stop him–stop that man with the angochha...,'

I discovered only later
much after he'd left
that when I was crying out
I was in fact quiet
just as all others were quiet
and instead of me
what cried out as a lone voice
in that crowded campus
was my Hindi.

*Translated by Harish Trivedi

X

PROMISES TO FULFIL

63

TWENTY-FIVE YEARS OF JNU: BETRAYAL AFTER A PROMISING START*

D. BANERJI

Institutional Memory and Its Erosion

An 'institutional memory' is an important element which enables an institution to hold on to the purpose for which it was created; it counters the inertia amongst some of its members to drag it down the beaten track. The forces of inertia are particularly threatening in the initial phases. Once the memory takes firm root, it becomes a cumulative process, almost an upward spiral. The institution becomes a national asset. I would venture to say that the struggle to protect the basic character of Jawaharlal Nehru University is a struggle between memory and forgetfulness. The occasion of the silver jubilee of the university, when 'forgetfulness' has taken a heavy toll, is an appropriate time to revive the memories of the early years of its life, when the commitment to its basic character was much stronger.

The distinctive character of the JNU philosophy

- A quarter-century ago, JNU was set up to develop its academic programmes around socially relevant themes: this implied an interdisciplinary approach to deal with different facets of problems, that often involved working on the frontiers of knowledge. While the windows were to be kept wide open for ideas from outside, the focus was on generating endogenous bodies of knowledge around the

*From Kanjiv Lochan (ed.), *JNU: The Years, An Anthology by the Silver Memoir Committee*, Bombay: Popular Prakashan, 1996, pp. 33-45. The essay has been edited for this volume.

identified problem areas. The mandate from Parliament was to make a net qualitative addition to the development of higher education in the country. India can justly be proud of daring to think in these innovative terms. There are few universities (if any) in the world, which have been established on such a mandate.

- JNU developed a distinctive organizational structure to fulfil the given mandate. There were Schools which covered different academic fields. Certain specific areas were chosen within the academic field of a school to build around them centres of study. The Centres in turn were the academic bricks for building the university.
- The Vice Chancellor was assigned the pivotal role of being the custodian of the distinctive character of the university. He was required to take considerable care to bring together a 'critical mass' of teachers who were to give shape to the Centres, the Schools and the university as a whole. They were required to possess almost impossible qualifications: social competence; interdisciplinary competence; and competence to work around the frontiers of knowledge in different fields.

The Formative Phase

One can dig out many 'original sins' committed during the early phase of the formation of the university. But here the effort will be to bring back memories of some of the aspects which gave an operational form to the distinctive character of the university. The School of Social Sciences (SSS), with its six Centres (two more were added later), is being referred to here, because the SSS was the centrepiece of the university.

That two of the original six Centres—the Centre for Studies in Science Policy (CSSP) and the Centre for Social Medicine and Community Health (CSMCH) were headed by persons with science backgrounds gives an indication of the character of the SSS. Some of the work conducted in the now much-maligned CSSP offer good instances. In the early 1970s, long before the Bhopal disaster, the chairman of CSSP, Professor B. V. Rangarao, was prophetic when he presented cogent data to assert the now well-recognized disastrous consequences of the extensive use of pesticides in India.

An outstanding feature of the university was that it had developed a mechanism for the democratic participation of teachers in academic decision-making. The tenure of Deans of Schools and Chairpersons of Centres was limited to two years, and Associate Professors were also made eligible to head Centres. Furthermore, the faculty acted as a collective for all decisions taken at the level of a Centre. The Chairperson was to convey the mandate given to him or her to the school-level bodies—the Board of Studies, the Committee for Advanced Studies and Research and the informal committee of the Chairpersons. The Chairperson also represented the faculty in the Academic Council (AC). The Dean, in turn, carried the mandate of the Chairpersons to the university-level bodies—the AC, the Executive Committee and the informal committee of Deans.

The records of early meetings of the AC show the excitement and eagerness of the members to zealously guard the distinctive character of the university—the JNU philosophy. The then Vice Chancellor, the late G. Parthasarathi, observed at an AC meeting that JNU would attach much greater importance to teachers who could enable an underprivileged student to move from say a grade of 45 to 50 than to those who could help a student from the privileged class to move from 60 to 85.

The AC was equally cautious in forming associations with other institutions. The recognition of courses at the National Military Academy for awarding a Bachelor's degree in Military Sciences triggered intense debate in the AC. The concern was that 'it was the thin end of the wedge to militarize JNU'. This too turned out to be prophetic. There was similar caution in accepting financial support from outside sources for academic activities. This sounds outrageous to the present exponents of academic and financial liberalization and globalization. The fear was (and the subsequent succumbing to the temptation to accept grants from outside more than vindicated it) that this would divert JNU into areas which were not central to its interests.

Yet another achievement of Mr Parthasarathi was to give an all-India character to the student body and create conditions for the student community to be self-governing. Apart from setting aside seats for SC/ST candidates, the university offered special support for those who belonged to poor families and to 'other Backward Castes'. Students of JNU ran their own union, along with the now deservedly famous election process, with a student-constituted Election Commission, which sternly implements the well-cherished code of conduct. When the President of the students' union V. C. Koshy was invited to address the first convocation ceremony of the university, he strongly disapproved of wasting so much money on such functions. He suggested the money be spent more wisely by supporting needy students. The university responded and has not held annual convocations since. Incidentally, JNU discarded the comical hoods and gowns for special convocations and, instead, uses a simple folded yellow shawl.

The university was prompt in implementing the recommendations of the Gajendragadkar Committee on student participation. It involved them at every level—Centre, School and AC. The students fully justified this trust and made substantial contributions to the deliberations of all these bodies. Such exposure must have helped many to acquire leadership positions, both political and otherwise.

Mr Parthasarathi was quite categorical about the role of the third component of the university community, namely the administration. It was meant to provide support to academic activities. One feels nostalgic about those days, when the administration responded promptly to the needs of teachers and students.

The Past Two Decades

The teaching community, particularly the Vice Chancellors and the Rectors who succeeded Mr Parthasarathi, are accountable for the spiralling erosion of the ethos of the university. The custodians not only lowered their guard but at times actually took steps which went against the basic character of the university. One example is the way the School of Environmental Sciences (SES) (which could have played such a pioneering role) was set up with the very active involvement of the Vice Chancellor who succeeded Mr Parthasarathi. It began with a big contingent of physicists. Then, there were two physiologists. Then a water treatment engineer joined as a Senior Fellow. To top it all, first a physical anthropologist and then a neurophysiologist were recruited to contribute to 'behavioural science' aspects. There was no cohesion among this disparate group. They found that the best course would be to carve out spheres of interest for each group and then see how they might be related to Indian problems concerning the environment.

The seeds of the decline were sown right at the beginning. There were some teachers who, having been selected because they swore by the JNU philosophy, yearned for discipline-based academic work. Unfortunately again, the 'critical mass' of the teachers, committed to the JNU philosophy, were not vigilant and strong enough to isolate such elements.

In the SSS, five of the eight Centres started MA programmes—economics, geography, history, political science, and sociology. This meant expansion of the teaching staff. Many of the teachers who came during this second wave were even further removed from the JNU philosophy, strengthening the discipline-based contingent. The Deans of the SSS and many Chairpersons of Centres almost unwittingly talked of the five MA teaching Centres as 'major Centres', implying that the other three were 'minor'. The coup that started with 'floor-crossing' thus became complete. The tenant became the owner and the owner was pushed into a one-room outhouse.

There has been virtually no interaction between scholars in the different Centres of the SSS. So strong has been class/caste demarcation between the 'majors' and the 'minors' that repeated initiatives from the CSMCH to work together with other Centres in fields such as medical sociology and anthropology, health economics, population studies, history of the medical and health services in India, regional planning in health, health administration and political economy of health, have gone unheeded. A frank observation from one of the most respected teachers of SSS best sums up the situation: 'If we divert our efforts to interdisciplinary areas, so stiff is the competition in our discipline, that we will be left out of the rat race and fail to have any position there.'

Incidentally, none of the students churned out by the science schools has had any exposure to such interdisciplinary areas as science and society, sociology of science, social responsibility of scientists and the history of science in India. Besides, the science schools are highly capital-intensive and very expensive to run. It is a tragic irony that JNU devotes so much of its very limited resources to running schools which are so far removed from the JNU philosophy. There is little money for so vital an institution as the university library. If that isn't enough, the science schools constitute four out of the seven schools, not to mention the Centre for Biotechnology. They thus get a disproportionately large representation in the key decision-making bodies of the university.

The nonchalance towards basic principles while making key academic decisions concerning the university is often reflected in the proceedings of the Academic Council. The most startling among them is the indulgence in a spree of recognition of military educational institutions. Apart from their obvious lack of relevance to the JNU philosophy, it raises a basic question of academic rectitude. How could JNU accord recognition to diverse educational programmes in far-flung regions about which it does not have even the most elementary expertise and has had to depend on outside consultants to advise it?

Another example is the recognition of an international training programme, the Post-Graduate Diploma in Population Studies, conducted by the Centre for Development Studies at Trivandrum and funded by the United Nations Population Fund (UNFPA). How could the AC and the Board of Studies of the SSS (in an emergency meeting conducted in the midst of the summer vacation) reconcile their recognition of the diploma with the fact that the participants come from different developing countries, with varied academic attainments in varied fields?

The third example is the offering of prime land on the campus to the National Institute of Immunology (NII) and the Indian Institute of Mass Communication (IIMC).

Mention may also be made of totally indefensible excesses by the student body in 1983, which provoked the entry of the police and closure of the university for one year. This was a watershed. Things have never been the same again. There was a breach of trust. It also made the authorities more authoritarian. It will take a long time to heal this wound.

The responsibility and response of the teaching community

Over the years, a number of myths have been built around JNU teachers. Quite undeservedly, they are often considered elites among the intellectuals of the country. Another myth projects JNU as a den of leftists and communists. In a lighter vein, it was observed that Mrs Indira Gandhi had set up JNU to dump all the leftists of the Nehruvian era at one place where they could indulge in their harmless and impotent pastime of intellectual gymnastics and acrobatics, while she went along with the more serious work of the state. Indeed, this group of 'leftists' forms a small minority. The bulk is formed by 'neutrals' who, if they have to subserve their personal interests, put on pink robes and join the leftists. The self-proclaimed red-blooded minority of leftists appear dominant because they are intelligent, hard-working, articulate, and outward-looking.

JNU still has some scholars of high calibre; however, the few who had the courage to stand out were banished by the establishment. They became non-persons, shut off from decision-making processes like faculty selection and formation of posts. They were intellectually ostracized. The majority of the teachers gave tacit approval to the treatment given to such 'troublesome' elements by remaining silent. So, on the day of reckoning, the teaching community will have a great deal to explain about its role in the decline of JNU.

What is to be done?

Even this very condensed account and analysis of developments at JNU during the past twenty-five years will provide the directions which ought to be adopted to revive and then reinforce the institutional memories of JNU. No attempt will, therefore, be made here to recount the steps that ought to be taken. They are self-evident. JNU remains a very valuable national asset. Better management of this asset is bound to yield very rich dividends.

Editors' Note: Much has changed at JNU since this piece was published in 1996, and at least some of the issues—such as the question of interdisciplinarity—have taken unanticipated shape in the newer, smaller centres.

64

INTERDISCIPLINARY/INTERDISCIPLINARITY[1]

DHRUV RAINA

In the late 1960s, interdisciplinarity arose as the alternative to the tapering successes and limitations of disciplinarity. The latter was recognized as a mode for production and reproduction of knowledge within a globalized university system. Thus it was not surprising that when JNU was established as a new university, those who conceived of it and wished to shape the future of its Schools, Centres, and research programmes, possibly recognized the limitations of disciplinarity against the background of rapidly changing frontiers of knowledge, and an equally changed social order marked by diversification, complexity, and growing inequality and conflict. It would indeed be self-defeating to measure the 1970s notion of interdisciplinarity by a retrospectively constructed idea of what it means today—as the philosopher of science cautioned, the rational reconstruction of theories or disciplines was a caricature of their history.

The schools at JNU were envisaged as interdisciplinary from the start. My conversations with faculty members involved with and committed to creating these interdisciplinary schools suggest that interdisciplinarity was imagined as the instrument for realizing a more comprehensive ideal of knowledge. Interdisciplinarity was seen as arising from the conversations between disciplines which enriched and enhanced each of them that worked through the complementarity of perspectives and was a stepping stone to the acquisition of robust knowledge. But there was another, still current, understanding of interdisciplinarity that suggests the application of a concept, a method, a set of techniques or theory from one discipline to another discipline, often resulting in the creation of a

---

[1] I am thankful to several colleagues for sharing their views, and express my gratitude to Dipankar Gupta, Gurpreet Mahajan, and Romila Thapar for their time. The usual disclaimer applies.

new field. Disciplinary identities were formed and sustained through self-referential communication and regulated by gate-keepers of disciplinary communities. Interdisciplinary practices entailed boundary crossing and transgressions that inspired the radically inclined and provoked the conservatives.

Within JNU, the quest for interdisciplinary research and teaching in the 1970s was definitely visible and audible. The School of International Studies, Environmental or Life Sciences could not but be interdisciplinary. The spectre of strong disciplinary identities hung over the Social Sciences, requiring self conscious efforts to develop the School on interdisciplinary lines. But we need to recognize that in the 1970s, the Indian university was possibly not yet entirely prepared for interdisciplinarity—in the field of history, for example, job vacancies in colleges and universities were announced strictly for ancient, medieval, and modern history. A university of the twenty-first century such as Ambedkar University, on the other hand, has been conceptualized as an interdisciplinary university, but has surely benefitted from the academic experience and discussion within wider disciplinary communities over the last four decades. We may say that Ambedkar University concretises in the social sciences some of the unrealized interdisciplinary aspirations of the academic community.

Within the School of Social Sciences at JNU, interdisciplinary teaching and research took a form that was possibly the most deeply debated. An important concern was the integration of strong disciplinary fields in the social sciences, for example, economics and political science under one institutional rubric. But the disciplinary paradigms were not exhausted; there was, and still is, much to be pursued within their frameworks. The logic of disciplinary evolution under such conditions is differentiation that eventually leads up to the formation of sub-disciplines. Consequently, as more faculty members were recruited in the School of Social Sciences during that founding decade, Centres began to emerge under quasi-disciplinary rubrics, but eventually retreated into reformed disciplines with improvised and innovative curricula and pedagogies that conferred distinct cognitive identities on their students. In another sense, the university's constant appeal to the ideal of interdisciplinarity was inculcated among its students as the 'ideology of interdisciplinarity'. Students recognized that research problems were customarily boxed into disciplines, and that the disciplines were self-limiting and far from comprehensive in the treatment of such problems. Interdisciplinarity thus remained an ideal in the early decades.

Furthermore, the structure of the curriculum so developed encouraged students to choose courses offered by Centres other than their own, even while they completed their core course requirements. The pressure for core course requirements was exacerbated by the wider context of academic professionalization. Universities and colleges were constrained by the orientation offered by disciplines, and recruitment into universities and colleges was based on discipline-based credentialization. Interdisciplinary degrees in the 1970s and 1980s were suspect in the marketplace—and the situation has not changed very much. Thus the 'disciplining' by disciplines was enforced due to forward linkages with the wider ecology of the higher-education system.

The ideology of interdisciplinarity was sustained by an informal institutional split between interdisciplinary teaching and research. Interdisciplinary teaching continues to be an ongoing experiment within the larger and smaller Centres of JNU—interdisciplinarity being more deeply entrenched within the smaller Centres where problems, themes and programmes are formulated at the outset in interdisciplinary terms. These smaller programmes really are Centres in the making. Amongst the larger Centres, the Centre for the Study of Regional Development within the School of Social Sciences is interdisciplinary. The debate within the smaller Centres was whether the curriculum was multidisciplinary or interdisciplinary. And it did take time and effort before these issues were effectively resolved in favour of interdisciplinarity.

On the other hand, interdisciplinary research was the default option that was pursued and cultivated due to an enabling environment that promoted conversations between Centres and Schools, and among students at informal locations that included hostels and dhabas spread across the campus. In other words, the wider ecology was receptive to interdisciplinarity even while the disciplinary boundaries were deeply entrenched—faculty members encouraged their students to take courses outside their centres and schools. Over the decades, the university did provide a salubrious climate for what one might call a narrow interdisciplinarity—an interdisciplinarity between disciplines sharing an elective affinity, or a methodological or epistemic family resemblance.

But some conversations just did not take place. Few attempts were even made to forge a broad interdisciplinarity between the natural sciences on the one hand and the social sciences, the humanities and/or cultural studies on the other. Some of the social sciences employed statistical and a limited range of quantitative techniques borrowed from the sciences or took recourse to remote sensing techniques and other data bases. This encounter was at best an instrumental or pragmatic interdisciplinarity which did not encourage cross-disciplinary conversations or create opportunities to break down the silos imposed by the 'two cultures' divide—that separates the sciences from the social sciences and the humanities. From the 1970s to the 1990s and possibly even up to now, the campus remained divided between criticism of science and scientism on the one hand and the sciences entertaining a suspicion of the interpretive flexibility of the social sciences. In other words, narrow interdisciplinarity (between the sciences themselves or just the social science disciplines) was more easily realized than broad interdisciplinarity.

However, over the decades a number of smaller centres kept on sprouting up within the ecology of the university, both at JNU and elsewhere. These centres were dedicated to instruction and research on specialized problems and concerns that required urgent academic attention, but the very nature of the problems needed disciplinary constraints to be surpassed. The Centre for Studies in Science Policy, followed by Community Health and Social Medicine, Educational Studies, Law and Governance, Women's Studies and, more recently, Discrimination Studies, Informal Economy and Media Studies made their appearance. What started off as less than a handful of interdisciplinary centres by the 1990s began to snowball into a wider movement, not just in the social sciences but in the other schools as well—with the School of Arts and Aesthetics emerging as a separate school followed by the School of Computational and Integrative Sciences. Similar processes possibly drove interdisciplinary specialization within the School of International Studies as the complexity of issues that plagued the emerging international order was recognized. This resulted not just in the blurring of political regions and economic consolidations but produced hybrid protocols of investigation.

Despite these developments, fortuitous or otherwise, forging broad interdisciplinarity has still been a problem. There appears to be the promise that the digital humanities and big data analytics might open up new windows for research and teaching but these developments are fairly recent and will take time to alter university practices. But here too one needs to ensure that the encounter does not merely produce a pragmatic interdisciplinarity which does little credit to any of the sciences and humanities. This concern begs serious deliberation and debate, for the 'two cultures' divide runs deeply through the subconscious of the university—just at a time when one anticipates that the divide itself poses impediments to the exciting research opportunities and possibilities available. In any case, JNU is a place where the divide could have been confronted and dismantled rather than endlessly sustained.

Despite the accomplishments, major or minor, of interdisciplinarity as a vocation, larger transformations in the mode of knowledge production have incontrovertibly altered the conditions of its reception. En route, the social sciences, humanities and other related schools and centres at JNU have played a significant role in contributing to the construction of the interdisciplinary identities for teaching and research.

65

TRANSLATION AND INCLUSIVITY

CHITRA HARSHVARDHAN AND MADHU SAHNI

This is an attempt to retrieve what was intended and what still largely remains a 'work in progress' with regard to integrating translation as a discipline into the programmes and discourse of the erstwhile School of Languages, (now the School of Language, Literature and Culture Studies) at JNU. All Centres teaching foreign languages, from the European to the Asian, also offer courses on translation and interpretation. At least two Centres, the German and the French and Francophone Studies, in fact, offer postgraduate degrees in translation and interpretation; English, Hindi, and Tamil Studies also offer courses on translation. This highlights the importance given to the process of, and theoretical reflexion on, translation in the various Centres of the school. Integrating translation into the mainstream programme was indeed remarkable for its time, since the institutionalization of translation studies, as has since occurred globally, was yet to take place. Yet, the execution of that intention and systemic evolution of the programme has been fraught with challenges.

The School itself was established in 1969, although most centres started functioning from 1971 onwards or emerged as new independent entities over the years. The intention of studying the language, literature and culture of other countries was to imbue students with a cosmopolitan worldview, 'inculcating in the students a world perspective and international understanding'.[1] This fitted in with the other distinguishing feature of the newly established university, as primarily a postgraduate and research institution. The pedagogical approach would be interdisciplinary

[1]JNU Act of 1966, Jawaharlal Nehru University, The First Schedule, p. 13 available at <https://www.jnu.ac.in/RTI/Act%20&%20Statutes/ACT.pdf> [accessed: 1 February 2019].

in promoting 'integrated courses in humanities, science and technology'.[2]

Translation was included in the curriculum after several queries from Indians settled in Germany for reliable and officially approved translation of documents such as marriage certificates and legal notices served on them.[3] In consonance with the proclaimed objective of the university to 'promote in the students and teachers an awareness and understanding of the social needs of the country and prepare them for fulfilling such needs',[4] an attempt was made to evolve a socially relevant programme which would, it was hoped, contribute to eventually generating employment on the one hand and on the other fulfil demands for bridging communication and technology gaps, also commercially, whilst meeting the requirement for making texts written in foreign languages accessible to researchers and scholars. Until then, this role was fulfilled by the INSDOC (Indian National Scientific Documentation Centre), established in 1952, where international scientific research was documented and translated for Indian scholars.

Translation was intended to disseminate knowledge generated in other languages.[5] Consequently, translation was perceived as a handmaiden to areas of research within the university. This created a dilemma of sorts, and complexities of an unanticipated kind. Interdisciplinarity, inherent to all translation, was one of the stated goals of the university as enunciated in the JNU Act,[6] yet hierarchies developed, since the complexity of articulating ideas originally expressed in another language into English was not always recognized and often dismissed as merely 'reproductive' work. The professional and academic quality of the translation course was questioned and viewed sceptically when it was first presented to the Academic Council. Some thought it too ambitious.[7]

Translation has the potential of transforming, subverting, democratizing and secularizing knowledge. It could lead to greater

---

[2]Ibid.

[3]Email correspondence with Professor Pramod Talgeri on 13 February 2019.

[4]JNU Act of 1966, p. 13.

[5]JNU–Report of the Working of the University 15 September 1973–14 September 1974, p. 9; see also JNU–Report of the Working of the University 1 September 1978–31 August 1979, p. 19.

[6]JNU Act of 1966, p.13.

[7]Email correspondence with Professor Pramod Talgeri on 13 February 2019.

inclusiveness, through strengthening peoples' participation in education. In an ex-colony like India the colonizer's language has persisted as the language of the elites and as the medium of instruction in higher education. By making important texts from all disciplines available in Indian languages, including English and translating Indian works into other languages, more equal access to domain knowledge would result in a multiplicity of viewpoints, ranging from the dominant to the marginal and peripheral, leading to greater communication and perhaps to alternative innovative solutions to problems within the nation and beyond. This aspect of translation has not been realized in the half-century of JNU's existence. It should have formed the cornerstone of the translation programme from the very outset. To be fair, all language centres at the School produce a few translators each year. But it is equally true that they often work for BPOs, translating mundane texts which require little or no research, the reading of parallel texts, or work with dictionaries. BPOs, undoubtedly the biggest employers of graduate and undergraduate students of the School of Languages, are problematic and exploitative, and fulfil neither the aims of university education nor lead to knowledge production. There is, hence, an urgent need to offer knowledge-building alternatives for which there are resources at the university and which are achievable given the interdisciplinary mandate that JNU was founded upon.

The increasing hegemony of English assumes that students will read all scholarly work in English, reducing translation to little or no significance. At JNU there is a Linguistic Empowerment Cell which aims at improving the English language skills of students. Does this empower students who do not come from an English-medium educational background? It could; but that is not ensured. Lisa Delpit contends that for students who are not participants 'in the culture of power, being told explicitly the rules of that culture makes acquiring power easier'.[8] In our context it would indicate that learning to write and read critically in the dominant academic language (here English) is crucial for students to function in the academic environment, hence this overrides the contrary argument that students should be able to express themselves in their own tongue in order to evolve intellectually. Some students may benefit from this, yet such an approach

[8]Lisa Delpit, 'The Silenced Dialogue: Power and Pedagogy in Educating Other People's Children', in *Education: Culture, Economy, Society* edited by A. H. Halsey, Hugh Lauder, Phillip Brown, Amy Stuart Wells, Oxford: Oxford University Press, 1997, p. 583.

may merely foster the creation of derivative knowledge. This by no means implies that they should not be taught in English, but in order to reach the level of students from all educational and financial backgrounds, there should be much more on offer. It surely makes more sense to ensure that all students have access to 'content' in the language they understand best before moving on to reading those texts in English. If indeed we have to create a level playing field, only one language such as Hindi, cannot be privileged over others. Despite government policies that underscore that all administration must be in regional languages, at JNU, all PhD and MPhil thesis titles have to be submitted in the Devanagari script.

The translation programme of the School remains incomplete. The School did propose establishing a separate postgraduate and research programme for Translation Studies under the XII Plan introducing areas that are fundamental to a holistically structured Translation Studies programme that is intensive in approach and comprehensive in design. The Translation Studies programme sought to:

- combine the theory and practise of translation
- sensitize participants to the inter- and cross-cultural rootedness of translated texts as well as to the interdisciplinarity of the act of translation itself
- transmit an understanding of the technological environment in which modern domain-specific and literary translation takes place

What made the proposal unique was the inclusion of Indian languages alongside foreign languages, with the long-term intention of translating across languages. English would continue as an equally important language of translation and communication, but as an equal and not as a hegemon.

Students could specialize either in translation, literary translation and editing, or interpretation or even a combination of these. Students would thus have wide choices ranging from research and teaching to translating, interpreting, and editing.

The plan was also to establish a translation validation/certification cell to validate/certify the authenticity of the translation with the original. This, in turn, required experts, both in the concerned languages and in specific domains. A panel of such experts would have to be approved and updated on a regular basis.

In order to train facilitators and teachers of translation, an MA-level course on Didactics of Translation, Translator Training and Materials Production was to be introduced, to be later developed into a one-year Postgraduate Diploma in Translation Teaching (PGDT) programme.

Something similar had already been introduced by the National Translation Mission (NTM), located at the Central Institute of Indian Languages, Mysore set up in 2006. One of the aims of the NTM was the 'promotion and publication of knowledge text translation in all major disciplines taught in colleges and universities' and the 'development of translation tools such as dictionaries and thesauri'.[9] The 2018–19 catalogue of the NTM publications seems to indicate that this objective was fulfilled to a certain extent as we find not only books from the sciences and social sciences, but also bilingual dictionaries, although here again the larger languages dominate (Nepali is the exception here).

The School of Language, Literature and Culture Studies is favourably placed to participate actively in the programmes of the NTM, given the collective experience it has at its disposal in the field of translation. From the 1970s, many centres had engaged in translation projects and lexicographical work: the German Centre collaborated with the Central Hindi Directorate and the lexicographers of the GDR to develop a German–Hindi dictionary; at the Russian Centre, Dr S. C. Mittal worked on a Russian–English dictionary of mathematical terms;[10] Dr S. J. Havewalla worked on a French–English–Gujarati dictionary supported by the Centre of French Studies, where another lexicographical project *Dictionnare Juridique Françias-Anglais* was undertaken by Professor K. J. Mahale.[11] In addition, the Spanish Centre translated 'The Short History of Mexico' from Spanish into Hindi, and a study on Mahatma Gandhi's life and message into Spanish.[12]

In the past few decades, translation activity and resources have definitely grown. To cite a few resources in Hindi: Abhay Kumar Dubey's six-volume *Samaj Vigyan Vishwakosh* published in 2013 offers access to a range of material for social scientists. Were we to look for

[9]'Aims and Objectives', National Translation Mission, available at, <http://www.ntm.org.in/languages/english/aimndobj.aspx> [accessed: 18 September 2019].

[10]JNU–Report of the Working of the University 1st September 1975–31st August 1976, p. 23 and p. 95.

[11]Ibid., p. 66.

[12]Ibid., p. 21.

lexicographical work, fundamental to translation projects, we do not find adequate resources. The IIT Mumbai offers an online resource, *Hindi WordNet* and a Hindi–English dictionary, similar to the *Wortschatz-Portal* of the University of Leipzig, though the latter is extremely extensive. The National Book Trust published a two-volume Hindi thesaurus. The Mahatma Gandhi Antarrashtriya Hindi Vishwavidyala established in 1997 for the promotion of Hindi as a world language hosts a webpage called *Hindi Samay*, where there is a section on translation. Here, we find texts by Simone de Beauvoir and Walter Benjamin translated into Hindi, though in both cases mediated through English rather than French and German.

Why was the proposed translation programme at JNU never introduced? Why do the existing Translation and Interpretation specializations of at least two centres and the several courses on translation offered in all the other centres of the SLL&CS not enjoy greater visibility? Looking back, it is striking that literary translation dominates. The other noticeable factor is that translations from foreign languages are predominantly into English. Knowledge texts are often informally translated for academic purposes, but are frequently not published. Over the years, those working professionally have probably tended to translate technical texts. However, there is no record of this available. One of the reasons for insufficient scholarly books in regional languages is the lack of lexical work, similar to what Abhay Kumar Dubey did in Hindi for Sociology, in other Indian languages. Although much has been translated into major Indian languages, the need for specialized glossaries and dictionaries remains. This will not only lead to equal academic opportunities for students from all language backgrounds but finally dismantle hierarchical learning structures.

XI

MEMORIES FROM AFAR

66

JÑĀNĀRAṆYER DINARĀTRI: REMINISCENCES OF A SEMESTER AT JNU

SALLY J. SUTHERLAND GOLDMAN AND ROBERT P. GOLDMAN

In the spring of 2010, while on academic leave from our home institution in Berkeley, California, we shared the remarkable and thoroughly enjoyable opportunity to spend a semester living and lecturing on the splendid, park-like campus of JNU under the auspices of the Centre for Historical Studies (CHS) under its then Chair, Professor Kunal Chakrabarti.

This unusual opportunity arose when one of us, Professor Sally Sutherland Goldman, was asked by Professor Chakrabarti to serve as a Visiting Professor at CHS while the other, Professor Robert Goldman, happened, serendipitously, to be holding, at that time, a Senior Research Fellowship from the American Institute of Indian Studies. We are both primarily Indologists specializing in the scholarly study of Sanskrit language and literature with special concentration on the great epics of ancient India, the *Rāmāyaṇa* and the *Mahābhārata*, and had had long histories of association with JNU as guest lecturers and participants in seminars and conferences both at CHS and the Centre for Special Studies in Sanskrit (CSSS) (now the School of Sanskrit and Indic Studies). We are not by training professional historians and, initially, Robert Goldman's affiliation was to have been with the CSSS. But aside from our more traditional philological interests, we are both keenly interested in and have published widely on the historical resonance of the epics and their receptive histories and influence on historical, social, political, religious and literary thinking across the longue durée of Indian cultural history. So, given Professor Chakrabarti's kind invitation, it made sense for Robert to shift his affiliation to CHS under the former's supervision and to join, informally, in the course that Sally had been asked to teach.

In this way, combining our areas of interest and expertise and those of the faculty and students of the ancient history section of CHS, we developed a semester-long course on Epic as History and Epic in History focusing on two related topics. The first of these was the tradition of the *Rāmāyaṇa* and the *Mahābhārata* as, among other things, itihāsas, or expansive narrative accounts of ancient historical events composed by legendary poet-seers who were, according to tradition, gifted with an omniscient command of the events that they were recording. The second was the powerful and continuing influence of these monumental works on Indian civilization's concepts of such critical matters as theology, aesthetics, social hierarchy, gender and statecraft, among others.

The course, which we entitled 'Epic in History, Epic as History: Reading the *Ramayana* and the *Mahabharata* as Documents of and Models for the Social and Political Life of the Indian Nation,' turned out, despite, or perhaps because, of its interdisciplinarity, to be surprisingly popular and became the venue for wide-ranging and stimulating discussions of history, cultural memory, and social thought. Our joint lectures, which were held each Monday during term for two hours attracted most of the students from the Ancient History programme and some from other sections in the Centre. Most gratifying and stimulating was the fact that many of the Centre's faculty also took to attending the lectures and participating in the discussion that followed, as did a number of CHS alumni who were pursuing academic careers at other colleges and universities in Delhi and even some very distinguished emeritus faculty including the incomparable Professor Romila Thapar.

One unexpected and thoroughly enjoyable as well as intellectually stimulating enrichment of our experience was that after most of the lectures, our colleague Professor Kumkum Roy, would organize an informal lunch cum adda at which many of the faculty would convene over tea, coffee and her lovely, homemade sandwiches to continue discussion of the topics that had been covered in class and beyond. This is one of our fondest memories of our stay at JNU.

Another aspect of the course which we found particularly enjoyable and stimulating was the tutorial sessions with the students enrolled in the class. In consultation with us, the students would select topics for research papers, which they would then submit for our comments and evaluation. We would then meet periodically with subgroups of the students for sessions during which they would present their revised papers for discussion. This is, of course, standard practice at JNU but is quite different from the way we work with our postgraduate students at Berkeley and it was interesting and instructive for us to be able to interact closely with the CHS postgrads.

One thing we noticed immediately between the students and us as faculty was the difference in the way in which the students at CHS related to us as compared with what we had come to expect from our students in the US. The JNU students initially struck us as far more reticent and deferential to their professors than are those under our supervision at Berkeley. This is no doubt at least in part to be explained as culturally conditioned as Indian students in general seem to be trained to be somewhat more deferential to figures of academic authority than are those in the US, perhaps at larger level a reflex of the culture of gurudevo bhava, etc. This tendency was also, perhaps, accentuated by the unfamiliarity on the part of many of the students in working with foreign professors.

We found the students—as one would expect at an elite institution such as JNU—to be highly intelligent and well-grounded in their studies, but a bit timorous in expressing their own, independent ideas to us whether in individual meetings or tutorial sessions. Thus, in their first tutorial papers we found the majority of the students to be relying a bit too heavily on their notes from our lectures and our own published work and seeming to be hesitant to cite opposing views or offer any of their own. This manifested itself during the office consultations and the first tutorial in the form of expressions such as, 'As you, sir/ma'am said/wrote'. We replied that we already knew what *we* had argued and were more interested in finding out what other ideas they had managed to uncover in their reading and what their own ideas were even or especially if they were different from our own. Happily, these exchanges encouraged the students to be a bit bolder in their self-expression, and we found that the second set of tutorials reflected a livelier intellectual dialogue as the students felt more confident about articulating their own findings and opinions.

Although undoubtedly our fondest memories of our sojourn at JNU are of the sparkling academic and intellectual exchanges with our colleagues at CHS, SCSS, and other units of the University, we would be remiss were we not to reflect a bit on the pleasures of life on the campus. For, through the good offices of Chair Chakrabarti, we were fortunate enough to secure a small but ideal apartment in the conveniently located Old Transit House (OTH) a short and (except during the summer months) delightful walk from what was then the home of the CHS in the old School of Social Sciences Building (SSS-I).

As suggested above, the campus seemed to us like a sort of academic Nandana Garden around which we loved to wander at intervals during our teaching responsibilities and our own research work on the translation and annotation of the critical edition of the *Uttarakāṇḍa* of the *Vālmīki Rāmāyaṇa.* Set within but delightfully apart from the noise and urban bustle of South Delhi, the campus offered us a calm and almost sylvan retreat from the chaos of the city, providing us with a rich array of sight and sounds. There are few more lovely sights to be found on any university campus that we have seen than the brilliant explosion of the bougainvillea blossoms and the flowering trees as the campus moves into summer. Then too there is the profusion of wildlife on the grounds, the great variety of charming wild birds—and not least the marvellous strutting peacocks and—to us city dwellers—the startling sight of the freely roaming nilgai. We also remember the sounds as well as the sights of the campus. On the one hand, we listened from our rooms and our little OTH balcony to the romantic cries of the peacocks and the lilting calls of the koels in springtime, while at the same time we heard in the dark of night the howling of the campus's myriad feral dogs and the thunderous, bone-rattling sound of the big passenger jets as they descended low over the campus on their approach to IGIA. Thinking back on it even now (jets and all) produces a kind of nostalgia for what was a happy time for us.

But although our recollections are tinged with a kind of nostalgic feeling for that time and that place, we should note that the JNU of 2010 is not, we are afraid, that of the present day. Since that time, campus disruptions and the politicization of India's institutions of higher education and especially JNU have wrought significant changes in the atmosphere of the campus. As foreign scholars who have had a particularly intimate relationship to and deep love of this crown jewel, as it were, in India's system of higher education, the intervening years have been rather painful. What was long regarded internationally as the foremost of India's elite academic institutions has become a target of political and public attacks that threaten to undermine the creative role of the university in the production and transmission of new, cutting edge knowledge in the sciences, social sciences, and humanities. This is a role that has, in the past, won it the high prestige that it has enjoyed. If Indian universities are to retain the high international reputation they have in many cases achieved, institutions like JNU must be accorded scholarly independence and be characterized by international standards of academic freedom.

But for now we congratulate JNU, its faculty and its students on its remarkable fifty years of academic achievement as we think back fondly on that brief, shining moment when we were privileged to live and work in the exciting intellectual atmosphere and charming surroundings of what, for us, will remain in memory at least, our jñānāraṇyer dinarātri.

67

SWEET CHAI AND RESTLESS THINKING

ARI SITAS

In *From Around the World in Eighty Days: The India Section*, written mostly at JNU during 2008–11, I cast myself as a post-colonial Phileas Fogg with a Senegalese side-kick, crossing the Arabian Sea to arrive in Mumbai and Gandhiland's shopping malls. Through India I came to redo exactly what the 1873 novel demanded—ride elephants, witness tigers, save Aouda from sati, so that as a character I mess up and go anywhere and nowhere and subsequently get stuck because there is no London to get to in the twentieth century. The book of poems was a tortured attempt to come to terms with the overwhelming experience of India facilitated by dozens of colleagues, creative people, students and activists who helped me during my encounter with India since the first trip to Delhi in 2003.[1]

Sixteen years on, the JNU I'd experienced in 2003 is under threat and so is secularism, critical reflection and the spaces for it. The analysis of what is going on now belongs elsewhere.

Astrid and I arrived in Delhi in January 2003 to be garlanded by doctoral students of the Centre for the Study of Social Systems, put in a rickety taxi and sent off to Aravali Guest House (because apologies, sir and ma'am, the International Guest House was not available). In no time, Professor Anand Kumar dispatched us and visiting students from all over the world in all possible directions of the city, Gandhian and Neo-Gandhian institutions, and before you could count to three, sent us to functions with colleagues of the social sciences and literature. Not to be outdone, Professor M. N. Panini had me in front of plenty of students and colleagues to test my theoretical parables about to be published in South Africa.[2] When we were finally ushered onto the return flight I

[1]Published in 2013 by the University of South Africa Press, Pretoria.

[2]Same publishers in Pretoria, 2004.

knew I would return, a fact that has recurred almost every year since, for short or lengthier times.

It all started in 2001 when a suave ex-president of the International Sociological Association (ISA) Professor T. K. Oommen pointed my way. We had met through the ISA and he had co-hosted me in Mumbai in 1995. Immanuel Wallerstein was the president of the ISA, and I was the president of the South Africa Sociological Association, so we were flown over to kickstart dialogues among different regions of the association. We met at the Tata Institute of Social Sciences and struggled to make our voices heard above the din of a murder of irrepressible crows. I was enjoying the benefits of post-apartheid euphoria, being voted into all kind of positions in the international scene and when Professor Schwengel and Dr Frank Welz of Freiburg University suggested a Global Studies Programme to Professor Oommen, he retorted that it could only be possible if South Africa was its third pillar. Of course, within South Africa it had to be Durban thanks to our helping Gandhiji on the way to his Mahatma-hood, and within that, the very corridors I was in charge of at the University of KwaZulu-Natal.

The programme was launched in 2002 and survives till today, thanks to the effort of dozens of colleagues. Little did I know that even at JNU it was not a very welcome programme due to a persistent critique of the very idea of globalization. Through it, I was to meet plenty of compeers: Susan Visvanathan, Surinder Jodhka, Dipankar Gupta, Harish Naraindas, Sujatha V, Maitrayee Chaudhuri, Vivek Kumar, Sukhadeo Thorat, Jayati Ghosh, and then colleagues at Delhi University and quite soon the newly formed Ambedkar University.

Two more long-term visits to JNU stand out: a stint in 2008, as a Fellow at the Jawaharlal Nehru Institute of Advanced Study and one in 2016, as the inaugural Bhagat Singh Chair in the Centre for Historical Studies. Through Professors Aditya Mukherjee and Mridula Mukherjee, I was introduced to key thinkers of the contradictions of post-Independence India and to some of my most treasured creative collaborators and friends.

The fellowship helped me through my thinking on prospects of reconciliation, and how to finish off my Mandela Decade volume; it also spawned the draft 'Charter for the Future of the Humanities and the Social Sciences in South Africa' (2011). The humorous and the tragic intermingled when a challenge on Gandhi was underway through

Dalit Scholars which I studied with interest. This did not prepare me for the company of two younger men who would follow every public engagement/seminar/talk of mine in the next four years to deride me each time I mentioned the Mahatma even if my focus was the burden of the Mandela myth.

On the creative front the list is also very long: Sumangala Damodaran (my key collaborator since then for award-winning works of word and music), Madan Gopal Singh, Susmit Sen, Pritam Ghosal, Ahsan Ali, Satchidanandan, Vivek Narayanan, Sabitha Satchi, Anuradha Kapur, Deepan Sivaraman, Maya Rao and, and, and.... During 2008–09, I was to also participate in academic discussions for the development of two schools in the newly-formed Ambedkar University: Creative Expressions and Development Studies. Through that and the care of Indu Chandrasekhar, our heterodox volume, *Gauging and Engaging Deviance 1600-2000* saw the light of day.[3]

The second long-stay was in 2016, as a Bhagat Singh Chair in CHS through which I was to teach a master's course with Professor Sucheta Majahan on 'nationalism'.[4] My host at Jawaharlal Nehru Institute of Advanced Studies (JNIAS) was to be Professor G. J. V. Prasad—the first real host of my poetry. Alas, 'nationalism' was a very unfortunate topic for reflection at the very moment when JNU was being singled out as the incubus of the 'anti-national'. Before I could utter Fanon or Nyerere, I was placed in front of thousands of protesting students and staff to speak on the theme as part of the defiant lecture series of the conflagration. It was a heady time from slogan to march, from march ('Ho Chi Minh/Bhagat Singh/we shall fight/we shall win') to theory and plenty of encounters with swathes of new people and invitations to speak until India decided 'enough!' and floored me with her microbiological powers: hepatitis A and a quick disposal back to the fairest Cape which lasted till the end of the year. During my recovery process I penned two pieces, one about Dr K's resurrection 'poem' which appeared on the fascinating website of the Indian Cultural Forum, and an oratorio ('For Small Things that Fall, Like

[3]Published in 2013 by Tulika Press, Delhi.

[4]These were more than heady times that I recall fascinating interventions that made me aware of the work among others of the late Bipan Chandra, Neeladri Bhattacharya, Janaki Nair, Ania Loomba, and Rajat Datta. Of particular significance was meeting Irfan Habib, a scholar who had influenced my understanding of history years ago.

a Screw'), a section of which was to be produced in Delhi by Anuradha Kapur and Deepan Sivaraman as *Dark Things* in 2018.

I was to return to JNU in late 2017 to speak at the launch of my friend Sumangala Damodaran's book *The Radical Impulse*, to visit friends and find out what was going on in the institution and now, where I am walking past the ever-busy security at the gate, the Kamal Complex market, the hostels and academic residences, to Admin and Freedom Square, emptied of sound, to the Social Science and History Buildings still abuzz with student life, the murals, the itinerant dogs and eerie peacocks and the restless nilgai, to pay my respects to a place that shaped both my intellectual trajectory and my structures of feeling.

There, by the market, memories of the sweetest chai and discussions with students: over my 'critique of arms' and their insistence that the Naxals were correct in the forests, and of course the debate around Nandini Sundar's *The Burning Forest*; by the chai place behind the Admin Block, whether Anderson or Chatterjee were right on nationalism; in the basement of SSS-II, over more chai and samosas, whether it was class or caste, and about Professor Jodhka's latest take on caste and Gopal Guru's pages on humiliation; at the chai place on the ground floor of the SSS-III where the Centre for Historical Studies is located, the similarities of my take on third spaces and Homi Bhabha's; by the canteen (with a library attached to it) a dosa and a dose of Fanon and the latest stuff on Gandhi and race, what with South African historians agreeing more or less with Arundhati Roy's introduction to Ambedkar, what about it, Professor? I retorted that people did not know that they are only right until 1911—Gandhi's attendance at the grand conference on race in London where he met W. E. B. Du Bois marked a significant shift. *Indian Opinion* started publishing Du Bois's critiques of race in Durban immediately thereafter.

In short, with every step, I was visiting memories of what a university could or should be: sweet chai and restless thinking.

XII.1. Who can stop us drinking tea? When the JNU administration decided to close down dhabas at night to control the sites of debate and discussion, students set up their own alternative tea stalls (April 2017).
Photo courtesy: Samin Asgor Ali

68

THE FIRANGI IN 306

DEBORAH SUTTON

It is ill-advised to compare my experiences as a PhD student to those of current and recent postgraduate research students. My memories of being a PhD student at JNU become more compelling and indistinct as the distance and disparity grows between my own academic position, and privilege, and the uncertain academic terrain negotiated by current young scholars. My memories reach back across almost two decades of my post-doctoral career and have been framed by the collective nostalgia of an enduring friendship network of JNU graduates and, finally, through the frequent visits to Delhi that afford far greater comfort than my Ganga-hostel room.

I arrived in 1997 to take up a Commonwealth scholarship at the Centre for Historical Studies. I avoided the competitive, tortuous selection process my peers had undergone and was parachuted, without a relevant MA or MPhil, directly into the PhD programme. I still had to negotiate JNU's brutal and complex bureaucracy. An autowallah dropped me at the Administrative Building ('the Pink Palace') after a long journey, and once I had found the relevant office, I was told that I had no scholarship. I was registered as a student only after a very kind IFS officer at the Indian Council for Cultural Relations intervened on my behalf. Thus began a relationship with the administration at JNU that routinely made me go all red in the face like an enraged memsahib. Initial registration was only a toe-hold. Twice a year, all JNU students were required to re-register themselves, to re-inscribe and revalidate our existence in the many offices of the many functionaries on campus. A sheaf of cards were collected at the Dean's office and, gradually, after each colour-coded card was stamped and signed by multiple officers, each was returned back into the labyrinthine system of JNU administration. (I'm ashamed that the only time I ever went to the sports centre was to register and then, four years later, to de-register). Registration invariably involved arriving at the office short of one, critical, ingredient (a signed photocopy, a photograph, a stamp) and a subsequent return visit with everything in order.

With hindsight (and I had to get quite far away to see this), laborious registration work brought certain boons. The first pleasure was the immediate gratification of completion. Walking out of any office with registration complete for another cycle created a feeling of elation approaching bliss. Another was a glimpse of how bureaucracies worked—a logistical and intellectual advantage to anyone who relies on bureaucratic records for research. With some help from professors at the Centre for Historical Studies, I began to understand a bureaucratic culture derived from the colonial apparatus that was so paralysed by the suspicion at its core that it struggled to carry out even ordinary tasks.

My archival research consisted of going through indices that mapped out the divergent and intersecting departments of the colonial archive—Revenue, Board of Revenue, Public, General, Home and, occasionally, Secret—searching for some mention of my own, fuzzily understood, subject. Bored of Revenue? (went the joke) Yes, I was. Very. My initial interest in Mysore shrank down to the Nilgiri Hills of the Madras Presidency and a focus on imperial cartography gradually morphed into agrarian history; a topic that I can now sheepishly (no pun intended) acknowledge, was simply more evident, more obvious, in the bureaucratic archive I was sunk in. The months I spent in the archives, in Delhi, Chennai and Udhagamandalam, were intensely enjoyable; a mixture of reassuring routine and the constant potential for 'discovery'—as I understood the term then in an unproblematized way. Long periods of archival research provided the perfect mix of industry and sociable leisure. My head would bob up constantly to check who was entering, passing by or leaving for chai. There was great camaraderie between scholars who shared both the delights of finding juicy materials and condolences when a sheaf of order slips were returned bearing the dreaded 'NT' (not transferred) or 'No light'. We ordered files in the hundreds; sometimes files called would be missing, others contained little more information than was contained in the index entry or, best and worst of all, a thick seam of relevant correspondence, reports and the promised pages of transcription and an aching hand.

My research closely followed the archive's grain (pace Ranajit Guha); tracing departmental indices, correspondences, reports, and orders.

Meanwhile, a generation of historians above and around us was beginning to manipulate the idea of the archive in a host of fascinating ways to create new agendas for history writing. I read and re-read Guha, Ajay Skaria, and Prathama Banerjee, attempting to graft their reflections on the archive, its temporalities and materials on to my own pedestrian research.[1]

Although the academic culture in the UK was ostensibly more egalitarian—and at JNU, the 'Sirs' and 'Mams' felt very awkward, there were small, creative subversions in India's rigidly hierarchical academic cultures. A friend told me the story of an undergraduate student in a Delhi University college who, having been unjustly marked by a professor whose dignity would not allow him to correct the class records, would, whenever he passed her, bow her head in a gesture of submissive civility and mutter a brief, violent term of abuse under her breath. Another friend told me about a classmate of his who would ask an elaborate question at research seminars and, as the speaker began to respond, would calmly stand, gather his things and leave the seminar room. Whether resistive or childish, these actions were unthinkable in the UK because we believed, erroneously, that we occupied the same, undifferentiated realm as our teachers.

It became apparent that the teaching and research culture at JNU was exceptionally warm and honest. Professors at CHS went out of their way to make me feel welcome, playing gracious hosts to a clumsy guest.

My memory of the campus consists of points and turns across glorious spaces of the campus: left from Ganga hostel to get to CHS, the dhabas and the library, and right to catch the 615 bus either to Munirka, to connect to Teen Murti, or to continue on to the National Archives on Janpath. A walk through the campus held the constant risk and promise of bumping into friends and heading for chai or lunch. A visit to the JNU library too often ended with my bringing books back to my room under the comfortable delusion that I would study not sleep. For proper work, it was better to turn right from Ganga and catch the 615 into the city.

Being a JNU student gave us the privilege of a bus pass. With a pass you avoided searching for two or five rupees and enjoyed a satisfying

---

[1]Ajay Skaria, *Hybrid Histories: Forests, Frontiers and Wildness in Western India*, New Delhi: Oxford University Press, 1998; Prathama Banerjee, 'Debt, time and extravagance: Money and the making of "primitives" in colonial Bengal', *Indian Economic & Social History Review*, Vol. 37, No. 4, pp. 423–45.

sense of entitlement. 'Mere paas pass hai' was always intoned to the blue line or DTC conductor with slight ennui. Teen Murti meant air conditioning and the chance of a seminar with free chai and snacks. JNU was an oasis in the tough, bewildering, and extraordinary city of Delhi. When the 615 turned right through the main gates on Aruna Asaf Ali Marg, I felt a palpable relief. JNU felt safe in a city that went to some lengths to make women feel uncomfortable. Living in Delhi created a state of hyper-vigilance in women. Most of us developed a pre-emptive death stare and these experiences cemented a feminism and collectivity the likes of which I have never experienced since. We were assaulted incalculable times on buses, on streets, in markets. There was a tedious repertoire of assault: the bus rub, the breast grab, the glancing punch between our legs, as we bent forward to look at books on a pavement stall in Daryaganj.

In my current teaching, I begin a lecture for first-year students on the Subaltern School by showing a photograph of a mural from the CHS canteen: 'Until deer have their own historians, histories of the hunt will glorify the hunter'.[2] Students in the UK know the lazy (and politically ambiguous) maxim that history is written by the victors. JNU taught me that history-writing should be a dynamic field of argument and not, as it so often is in Western Europe and North America, a set of comfortable reaffirmations of the geographical, cultural, and social shape of the nation state. Being a student in CHS gave me insight into history as a vibrant field of discussion in which nothing, and nobody, could, or should, be regarded as authoritative.

Our exposure to an extraordinary range of scholarship, created a community that was animated by ideas and our own sense of being at the centre of the world. Being at JNU, and Delhi, gave us access to exciting speakers and ideas. It is clear now that the seminar culture at JNU was incredibly aggressive. We watched in awe as luminaries in the field of historical scholarship fielded politely eviscerating questions. One CHS professor told a visiting professor from Oxford that, 'she was charming but trite'. A brilliant student pointed out to another Oxford professor that the problem with her argument was that it was 'irrefutable' (and therefore pointless).

[2]Old SSS-I Building canteen, All India Students Association poster, 2011.

Not only were we at the centre of the world, we were taught by academics who could help us negotiate the extraordinary scholarly terrain we inhabited. Bappa, as Professor Sabyasachi Bhattacharya was generally called, gave me the best advice I ever received, then or since. Faced with my infernal whining about my research, my writing and my uncertain future, he told me, with great courtesy, 'If you are not having fun, then find something else to do.' This advice, passed on many times, has become one of my most cherished maxims.

Bappa's comment expressed a distinct characteristic of the academic culture we inhabited at JNU. Despite the doughty and intimidating range of scholarship in which we were immersed, we felt a lightness that now strikes me as remarkable. Visitors from the fiercely competitive graduate school cultures in the US seemed, by comparison, weighed down by a need to broker their scholarship. They pinned down their own work in relation to (then) dominant intellectual landmarks and explained the significance of their work with poker-faced sincerity. As an early career academic back in the UK, I was taken aback by colleagues in England who would carefully and slowly explain to me that their work was 'post (-) colonial' (with a hyphen in a parenthesis between post and colonial implied by their tone) and that they were very interested in the 'Subaltern approach'. Had I heard of it? For all the difficulties that the administration at JNU placed on scholars and students, the institutionalised academy did not weigh heavily on the intellectual culture at JNU. We were, as Bappa hoped, having a great deal of fun.

Being a student at CHS gave me four years of exhilarating, exhausting, and important education. JNU taught me what a university is: an academic community united by a common purpose. That common purpose was never consensus. In the hostel mess, along with our food, we collected sheets of densely argued political tracts produced by political groups on campus. These tracts testified to the appetite for connecting thought and activism and sometimes mapped factions that split with kaleidoscopic complexity. The intellectual culture of JNU necessitated disagreement, arguments, and discomfort. The solidarities created at JNU never meant universal agreements but they did entail the necessity of allowing speech and listening. Carefully.

I have always relished the various mythologies that swirled around and about JNU. Even those of us with the thinnest political credentials revelled in the institution's reputation for political and social activism. The concomitant stories about our debauchery we regarded as amusing (possibly aspirational). They certainly did not reflect our quotidian routine of water hoarding, chai drinking, chatting and occasional rum drinking. During the last five year, these mythologies have been aggressively reframed, and deployed with some effect on social media platforms, to caricature JNU as, at best, a bubble of liberal and out-of-touch privilege and, at worst, a haven of 'anti-national' activities. The emergence of a state that wields its formidable power to attack a university and the police incursion at the beginning of 2016 marked a sea change at JNU's history. The closure of the campus and the arrest of four students on charges of sedition demonstrated the vulnerability of any public institution in the face of violent, exclusionary state politics. The fantasized extremism is garnish to an attack aimed squarely at the university as a complicated, heterogeneous place of thought and debate.

69

LOOKING BACK

QUOC ANH NGUYEN

Looking back after almost fifteen years, travelling around the world, setting up different kinds of businesses, I would certainly say my two years (2002–04) at JNU shaped the very core of my intellectual life.

In JNU, I learnt many things. Let me recount only five. First: I learnt how to overcome any challenge thrown straight at your face, most of them unexpected. To begin with, it was the infrastructure of the school in 2002. I was staying in Jhelum hostel, sharing a room with another student, having dinner in the common room, and sharing bathrooms with practically everyone. I still remember most of the bathroom doors were broken or there were no latches. And we took cold showers in the winter with the door half open. Can you picture that?

Having spent those years, having negotiated difficult conditions, I don't really understand why members of staff in Vietnam complain about crushed bedsheets in fancy hotels. Even with all the difficulties I faced, it was still the best decision to stay on the campus, and not rent a room outside. For it was not an experience to be missed. The most vivid memory I have is of the dining room—the mess as it was called. Every night after dinner, it transformed from a messy room with leftover food into a battleground of ideas, where some of the most intense debates I have ever witnessed took place. I still remember listening to spirited arguments while chewing the last bits of my chapatti.

Second: I learnt the value of intimate yet public spaces of socialization. 'That is the café you told us about?' my students from Vietnam on our collective trip to India would ask me in bewildering disbelief. All they could see were a few large rocks under the trees near the Ganga hostel bus stop at JNU. How could I capture for them what Ganga Dhaba meant for us as students?

'Yes it is, and that is where much of my learning took place at JNU,' I said with a nostalgic smile. Yes, only a few rocks, but seated there on those rocks, sipping tea and munching snacks, I was part of many passionate and lively discussions. Ganga Dhaba was our designated place to hang out after dinner, and being there was a heady experience. When I returned to my room at night, ideas would be dancing in my mind. What an intellectual experience it was. Years later, having worked in different organizations with wonderful facilities, I still look back to JNU with nostalgia: nowhere have I found a comparable spirit of discussion or level of dialogue.

Logistically, the infrastructure of any university, with all modern facilities, could be easily built in a year or two, but the heart and soul of an institution requires a lot of time to nurture, and they require spaces of nurturing. Open spaces where students can freely socialize, speak their minds, inspire and be inspired. In my time at JNU, such spaces were the dhabas of JNU, where diverse ideas could freely intermingle, generating new ideas, firing minds.

Third: A bigger challenge would come from the intellectual demands of the courses. If you think you know good English, think again, when you start reading Derrida, Hayden White or Heidegger. There were times I was so confused looking at the texts that I was not even sure if they were written in English or Latin. On top of that, my group of five friends would drive me crazy when they discussed concepts such as signifier/signified, deconstruction, analogy, allegory, metaphor. You can imagine my face at that time: being there but not really there, having absolutely no idea what these aliens were talking about. So I channelled my survival skills again: if they needed two hours to read a book, I needed twenty. I photocopied my readings so that I could go through them over and over again. The photocopywallah in CHS, Ashish da, must have made a fortune out of my drive for books (we all conspired to help each other, to overcome the copyright limit of photocopying no more than 20 per cent of the book). Thinking back, I have no idea how I could understand those texts, which I still use once in a while, possibly only to scare my students here in Vietnam.

It was not just the language and the texts; I struggled for months with the whole new way of looking at history: exploring how it was constructed and for whose benefit. The most memorable piece of my memory is an afternoon discussion with Professor Romila Thapar, during which we learned how history should be interrogated and her six questions are still at the very core of my critical thinking points, even more needed today with the wide spread of fake news. I don't remember how many courses I took but every professor had his or her own distinctive personality. Years later, I had an opportunity to host some of them in Vietnam and we were able to share endless laughs about those lectures. 'I didn't know that my lecture is so powerful as to induce sleep in just minutes' said one professor to me once when I was dozing in the class after a late night.

Fourth: In JNU I came to recognize the meaning of friendships. It was there that I built some of the most amazing friendships during the formative years of my life. It was a time when there were no Facebook, Instagram or any form of social media. Even when we said goodbyes, the only means of communication was just a simple email. We didn't have a graduation party: we just got the final results and set off, parting ways, not sure when and how we would see each other again. We were all thinking of our uncertain futures, unable to spare any neuron to think of how we could possibly stay in touch. Yet true friendship could only be tested with time.

Thirteen years after our graduation, I met one of my friends, Uditi, in a London pub. We connected in minutes as if we had never left JNU. The same kind of conversations, laced with a slightly higher level of sarcasm, about everything under the sun. How could all those years disappear? Time can separate; it can erode bonds that connect people together. But spatial and temporal separation had not changed our friendship, formed through endless discussions, jokes, and parties.

Our times with Mandakini, in her tiny Maruti car, also made up for an amazing story. Five of us close friends would cram into the car and drive around Delhi, enjoying every bit of our discussions over numerous lunches hosted by her mom, sometimes with her sister around, and her very fat cat.

The two Adityas, who argued endlessly and tirelessly. It was through them I learned the importance of engaged conversation, and the value of rich intellectual dialogues. But, in reacting to their never-ending discussions, I also learned the value of brevity. When I joined the business world, I made a rule that no one could take more than three minutes to state an argument. They now know that many of the 'crazy' rules of my company originated from my experiences at JNU.

Fifth: In JNU I began to understand the meaning of cultural diversity.

Before coming to India, I had heard a lot about the country. I knew of the idea of unity in diversity, and I was aware of the differences in languages and cultures in different parts of India. But living in JNU was a different learning experience.

I had travelled to most states of India to get a first-hand experience of the differences in languages, cultures, and peoples even before joining the university; but it was only at JNU that I could feel diversity in a real sense. I confronted different mindsets in action. I was initially persistently surprised at what I heard. I could not understand how people could think so differently, how my ideas were often so radically different. More than once I screamed out: how on earth can you think like that? Isn't it so obvious? Isn't this just common sense? No, nothing is obvious, nothing is common sense. People think differently. Our reference points are different. To understand each student, each friend, you have to know about his or her specific background. During those years at JNU, I learned to investigate how different opinions were formed; I learned to examine distinct layers of someone's ideas, see the particular cultures that shaped a student's mind, and the way the economic and family background had a formative influence.

Looking back, it appears, being at JNU itself was a great opportunity to see how and why diverse perspectives get formed. The ability I acquired not to jump to any conclusion based on just what someone says but to step back and examine the whole process of opinion formation, helped me tolerate diverse ideas, no matter how radical their difference. Moreover, this curiosity enabled me to decide whether I should engage with a contrary idea or not and, if yes, then how do I begin to engage. I remember once a friend came up to ask 'why do you use chopsticks? Have you no respect for food?' I was taken aback, but laughed and tried to understand why he had made the statement, what it reflected about cultural difference.

The tolerant culture of JNU is seen at its best in the protests and marches where varying ideas are tested in front of a thousand minds. At such times, there was lots of slogan-shouting and much discussion: we heard speeches, listened to different speakers, saw ideas being challenged and defended. For me, such times of students' action were enriching, and the discussions exciting. But the time of election was special. Members of as many as four different students' associations would come to my room in an evening, to persuade me to vote for them. It was a great chance to ask them questions. Some certainly did not share my socialist values.

We all learn as we grow older that a happy life is not the result of materialistic pursuits: material pleasure fades quickly. Happiness resides in the memories formed through experiences. For me the experiences at JNU are part of my most precious memories. I return to them, delight in them and writing this story has offered me an opportunity to relive those wonderful moments.

XII

THE SPIRIT OF JNU

70

THE WORLD OF JNU

HAPPYMON JACOB

It was in the sultry summer heat of June 2016 that I hiked up to a small piece of land in the Jammu division of J&K called 'Chicken neck', a heavily militarized area manned on the Indian side by the Border Security Force (BSF) and the Pakistan Rangers on the other. Surrounded on three sides by Pakistani soldiers, and witness to deadly tank battles during the 1965 and 1971 wars, the area, referred to by the Pakistanis as 'dagger', (meaning that it is piercing into the Indian territory) is not an easy place for civilians to gain access to or for men and women in uniform to guard.

I was on a field visit there and was received by a uniformed man in his mid fifties. 'How's JNU doing these days?' he asked me before enquiring how I was at the end of a rather tiring journey. A sharp, tall, and soft-spoken Deputy Inspector General (DIG) of the Border Security Force (BSF), at least a dozen years senior to me, turned out to be a former student of JNU, and we hit it off instantly. We were in a war zone—well, almost. Machine-gun fire occasionally resonated in the hot dusty air, and my BSF contacts had warned me of the possibility of firing breaking out anytime. I was advised to stay indoors, talk to the officers and return to the sector headquarters in Jammu, in 'one piece'.

The BSF officer ignored the mayhem and the advice of his colleagues and took me on a drive around the chicken neck area, showing me around the strategically important piece of land. We were sitting in a bulletproof jeep, with him in the driver's seat, travelling behind the mud-bunds built to withstand Pakistani firing, ducking enemy gaze, while discussing Ganga Dhaba and Gopalan's canteen. I returned two days later and have never met or spoken to him again, but his hospitality and his fond memories of JNU from the mid 1980s remain fresh in my mind.

Over the years, I have encountered several others like him. A senior IPS officer in Delhi fondly remembered his supervisor, Zoya Hasan, while having an off-the-record conversation with me on the home ministry's approach to the India–Pakistan border. Sanjay Kumar from the School of Languages was my 'two a.m.' man while I was away on my sabbatical at the Central European University in Budapest in 2017 (Sanjay lived in the old town with his Hungarian wife and two kids and he was, indeed, my lifeline in an unknown city in the heart of Eastern Europe with its often unfriendly attitudes towards outsiders); Anup Sam Ninan was my beer-buddy while on sabbatical in Berlin—both from JNU.

These people shared something in common—whether they were bureaucrats, politicians, academics, journalists or those working in the NGO sector. Age, gender, rank, and professional differences tended to disappear when one JNUite met another in any corner of the world. You can take a JNUite out of JNU, but you can't take JNU out of the JNUite, goes the cliché. There is an immediate connect that gets established, something non-JNUites find difficult to fathom. So what explains this JNU-ness that one finds even among those who left the campus decades ago?

The cult of JNU

JNU, they disparagingly say, is an ivory tower. I agree, in an unapologetic way, and I think it should remain so, as should all institutions of higher education. A university should provide you with a space where you experiment with ideas, debate them, dispute them, dump them, acquire new ones and then go back into the world to live those ideas. That's what JNUites do, always with a tinge of nostalgia.

Wherever they may be and whatever they might do, those who studied at JNU take pride in having belonged to the place, and long to compare their memories and experiences with yours. 'During my time in the 1980s, there were hardly any trees on the Campus', some of them would tell me (I joined JNU for an MPhil degree in 2002). 'Oh, it's a forest now', I would respond. 'Does Francis still run the canteen in SSS?' 'Not anymore'. Onlookers are often puzzled by these seemingly inane conversations. Indeed, inane they are except for those who once belonged to the hallowed space of JNU.

What does JNU do to someone from the country's hinterland that s/he remembers it or lives by its credo for the rest of his/her life? What is it that unites the world of JNU? Certainly, it is not the hostel food or the standard of accommodation, of which the less said the better!

There is the inexplicable JNU connect which magically brings people together. Then there is the pride of having belonged to a coveted place, the nation's best public-sector university which you can only become part of by competing in a serious (at least until recently) national-level examination. JNU is also about both witnessing the unfolding of national politics in the capital from an arm's length, and occasionally participating in it. Sometimes even shaping it.

A senior Delhi-based journalist, whose columns on economic issues are a hit today, was my contemporary at JNU. He recently recounted what the university did for him: 'JNU gave me political capital'. 'What does that mean?' I asked. 'Not only did I start grasping the unstated politics behind what happens in the country on a day-to-day basis, but equally importantly, JNU gave me a certain political confidence—to challenge and expose the established political canons, and to arrive at my own political conclusions.'. And in a world of half-truths, un-truths and fake news, the lack of political confidence is a deadly shortcoming.

This point needs to be restated given the high premium placed on 'social capital' in a country like ours especially in our institutions of higher education. As a young student, JNU requires you to have no social capital, JNU *is* the social capital for its students. For those who lack proficiency in English, the inability to converse in English hardly matters since it's your ideas that matter. As a saying on the campus goes—'What matters is not the language in which you say it, but what you say.' The lack of a privileged background becomes completely irrelevant for a JNU student. As a matter of fact, frontloading your privileged background could even backfire. Interactions with faculty are unmarked by hierarchies. And of course, the learning that takes place outside the classrooms is as important as the lectures and discussions inside the classrooms.

However, I think what distinguishes JNU is its anti-establishment streak, which translates into an abiding unwillingness to accept the conventional wisdom about society, state and government. Most JNU students go back into the world having imbibed this anti-establishment streak, though in varying degrees.

For the JNUites out there, the world of JNU is a unique socio-political space, a Weltanschauung, where democracy and egalitarianism are a daily practice, and knowledge is applied in all professional engagements.

Public intellectualism is yet another unique hallmark of JNU. In public forums, JNU faculty typically challenge the conventional wisdom on how the country should be governed. They highlight how official policies are often discriminatory, argue that majoritarianism eats into the vitals of our democratic polity, and show that warmongering and imagined enemies are often cheap strategies adopted by the ruling classes to deflect attention from the real issues haunting the country. Ironically, the very same government that despises JNU's anti-establishment streak, often looks for its advice and counsel. I have been asked several times as to why I am so critical of the government's institutions and policies and my typical answer has been that 'because we deserve better'. Even though a public intellectual is often viewed as a nuisance by the powers that be, they are an essential ingredient of a healthy democracy. It is also a responsibility that those of us who have had the privilege of higher education have towards our society. And JNU faculty have traditionally displayed a strong inclination towards such public intellectualism.

Fifty years since its establishment, JNU must be proud of what it has done for the nation, how its faculty has shaped contemporary debates of national importance and how it remains a beacon of hope in a milieu of hyper-nationalism and politically motivated disinformation.

So every time I step out of the JNU campus into an uncertain world, I hope to encounter someone with a similar world view, who I may or may not agree with, but with whom I can have a decent conversation... someone from JNU.

71

SARASWATI, MAHISHASURA, AND DURGA: LOVE, JNU, AND A MYTHOLOGY OF DISSENT

KANAD SINHA

Saraswati Puja, the worship of the goddess of learning, is an extremely popular festival in Bengal. Studying is prohibited on the day, mischief and whims of the students are treated with indulgence, turning schools into centres of festivities. The occasion is also known as the 'Valentine's Day of the Bengalis'. Though we hardly knew what Valentine's Day was, Saraswati Puja created a colourful fantasy in our adolescence. This was the day when the boys would be allowed inside the girls' schools and vice versa. Often, kurta-clad schoolboys approached the sari-wearing schoolgirls, to initiate new love stories.

The Saraswati Puja of 2016, supposed to be the last one of my formal student life, became special in a different way. My university was suddenly all over the national news. The JNU Students' Union President Kanhaiya Kumar had been arrested on the charge of sedition. Students and teachers gathered spontaneously at the Administrative Block where the crowd was addressed by many national-level leaders expressing solidarity with JNU. Until then, JNU was perceived as the premier university of the country. It suddenly began to be portrayed as a hub of sedition where, on 9 February, some students allegedly raised 'anti-national' slogans during a cultural event on Kashmir.

The JNU students, in the following days, were verbally abused, physically attacked and humiliated, threatened with rape and mob lynching. Everybody—friends, relatives, neighbours, shopkeepers, auto drivers, co-passengers, and the 'common man'—was judgemental and condescending about an institution which supposedly nurtured a stand against the unity and integrity of the Indian nation. Many news anchors complained on air how hard-earned public money was being wasted on 'ungrateful elements' who were against their own country while 'soldiers were dying in the frontiers'. It was decided that the JNU students didn't actually study; there was growing curiosity about what went on in the enclosed campus. Colourful images came, including the one of the BJP MLA Gyandev Ahuja who imagined constant bacchanalia of naked dance, rave parties and other frivolities, daily producing a huge number of used condoms, alcohol bottles and 'abortion syringes'![1]

Amidst this crisis, an overwhelming number of JNU students and teachers stood in unprecedented solidarity to resist attacks against the autonomy of the campus space and for the fundamental right to freedom of speech, enshrined in the Indian Constitution. Umar Khalid and Anirban Bhattacharya, the main organizers of the disputed event, were soon arrested. A huge number of JNU students and teachers, alongside students and sympathizers from other institutions, came out on the streets against the crackdown, the vilification of the institution and criminalization of dissent. The ensuing debates raised fundamental questions regarding what nationalism meant. Reputed academicians from JNU and other places were invited to conduct open-air classes on nationalism every afternoon in the Administrative Block, now known as the 'Freedom Square'.

The arrested students had to be released soon. Kanhaiya's speech defining the movement's goal as azadi (freedom) in India, not azadi from India, was all over the news. However, JNU, a leading educational institution that promoted free thinking, now was being alternatively represented as a space where communism was the dominant doctrine, dissent was a manifestation of Left-leaning insurrectionary tendencies, and where religion in general and Hinduism in particular was under constant attack. Though the movement united all secular democratic forces for protecting the Constitutional cornerstone of Indian democracy from fascist onslaught, and not for replacing the current regime with a communist revolution, the perception thrived and was reified by Smriti Irani, the Human Resource Development Minister at that time. She alleged in the Parliament that the JNU culture supported the consumption of beef and valorized Mahishasura, the buffalo demon antagonistic to the great goddess, during the Durga Puja. Makarand Paranjape, who teaches English at JNU, had been among the few JNU teachers criticizing the movement from the start. Despite that, he was invited as a speaker in the open-air

[1]Dipsikha Thakur, '3,000 Condoms and Other Tales from the Crypt', *Outlook*, 25 February 2016.

teach-in series. His lecture expectedly went into an all-out attack on left-wing politics. He accused JNU of being a Left-hegemonic place where any non-Left element is either brainwashed or bullied, and lamented the lack of 'mediality' between the two extremes of the political spectrum.

In short, there was a myth created around JNU's celebrated culture of dissent, like the Puranic myth of endless feud between the Devas and the Asuras, culminating in the churning of the ocean of milk. The churning produces the poison of hegemony, which is forced down the throat of the demonized political right. The elixir of immortality, Freedom of Expression, becomes the exclusive privilege of the political Left. The jhola-carrying, beard-wearing, kurta and jeans-clad JNU leftists thus enact the hegemonic role of the very Brahmanical gods they pathologically detest. God-fearing, right-leaning nationalist Hindus spend their days at JNU as a bullied minority like the demonized Asuras condemned to the eternal underground (Patala). The left wing plays with their religious sentiments, craving for the meat of every cow and worshipping every buffalo, at the cost of the Mother Cow, the mother goddess, and—therefore—Mother India.

This myth can be shattered by bare political facts. ABVP, the Sangh Parivar's student wing, has traditionally been dominant in most of the science schools, whereas the Left groups are stronger in the humanities schools (except the Sanskrit Centre) at JNU. This betrays a picture where one group is totally bullied or brainwashed. Yet, mere electoral data may not adequately address the myth. Therefore, I shall move from believed mythology to lived experience.

Dissent is an important content in the public life of JNU, a university committed to the development of critical thinking and thus encouraging constant questioning. Inside the classrooms of the Centre for Historical Studies, we learnt to question the various narratives of the past, the sources we use and their perceived 'authenticity', even the very nature of our discipline. However, the JNU culture also relates the academic training with life. Therefore, it is a space which will constantly draw one out of the inertia of inherited social conventions. Your academic understanding of social institutions will often lead you to question the status quo and problematize the sacrosanct. Questioning goes beyond the classrooms to the streets, the various dhabas, and the hostel rooms. Nationalism or communism, religion or caste, patriarchy or monogamy, none remain unquestioned. However, a fine line separates questioning and rejecting, criticism, and demolition. That is the line which defines 'mediality'. The line was not at all blurred at JNU. Rather, it defined the institution.

Despite being a declared non-Marxist, I have survived and thrived at JNU for seven years without being bullied or brainwashed. Rather, JNU provided me the greatest room for the articulation of my liberal democratic ideas catering to secular centrism. Even if I look at not the secular but the religious, not the communist slogans but religious festivals, an interesting picture emerges. I had started this essay with the celebration of Saraswati Puja at JNU. Isn't it surprising that a campus of so called 'Left hegemony', where Brahmanism and casteism are denounced every moment, would have a vibrant celebration of a festival worshipping a Hindu goddess? Yet, the Saraswati Puja is celebrated with much enthusiasm. Every hostel committee at JNU celebrates Diwali, and Holi at JNU is a grand spectacle. The Durga Puja is held annually with massive participation. Onam, Lohri, Pongal, Bangla Nababarsha, and other regional festivals have their space on the campus life, and so do the non-Hindu religious festivals like Eid and Christmas. The religious Hindu (or non-Hindu) does not live in constant fear at JNU like the believers did in Stalinist USSR.

The culture of dissent at JNU is not a culture of demolition, but a culture of nuancing and questioning the given. Thus, in the Saraswati Puja, many leftist atheists participated in the festivities, while the believers performed the rituals. The rituals were not necessarily unquestioned. Among the various students whom I had seen officiating as priests, there was a beef-relishing Brahmana, a low-caste Sanskrit scholar, two women, and a history student who discarded his sacred thread (yours truly). A devout Himachali Brahmin volunteered to cook the meat for the Eid celebrations on the campus. Similarly, Durga Puja was celebrated at JNU, as was the controversial 'Mahishasura Shahadat Divas'—on 'Vijaya Dashami'—organized by one political group.

The battle between Durga and Mahishasura is one of the three central myths of the *Devi Mahatmya*, a Puranic text which brought back the goddess of the old fertility cults into mainstream Hinduism. No religious text has emphasized the power of the feminine more strongly than the Devi Mahatmya, and the gripping story of the triumph of the Mother Goddess of pre-Vedic fertility cults over the fertility potentials of the shapeshifting hyper-masculine buffalo demon or the self-regenerating

Raktabija can fire up the imagination of many feminists. Moreover, being a Bengali, I naturally relate to the Durga Puja as a significant cultural spectacle transcending religious boundaries. Yet, Mahishasura's martyrdom is indeed celebrated in certain tribal and Dalit myths. While the political Right was outraged by the worship of the demonic Mahisha and the representation of Durga as a seductress employed to bring about the fall of that demon king, the typical mediality of this campus provided a room broad enough to accommodate both the Goddess and the demon.

In fact, the worship of Mahishasura is integral to traditional Durga Puja. Moreover, the *Devi Mahatmya* itself emphatically claims that the goddess is manifest in all the women of the universe (definitely including seductresses). Seduction, in the Purana, has indeed been crucial in the way the Goddess lures the demons Shumbha and Nishumbha towards their destruction. In Bengal, the great goddess of scriptural authority transforms into a Bengali folk reincarnation, representing the annual homecoming of a daughter victimized in a troubled marriage. The musical genre of agamani songs often tells the story of Uma (Durga)'s suffering in poverty and domestic violence because of her poor, irresponsible drunkard husband (Shiva). The goddess re-emerges there not as a source of authority, but as the co-sufferer of innumerable helpless women. In an integrative, assimilative, and accommodating 'Indian culture', all varieties of myths deserve a place. The JNU campus retains its capacity to listen to another voice where Durga and Mahishasura share the plight of being victims of patriarchal Brahmanism, one being used as a helpless tool to eliminate the other.

The 'culture of dissent' at JNU is much more nuanced and multicoloured than the myth created around it would make you believe. The admission process made it possible by assuring a substantial presence of the socially marginalized: a majority of women over men, deprivation points for those coming from underdeveloped districts, strict implementation of various kinds of reservations, and a subsidized education affordable for all. Therefore, the admission policy committed to social justice and critical thinking has been one of the first targets of the authorities trying to destroy the excellence of JNU.

JNU's culture of dissent is a liberating experience. As the ambit of the liberation extends to the field of gender relations and sexuality, the social status quo often responds with another mythology of anxiety. Gyandev

Ahuja's condom-count may not be just the individual's act of stupidity, but the expression of suspicious anxiety about a campus which does not judge women for their dress, does not consider virginity as sacrosanct, does not fight shy about discussing sexuality and desire openly, is not schizophrenic about free mixing between the sexes, and refuses to ostracize transgenders and homosexuals. JNU also reconstructs and deconstructs people's relationships, at times resulting in a medley of complex relationship issues. Yet, what is remarkable about this campus is the unrelenting belief in a culture of love. If there is any sphere where the campus is hegemonic it is in its uncompromising support for love over hatred.

Therefore, Valentine's Day has also been very special at JNU. And no Valentine's Day was as special as the one in 2016 when, amidst the flowers blooming as part of the amazing JNU spring, more than 5,000 people stood hand in hand forging a nonviolent human chain, in a resolve to defend everything JNU stands for. Against the tirade of attacks, threats and abuses, morphed videos and provocative speeches, controversial recruitments and attempts from the top to destroy it, JNU still stands for a unique space that mingles dissent and love, questioning and co-existence, holding hands to shatter many myths and to give rise to new ones.

72

ON MANY WAYS OF BEING A JNUITE

YOGENDRA YADAV

For the first time, I felt like calling myself a JNUite.

It was around midnight of 5 January 2020. I was standing outside the JNU main gate. The masked goons had finished ransacking the campus and had been honorably escorted out under the nose of Delhi police. The hecklers and bouncers, who were providing a cover through the evening both to their friends inside as well as to the Delhi police had also dispersed. Mission accomplished, streetlights were mysteriously switched back on. Just when you would expect the campus residents to retreat into the safety of their homes and hostels, the JNU community marched in a peaceful procession, teachers standing shoulder-to-shoulder with their students, all raising slogans. They forced open the university gate. The JNU community reclaimed the space that had been desecrated a few hours ago.

I felt so proud. I felt I belonged here. Like never before.

For thirty-seven years I had resisted calling myself a JNUite. Maybe it was just my nature. I am uneasy with clannishness of any kind—caste, community, club, school, village, nation, party, anything—and am happier with milder forms of identification. That is how it was with Khalsa College, Sri Ganganagar, from where I came to JNU, and with the Panjab University, Chandigarh, to where I moved. So, wearing my two years at JNU (1981–83) as a badge for the rest of my life made little sense. Besides, I find it hard to suspend real-life memories and participate in collective nostalgia and myth-making. I could not help noticing, for example, how the periodization of the 'Golden age of JNU' kept shifting every decade or so. Finally, I just cannot stand institutional snobbery by any name—Stephanian, Oxonian or JNUite. 'Kabul me gadhe bhi hote hain' (Kabul breeds not just horses, but donkeys as well) used to be my favourite line to debunk any institutional hype. That's why, even though some of my best friends and colleagues were from JNU, I kept off from all formal and informal gatherings of 'JNUites'.

There must have been a cultural unease as well. Having come from a small town, Sri Ganganagar in Rajasthan, I could not relate to JNU's dominant culture. Insiders saw it as radical, progressive, and cosmopolitan. To an outsider like me, it came across as alien and anglicized, if not deracinated. But the beauty of JNU was that you could create your own oasis. Like every newcomer, I was courted by various student groups and sheltered by seniors. (Anyone who believes that ragging contributes to senior-junior bonhomie should be exposed to this beautiful aspect of JNU's student culture). JNU is where I made the few friends that I can claim. This is where I discovered India, learnt something about Odiyas, Telugus, and of course Biharis. This is where I discovered that I was a Yadav! (How come a Yadav like you is so soft-spoken?) Campus life gave people like me space to form cultural enclaves. Reading *Raag Darbari* and Phanishwarnath Renu was a way of getting back at English-speaking radicalism. Not smoking and not drinking, not even chai, was my private rebellion against the dominant ways of rebelling at JNU. I would drink a glass of milk and carried some homemade laddoos or gur to make a point, perhaps to myself.

My intellectual differences with JNU's Marxism must have compounded my unease. I did not learn about Marx first at JNU. History of political philosophy was my favourite paper in BA. And my father's library had enough books on Marx and Marxism. Given this background, I found the dominant version of Marxism taught at CPS/SSS rather formulaic, if not polemical. J. D. Bernal's *Science in History* was not my idea of how to read Greek philosophic texts. Nor did Rajni Palme Dutt's *India Today* look like a good advertisement for the Marxist interpretation of politics in India in 1980s. Even though I lacked the courage and skills to argue with my teachers, much of my early encounter with Marxist orthodoxy felt like someone was using sandpaper on my skin. I did all right with my grades, rather well given my limitations with English, but it felt like intellectual regress. Sometimes, I did wonder if all that I had learnt so far about logical reasoning was pointless.

Fortunately, some teachers helped me recover from this intellectual shock. I remember Sudipta Kaviraj and Rajeev Bhargava in particular. Their exposition of sophisticated strands of Marxist thought reassured me that intellectual crudity was not a virtue. Even though I cannot recall much of what we studied about Lukács, Althusser or Gramsci, it did feel like a breath of fresh air. Listening to Sudipta Kaviraj in the classroom was unlike anything I had experienced before. (I was so much in awe of his brilliance that for years I would stammer in his presence!). Rajeev Bhargava was more accessible, yet no less rigorous. He restored my belief, inherited from my father, that an argument needs to stand on its own legs. They inoculated me against polemics, political correctness, play on words, jargon or angrezi that passes off as intellectualism in our country. My intellectual debt to both these teachers has grown further over the last four decades. Yet it did not endear me to JNU, for I saw them as exceptions. The more I learnt from them, the greater was my distance from JNU's Marxism. Besides, the dominant Left academic establishment invited the anti-establishment streak in me.

All this must have fed into my politics at that time. If Marxism dominated the classrooms, SFI-AISF dominated the politics of the campus. It is difficult now to understand the nature of Left dominance in the days prior to the collapse of Soviet Union. I don't quite recall how I got drawn into the anti-establishment student politics on the campus. It must have been a mix of intellectual, cultural and personal influences. Unlike many of my contemporaries, I couldn't possibly romanticize the Soviet Union or applaud the practice of Indian communists. While I applauded the idealism of the naxalites, their theory and political practice left me intellectually and morally cold. Nor could I stand anyone who ridiculed Gandhiji, which was very much in vogue in campus politics those days.

I drifted towards Samata Yuvjan Sabha (SYS), the student wing of Samata Sangathan. The trio of Sunil Gupta (or Sunil ji as he was known), Chengal Reddy and Jasvir Singh represented the SYS at JNU. In particular Suniljі, then a doctoral student at the CESP/SSS was an inspiration. His intellectual brilliance, personal simplicity and deep idealism left a profound impression on me and inspired me to take to politics. My association with SYS brought me to Kishen Pattnayak, my political guru and Sachchidanand Sinha, an enduring intellectual influence. I already had some exposure to and respect for the socialist tradition, thanks to my father. But it was at JNU that I began to relate to the political and intellectual legacy of Jayaprakash Narayan and Rammanohar Lohia. Post-JNU, this association grew deeper as I did research on India's socialist tradition and worked closely with Kishen Pattnayak in Samata Sangathan and Samajwadi Janparishad.

All this does not fit the profile of a stereotypical JNUite. So, while I kept a beard and often carried a jhola, I stayed away from this label. Until this year.

To be fair, it has been a gradual transition. Over the years, I feel less alienated from JNU's Left. In part, this is because the world has changed. Marxism is no longer the dominant academic establishment within and outside India. Soviet Union does not exist any more. The CPI(M) does not rule West Bengal and Tripura. It would be silly to retain older battle lines in this new world. JNU has also changed. It is intellectually and politically more diverse. Unlike our times, it is possible, indeed necessary, to talk about caste and gender now. You do not mock Gandhiji or dismiss culture. Political economy has taken a back seat, sometimes too far back for my comfort. While retaining its social diversity, the student community of JNU is now politically more diverse, including the NSUI and the ABVP. The public culture of JNU campus is also far less anglicized. Most of the political speeches are in Hindi.

Perhaps I have changed too. With hindsight, I have come to see the most valuable contribution of the Left to India's political life: notwithstanding its disdain for 'bourgeois democracy' and contempt for culture, the Left helped maintain the democratic character of our democracy, and pro-people orientation of our public culture. It may not be the vanguard of an impending revolution, but the Left is a necessary ally in the historic project of reclaiming the republic. Gradually, I have come to put my experience at JNU in perspective. For all my unease, difference and alienation, JNU has shaped both the passions of my life—ideas and politics. Just as there is no one way of being an Indian, there is no one way of being a JNUite.

Above all, JNU encouraged and equipped us to lead a life of the mind. But for JNU, a small-town boy like me would not have had exposure to some of the leading minds of the country, neither in the classrooms nor in the famous late-night debates. While the ideological orthodoxy of JNU tried to impose itself, it did so by engaging with its opponents. While we were nudged to favour a Marxist reading of Indian politics, we were also required to read Rajni Kothari. You may not be a Marxist—and I have never been one—but you cannot deny the intellectual contribution of the Marxists who injected some sense and relevance in our social sciences.

Within the discipline of Political Science, JNU's dominance and its influence on the syllabi of other universities saved Indian political science from being colonized by the American science of politics. Once I turned an academic and had an opportunity to visit many other institutions in the country and abroad, I came to appreciate JNU as a centre of academic excellence, as a national asset. It still is one of the few Indian academic institutions that command global respect.

Similarly, I have come to take a more positive view of the left-wing student politics of JNU. For all its faults, it has had the virtue of connecting the Indian youth, many from privileged backgrounds, to the realities of the country they live in. Unlike most universities in the country, campus politics at JNU was peaceful and democratic. It meant considerable space for those like us who did not toe the official Left line. JNU politics made it possible for young men and women with ideas and ideals to take to politics. JNU as an institution has provided a space for innumerable students from underprivileged background to build not just a successful career but also lead a political life. No wonder this small institution has contributed a disproportionately large number of leaders to India's public life, from revolutionary activists to parliamentary politicians. But for my exposure to student politics at JNU, I would not be in public life today.

Thus my assessment of JNU kept shifting over the years. Yet I continued to be a detached observer. Not a JNUite.

The last four years have changed it all. As the attempt to tarnish brand-JNU gathered momentum, my reluctance to identify with it has faded away. The present regime, desperately in need of internal enemies, has zeroed in on JNU as its prime ideological target. We have witnessed a multi-pronged attack on JNU by the state. When the regime realized that it lacked the intellectual resources to take JNU on in a debate, it resorted to defaming and demonizing the institution with the help of a pliant media. Kanhaiya Kumar and Umar Khalid became the symbols of this attack. This was accompanied by a political onslaught on campus politics and followed by a bureaucratic onslaught. The present Vice Chancellor was thrust upon the university to complete the demolition job, of changing the character of JNU forever. The goonda attack under police protection in January 2020 was the final act—the physical attack—in this long process of institutional destruction.

In the face of this relentless onslaught, today JNU symbolizes whatever this regime does not want or cannot handle. Now JNU does not stand for any ideological orthodoxy, it stands as a symbol of democratic dissent. The battle is not Left vs Right any more. Post the physical assault, it is simply right vs wrong. JNU is being targeted because it thinks, because it asks inconvenient questions, because it refuses to become either a kindergarten or a coaching factory, because it dares to be political. This leaves any citizen with no option but to stand up to this barbarity. If the regime wishes to turn JNU into any other university, the only response is to turn every university into a JNU. Now JNU is not just a resource for the battle to reclaim the republic, it is one of the key sites of this battle.

That is why I stand as a proud JNUite. So must you, even if you never studied there.

73

MY UNIVERSITY EXISTS WITHIN ME

AVIJIT PATHAK

I am aware that I am writing this essay at a time when not everything is fine with the state of higher education in India. We are seeing an organized attack on public universities. While those in power suspect the domain of critical and reflexive thinking, and even degrade it as 'anti-national', the market is allowed to invade the domains of knowledge. With the celebration of market-oriented techno-managerial skills, the meaning of education—particularly, if we look at the culture of private universities and institutes of technology and management—is becoming increasingly instrumental. 'Productivity' matters; thinking suffers.

And this seems to be the reason why I become immensely impassioned when I reflect on my own university days—the place that nurtured me as a young learner, and enabled me to evolve as a teacher. Its 'fall', I know, would shatter me. My attachment with the university is not instrumental, and so the rationale of the market or the fetish of 'nationalism' cannot measure it. In fact, I experience the soul of my university; it has transformed me; it is not merely a physical site; it exists within me. It is no wonder that I look at my university with a sense of deep gratitude—its culture of learning, its dialogic spirit, its politico-ethical sensibilities, its natural landscape, and its mode of communion.

Learning to Think and Reflect

1979 was a turning point in my life. As a student of this university, I began to learn the fundamentals of my discipline. But then, reading Durkheim and Weber, or writing a term paper on Marx was not the essential substance of my early experience at JNU. I learned something more. To begin with, I acquired the courage to interrogate the 'taken-for-granted' hierarchy of knowledge traditions—say, natural sciences vs. humanities or social sciences. When the cognitive power of 'heroic' science or its technological gains are highly valued by a society willing to modernize and industrialize, it is not easy to see beyond the hegemonic science, and find liberating possibilities in history, literature, sociology and political philosophy. However, JNU made it possible. I saw self-confident and critically engaged students and researchers in the domain of social sciences, international politics and literature. And I realized that its great professors—historians, sociologists, political theorists and economists—were the ones who contributed immensely to the making of this wonderful university. Well, there were good science schools—life sciences and computer sciences. However, the predominant character of the university, as I felt, was that of critically nuanced social sciences and humanities.

I experienced the worth of being a student of social science—without any stigma or a sense of loss. This positivity filled my mind with a high degree of creative energy. Reading books, moving around the library with great joy, writing pamphlets on culture and politics, listening to extraordinarily illuminating talks delivered by the likes of Bipan Chandra, Sudipta Kaviraj, Amit Bhaduri, Namwar Singh, and others: we celebrated the culture of social sciences. And it became clear to us that we were doing something deep, meaningful and relevant. In a society that compels us to suffer from chronic career anxiety, and strive for 'safe' options and 'right' courses in science and technology, it was not easy to remain eternally excited by Antonio Gramsci's *Prison Notebooks*, Herbert Marcuse's Freudo-Marxism, or Raymond Williams's essays on culture and revolution. Yet, JNU made it possible. It altered my way of looking at the meaning of education—something that a generation obsessed with 'placement and package' would not be able to comprehend. JNU was different. It nurtured the 'madness' of creativity.

Generally, we grow up with a notion of discipline—regulated, observed and controlled by an external agency. We tend to believe that we can work and perform only if there is some external authority to pressurize us. Freedom, we presume, is not something we should expect from the sphere of work. 'Discipline' vs. 'Freedom'—the JNU I am fond of broke this binary. As a student I sensed what it meant to be responsible without the fear of any external authority. And I realized the beauty of freedom—the freedom to relate, work and give my best. A relaxed environment in our hostels, all sorts of discussions and addas in the library canteen and the

Ganga Dhaba and, above all, the absence of mandatory attendance—we breathed freedom. And yet, we attended classes with absolute regularity, visited the library frequently, and wrote our assignments with a high degree of sincerity. Possibly, the finest gift that this university offered me was this assurance: your freedom is your responsibility; your responsibility is your freedom; and learning is a celebration. Sometimes, I feel this experience of responsible freedom would not be understood by those who have normalized the culture of surveillance, and no longer feel shocked at the all-pervading presence of CCTV cameras. It is really difficult to believe that we attended classes precisely because we loved to learn; it is not easy to believe that men and women can mix so freely, yet retain their autonomy, grace and sanity. Yes, JNU was radically different. It was a model—a domain of possibilities, a ray of hope in a bureaucratically-controlled/patriarchal/conservative society.

Possibly, this blend of freedom and responsibility was reflected in the culture of politics that our university nurtured. Yes, for me, it was a refreshing departure. No to lumpenism. No to violence. But a celebration of debate and dialogue, critical thinking and ideological reflection. Who could imagine this sort of political culture when colleges and universities were characterized by ugly politics and brute power? Yes, JNU made it possible. In fact, as a student I learned a great deal about political philosophy and international politics while reading argumentative pamphlets, listening to speeches delivered by the likes of D. P. Tripathi, Sitaram Yechury, Anand Kumar, and David Thomas. I learned about the diverse shades within the Left movement: 'official' Marxism and Trotskyism, and Maoism and Parliamentary Left. And I also witnessed the intellectual challenges that self-confident 'Free Thinkers' used to pose before the leftists. And then, there were socialists; they enabled me to take active interest in Gandhi, Lohia and JP; and some of these socialist leaders like Jasvir Singh and Sunil Gupta enchanted me; their honesty was remarkable. For me, the political culture I witnessed at JNU was an integral part of its pedagogy. As students of humanities and social sciences, we learned to engage with the discourse of power. We learned to think politically. No wonder, from posters to pamphlets, and from late-night hostel meetings to film shows, it was difficult to escape politics. It is, however, a different story that these days 'technically skilled', but politically illiterate graduates—the fancy products of the emergent education shops—would not understand the significance of the political context of learning.

Regionalism or parochialism has destroyed many of our universities. What, however, has elevated JNU is its cosmopolitanism. In fact, my own mental horizons began to expand after coming to JNU. Finding a roommate from Haryana, watching a movie with a friend from Kerala, sharing a book with a student from Australia, learning about Muktibodh's poetry from a bright student from Madhya Pradesh, and working with a supervisor who radiated the best of Sikhism: I have no hesitation in saying that JNU helped me realize the meaning of our shared humanity. I began to see beyond cultural stereotypes. I didn't forget my language or religion but I became aware of the vastness of the world and its diversities. Instead of just a bookish knowledge of 'unity in diversity', the very mode of living at JNU was an experience of horizons fusing together. When cosmopolitanism elevates us, we cultivate the most important faculties of learning culture—empathy, humility, openness and the art of listening. I am eternally grateful to my university for keeping my humanity alive. It has saved me from the madness we see in our times: violence in the name of regionalism, casteism, parochialism and militant nationalism.

Realizing the Meaning of the Vocation of Teaching

1990 was yet another eventful year. It was the year I joined the university as a faculty. The progression—from a student to a teacher—aroused in me a sense of pedagogic responsibility: I ought to serve my university; I ought to give my best; and I ought to evolve through my sustained engagement with the place. My prayers became part of my being. Once again I experienced freedom—the freedom to evolve my course, the freedom to experiment with ideas, and the freedom to work on new modes of evaluation and assignments. My colleagues gave me suggestions; we debated and learned from one another. And I realized that it was this ethically enriched freedom that enabled me to work hard with joy and creativity. Teaching was never a burden, a routine exercise, or an official duty. Working on every lecture, engaging with students, sharing books and research papers with them, and continually learning and unlearning, I found my vocation. I could transcend the binary of 'work' vs. 'play'. Teaching and research were deeply integrated. Never did I feel teaching as an obstacle to the cultivation of research.

With deep gratitude I recall my association with young students. Their civility, intellectual zeal and alertness have always enriched me. They have made me realize that teaching is a continual process of learning. A foggy winter morning...9 a.m. class...and the classroom is full (without mandatory attendance), imagine the beauty of this communion. Furthermore, they made me work on my pedagogy. Otherwise, how can I possibly engage with this splendid heterogeneity? I see a tribal girl from Jharkhand, a young boy from Kolkata's Presidency College, an LSR feminist and a Dalit Maharashtrian. How do I communicate? How do I teach so that none feels excluded? And how do I relate so that an inclusive environment is created? I believe that at JNU a teacher has to be extraordinarily reflexive and sensitive to engage with this heterogeneity. It is a great challenge to take. The one thing I do know: My association with them has made me humble; I have learned to value the therapeutic power of empathy and care.

Yes, the students are political. And at times, ideological indoctrination prevents them from growing and evolving. If you are an Ambedkarite, you do not want to hear anything nice about Gandhi. Or you are a Marxist; and you do not wish to hear anything about Swami Vivekananda. I will not deny that I have felt the negativity of ideological rigidity (or is it the burden of 'political correctness'?) in our classrooms. However, I do not give up. For instance, while teaching a course on Modern Indian Social Thought, I encouraged my students to read Periyar as well as Sri Aurobindo, and Tagore's reflections on the Upanishads as well as Dr B. R. Ambedkar's *Philosophy of Hinduism.* Although it generates intense debate and even emotional turmoil, I have allowed myself to pass through it. I do not negate my own politics but, as a teacher it is my responsibility to tell them about diverse and conflicting worldviews. My task is to sharpen their abilities to listen—and listen to the viewpoints of even their intellectual opponents. It was the same academic culture that further activated my interest in education and pedagogy, politics and ethics, and diversity and pluralism. I have not arrived. I am still walking.... And it is a wonderful walk.

No, JNU was not perfect. I have always believed that we need honest self-introspection; we should not hesitate to admit our shortcomings. First, possibly due to a sense of intellectual pride and the appeal of an alternative culture we were becoming insulated from the larger society. The communication between JNU and regional centres of learning was missing; there was also a gap between 'metropolitan' intellectuals like us and people whose cultural idioms were different. Did JNU become a privileged island? Second, I wonder whether there was some sort of subtle hegemony that didn't allow other intellectual traditions to evolve? Was it a world of the 'left-of-centre' Nehruvian intellectuals? Were we always democratic in understanding the other voices—even the voices of Gandhi and Tagore while looking at the world? And third, were we becoming too proud? Were we taking things for granted? I must admit that some of us—students as well as teachers—were not truly serving the university. Using the university as a mere platform for utterly instrumental career pursuits (collaboration, projects, foreign trips, networking) and negating the primary task of nurturing a new generation of young researchers; or students not attending the classes and misusing the doctrine of 'rights' and 'freedom', or dividing themselves on the basis of caste identities: I have been often anxious about these dangerous trends.

Walking Through a Difficult Terrain

This self-critique emanates from my love. How can I forget that the university has become part of my being? While we must work on ourselves to heal the wound, we cannot deny that these days there has been an organized attack on a public university like ours. As the mix of militant cultural nationalism and neoliberalism emerges as the dominant ideology, everything positive about JNU—its critical consciousness, its culture of debate and its broadly humanistic traditions—is under threat. The propaganda machinery manufactures the 'public opinion' against the university. And what is really sad is that it affects the functioning of the new administration. We are passing through a tragic metamorphosis: from trust to surveillance, from decentralization to absolute centralization, and from dialogue to loyalty. With the breakdown of communication between the authorities and the academic bodies, stubborn and non-democratic administration, and unhappy students and teachers, the university is becoming increasingly toxic. With birds and flowers, and trees and peacocks, the physical landscape continues to look immensely promising. However, the presence of security guards even at Academic Council or Board of Studies' meetings, and the persistent efforts of the administration to silence dissenting voices have polluted the mental landscape of the university. It is painful to watch this politics of organized conspiracy which creates fear and suspicion, and mars the beauty of free-floating conversations and informal relationships.

Possibly, this too will pass; and our university will be able to renew its positive spirit and creative life energy. With this hope I continue to come to the class, meet my students, work with them, and acquire the courage to write this essay.

74

IF YOU COME TO JNU

A. LOZAANBA KHUMBAH

If you are coming to JNU
make sure you come in July—
late July or early August;
the monsoon rains will have arrived
turning the campus green
and ready for young minds to take up residence.

If you have come to JNU
do not hurry, take your time;
look around and breathe it in—
the place you stand is holy ground!
Feast your eyes on the walls—
well, whatever remains upon them:
they will tell you stories
of the world we live in
and of what this university used to be.

In the evening
come to the dhaba, grab a cup of tea
and join at one of the tables;
or, maybe, just listen:
if you have an ear for voices
you may catch a debate—
persistent, unyielding, respectful;
or some shrill music of protests—
see if they are similar to the ones on TV
if you understand their cause
you may join their chorus to change the world.

Come share our food in the mess
    it is usually dal and sabzi, roti and rice
    nothing very special—but we thrive!
    for we do not live by bread alone:
    it is words and ideas, dreams and aspirations,
    the hunger to learn—
    that is what makes us human;
    and the space to freely express them—
    that is what defines JNU.

So when you come to JNU
    do not be afraid: we are not a threat;
    what you see on TV is only an illusion of the truth.
    Anyway, what remains is a past
    struggling to stand up to the present
    and stripped of the future;
    we are remnants, survivors,
    captives in our own beloved campus.
    Do not be afraid of JNU—
    we are a crumbling institution,
    overtaken, trampled upon and cast down.

Yet when this place is overrun
    the walls painted lifeless
    and the cries of protests silenced;
    even if you tear down these buildings
    and raise up new ones,
    know this:
    JNU is an idea—
    it knows no constraint
    of space or time,
    nor submits to the rule of regimes.

So shed no tears for JNU.
    For the idea that brooded in its spaces
    like a hen over her eggs,
    will give birth to brave women and men
    who will speak forbidden tongues
    and shape new times of freedom.

July 2018

75

REFLECTIONS ON THE STATUE OF JAWAHARLAL NEHRU AT JNU

ANIL BHATTI

I

The so-called Old Campus of JNU had a centre which facilitated communication. The multipurpose central building, which had a bank, a post office, a students' mess, and a faculty club, for some time also had rooms for the new faculty of the erstwhile School of Languages and, among other things, a central canteen which became a kind of adda comparable to old coffee houses.

When we shifted to the New Campus around 1973–74, this absence of a central meeting place disturbed me initially, but only because communication became difficult. The architecture of the place led to an isolationist self-sufficiency in faculty buildings whose solidity consolidated the borders between disciplines. This was odd in a university which spoke so much about interdisciplinarity. The adhocism of decision-making at JNU, I thought, was related to this. From the very beginning, the idea of having an art gallery at JNU was raised in many discussions. It was argued repeatedly that the university should promote art and make it accessible for the academic community. To initiate this, G. Parthasarathi, the first Vice Chancellor, bought a painting by Vivan Sundaram on the recommendation of the faculty. Another such idea was to create something like a sculptor's park, with a statue of Nehru flanked by other statues. But these remained stray ideas. The political graffiti and murals on the walls of the faculty buildings ultimately became the living open-air galleries of JNU. The statue came much later.

II

If you walk from the Dakshinapuram residences on JNU campus down to the main administration building (the Pink Palace in folklore), you will most probably take a shortcut, which like all shortcuts in planned landscapes is a subconscious revolt against the tyranny of the eternal right angle of the tarred road, and you will see the statue of Jawaharlal Nehru at an angle to the stairs leading to the main entrance to the Admin Block (as it is also called). The statue does not stand as if it were slightly at an angle. It does not dominate but invites you to halt before you move on. A reminder to pause in your purposeful march on your business and see how Nehru in his bronze garb, achkan flowing, walking stick tucked in under the armpit strides optimistically to a future you and he are supposed to realize. At the foot of the statue on the pedestal you will have occasion to read and ruminate over his words which are a kind of official motto of JNU:

> A University stands for humanism, for tolerance, for reason, for progress, for the adventure of ideas and for the search for truth. It stands for the onward march of the human race towards even higher objectives. If the universities discharge their duty adequately, then it is well with the nation and the people.

Nehru had penned these words for Allahabad University in 1947. And if you belonged to that generation you would have empathized with the Victorian pathos of Nehru's words, so similar to his other iconic speech that ushered India into freedom at midnight and the Transfer of Power in 1947. To a later generation, which had seen the students' revolution of the late sixties the words may have sounded old fashioned. But, such is the way the dialectics of history work, they now seem strangely apposite. The rest of Nehru's Allahabad address continues:

> But if the temple of learning itself becomes a home of narrow bigotry and petty objectives, how then will the nation prosper or a people grow in stature? A vast responsibility, therefore, rests on our universities and educational institutions and those who guide their destinies. They have to keep their lights burning and must not stray from the right path even when passion convulses the multitude and blinds many amongst those whose duty it is to set an example to others. We are not going to reach our goal through crookedness or flirting with evil in the hope that it may lead to good. The right end can never be fully achieved through wrong means.

XIII.1. There he is, in confident mid stride: the statue of Jawaharlal Nehru nestled amongst the kikar trees near the Administrative Block.
Photo courtesy: Samin Asgor Ali

It is a disturbing, theologically coloured anticipation of our contemporary situation. Thus, yesterday's staid, conventional, liberal rhetoric becomes today's avant-garde demand for freedom in the beleaguered university. It coalesces in my mind now with the other famous statement in a university, at the Humboldt University of Berlin where the statues of Alexander von Humboldt and Wilhelm von Humboldt in front of the main building prefigure Karl Marx's famous eleventh thesis on Feuerbach engraved in the great entrance hall, reminding us: 'The philosophers have only interpreted the world, in various ways; the point is to change it.'

These two public statements in two different universities with different pasts are nevertheless strangely similar and apposite now. We are passing through a phase where we have now again to defend and assert the right to interpret in an atmosphere of political repression before we can again stride confidently into a future where we could realize the promises of India's freedom struggle. One of these was the establishment of institutions which can stand against unreason, against assaults on the freedom to think and speak independently and against the imposition of an unworthy present over the hope of achieving a real, substantive democracy in the future.

III

On one of the occasions when the JNUTA (under the presidentship of Professor Ajay Patnaik) organized a function to protest against the loss of freedom at JNU, I had the opportunity to say a few words. The rostrum was situated in the area in front of the steps to the administration building, today's Freedom (azaadi) Square. Behind me was the statue of Nehru and diagonally to the front were the basement rooms of the administration building, now heavily barred. Earlier they had served as openly accessible car parks for the administration and at times also for visitors. But during the academic year 2004–05 they housed an atelier in which the sculptor Biman Das hewed out the nine-foot statue of Nehru. It was not the function of the statue to awe the viewer. It was, if anything, pleasantly understated.

From the atelier to the future site for the statue and back, it seemed to me, one could draw an imaginary diagram. Opening up an alternative architectural space of the campus. From the statue one could draw an imaginary line to what was once an open atelier and now is a barred space. This may well symbolize a closure and a comment on the direction the university has gone under the present dispensation.

Placed in an eccentric location, the statue is at a point which forms an imaginary triangle with the library and the Parthasarathi rocks.

IV

I became involved in the Nehru statue project around the time Professor G. K. Chadha became the Vice Chancellor, Professor Balveer Arora became Rector and I was the Dean of the School of Arts and Aesthetics (SAA). Dr Karan Singh, Chancellor of the university, was also consulted as he had wanted the statue installed for a long time. He stated in an interview:

> Soon after I had the privilege of being appointed Chancellor of the Jawaharlal Nehru University (JNU) by the President K. R. Narayanan in 2002. I visited its 1000 acres campus, surely one of the finest in India. While I was very impressed with the way it had been developed, I noticed that there was not a single statue in memory of the man after whom the university was named, Pandit Jawahar Lal Nehru. Therefore I initiated the project of installing a really good statue of Panditji. The Vice Chancellor and the university authorities readily accepted the suggestion and we proceeded to install a large and an impressive statue by the famous sculptor Bipon Dass, (*sic*) which has become the university's landmark.[1]

There was no separate budget for the statue, so funds had to be found from somewhere and reallocated under Arts and Aesthetics. I have an amusing memory of signing papers prepared by Dr Chandrasekhar, the then Coordinator of Academic Affairs, for the honorarium paid to the sculptor Biman Das.

Some of us, I remember Professor Chadha, Dr Karan Singh, Professor Balveer Arora would go down to this basement room and comment on the statue in its nascent state. On the likeness, the flow of the achkan, the stance. Occasional doubts were also expressed. Should the figure have this resolute marching stance or should it not rather express the thoughtful pose so cultivated by Nehru. A meditative Nehru versus a militant Nehru? All this was heard by the sculptor with great politeness. But with the motto all were in agreement.

The statue is of course a statement. But it is different from the statues in other universities because of this oblique, eccentric location slightly off-centre with the age-old Aravalli rocks behind it. And because the motto at

[1]'Karan Bats for "Unknown Soldier" Monument', *Kashmir Times*, 26 July 2017.

the base of the statue itself gives the construction an emblematic structure demanding interpretation. As in a classical emblem, the motto as text interprets the action of the visual figure and gives it a unique meaning.

The statue was unveiled by the then Prime Minister, Dr Manmohan Singh, in the presence of Shri Arjun Singh, Union Minister of HRD and Dr Karan Singh, Chancellor of JNU and Professor Chadha's successor, Professor B. B. Bhattacharya and Professor Balveer Arora's successor as Rector, Professor Rajendra Prasad on 14 November 2005.

V

The imaginary triangle I suggested creates its own mesh as an imaginative, oppositional alternative field to the existing field of power. It asks the Brechtian question: Whose university is the university? Whose world is the world?

Read thus, the statue reaffirms the theoretical position that the university, like India, should be looked upon as a palimpsest. It fights against the logic of erasure which is contained in the drive for purity of an original, authentic, homogeneous order of society postulated by ideologues. As against this, the university develops the critical art of inheritance which shows how to combine past and present, establish links in and out of the plenitude of the world to derive that critical assemblage which will enable us to shape a better world.

At the time it was being sculpted the aesthetics of the statue often came up for discussion. Was it not too old-fashioned? Was it not fashioned in an outdated realistic mode? Would not an abstract statue be more in keeping with JNU's avant-garde function? This question was never resolved.

There it stands now. In front of ancient rocks of the Aravalli range, together now part of our palimpsestic present. With a confident striding Nehru symbolizing JNU's place in a future, substantive democracy, an ever tolerant, inherently pluralistic India.

ACKNOWLEDGEMENTS

This book took shape during a conversation at the beginning of 2019 on ways of remembering an institution that had completed a very creditable fifty years. It was quite by chance that several members of the Centre for Historical Studies came together, not just to celebrate the Golden Jubilee in print, but to engage with ways of remembering. Could we, by 14 November 2019, the birth anniversary of the man in whose name the University came up, put together several images of the past, fragments of life, insights into institutional functioning, the histories of specific schools and programmes—all expressed in a personal voice? In some ways, our training was of less use, since we had to work with and through multiple voices and perspectives, reconcile conflicting memories, and yet hold together the coherent narrative that JNU has become. We had to find a way of not slipping into nostalgia, yet retain the warmth, pain, and humour of the various tellings; not exceptionalize JNU and yet find that which would be of worth to institution builders and administrators within the beleaguered space of public universities in India. As members of the Centre for Historical Studies (CHS), we, in particular, felt the obligations and burdens of this act of remembering.

Circumstances simply did not permit us to meet the November 2019 deadline, since ground realities were changing, sometimes dramatically, on an almost daily basis. But the volume has only improved as a consequence and it is a collective effort in the truest sense of the term, involving multiple meetings, phone calls, emails, and deadlines. We are indebted to all those who have made the university what it is, though there are some people in particular whom we would like to thank.

This book would simply not have been possible without the support, generosity, intellectual inputs, cautions, editing, translation, and typing assistance of Kumkum Roy. Her room became our home for well over a year, and she kept us cheerful and well fed, with an excellent supply of snacks and tea. Her decision to remain unacknowledged as a co-editor was only reluctantly accepted by the rest of us. Still, she shared our interest in and anxiety about preserving an institutional memory, and performed even the littlest of tasks with great panache and humour. We cannot thank her enough for undertaking this journey with us.

Aienla Ozukum and Aleph Book Company proved to be the ideal editor and publishers for a book like this. Aienla has put up with editors who have given the word 'deadline' a completely new meaning, and has accommodated all our requests, provided constant encouragement, and has shown saintly patience in her interactions with all of us. We thank her for enabling this very special collaboration.

For photographs our list of debts is long. N. Ram made it possible to get the image of G. Parthasarathi from *The Hindu* Photo Archive with great ease. Gyan Prakash helped in accessing some of the images from the 1970s. S. A. Huda and Chandrashekhar Tibrewal enthusiastically offered access to their collection of old photographs of JNU. Samim Asgor Ali has done more than expected from a photographer busy chronicling the story of our times at JNU and outside. He has generously offered access to his large image archive for our use, and has edited and improved the quality of all photographs reproduced in the volume. Many others provided photographs that made such a profusely illustrated book possible: Akash Bhattacharya, Antony Thomas, Cherian Samuel, Devayani Prasad, Gul Mooni, Joy L. K. Pachuau, Jyotindra Jain, Mario Da Penha, Mudit Trivedi, Naman Ahuja, Nirmala George, P. Bilimale, Pangertoshi Walling, Ram Ramaswamy, Seema Chisti, Sthira Bhattacharya, Surya Prakash, Vidur Krishnan.

Ann Ninan took on the thankless task of proofreading and some editing, as her own contribution to JNU and its institutional memory. We thank her for her invaluable inputs. Our thanks also go out to Shivangi Jaiswal for assembling old school and centre prospectuses, and in obtaining other essential materials and to Sonali Verma and Megha Sharma for retyping and other chores. Muthuraman personally took contracts to those who were not on email. Neeti Nair generously offered her scans of Saiyidain papers, and Ensminger's Oral transcript from the Rockefeller Archives, Tanmoy Sharma photographed the necessary files from the Ensminger papers at Yale University Archives. The PRO of JNU, Poonam S. Kudaisya, helped us in our venture, and gave us access to the early architectural designs. Kanjiv Lochan graciously facilitated the reprinting of three articles from the JNU Silver Jubilee volume of 1996.

To all those who have contributed to this volume, and who adhered to the impossible schedules we laid down, a very sincere thanks. There were many others whom we approached, but were unable to participate due to the very short notice. Our volume would have been fuller, richer and more complete with their contributions. We can do no more than signal in this brief preface the absences and silences that are a result. There were people, events, processes, centres, schools, and political associations (such as the Birsa Ambedkar Phule Students' Association [BAPSA]) that we would have liked to represent better in this volume on fifty years of JNU. Indeed, some newer questions relating to identities more generally, and their contributions and challenges to campus life and culture, have been only acknowledged in passing. The larger-than-life presence of the social sciences and language/literature at JNU has also meant that life sciences, environmental sciences, computer schools have received less space, and that imbalance is regretted. We would have liked to have had a much greater representation of our staff in this volume, but despite our best efforts, this was not to be. We have included only a tiny sample of writings in Hindi, and are aware of severe shortcomings on the language question: neither all languages spoken nor taught on the campus find representation here. Another significant absence pertains to the extra-academic activities and achievements of JNU. Given the very short time frame, such shortcomings were inevitable.

NOTES ON THE CONTRIBUTORS

Abhijit V. Banerjee is the Ford Foundation International Professor of Economics at the Massachusetts Institute of Technology. In 2003 he founded the Abdul Latif Jameel Poverty Action Lab (J-PAL), along with Esther Duflo and Sendhil Mullainathan. Banerjee has been a Guggenheim Fellow, an Alfred P. Sloan Fellow and has won the Infosys Prize. In 2019, he was awarded the Nobel Prize in Economics with Esther Duflo and Michael Kremer. He is the author of a large number of articles and four books, including *Poor Economics* (www.pooreconomics.com), and has directed two documentary films. He completed his MA in Economics from JNU, 1981–83.

Akash Bhattacharya is currently a Senior Lecturer at the School of Education, Azim Premji University, having finished his MA, MPhil, and PhD from the Centre for Historical Studies, Jawaharlal Nehru University (2009–17). He has conducted research on a range of themes, including histories of education, vernacular literary histories, and the politics of history writing.

Albeena Shakil is Associate Professor of English at OP Jindal Global University. She is the author of *Understanding the Novel: A Theoretical Overview,* Primus Books, 2015, and has been a Fellow of the Indian Institute of Advanced Study, Shimla, where she edited *Summerhill: IIAS Review*. She was president of the JNUSU in 2001–02 and was a member of the first Gender Sensitization Committee Against Sexual Harassment (GSCASH) at JNU in 1999. She was a JNU student from 1997 (MA) to 2005 (submission of PhD).

Alok Bhattacharya is a Professor of biology at Ashoka University. He obtained his BSc and MSc degrees in Chemistry from Delhi University and IIT Kanpur respectively, and his PhD from JNU. He was a Professor in the Schools of Life Sciences & Computation and Integrative Sciences at JNU until February 2019. He has published over 200 research papers, review articles, and book chapters. He has been awarded the Robert McNamara Fellowship (World Bank), the Rockefeller Biotechnology Career Development Award, the Shanti Swarup Bhatnagar Prize, and the J. C. Bose Fellowship.

Amit Sengupta was the 'Independent' President of JNUSU, 1989–90. He led a rainbow coalition of independent students, along with the Left, socialists, and liberals. He resigned in support of the Mandal Commission and affirmative action for the marginalized classes. Since then, he has worked as a journalist and senior editor with several mainstream newspapers and magazines. He was also Associate Professor, English Journalism, IIMC, Delhi and Visiting Professor, MCRC, Jamia Millia Islamia, Delhi. He is currently Executive Editor, *Hardnews* magazine: <www.hnfp.in>

Anil Bhatti is Professor Emeritus, Centre of German Studies, JNU. He joined JNU in 1971 and taught German Literature, Culture, Philosophy in comparative cultural contexts between Europe and India. He was Dean of the School of Languages and the School of Arts and Aesthetics at JNU. He has written variously on Goethe, August Wilhelm Schlegel, Peter Weiss, Pluriculturality of the Hapsburg empire, Marxist Aesthetics, and of late on the concept of similarity in Culture Theory. He was awarded the Research Prize of the Alexander von Humboldt Foundation in 2011.

Ankita Pandey teaches Political Science at Indraprastha College for Women, University of Delhi. She did her MA (2003–05) and MPhil (2005–07) at JNU and completed her PhD at the University of Oxford, which was entitled 'Movement Allies: The Politics of Civil Rights Activism (1960–80)'.

Ari Sitas is a South African sociologist and writer. He was the inaugural Bhagat Singh Chair at the Centre for Historical Studies, JNU, in 2016, and the titular Gutenberg Chair at the University of Strasbourg in France in 2019. He received the National Order of Mapungubwe from the South African Presidency. He directs a multi-institutional research programme involving six universities that explores the movement of people, material and symbolic goods in Afro-Asia between 700–1500 CE. One of his initiatives, an ensemble of South African and Indian composers and poets, has won the Humanities Award of the National Institute for Humanities and Social Sciences.

Ashish Das joined JNU as project assistant in the Centre for Political Studies and then got on offer to open a photostat shop in 2001. He runs his shops on the ground floor of the School of Social Sciences Building I & III (SSS-I and III). Mostly students of Centre for Historical Studies, Centre for the Study of Regional Development, and Centre for Political Studies avail of his services.

Atiya Habib Kidwai was a founding faculty of the Centre for the Study of Regional Development, JNU in 1971. She is a professionally trained Regional Planner from the Indian Institute of Technology, Kharagpur. She received her doctoral degree from JNU. She has been a recipient of the Rhodes Visiting Fellowship to Oxford University (1973) and the Senior Fulbright Fellowship to the University of Chicago (1981–82). She has served as a Visiting Professor at the School of Planning and Architecture, Delhi for five years.

Avijit Pathak is Professor of Sociology at JNU. He has written extensively on modernity, cultural politics, social thought, and education. He was a student of JNU from 1979–87. His many books include *Social Implications of Schooling: Knowledge Pedagogy and Consciousness* (2013); *The Chaotic Order: An Unknown Teacher's Pedagogic Travelogue* (2015); *Ten Lectures on Education* (2018), which have been published by Aakar Books.

Ayesha Kidwai is Professor of Linguistics at JNU. She joined JNU as an MA student in Linguistics in 1988, completed her PhD in 1995, and has been on the faculty of the Centre for Linguistics since 1996. She has published in several areas of linguistics—both theoretical and descriptive—and language policy. She is also a translator, and was President of the JNU Teachers' Association in 2017–18. She was awarded the Infosys Prize in 2013 for her work in theoretical linguistics.

A. Lozaanba Khumbah is pursuing a PhD from the Centre for the Study of Regional Development, School of Social Sciences. His research looks at the ways access to market is transforming the traditional practice of shifting agriculture in the hills of Manipur. He finds poetry an effective medium to convey mystery, beauty, and hope in everyday life.

Birendra N. Mallick received the Calcutta University Gold Medal (MSc Physiology, 1979). He completed his PhD from AIIMS and joined the School of Life Sciences (SLS) in 1986. He has published over 130 research papers and book chapters, has written/edited four books and has delivered more than 300 invited lectures in India and abroad. He has received the Shakuntala Amir Chand Award (ICMR, 1992), National Bioscience Award (DBT, 1999), Shanti Swarup Bhatnagar Award (Medical Sciences) (CSIR, 2001) and J. C. Bose National Fellowship (DST, 2010).

Chitra Harshvardhan was a student at the Centre of German Studies, JNU, between 1977–81, and began teaching at the CGS from late 1981. She teaches translation theory and consecutive and simultaneous interpretation. She has also translated and co-translated books and articles from German into English. Her publications include a book on *Diplomacy for Conservation or Commercial Gain? A Case Study of German Environmental Aid to India, 1990-2002* (VDM Verlag, 2009), and several articles.

D. Banerji was chosen to set up the Centre of Social Medicine and Community Health in the School of Social Sciences at JNU in April 1971 to develop an academic programme that uses an interdisciplinary approach, which amounted to developing a new grammar of public health. This was articulated in his work *Health and Family Planning in India: An Epidemiological, Socio-cultural and Political Perspective.* A medical doctor by training, Professor Banerji's seminal work in the formulation of the Tuberculosis Programme, and in analysing the political economy of the health services is well recognized nationally and internationally. He continues to be associated with the Centre as Professor Emeritus after retiring in 1990.

D. Raghunandan (JNU 1975–82, Centre for Study of Social Systems) leads the Centre for Technology & Development, an NGO active in participatory development and application of technologies for pro-poor rural industries. He also volunteers with the Delhi Science Forum and writes on policy studies, notably in climate change and environment.

Deborah Sutton was a Commonwealth Student at the Centre for Historical Studies from 1996 to 2001. She is now Senior Lecturer in Modern South Asian History at Lancaster University in the UK. Her publications include *Other Landscapes: Colonialism and the Predicament of Authority in Nineteenth-Century South India* (Nordic Institute of Asian Studies Monographs, 2009).

Dhruv Raina is Professor at JNU. He studied physics at the Indian Institute of Technology, Mumbai and received his PhD in the philosophy of science from Göteborg University. He has co-edited *Situating the History of Science* (1999) and *Social History of Sciences in Colonial India* (2007), *Science Between Europe and Asia* (2010). He is the author of *Images and Contexts* (2003) and co-authored *Domesticating Modern Science* (2004) and *Needham's Indian Network* (2015).

G. Arunima teaches in the Centre for Women's Studies, JNU, and has researched and published on both historical and modern contexts in India, focusing particularly on cultural, visual and material texts, and rethinking the politics of the contemporary. She has written *There Comes Papa: Colonialism and the Transformation of Matriliny in Kerala, Malabar, ca 1850-1940* (Orient Longman, 2003), and has recently translated Rosy Thomas's biography of her husband, playwright C. J. Thomas, from Malayalam to English (*He, My Beloved CJ*, Women Unlimited, 2018).

Girija Kumar was the first librarian of JNU, and the first President of the JNU Officers' Association. He also served as a President of the Indian Association of Academic Librarians. He is the author of *Politics, International Relations and Law: Scope, Methodology and Classification* (1965), and *Ranganathan, Dewey and C.V. Raman: A Study in the Arrogance of Intellectual Power* (1991).

Gopal Guru was Professor, Centre for Political Studies, JNU, and is currently Editor, *Economic and Political Weekly*. He has written essays on social justice and the political realism of B. R. Ambedkar, on touch and political phenomenology. His books include *Humiliation: Claims and Context*, (ed.), (OUP, 2009), *The Cracked Mirror: An Indian Debate on Theory and Experience* (with Sundar Sarukkai) (OUP, 2012), *Experience, Caste and the Everyday Social* (with Sundar Sarukkai) (OUP, 2019). He received the Malcolm Adisheshiah Award in 2014.

Gyan Prakash is the Dayton-Stockton Professor of History at Princeton University and was a member of the Subaltern Studies collective. Prakash received his master's degree in history from JNU in 1975, and his doctorate in history from the University of Pennsylvania in 1984. His field of research concerns urban modernity, genealogies of modernity, and problems of postcolonial thought and politics. His books include *Bonded Histories:*

Genealogies of Labor Servitude in Colonial India (1990); *Another Reason: Science and the Imagination of Modern India* (1999), *Mumbai Fables* (2010), and *Emergency Chronicles* (2018).

Happymon Jacob is now Associate Professor of Diplomacy and Disarmament Studies at the School of International Studies. He completed his MPhil from JNU in 2003, and his PhD in 2009. He is a columnist with *The Hindu*, and hosts a weekly show on national security at *The Wire.in*. His most recent work is *Line on Fire: Ceasefire Violations and India-Pakistan Escalation Dynamics* (OUP, 2019).

Harbans Mukhia taught medieval history for forty-four years at Delhi University and JNU. Of these, the thirty-three years at JNU were crucial in his evolution as a student of history and a teacher. Among his writings, *Historians and Historiography During the Reign of Akbar* (Vikas, 1976) and *The Mughals of India* (Wiley, 2004) deserve mention, besides several edited volumes on a range of themes. His essay, 'Was There Feudalism in Indian History?' queried the durable orthodoxy of 'Indian feudalism' and led to a prolonged international debate resulting in two books: *Feudalism and Non-European Societies* (Frank Cass, 1985) and *The Feudalism Debate* (Manohar, 1999).

Imrana Qadeer retired from JNU in 2006 as Professor at the Centre of Social Medicine and Community Health, School of Social Sciences. She was at the Centre for Women's Development Studies as J. P. Naik Fellow for two years and is now a Distinguished Professor at the Council for Social Development, New Delhi.

Jairus Banaji studied Classics, Ancient History and Modern Philosophy at Oxford in the late 1960s. He was at the Centre for Historical Studies, JNU in the early seventies (1972–75). Ten years later, he returned to Oxford to do a DPhil in Ancient History. This was later published as *Agrarian Change in Late Antiquity: Gold, Labour and Aristocratic Dominance* (2001). More recently, he has published *Theory as History* (2011) and *Exploring the Economy of Late Antiquity* (2016). His latest book, *A Brief History of Commercial Capitalism*, has been published in September 2020 by Haymarket.

Janaki Nair taught history at the Centre for Historical Studies, JNU. She completed her MA at JNU in 1983, and her PhD from Syracuse in 1991. Her publications include *Women and Law in Colonial India* (Kali for Women, 1996), *Miners and Millhands: Work, Culture and Politics in Princely Mysore* (SAGE, 1998), *The Promise of the Metropolis: Bangalore's Twentieth Century* (OUP, 2005) for which she won the New India Foundation Prize. She has also made a film, *After the Gold* (1997).

Jayati Ghosh is Professor of Economics at Jawaharlal Nehru University, New Delhi. Her research interests include globalization, international trade and finance, employment patterns, macroeconomic policy, gender issues, poverty, and inequality. She has authored and edited a dozen books and around 200 scholarly articles, and has received several national and international prizes. She has advised governments in India and other countries, is regularly consulted by international organizations and is member of several international commissions. She writes regularly for popular media like newspapers, journals, and blogs.

Jyotindra Jain, founder-Professor and Dean of the School of Arts & Aesthetics, JNU, has been a Visiting Professor at Harvard and Humboldt University, Berlin. A scholar of Indian art and visual culture, Jain has published extensively in these areas of his specialization. His books include *Kalighat Painting: Images from a Changing World* (Mapin, 1999); *Indian Terracotta* (India Book House, 2004); *Jangarh Singh Shyam: A Conjuror's Archive* (Mapin, 2019).

Kamal Mitra Chenoy joined JNU in 1990 as an Assistant Professor and retired as Professor, Comparative and Indian Politics, School of International Studies, JNU. He was a student of the Centre for Political Studies JNU, and his teachers included Rasheeduddin Khan, C. P. Bhambhri, Sudipta Kaviraj, Zoya Hasan, Balveer Arora, Ashwini Ray, among others. He was the first Vice President of JNUSU. He was at the JNU Post Graduate Centre in Imphal from 1976–77. His publications include *The Rise of Big Business in India* (Aakar Books, 2015).

Kanad Sinha teaches at the Department of Ancient Indian and World History, Sanskrit College and University, Kolkata. He completed his PhD from the Centre for Historical Studies, JNU, on 'From Dāśarājña to Kurukṣetra: Making of a Historical Tradition' in 2018. He has co-edited the book *State, Power and Legitimacy: The Gupta Kingdom* (Primus, 2019), with Kunal Chakrabarti. He has published in *Studies in History, International*

Journal of Hindu Studies, and *Studies in Humanities and Social Sciences.*

Kanhaiya Kumar, member of National Council of Communist Party of India, received his doctorate in African Studies from JNU in 2019. He was elected as President of Jawaharlal Nehru Student Union in 2015. His autobiography, *Bihar to Tihar: My Political Journey* was published in 2016.

Kanjiv Lochan was a student at JNU from 1988 to 1999, when he completed his PhD from CHS. He is the author of *Medicines of Early India* (Chaukhambha Sanskrit Sansthan, 2003), and has edited the *Encyclopedia of Ayurveda.* He edited and translated a number of Sanskrit Ayurvedic texts, including the first English translation of the *Bhaishajya Ratnavali.* Currently, he teaches history at Ranchi University, Jharkhand.

Kavita Krishnan did her MA at Centre for Linguistics and English, School of Languages at JNU from 1993–95, and submitted her MPhil in 1997. She was Joint Secretary of JNUSU in 1995–96. She has served as the All India President of AISA, and is currently a Politbureau member of CPI (ML) and Secretary, All India Progressive Women's Association.

Kedarnath Singh was born in a village in Ballia District, UP. He studied in Banaras Hindu University, completing his MA in Hindi in 1956 and PhD in 1964. After teaching for some years in different colleges, he joined the Centre for Indian Languages at JNU and taught there till his retirement. He has written many books of prose and poems, and has been honoured with several prestigious awards including the Sahitya Akademi Award (1989) and the Jnanpith Award (2013).

Kuldeep Kumar is a Hindi poet and a bilingual journalist who writes on politics and culture in Hindi and English. He studied Ancient Indian history and Hindi literature at Jawaharlal Nehru University from 1973–80. Presently, he writes a fortnightly column in *The Hindu* and *Outlook* (Hindi).

Kunal Chakrabarti joined the Centre for Historical Studies, JNU, as an MA student in 1974, and retired as Professor of Ancient History in 2019. His areas of interest are social history of religion, regional histories and early textual traditions. His books include *Religious Process* (OUP, 2001), *Historical Dictionary of the Bengalis*, co-authored with Shubhra Chakrabarti (Scarecrow Press, 2013) *State, Power and Legitimacy: The*

Gupta Kingdom, co-edited with Kanad Sinha (Primus, 2019).

Kusum Lata Sharma, who writes under the pen name Tamanna, worked at JNU from 1975 to 2013. Appointed as a clerk-cum-typist, she rose to be Office in Charge. During her long career spanning thirty-eight years, she served in various departments including the Library and the Archives of Contemporary History. Apart from her administrative experience, she is recognized as a writer.

L. N. Malik obtained a Master of Library and Information Science degree after completing post-graduation in Sanskrit from Delhi University. With diplomas in German, French, and Spanish, he was employed by JNU to organize the European languages reading materials in the library where he worked from 1971 to 2001. He continued to offer his expertise to libraries of several newly established centres of the university after retirement. He also helped digitize the library of the JNU Academic Staff College.

Lalthuamliana completed an MA History (Modern India) from CHS in 1979. He then joined the State Bank of India in 1980 and retired as Assistant General Manager in 2016. In this time, he worked in various capacities as Branch Manager of rural, semi-urban and urban branches in Mizoram, Regional Manager of Mizoram Region and as Chief Manager of Hazaribagh, main branch in Jharkhand. He was a member of the IT team which implemented Core Banking Solution (networking of branches) in State Bank of India while working at Belapur. He lives in Aizawl.

Lateef comes from a small village in Sultanpur, UP. Born in a large but poor family of eleven members, he started working at the age of nine in hotels, canteens, and food industries in various places. He came to JNU in 1992 and worked for nearly twenty years in Mr Rao's canteen, School of SSS-I. Now, he runs his own canteen on the ground floor of the SSS-III.

Madhu Sahni studied at the Centre of German Studies, JNU, between 1975–80 and 1982–84 and has been teaching there since 1984. Her research interests include feminist literary studies, literary translation and critical language pedagogy. In 2000 she published *Zum Geschichtsverständnis Heinrich Manns in seiner essayistischen Arbeit 1905–1955*. She edited the Goethe Society of India Yearbook between 2012–15 and has, along with Namita Khare, edited an anthology of translated texts from German into Hindi (*Ek Ajnabi se Mulakat. German Bhashi Stree-lekhan* 1945–2014,

Sampark, Kolkata, 2017).

Mario da Penha is a historian and an activist. Previously educated at St. Xavier's College, Mumbai, and at the Centre for Historical Studies, JNU, he is now a doctoral candidate at Rutgers University, New Jersey. His research interests are in the history of the third gender in the Maratha- and colonial-era Deccan. Apart from his academic pursuits, he is involved in queer organizing, both in India and the United States. He was also part of Voices Against 377, which helped fight India's anti-sodomy law in the courts.

Mohan Rao, a medical doctor, specialized in public health, taught at the Centre of Social Medicine and Community Health, School of Social Sciences for thirty-one years till his retirement in 2018. His publications include *From Population Control to Reproductive Health: Malthusian Arithmetic* (Sage Publications, 2004) and *Public Health and Private Wealth: Stem Cells, Surrogates and Other Strategic Bodies*, co-edited with Sarah Hodges (OUP, 2016).

Mudit Trivedi is a graduate student at the Department of Anthropology, University of Chicago. He completed his MA and MPhil at CHS, JNU, in 2004–08, where he learned from the complex landscapes of the campus, past and present. Trained as an archaeologist, he has worked on the Delhi Palaeolithic, the emergence of complexity and urbanism in the Ganga plains and the megalithic and Iron Age of Karnataka. Since 2014, he has led an archaeological survey and excavation project, in collaboration with the Department of Archaeology and Museums—Government of Rajasthan, on the archaeology of urbanism and conversion to Islam in Mewat.

Mukul Mangalik teaches History at Ramjas College, University of Delhi. He retains an abiding interest in the histories of railway labour and the working lives of shepherds in the Garhwal Himalaya, hoping to return as well, to footloose travel and freelance work, speaking, writing, and filming along the way.

Nagesh Hegde is a journalist who worked for twenty-six years for the *Deccan Herald* group, Bengaluru. His writings in Kannada on science and environment have been incorporated as textbook lessons for schools and colleges. He has received many important awards in journalism and literature in Karnataka. He has the unique record of running a science column (in *Prajavani*, a Kannada daily) which is in its thirty-sixth year. He is currently a Visiting Professor in IIJNM. He was a student of JNU from 1972–75 and then again from 1977–80, when he completed his MPhil.

Naman P. Ahuja, Dean of the School of Arts and Aesthetics, JNU, is a curator of Indian art and editor of *Marg* publications, Mumbai. He specializes in Early Historic archaeology, Indian iconography and the history of the interpretative frames of Indian art. His books include *India & the World: A History in Nine Stories* (Penguin Random House, 2017); *Art and Archaeology of Ancient India: Earliest Times to the Sixth Century* (Ashmoleon, 2018).

Neeladri Bhattacharya joined the Centre for Historical Studies, JNU, as an MA student in 1973, and retired as Professor of Modern History in 2017. His recent publications include *The Great Agrarian Conquest: The Colonial Reshaping of a Rural World* (Permanent Black, 2018), and *Landscape, Culture and Belonging: Writing the History of Northeast India*, co-edited with Joy Pachuau (Cambridge University Press, 2019).

Niraja Gopal Jayal is Professor at the Centre for the Study of Law and Governance, JNU. Her *Citizenship and Its Discontents* (Harvard University Press, 2013) won the Ananda Kentish Coomaraswamy Prize in 2015. She is the author of *Representing India: Ethnic Diversity and the Governance of Public Institutions* (Palgrave Macmillan, 2006), and *Democracy and the State: Welfare, Secularism and Development in Contemporary India* (OUP, 1999); and co-editor of *The Oxford Companion to Politics in India* (OUP, 2010).

Prabhat Patnaik, who held the Sukhamoy Chakravarty Chair at the Centre for Economic Studies and Planning, JNU, at his retirement, is currently Professor Emeritus at that Centre. Before joining JNU in 1974, he taught at the University of Cambridge, UK, and was a Fellow of Clare College. His areas of interest are Macroeconomics and Development Economics. His books include *Whatever happened to Imperialism and Other Essays* (Tulika, 2003), *The Retreat to Unfreedom* (Tulika, 2003), *Accumulation and Stability Under Capitalism* (Clarendon Press, 1998), *The Value of Money* (Columbia University Press, 2008), and *A Theory of Imperialism* (co-authored with Utsa Patnaik, Columbia University Press, 2016).

Prabir Purkayastha is an engineer and science activist. He has worked in the energy and information technology sectors for more than four decades. He is the Founder Editor of the news portal, *Newsclick.in*, the President of Free Software Movement of India and a founding member of Delhi Science Forum. He is the co-author of *Uncle Sam's Nuclear Cabin* (Leftword Books, 2007), and *Enron Blowout: Corporate Capitalism and Theft of the Global Commons* (Leftword Books, 2002), and has written a number of articles and papers. He was a PhD student at JNU's School of Computer and System Sciences.

Purushottam Agrawal has been Professor, Centre of Indian Languages, JNU, Visiting Professor at the Faculty of Oriental Studies, Cambridge University (UK) and at El Colegio de Mexico, and has served as member, Union Public Service Commission of India from 2007–13. His publications include *Akath Kahani Prem Ki: Kabir ki Kavita aur Un ka Samay* (Rajkamal Prakashan, 2009), *Hindi Serai: Astrakhan via Yerevan* (2013), and *Padmavat: An Epic Love Story* (Rupa Publications, 2018).

Pushpesh Pant, author, columnist, broadcaster, anchor, independent producer of documentaries, and sometime teacher, was born in 1946 in a small Himalayan town. Schooled at home and later in Nainital and Delhi, he studied history, international relations and law at Agra University and later at the University of Delhi. He has taught and researched for over four decades at Jawaharlal Nehru University, and published over fifty books, of which twenty deal with food. *India: The Cook Book* made it to the *New York Times* bestsellers' list in 2010 and has been translated into Dutch and German. His most recent book is *Indian Vegetarian* (Phaidon, 2018).

Quoc Anh Nguyen did his MA at the Centre for Historical Studies, JNU (2002–04). After graduating, he joined Vietnam National University to teach South Asian History. Since 2010, he has been working as the CEO of Headstart Research Centre, conducting independent researches on Neuroscience and Language acquisition. Besides education researches, the centre is training 5,000 university students every year in the art of communication, critical thinking and problem solving.

Rakesh Batabyal completed his PhD from the Centre for Historial Studies, JNU in 1996. He currently teaches at the Centre for Media Studies at JNU. He has been a fellow of the Indian Institute of Advanced Study, Shimla (1996–99), National Institute of Panjab Studies (2004), and was the Inaugural Chair of Contemporary Indian History at Tokyo University (2010). His publications include *Communalism in Bengal: From Famine to Noakhali 1943–43*, (Sage Publications, 2005), *The Penguin Book of Modern Indian Speeches* (Penguin Books, 2007) and *JNU: The Making of a University* (HarperCollins, 2015).

Ram Ramaswamy is presently Visiting Professor at the Department of Chemistry, Indian Institute of Technology, Delhi. From 1986 until his retirement in 2018, he taught in the School of Physical Sciences, and the School of Computational and Integrative Sciences. Ramaswamy's research interests include aspects of chemical dynamics, classical and quantum chaos, semi-classical quantization, and disordered systems and statistical physics. He is the author of nearly 200 peer-reviewed publications and has edited about thirty books and conference proceedings. He is an elected Fellow of TWAS, The World Academy of Sciences, the Indian National Science Academy, New Delhi, and the Indian Academy of Sciences, Bangalore.

Ranjan Ghosh completed his MA in history from JNU and PhD from Calcutta. He worked with a trade union in Jharia coalfield for ten years, and is currently working with an NGO in the same area.

Ritoo M. Jerath joined the Centre of Russian Studies as a student in 1976. Her PhD was on 'The Social Protest in the Pre-October Poetry of V Mayakovsky', and she joined CRS as a faculty member in 1990. She was an active participant in all aspects of JNU life, from being Warden, Godavari Hostel, member of GSF, GSCASH and JNUTA, until her death in 2017.

Robert P. Goldman is the William and Catherine Magistretti Distinguished Professor of Sanskrit at the University of California at Berkeley. He is the General Editor and a principal translator of the critical edition of the *Vālmīki Rāmāyaṇa* prepared over a period of fifteen years by scholars at the Oriental Institute of Baroda. He is a Fellow of the American Academy of Arts and Sciences and was the recipient of the President of India's Certificate of Honour for Sanskrit (International) in 2013.

Rohan D'Souza is Associate Professor at the Graduate School of Asian and African Area Studies, Kyoto University, Japan. He was elected General Secretary of the Jawaharlal Nehru University Student's Union (1989–90), on the political platform of the All India Student's Federation. He completed his PhD from the Centre for Historical Studies, JNU in 1999. From 2003–15, he was Assistant Professor at the Centre for Studies in Science Policy in the School of Social Sciences, JNU. He also served a term as Secretary to the Jawaharlal Nehru University Teacher's Association and was elected to the University's Executive Council.

Rohit Azad teaches at the Centre for Economic Studies and Planning, JNU. He is the author of *It's Not Over: Structural Drivers of the Global Economic Crisis* (OUP, 2013), and has co-edited *What the Nation Really Needs to Know* (HarperCollins, 2017), and *A Quantum Leap in the Wrong Direction* (Orient BlackSwan, 2019)

Romila Thapar has researched and written on Early Indian history, specializing in social and cultural history and historiography. Her latest book is *Indian Cultures as Heritage: Contemporary Pasts*, published in 2018. She is Professor Emerita of History at the Jawaharlal Nehru University New Delhi, where she taught from 1970, when it was founded, to 1991 when she retired.

Sally J. Sutherland Goldman is a Senior Lecturer in Sanskrit at the University of California at Berkeley. In 2012, she was awarded the prestigious Distinguished Teaching Award at Berkeley. She is the co-author of the *Devavāṇīpraveśikā: An Introduction to Sanskrit Language*, co-annotator of the first book of the epic, the *Balākāṇḍa*, Princeton University Press, 1984, co-author of the fifth book, the *Sundarakāṇḍa* 1996, the sixth book, the *Yuddhakāṇḍa*, 2009, and the seventh book, the *Uttarakāṇḍa*, 2017. Her areas of interest are gender and narrative, epic, classical Sanskrit literature, the Sanskrit grammatical tradition, and the Vedas.

Shipra Nigam is a consultant economist based in Delhi. She has studied economics in Hyderabad Central University and Centre for Economic Studies and Planning, JNU.

Sohail Hashmi joined the MA at CSRD in 1972. His scholarship was stopped and he was arrested during the Emergency, 1975–77. Later, he dropped the PhD in 1981 to work full-time with CPI (M) for ten years. In 1991, he moved into electronic media, worked with PTI TV, Home TV, BiTV etc., also as Media Advisor to the National Literacy Mission, ran Leap-Years, a creative centre for children. He also makes documentary films and conducts heritage walks. He is founding Trustee of Sahmat, a platform to defend creative freedom.

Sonajharia Minz has been teaching at the School of Computer and Systems Sciences, JNU, as Assistant Professor from 1992, and as Professor from 2005. Her research interests include data analytics, machine learning, spatial analytics, and Big Data. She regularly publishes in international journals in the area of data mining, soft computing, knowledge engineering and geo-informatics. She has co-edited two volumes of essays *Pearls of Indigenous Wisdom: Selected Essays from Lifetime Contributions by Bishop Dr Nirmal Minz,* 2007; *Indigenous People of India, Problems and Prospects: Essays in honour of Bishop Dr Nirmal Minz, an Adivasi Intellectual,* 2007. Her pursuit of equality and justice motivate her to stand with the issues of the tribals, the deprived, and the marginalized. She is presently Vice Chancellor, Sidhu Kanhu Murmu University, Jharkhand.

Sudhir K. Sopory is currently SERB Distinguished Fellow at the International Centre for Genetic Engineering and Biotechnology (ICGEB), New Delhi. He obtained his PhD in 1973 from the University of Delhi and has held post-doctoral/visiting scientist stints in Germany and USA. He was at JNU from 1973–96 and later as Vice Chancellor from 2011–16. From 1997–2010, he worked at ICGEB, as Group Leader, Director, and later as Arturo Falaschi Emeritus Scientist. He has edited thirteen books and published over 230 scientific papers in international journals and sixty book chapters. He has received many honours and awards including the Padma Shri, S. S. Bhatnagar Award, Birbal Sahni Medal of the Indian Botanical Society, and Life Time Achievement Award of the Indian National Science Congress and Biotechnology Society.

Sudipta Kaviraj received his PhD in Political Science from JNU, and taught at the Centre for Political Studies from 1971 to 1991. He teaches Indian Politics and Intellectual History at Columbia University. His books include *The Unhappy Consciousness* (Oxford University Press, 1995); *The Enchantment of Democracy and India* (Permanent Black, 2014) *The Invention of Private Life: Literature and Ideas* (Columbia University Press, 2015).

Sukhadeo Thorat is Professor Emeritus, JNU. He is Former Chairman of University Grant Commission, Indian Council of Social Science Research, and Chairman of Indian Institute of Dalit Studies, New Delhi and Institute for Social and Economic Change, Bangalore. He is the recipient of the Padma Shri, the Mother Teresa International Award, and Babasaheb Ambedkar Ratna Award. An economist by training and a specialist on agricultural economics and studies of social exclusion and discrimination, he was at JNU between 1973 and 2014.

Sumangala Damodaran is a Professor of Economics, Development Studies and Popular Music Studies at Ambedkar University Delhi. Her research and publications fall broadly within the rubric of industrial and labour studies and more specifically on Industrial organization, global value chains, the informal sector, labour and migration. Apart from her academic involvements as an economist and social scientist, she is also a singer and composer. Her archiving and documentation of the musical tradition of the Indian People's Theatre Association from the 1940s and 1950s has resulted in a book *The Radical Impulse: Music in the Tradition of the IPTA* (Columbia University Press, 2017), and an album titled *Songs of Protest.* She has performed in different parts of the country and abroad.

Surya Prakash is at the School of Life Sciences, JNU. An ardent birder and naturalist for over thirty-five years, he has identified many varieties of rare birds and butterflies at JNU, and along with WWF-India, documented the faunal diversity of Delhi. A wildlife writer, he has contributed to many leading nature magazines, scientific journals, and electronic media.

Tiplut Nongbri was formerly Professor of Sociology at the Centre for the Study of Social Systems and founder Director, North East India Studies Programme, School of Social Sciences, JNU. After retirement from JNU in 2016, she was appointed to the Dr Saifuddin Kitchlew Chair attached to the Centre for North East Studies and Policy Research at Jamia Millia Islamia, New Delhi where, besides teaching and supervision of MPhil and PhD scholars, she is engaged in research and writing.

Udaya Kumar is Professor at the Centre for English Studies, JNU. He was a student of the MPhil. English programme of the Centre for Linguistics and English during the years 1982–84. He joined JNU as a faculty member in October 2015. Before joining JNU, he worked at the University of Delhi, Centre for Studies in Social Sciences, Calcutta and the University of Poona. His publications include: *The Joycean Labyrinth: Repetition, Time, and Tradition in Ulysses* (OUP, 1991); *Writing the First Person:*

Literature, History, and Autobiography in Modern Kerala (Permanent Black, 2016).

Vijay Singh Rathor served in the administration of JNU from 1975. He worked at the Public Relations Office and fondly remembers the vibrant atmosphere on campus, its students and faculty, and his interactions with international delegations.

Vipul Jhingta has done his MA in Ancient History from JNU, from 2014–16. He has various research interests and is currently pursuing independent research on Tibetan civilization.

Yogendra Yadav, a former academic, is now a full-time political activist. As an academic he taught at Panjab University, Chandigarh, did research at Centre for the Study of Developing Societies, Delhi, revived National Election Study and founded Lokniti, a network of scholars. After shifting full-time to public life, he has been involved with farmers' movement and the movement for equal citizenship. He was among the founders of Aam Aadmi Party and is the founder National President of Swaraj India.

Zos Bhatia née Hauhnar worked under the supervision of the late Professor P. K. Das in the Division of Southeast Asian and South West Pacific Studies, School of International Studies. After submitting her PhD thesis in 1998, Zos Bhatia moved to Dharamshala in Himachal Pradesh and taught English in a school for Tibetan refugee children for over a decade. She enjoys reading, watching whodunits and Coen Brothers films and going for long rides in the countryside.

ANNOTATIONS

Balveer Arora was Professor of Political Science at the Centre for Political Studies, Jawaharlal Nehru University (1987–2010). He was also the Rector and the Pro-Vice Chancellor of JNU between 2002 and 2005.

P. K. Bahri was the retired High Court Judge who was appointed to inquire into an incident involving a skirmish between students and two army officers, one of whom was alleged to have brandished a revolver at an Indo–Pak mushaira organized on the campus on 29 April 2000.

Bappa was the 'dak naam' (or pet name) of Sabyasachi Bhattacharya, former professor of economic history who taught at the Centre for Historical Studies, 1972–2003.

Amit Bhaduri was Emeritus Professor of the Centre for Economic Studies and Planning where he taught economics between 1973 and 2001. He recently relinquished his Emeritus Professorship to protest events that unfolded on 5 January 2020.

Krishna Bharadwaj established the Centre for Economic Studies and Planning in 1973. She lived and taught at JNU for twenty years.

G. K. Chadha taught economics at the Centre for the Study of Regional Development, JNU and was Vice Chancellor of JNU (2002–05).

Bipan Chandra was among the founding members of the Centre for Historical Studies in 1973, where he taught until 1993. He was Professor Emeritus until he died, and was the author of several widely circulated books such as *India's Struggle for Independence, History of Modern India, Nationalism and Colonialism in Modern India,* etc.

Chandu was how friends called Chandrasekhar Prasad, an alumnus of JNU, twice president of JNUSU, and member of AISA. He returned to his native Siwan, Bihar, after his studies at JNU where he was shot dead on 31 March 1997, along with another colleague.

Gopalan's Canteen is a canteen that was first housed within the JNU library premises but now with its own building, adjacent to the library. The only place on campus that functions seven days a week serving south Indian snacks.

P. C. Joshi was the first general secretary of the Communist Party of India. He was responsible for setting up the Archives on Contemporary History housed in the JNU library.

Ratna Kapur Feminist legal scholar, who has taught at OP Jindal Global University, Sonepat, Queen Mary University of London, and has been visiting faculty at International Global Law and Policy Institute at Harvard Law School.

Anjan Mukherji retired from JNU as the Reserve Bank of India Professor of Economic History and is Professor Emeritus, JNU.

Munirka formerly a village located to the north of JNU's Main Gate, is today a bustling residential and business locality

T. K. Oommen was Professor of Sociology at the Centre for the Study of Social Systems, JNU at CSSS JNU, and currently Professor Emeritus.

Moonis Raza was a regional planner and geographer and one of the co-founders of JNU. He is also credited with overseeing the landscaping of the new JNU campus and the naming of hostels.

Lotika Sarkar taught at Law Faculty, DU and was the founding member of Centre for Women's Development Studies and Indian Association for Women's Studies.

Namwar Singh, acclaimed author, literary critic, and professor of Hindi literature, was the first chair and founder of JNU's Centre for Indian Languages and later appointed as Professor Emeritus of JNU.

Ashok Singhal was the international working president of the Vishva Hindu Parishad for over twenty years.

Sapru House, located on Barakhambha Road, New Delhi, currently houses the Indian Council of World Affairs (ICWA). Many institutions such as Institute of Defense Studies and Analysis, as well as JNU's School of International Studies were initially located here.

Teen Murti or Teen Murti Bhavan was the former residence of Prime Minister Jawaharlal Nehru. It houses many institutions, including the Nehru Memorial Museum and Library, which has a rich collection of books and private papers, and other documents. NMML has been the second home of many research students of JNU.

Praveen Togadia was formerly the International Working President of the Vishwa Hindu Parishad.

615: A bus route that begins from Poorvanchal at JNU and ends at Minto Road, Connaught Place.